W9-DET-741

CONVERTIBLES

HISTORY AND EVOLUTION
OF DREAM CARS

BARNES
& NOBLE
BOOKS
NEW YORK

Texts
Giuseppe Guzzardi
Enzo Rizzo

Editors
Valeria Manferto De Fabianis
Laura Accomazzo

Photographic research
Laura Accomazzo

Graphic design
Patrizia Balocco Lovisetti

Translation
C.T.M., Milan

English translation editor
Jay Lamm

© 1998 White Star S.r.l.
Via Candido Sassone, 24
13100 Vercelli, Italy.

This edition published by Barnes & Noble, Inc.,
by arrangement with White Star S.r.l.,
1998 Barnes & Noble Books

All rights reserved. This book, or any portion
thereof, may not be reproduced in any form
without written permission of the publisher.

Library of Congress
Cataloging-in-Publication
Data available

ISBN 0-7607-1118-6
M10987654321

Printed by Pozzo Gros Monti, Italy
Colour separations by Fotomec, Turin, Italy
and Fotolito Bassoli, Milan, Italy

CONTENTS

1 top This 1900 photograph shows the Benz 3 1/2 HP vis-à-vis which, as suggested by the name, had facing seats. Note the vertical steering column with the small horizontal wheel and grip, as used on trams.

1 bottom The picture shows the front of a little known Porsche 356 version "A": it is the Convertible D, where the letter D stands for Drauz, the name of the coach-builder who designed this particular version. This model was only produced between 1958-59 and replaced a more famous 356, the Speedster. It was only fit with a 1.6 liter, 60 HP engine. 1330 examples of the Convertible D were produced.

2-3 This is the front of a Mercedes Benz 770 K "Grosser Mercedes" from 1937. The picture clearly shows one of the symbols traditionally applied to luxury cars, the large chrome radiator grill, here in a neo-classical design. Note also the elegant design of the support for the headlights and horns beside the cushion-like curves of the fenders.

4-5 In this custom Cadillac Eldorado from 1959, the roof leaves the part of the cabin reserved for the driver uncovered. This might be considered an example of the old Sedanca design, but it actually was a precursor of what is now called targa bodywork. The picture highlights the rear fins that were a distinguishing feature of the 1950's American convertible coupés.

6-7 The Mercedes 300 SL, one of the most beautiful roadsters of all time. It was derived from the Gullwing coupé and was one of the most important luxury open tops of the 1960's. Its particularly powerful 3 liter engine enabled it to exceed 130 mph with ease. This model was a harbinger of the Mercedes SL series, a point of reference for all modern sports cars.

PREFACE

The convertible is to the car what the thoroughbred is to the horse. The comparison of the convertible with this most noble of animals is also valid for the spirit they share which evokes the desire for open spaces, freedom and riding at full speed with the wind in one's hair. But convertibles are much more: They are a legacy of recent world history, bearing an intrinsic message that no other type of car can and a tangible symbol of the moods, wishes and social habits of the western world.

They have survived dictatorships, recessions, revolutions, reconstructions and wars, often being used as a symbol of, if not a participant in, moments of contemporary history.

There have been very many books dedicated to this elite type of car: Some are monographic works on famous models, from enormous convertible sedans to small, fleet-footed sports cars; some illustrate the production of a certain type of open top while others analyze a precise period, a dominant style or perhaps production from a particular part of the world. Those that remain deal with technological, formal and production aspects.

This book, "Convertibles", attempts to fill the gap created by the lack of an all-round history of the open-topped car from its origins up to the year 2000, from when cars were open-topped from necessity rather than choice up till the most recent stylistic innovations.

It has been like excavating through geological strata while bouncing from one side of the globe to the other, analyzing works of designers from France, Germany, Great Britain, Italy, the United States and occasionally Japan and even China.

Our research has led to the production of nine chapters, we hope sufficiently detailed, or at least enough so, to encourage other publications to deal with open-topped motoring in all its aspects. Our history is presented chronologically and the chapters are divided into design periods in the various areas of the world.

The second part of the volume is dedicated to the description of models that we consider particularly significant. To have to leave out some has been a real torment. Leafing through these very best, one notices how much has changed in terms of shape and contents over ninety years, though not the desire to dream. Yesterday, as they do today, convertibles and roadsters represented a cocktail of daring, irony and status for their owners; for their designers, they were the best opportunity to experiment with new ideas or to show the best of oneself. The result is that open-topped cars have always occupied the most elite position in the world of car fashions for their nobility, elegance and imaginativeness of design.

We hope readers will excuse us for any imperfections and for the inevitable omissions.

Giuseppe Guzzardi

Enzo Rizzo

8-9 The Chevrolet Corvette is the definitive American sports car, the Ferrari of the United States. The photograph shows the 1997 version, the fifth generation that made its debut 44 years after the first series. It maintains the original characteristics that have made Corvettes so famous: the body made from fiberglass, a long hood, a trim rear end and the famous Chevrolet Smallblock V8 engine.

9 This poster from the end of the 19th century illustrates one of the possible uses for the heir to the carriage - a Sunday outing for the family. The car in the foreground is an 1898 Peugeot and, unlike many models of that time, the seats neither face each other nor are back to back; they herald the common configuration used today.

10-11 This picture shows the looming profile of one of the most desirable English cars of all time, the Jaguar E-Type. This car has many features worthy of note; the characteristic spoked wheels, the lights protected by transparent covers, the long hood which hid first the 6 cylinder in-line engine, then the V12 in the 1970's, and the cuttlebone-shaped back end which was soon taken up by Alfa Romeo's Duetto, later known as the Spider.

12-13 The Ferrari F50 is an open top but not a convertible, as it was only produced with a hard top that made this road monster resemble the prototype sports cars of the 1960's and 70's. The mid-mounted engine was a 4698cc V12 capable of producing 520 HP. The car's top speed was 203 mph and 0-60 acceleration was an incredible 3.8 seconds.

THE CAR IS "BORN" OPEN-TOPPED
LATE 19TH CENTURY CARRIAGES

One Sunday morning towards the end of the 1800's in one of any of the large cities in the industrialized nations, a well-bred gentleman approaching what is discreetly called "middle" age is walking down the high street.

In his right hand he carries his gloves and in his left the newspaper he has just bought from the paper-boy waiting, as usual, outside the church for those who - like the gentleman above, having listened attentively to the sermon - are looking forward to the enjoyable Sunday routine of an aperitif, lunch at the club and a leisurely perusal of the paper.

Walking towards him on the other side of the road are two elegantly dressed young ladies, close enough for the gentleman to appreciate their features and fashions, one dressed in dark red and the other in bright blue and white. It is a clear, warm day that encourages thoughts of a trip into the countryside, a picnic perhaps if you

15 bottom The subject of the drawing is a broken down vehicle being drawn by a horse. The vis-à-vis seating arrangement was the most common on open carriages and stagecoaches.

14-15 R.E. Olds, one of the main characters in the early development of the car, at the wheel of his first model, non-topped, built in 1897.

15 top The Peugeot Vis-à-vis dates from 1897. Its name indicates that the passengers sat opposite one another. In other models of the period the seats were laid out differently: The 1897 Oldsmobile had opposed seating, i.e. they sat back to back, but generally the padded seats faced one another. The configuration dictated the position and unfolding of the soft cover.

14 top left Karl Friedrich Benz's 1888 tricycle was called Model 3. A seat for the third and fourth passengers was placed in front of the rider. The power given by this tricycle's motor was 1.5 HP.

14 bottom This 1894 Peugeot was powered by a Daimler engine. Peugeot and Panhard & Levassor were among Gottlieb Daimler's first enthusiastic supporters and brought the passion for motor vehicles to France.

like that sort of thing. On the other hand maybe a relaxing afternoon at the club would be better. All of a sudden, a burst of noise shatters the quiet with the same effect on the man's mood as a hammer on a crystal glass, and before he has time to realize what is happening, he finds his trousers and gaiters covered in mud. The scoundrel responsible, with less respect for good manners than for the rules of the road, has just driven by in one of those horrible motorized carriages that have been severely testing the civility of the well-to-do for some time. Annoyed, the man tries in vain to clean off the mud.

The two ladies, seeming much less fashionable to him now, hide their laughter behind their hands and turn their heads in the direction of the daredevil already hidden behind a large ·cloud of smelly smoke.

The gentleman is by no means conservative; on the contrary, he considers himself something of a liberal spirit. But there is a limit to everything: If these young madcaps want to play with these useless, costly contraptions, let them do it in the countryside or in areas which the authorities should have reserved for these childish pastimes some time ago.

Fortunately this fashion, like all others, will pass and the reassuring clip-clop of horses' hooves will return.

Resigned but not cheered, the gentleman continues his dignified walk to the club.

But his hopes are poorly placed. The thoughtless young man of good family, with his cap pulled tight down on his head, will shortly win the battle. Only a few years hence, horse transport will remain the prerogative of the nostalgic provincial nobility who are unwaveringly tied to their coach and four despite it being obsolete, useless and dangerous. Instead, the noisy, clumsy rig that is no more than a cutdown carriage adapted to carry what is called an "internal combustion engine" will invade the world, continually improving its technologies and changing shape - first following, then creating, its own stylistic trends: the car.

16 top left Karl Friedrich Benz (1844-1929) was one of the great figures in the history of the car.

16 bottom left The poster showing Benz's tricycle was the first advertising of a motor vehicle and dates from 1888. The cost of the Patent-Motorwagen was 2,750 marks.

16 center Gottlieb Daimler (1834-1900) built the first car, the Motorwagen, in 1886. The Daimler name was later linked with that of Benz to create one of Germany's most famous industrial brand-names.

16-17 The picture shows the motor of the first road-going automobile: the Benz Patent-Motorwagen. It was built at the end of 1885 and tested in 1886. The engine had a single 990cc cylinder capable of producing less than 1 HP. It had no fuel tank so Benz's son, Eugene, had to run after his father with a bottle to top up the motor. Karl Benz's family supported him in his obstinate wish to build internal combustion engines. In 1888, his wife, Bertha Ringer, loaded her children on one of his cars and drove from Mannheim to Pforzheim to demonstrate the reliability of her husband's vehicles!

17 top These are the drawings Benz included in his application for the patent number 37435, which was awarded to him on 2 November 1886.

17 center The Benz Velociped of 1894 shows the first attempt to rationalize the layout of the components.

17 bottom The Curved Dash Oldsmobile of 1903 can be considered one of the two most important early cars with the Ford Model T. Finally the wheels were of equal size.

Can the hero of this story really already be called a "car"? That is a controversial question. We believe that the automobile became a car from the moment it had four wheels, an internal propulsion unit (internal combustion engine not a steam-driven motor), a steering wheel (not a lever system or handlebar) and was able to carry at least one passenger as well as the driver, seated and facing in the direction of travel. After a long series of prototypes, sometimes ingenious, sometimes absolutely mad (like the mechanical horse with six hooves), the car began to develop in a fixed direction. The first examples, produced in 1886 by Gottlieb Daimler and Karl Benz, can be considered an excellent starting point due to the chain effects that they generated. It did not take long for Daimler's ideas to arrive in France thanks to Panhard & Levassor and Peugeot, in Italy through Giovanni Agnelli, in England through a branch of Daimler's own company and in the United States through the piano manufacturer Steinway, while Benz became the world's most important carmaker producing over 600 machines a year. Today's cars therefore descend from a German lineage. But it was in England and above all France that the motoring fever took rapid hold, finding enthusiasts in every social stratum. In Italy, too, passion for the car was not slow in arriving while the reaction of industry and America was reluctant. Once started, though, the US market was unstoppable: 4,192 cars were sold in 1900 but three times that number were sold in 1903. By 1914 there were over one and a half million cars in the world, almost all of them open-topped.

Most of today's most important manufacturers came into being during this period: Buick, Cadillac, Ford, Fiat, Mercedes, Oldsmobile,

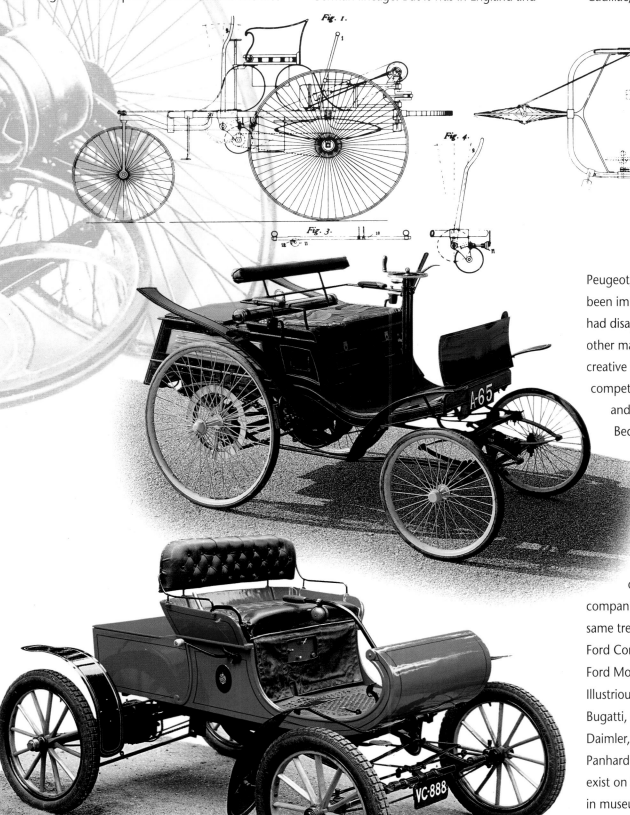

Peugeot, Rolls Royce, while others which had been important at the beginning of the century had disappeared, failed, been swallowed up by other marques or just did not have the necessary creative force to keep up with the increasingly competitive market both technologically and organizationally.

Because of its enormous potential the car market turned into a battlefield without rules where unlawful patents, stolen industrial secrets and company takeovers were the norm. Ruling figures such as Daimler and Benz and August Horch, later founder of Audi, were thrown out of their companies. Even Henry Ford once received the same treatment, being released from the Henry Ford Company before going on to found the Ford Motor Company.

Illustrious and famous marques like Atala, Austin, Bugatti, Cord, De Dion-Bouton, De Soto, Daimler, Dixi, Duesenberg, Isotta-Fraschini, Panhard & Levassor and Studebaker now only exist on the shining radiators of beautiful models in museums and receive fleeting admiration from readers of colour-plated volumes on the history of veteran and vintage cars.

THE VERY FIRST CARS AT THE TURN OF THE CENTURY

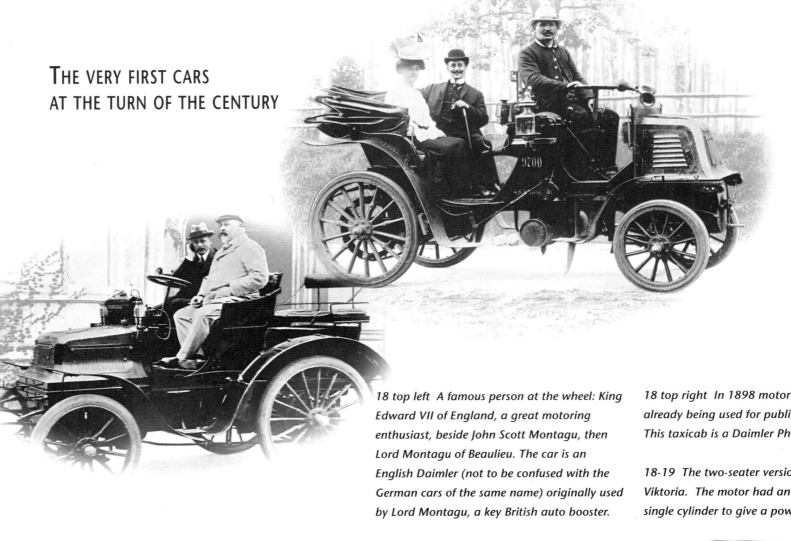

18 top left A famous person at the wheel: King Edward VII of England, a great motoring enthusiast, beside John Scott Montagu, then Lord Montagu of Beaulieu. The car is an English Daimler (not to be confused with the German cars of the same name) originally used by Lord Montagu, a key British auto booster.

18 top right In 1898 motor vehicles were already being used for public transport. This taxicab is a Daimler Phoenix-Wagen.

18-19 The two-seater version of the 1893 Benz Viktoria. The motor had an amazing 2.9 liter single cylinder to give a power of only 6 HP.

Before chassis could be designed specifically for the requirements of a car, it was necessary to wait until industrial production turned serious during the first decade of the century. In the meantime horse-drawn carriages had to satisfy the feverish activity of inventors and mechanics and were continually cannibalized. They were stripped right down to make space for the motor, radiator, auxiliary parts and control systems with the result that they no longer had anything in common with their original equestrian models. It goes without saying that the first cars had large wheels with spokes and wooden, tireless rims (or spokes and bicycle tires), large springs to absorb the unevenness of the roads, and interiors like wooden shells with seats not always padded or covered in leather, which caused easily imaginable problems to the base of the spine of the intrepid drivers. Progress always demands some sacrifices.

The motor was huge and noisy in proportion to its power output. The internal combustion engine was almost immediately adopted, although numerous attempts used electric, steam or gas-driven propulsion units. It was positioned indifferently at either end of the machine or under the passenger cab. The steering column was visible and topped by an almost horizontal, large diameter steering wheel, originally with a grip similar to that of a tram.

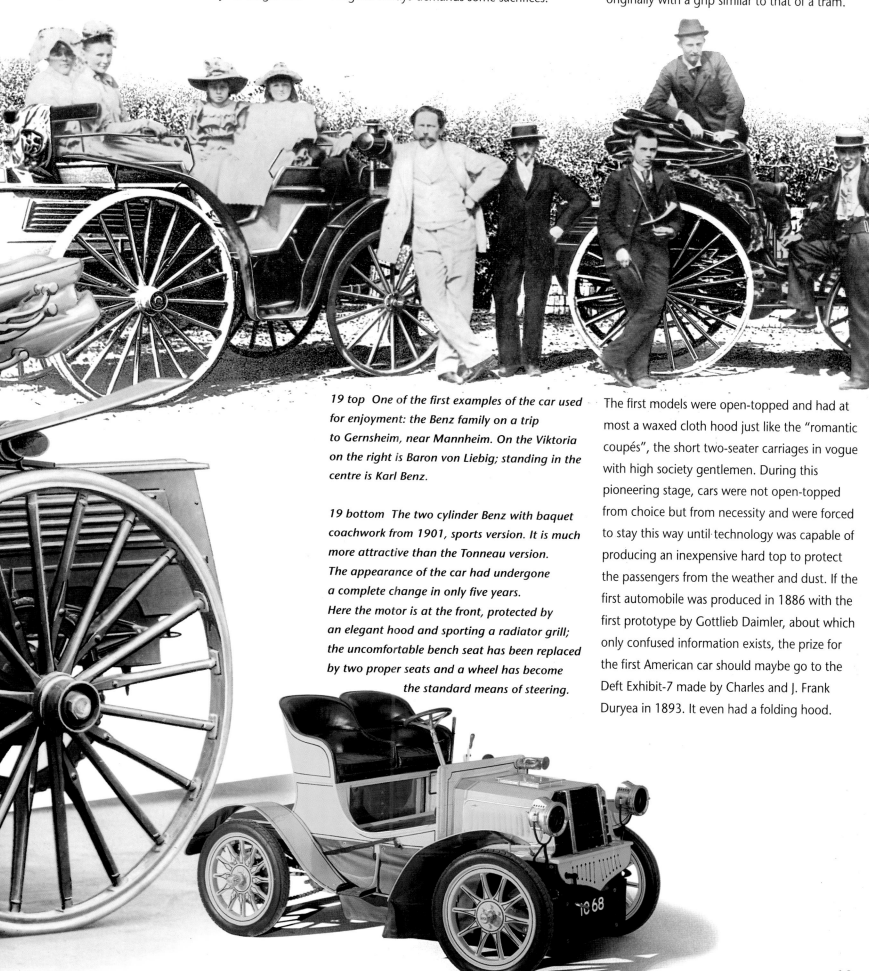

19 top One of the first examples of the car used for enjoyment: the Benz family on a trip to Gernsheim, near Mannheim. On the Viktoria on the right is Baron von Liebig; standing in the centre is Karl Benz.

19 bottom The two cylinder Benz with baquet coachwork from 1901, sports version. It is much more attractive than the Tonneau version. The appearance of the car had undergone a complete change in only five years. Here the motor is at the front, protected by an elegant hood and sporting a radiator grill; the uncomfortable bench seat has been replaced by two proper seats and a wheel has become the standard means of steering.

The first models were open-topped and had at most a waxed cloth hood just like the "romantic coupés", the short two-seater carriages in vogue with high society gentlemen. During this pioneering stage, cars were not open-topped from choice but from necessity and were forced to stay this way until technology was capable of producing an inexpensive hard top to protect the passengers from the weather and dust. If the first automobile was produced in 1886 with the first prototype by Gottlieb Daimler, about which only confused information exists, the prize for the first American car should maybe go to the Deft Exhibit-7 made by Charles and J. Frank Duryea in 1893. It even had a folding hood.

The turn of the century was still an experimental, pioneering period but the greats of the car industry were nearly all already enrolled in the "Hall of Fame". There was Nikolas August Otto, traveling salesman and father of the four-stroke Otto cycle engine; Gottlieb Daimler, gun manufacturer, whose name will always be linked with that of Karl Benz, mechanic; Ransom E. Olds, another mechanic, who was among the first in the United States to believe in a vehicle with an internal engine and to create a marque which is still today one of the largest, Oldsmobile; Giovanni Agnelli, a founder of FIAT, who was a cavalry officer; Schmidt and Stoll, knitwear industrialists whose managerial activities were the origin of Audi; and the greatest of them all, Henry Ford, a locomotive repairman.

20 top Cavalry officer Giovanni Agnelli, key founder of Fiat, with the engineer Marchesi. They are inside the factory in Corso Dante in Turin, the first address of Italy's most important car manufacturer, founded on 11 August 1899. The photograph was taken in 1904. Agnelli was one of the first supporters of Daimler's and Benz' work and took their results to Italy.

20 bottom The picture shows the feverish activity in the Fiat factory in 1900.

20-21 top The first emblem of the "Fabbrica Italiana di Automobili Torino" (FIAT) displayed at the factory under an Art Deco floral design.

20-21 bottom The first Fiat was called the 4 HP though in reality the power was actually 3.5 HP. The body was called Duo and designed by the horse-drawn carriage builder Marcello Alessio. It could seat three passengers face to face though the customer could choose other configurations. The 679cc, two-cylinder, horizontally mounted engine was designed by Aristide Faccioli and placed in the rear.

21 top left The darker, parallel lines in the design drawings of the 4 HP show the chain-driven transmission. The fuel tank was placed under the main seat.

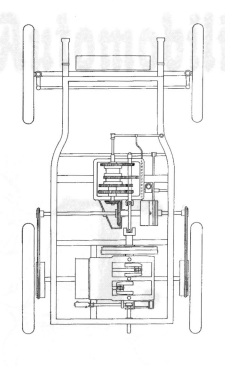

21 bottom left The first Fiat, the 4 HP, seen from below. The steering gear can be seen, which was controlled by a rod similar to those used on trams. At the front, the radiator coil can be seen.

21 right In Italy too the car builders discovered advertisement: This is Fiat's first. Note the colours that were used on cars, like the red on the touching spoke wheels with white tires.

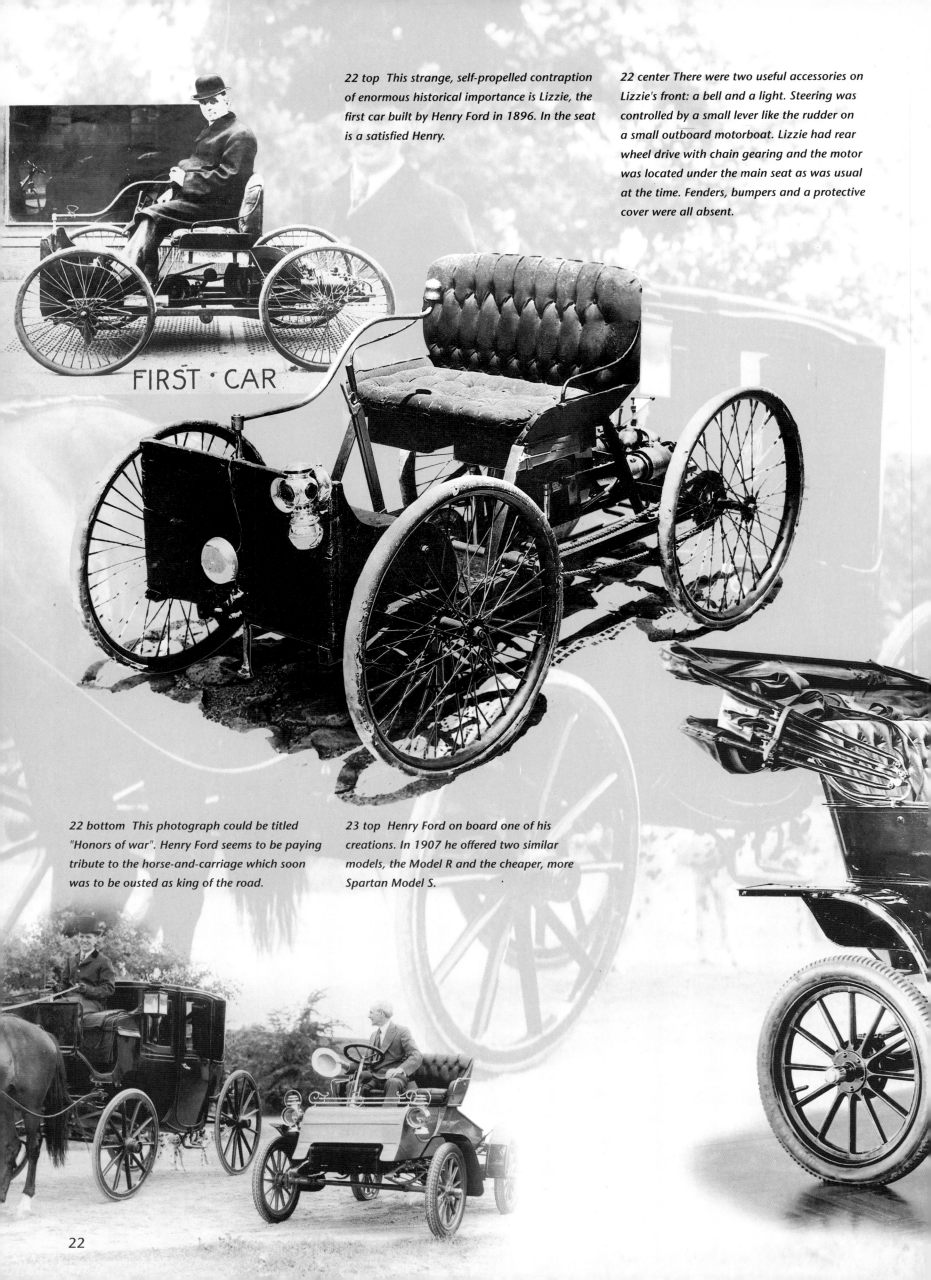

FIRST · CAR

22 top This strange, self-propelled contraption of enormous historical importance is Lizzie, the first car built by Henry Ford in 1896. In the seat is a satisfied Henry.

22 center There were two useful accessories on Lizzie's front: a bell and a light. Steering was controlled by a small lever like the rudder on a small outboard motorboat. Lizzie had rear wheel drive with chain gearing and the motor was located under the main seat as was usual at the time. Fenders, bumpers and a protective cover were all absent.

22 bottom This photograph could be titled "Honors of war". Henry Ford seems to be paying tribute to the horse-and-carriage which soon was to be ousted as king of the road.

23 top Henry Ford on board one of his creations. In 1907 he offered two similar models, the Model R and the cheaper, more Spartan Model S.

Henry Ford was very active in the automobile industry right from the start. His first model was called the Quadricycle and it is believed to have been first produced in 1896.

Olds however was already traveling around in his first four-seater, a real, working, reliable long distance car, inflicting every kind of torture on it. This open-topped car, the Curved Dash, was second in importance during the pioneering era only to the Ford Model T.

The first Quadricycle was a perfect example of the minimalism characteristic of handmade prototypes. It had large wheels, a rear-mounted two cylinder engine (later in the center under the seat), and a horizontal steering lever.

Two years later, the new model was better finished and even had a padded seat. The model produced in 1901 by the Detroit Automobile Company also had a steering wheel. The Ford Motor Company was established in 1903 and its first car was the Model A. This was replaced by the Model C and in 1906 by the Model N.

23 bottom The Ford Model T, probably the most important car in the history of the automobile, the car that motorized America. There were very many versions: two and four-seaters, tourers and roadsters, even pick-up trucks. The typical features of an efficient car are already all there plus the novelty of cross suspension. In this 1909 touring version, which cost 850 dollars, the oil lamps were standard.

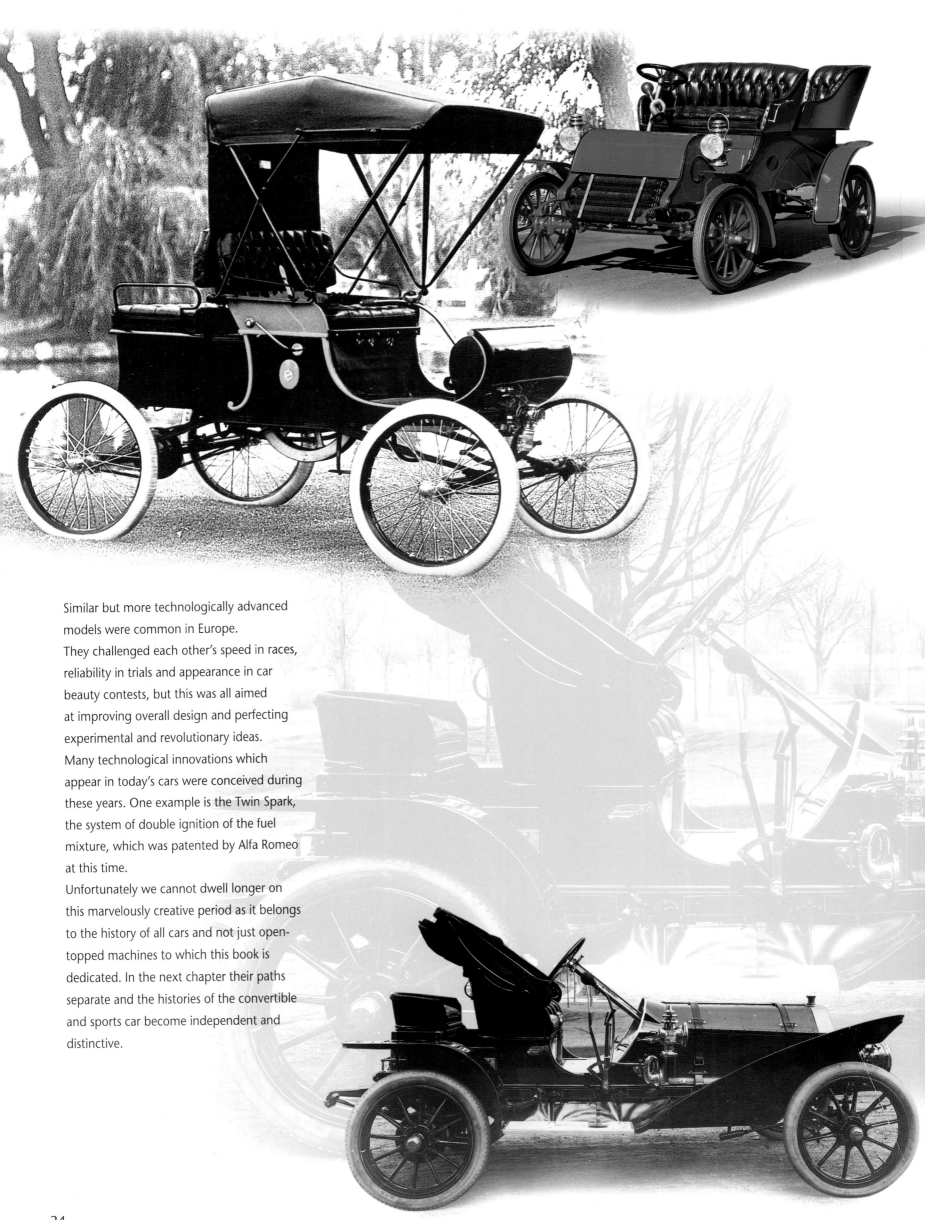

Similar but more technologically advanced
models were common in Europe.
They challenged each other's speed in races,
reliability in trials and appearance in car
beauty contests, but this was all aimed
at improving overall design and perfecting
experimental and revolutionary ideas.
Many technological innovations which
appear in today's cars were conceived during
these years. One example is the Twin Spark,
the system of double ignition of the fuel
mixture, which was patented by Alfa Romeo
at this time.
Unfortunately we cannot dwell longer on
this marvelously creative period as it belongs
to the history of all cars and not just open-
topped machines to which this book is
dedicated. In the next chapter their paths
separate and the histories of the convertible
and sports car become independent and
distinctive.

24 top left This Curved Dash Olds Runabout from 1902 has the top unfolded. Runabout was a frequent term at the beginning of the century and referred to short wheelbase vehicles as opposed to tourers, which were bigger and more spacious. Genetically and historically, runabouts were the forerunners of two-door convertibles, roadsters and sports cars. Tourers, on the other hand, were the precursors of torpedoes, four-door convertibles and cabriolets. The Curved Dash was the first mass-produced automobile in the US. The engine was single cylinder and produced 4 HP.

24 top right Cadillac was founded in 1902 as a result of the reorganization of the Henry Ford Company. The Model A Tourer in the picture, its first model, was presented at the 1903 New York Auto Show and found great success: 2,286 were sold. It was similar to the first Ford Model A (not to be confused with the later Ford Model A introduced in 1928).

24 bottom Compared to the Curved Dash, the Oldsmobile Touring of 1905 has a longer wheelbase.

25 top One of the first Peugeots, the 1892 Vis-à-vis. Note the mostly floral decorations on the sides and top. There are also patterns on the fenders.

25 bottom Horch was a very important marque in the first stages of the history of the car. This tonneau, built between 1900 and 1905, had a powerful 2.5 liter engine which could produce 12 HP. Maximum speed was 22 mph.

IN THE OPEN AIR WITH RUNABOUTS, ROADSTERS AND TOURING CARS

Shortly after the turn of the century, the paths of cars with and without a hard top began to separate: sedans had finally come into existence. For the purposes of this book two types of semi-open hard tops shall not be dealt with (a decision taken not without remorse). They are the partially open limousines called "landau-landaulet", which derives from the term for horse-drawn vehicles that were in part uncovered, and cars on which the rear part of the top could be rotated as though it were the lid of a trunk; these models were the antecedents of the modern "Targa" like the Porsche 911, C4 Corvette, Honda del Sol and Fiat X1/9, cars with a removable hard top. For the most part, the motoring literature assigns the birth of the convertible and sports car such as they are to the mid 1920's, but in

26 top This unusual 1904 parade shows Buick salesmen taking their cars from the Flint factory to their dealerships. Buick was a new marque and the factory had only recently been converted to car production from the assembly of agricultural carriages.

26 center After only three years, Buick was second in sales to Ford. The photograph shows a Model H Tourer of 1907.

26 bottom The Ford Model N; its importance lies in being the precursor of the Model T. It was a small runabout which reached the high speed of 28 mph.

addition to moving this date back by at least ten years without hesitation, the authors would also like to draw attention to developments that occurred between 1900 and 1910. There were certainly many significant models but, more importantly, the stylistic evolution and technological innovations were numerous. Most of them had their origin in the design centers in the United States.

There were three types of car that had no hard top (excluding racing cars): runabouts, roadsters and touring cars.

Runabouts were tiny two-seaters with or without a top for which the body was the mainstay of the machine. The motor had either one or two cylinders though may have been electrically or even steam-driven. Their short wheelbase made them the precursors of the European and

27 top This 1907 Cadillac Model G is fitted with a top. The picture is interesting because it shows how the protective cover, called a "cape cart top", precursor of the proper top, was fitted. It had to be fixed in place each time it was used by means of three metal supports and tie rods at the side. It cost 120 dollars.

27 center Queen Margherita of Italy in a Fiat Brevetti, known as a Cabriolet Royal and built between 1905-12. It is a typical Landau with the rear part that could be open or covered with a folding hood. Two passengers could sit in front, like in a carriage, while the driver and companion were protected by a hard top without protection at the sides.

27 bottom The inclined windshield is noticeable on this 1912 Buick Model 22. It reduced the car's air resistance.

American mini-convertibles of the 1920's but they were still very much tied to the tradition of the horse-drawn carriage. They became very popular throughout the industrialized countries. A step up from the small unpretentious runabouts were the noisy roadsters. These were only slightly longer but certainly more powerful; besides the two front seats, roadsters also often provided a highly risky and uncomfortable jump seat which, it is left to the reader to decide why, was known as the "mother-in-law's seat". Finally touring cars, sometimes known as 'baquets' or 'phaétons', also had romantic links with horse-drawn vehicles through the shape of their body: The French name 'phaéton' was remarkably apt as it means a wooden tub. Compared to runabouts and roadsters they were large, comfortable, powerful and elegant. The 3-4 liter motor often had four cylinders and the car could carry at least four passengers seated high above the ground with those at the rear raised even further. The interior resembled a small salon with two sofas or two armchairs and a sofa or four separate armchairs. The hood was often missing, the windshield always, and depending on the level of comfort required, often the side doors too, particularly the front ones. Production of runabouts was high on both sides of the Atlantic. Sometimes a long wheelbase version (or touring car) existed.

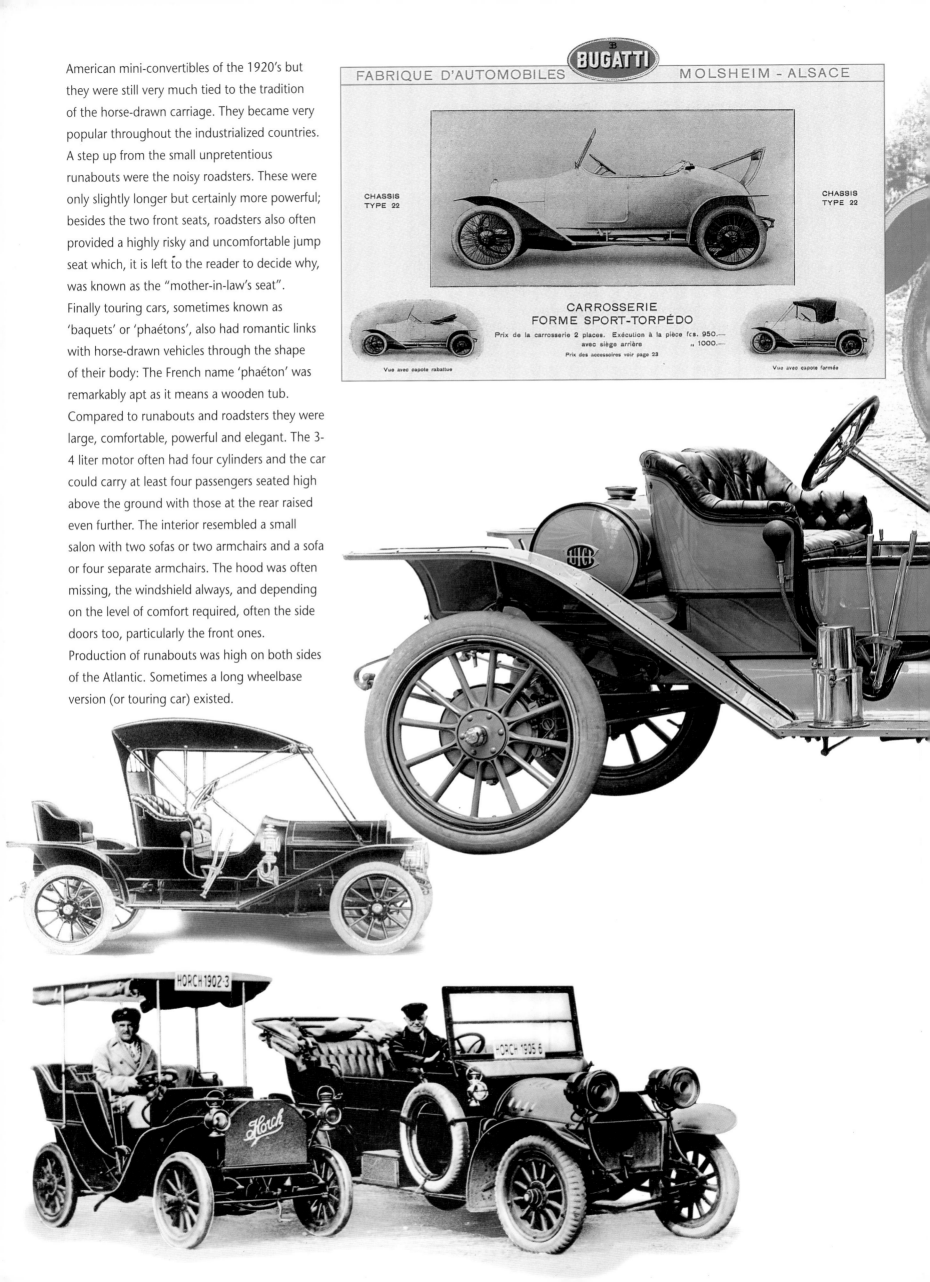

BUGATTI

FABRIQUE D'AUTOMOBILES   MOLSHEIM - ALSACE

CHASSIS TYPE 22   CHASSIS TYPE 22

CARROSSERIE
FORME SPORT-TORPÉDO
Prix de la carrosserie 2 places. Exécution à la pièce fcs. 950.—
avec siège arrière   „ 1000.—
Prix des accessoires voir page 23

Vue avec capote rabattue   Vue avec capote fermée

28 top The Bugatti Type 22 looked good in the company catalog. It was a simple design, far from the elegance of the Atalante Type 57, and was described as having a sport torpedo body. In truth, it resembles a runabout, precursor of the roadster. Note the jump seat ("mother-in-law's seat"), which was offered as an option at 50 francs.

28-29 The Buick Model 26 from 1911 of which 1,000 examples were sold. It is representative of the first roadsters, sporty but well-finished. There is no roof but the shapes of the fenders and footboard are interesting - they are just beginning their evolution into the soft, rounded, tapered forms representative of Futurism.

28 left This 1909 Cadillac offered a cover for the runabouts while the rear seat left the passengers to the mercy of the weather; this was why it was reserved for mothers-in-law. Right from its founding, Cadillac distinguished itself for the care it took in construction.

28 bottom The photograph was taken long after the models were produced (the dates are shown on the license plates); Augustus Horch (left), founder of the company of the same name, is sitting at the wheel of a Tonneau. These models were generally called Breaks and were more ungainly than functional. To Horch's left is Dr. Stöss at the wheel of a much more elegant Doppelphaeton.

29 top The 1912 Buick Model 24 roadster differed from the Model 26 by its sensible raincover.

29 center Louis Delage, founder of the company of the same name, together with Augustin Legros and one of his first cars. The company was established in 1905 and used components from one of the most prestigious and reliable manufacturers of the period, De Dion-Bouton.

29 bottom The flags on the windshield give a clue to the occupants: they are Franklin Delano Roosevelt and his wife, Eleanor, in a 1912 Cadillac.

An overview of these various models would start with the oldest car still running produced in Great Britain - the Daimler AD 1897. Daimler in this case was the German company's British branch, later to be taken over by Jaguar, which still uses this marque for its top-of-the-range sedans. Two years after its initial production, the Daimler AD 1897's direction bar was replaced with a steering wheel. In 1900 the Austrian diplomat Herr Emil Jellinek, whose genius and passion for motors was later to pass him into history with his daughter Mercedes, commissioned a beautiful racing Phoenix to be made entirely of steel from the German Daimler. In 1903 the 24-32 HP Short Wheelbase Fiat went on sale (the Long Wheelbase version was a touring car) as did the Packard Model F (showing a distinct lack of imagination in name) which had an unusually modern sheet metal body. There was also the single cylinder Overland and the 1903 Rambler which was perhaps more of a touring car with its extraordinary seating arrangement; besides the usual two places in the front, two children could sit at the feet of the driver and his passenger while there were two more seats behind facing in the opposite direction, all in a very restricted space. Finally there was the De Dion-Bouton which had a well-profiled motor compartment. In 1904 came the "Colonel's car", the Pope Tribune, also single cylinder; the following year brought the Overland Model 17 with a high seat back and a radiator, and the Ford Model N, the precursor of the Model T which will be dealt with separately.

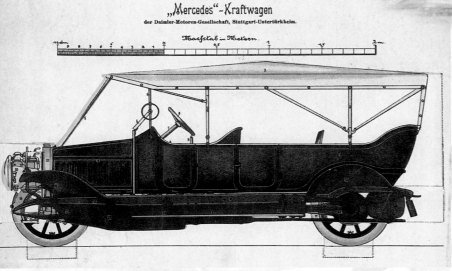

30 top Miss Mercedes Jellinek did not build cars but her name is one of those that will never be forgotten in the history of the car. Her diplomat father Emil was a devotee of motors and had a sharp commercial instinct. He commissioned increasingly powerful versions of Daimler engines which achieved brilliant racing victories and a consequent avalanche of publicity. Although Daimler were not keen on this type of exhibitionism, they could not say no to such an important customer even when he started to call his cars after his daughter. This was the origin of the name Mercedes.

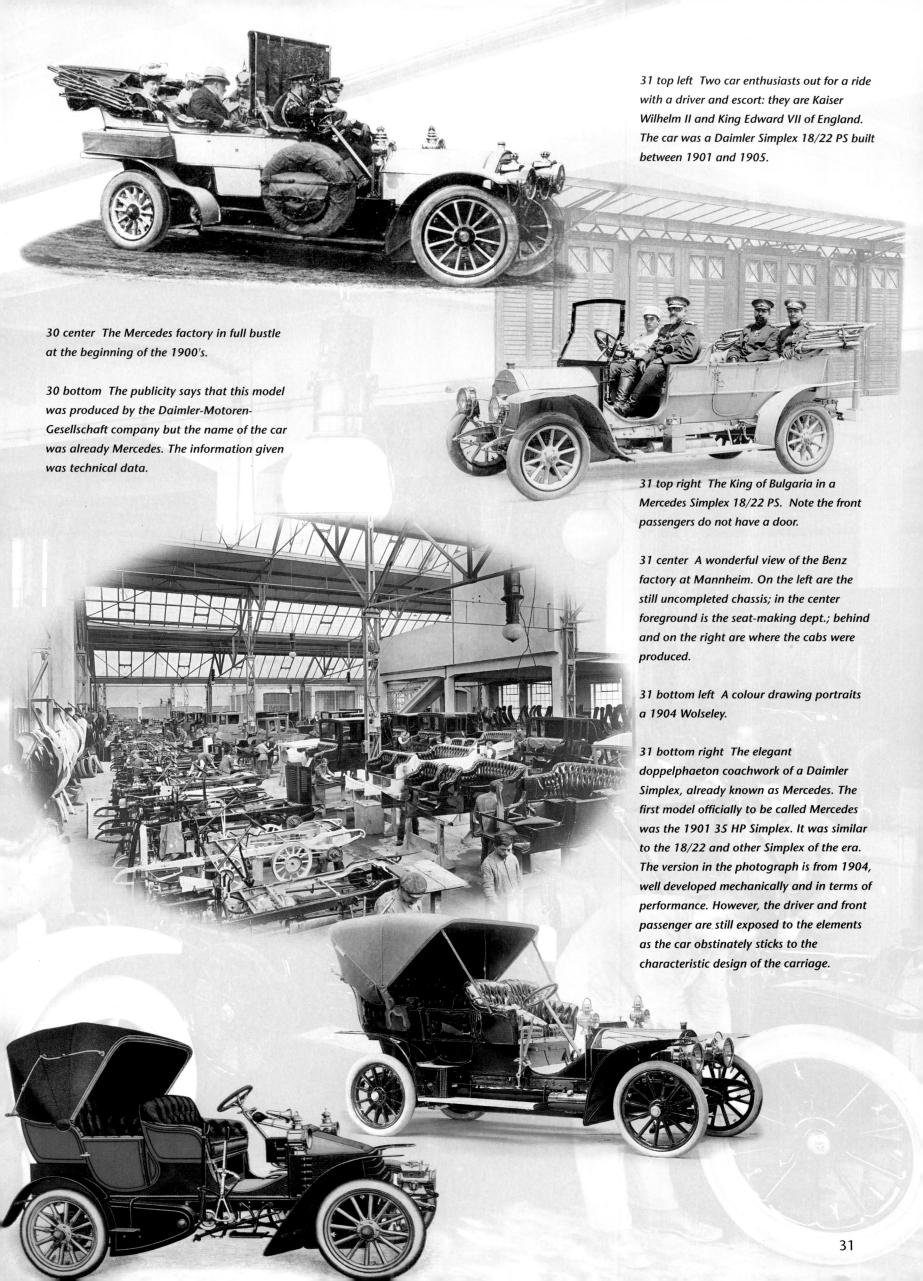

31 top left Two car enthusiasts out for a ride with a driver and escort: they are Kaiser Wilhelm II and King Edward VII of England. The car was a Daimler Simplex 18/22 PS built between 1901 and 1905.

30 center The Mercedes factory in full bustle at the beginning of the 1900's.

30 bottom The publicity says that this model was produced by the Daimler-Motoren-Gesellschaft company but the name of the car was already Mercedes. The information given was technical data.

31 top right The King of Bulgaria in a Mercedes Simplex 18/22 PS. Note the front passengers do not have a door.

31 center A wonderful view of the Benz factory at Mannheim. On the left are the still uncompleted chassis; in the center foreground is the seat-making dept.; behind and on the right are where the cabs were produced.

31 bottom left A colour drawing portraits a 1904 Wolseley.

31 bottom right The elegant doppelphaeton coachwork of a Daimler Simplex, already known as Mercedes. The first model officially to be called Mercedes was the 1901 35 HP Simplex. It was similar to the 18/22 and other Simplex of the era. The version in the photograph is from 1904, well developed mechanically and in terms of performance. However, the driver and front passenger are still exposed to the elements as the car obstinately sticks to the characteristic design of the carriage.

31

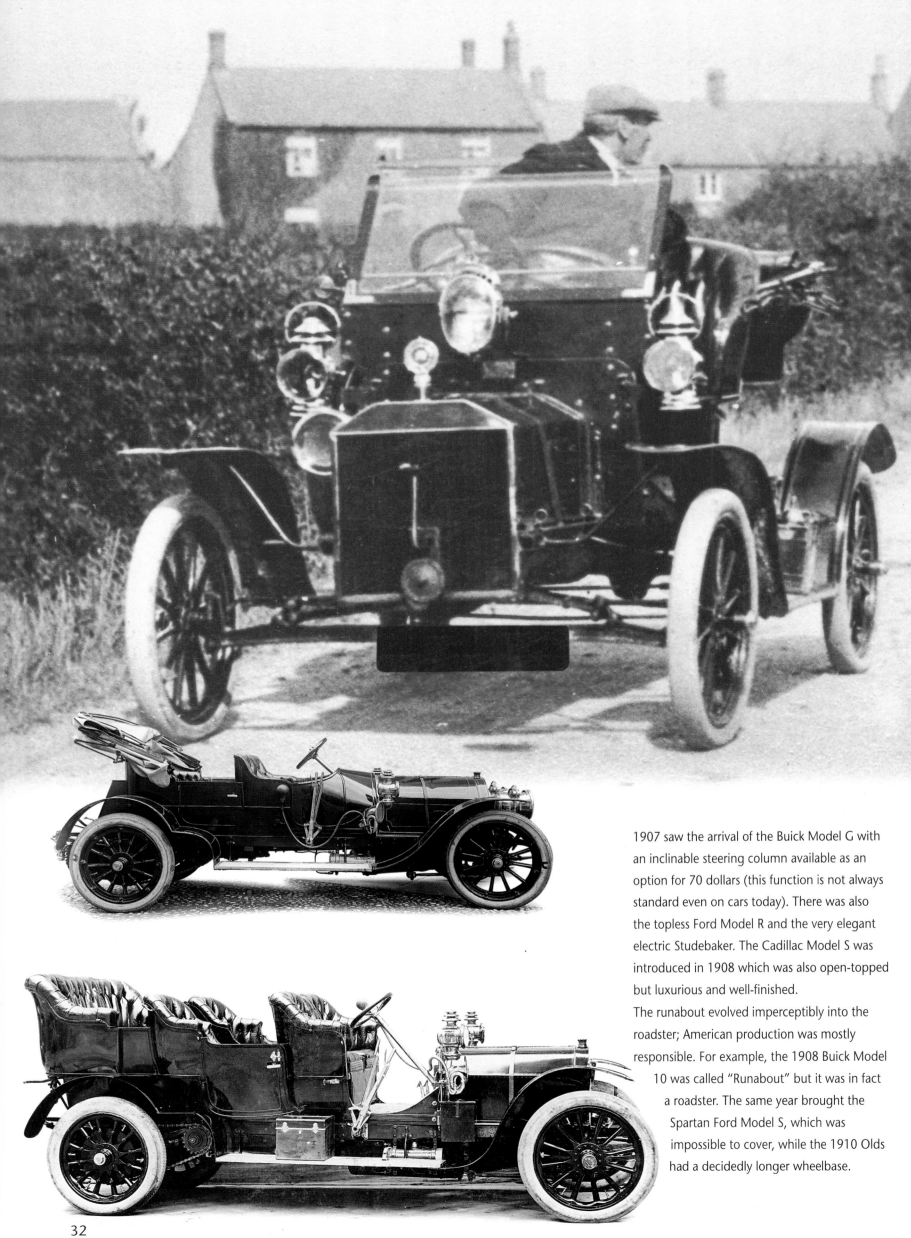

1907 saw the arrival of the Buick Model G with an inclinable steering column available as an option for 70 dollars (this function is not always standard even on cars today). There was also the topless Ford Model R and the very elegant electric Studebaker. The Cadillac Model S was introduced in 1908 which was also open-topped but luxurious and well-finished.

The runabout evolved imperceptibly into the roadster; American production was mostly responsible. For example, the 1908 Buick Model 10 was called "Runabout" but it was in fact a roadster. The same year brought the Spartan Ford Model S, which was impossible to cover, while the 1910 Olds had a decidedly longer wheelbase.

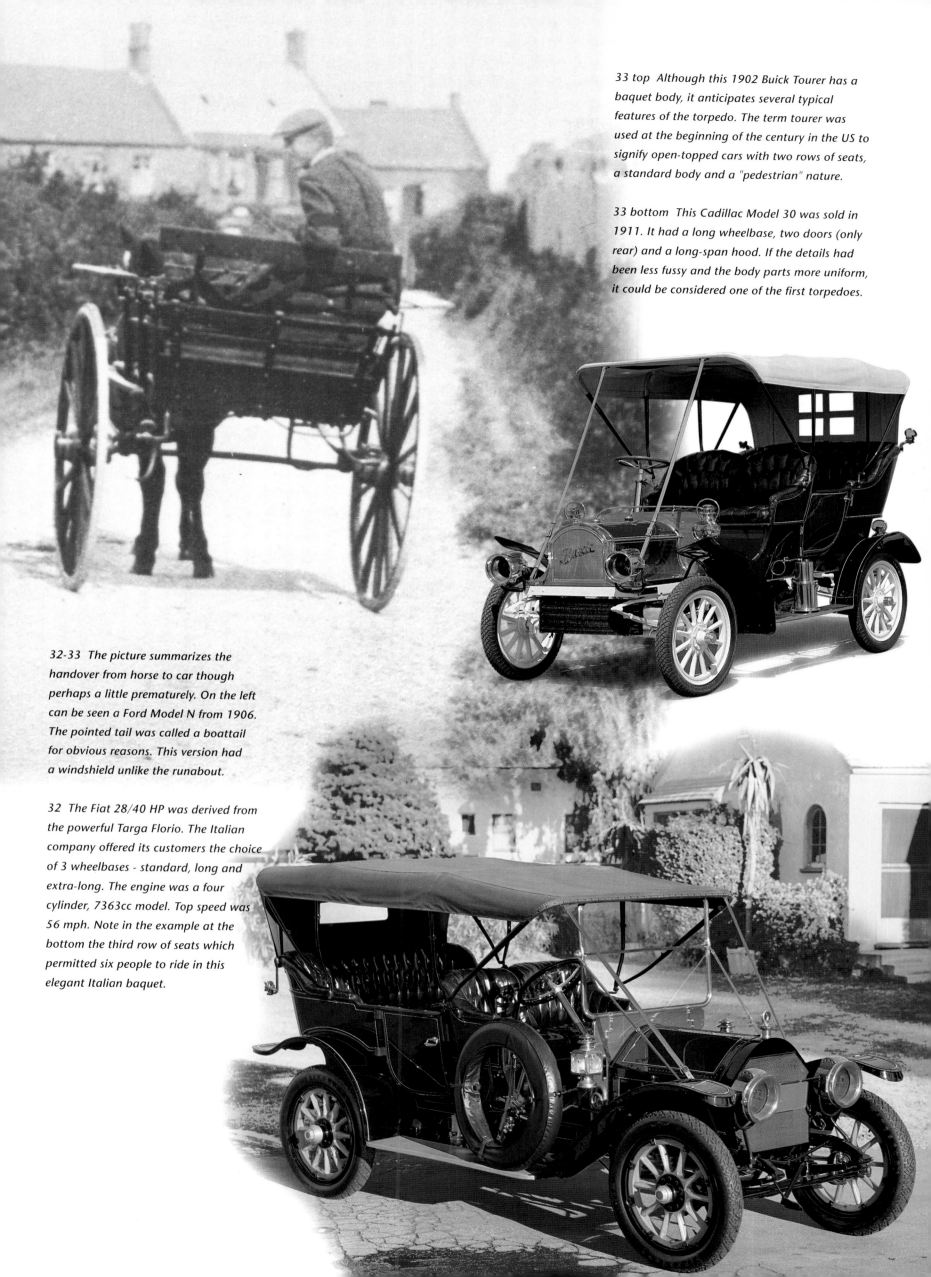

33 top Although this 1902 Buick Tourer has a baquet body, it anticipates several typical features of the torpedo. The term tourer was used at the beginning of the century in the US to signify open-topped cars with two rows of seats, a standard body and a "pedestrian" nature.

33 bottom This Cadillac Model 30 was sold in 1911. It had a long wheelbase, two doors (only rear) and a long-span hood. If the details had been less fussy and the body parts more uniform, it could be considered one of the first torpedoes.

32-33 The picture summarizes the handover from horse to car though perhaps a little prematurely. On the left can be seen a Ford Model N from 1906. The pointed tail was called a boattail for obvious reasons. This version had a windshield unlike the runabout.

32 The Fiat 28/40 HP was derived from the powerful Targa Florio. The Italian company offered its customers the choice of 3 wheelbases - standard, long and extra-long. The engine was a four cylinder, 7363cc model. Top speed was 56 mph. Note in the example at the bottom the third row of seats which permitted six people to ride in this elegant Italian baquet.

Then in 1908 appeared what can probably be considered the most important model in the history of the car, the Ford Model T. More than fifteen million examples were made in the twenty years to 1928; it was the car that motorized America, revolutionized the relationship between the industry and the workforce (Ford workers were paid most and worked least) and introduced the concept of the assembly line with success (the idea struck Henry Ford while he was watching the organization of work in a Philadelphia slaughterhouse). Model T's were produced in all versions: runabout, touring car, roadster, various torpedo versions, a landau and even a pickup truck. Further examples of these years were the 1911 Buick Model 38 and Cadillac Roadster, the latter less Spartan than previous models and more comfortable even boasting doors and a top; then there was the odd Chevrolet Royal Mail from 1914, available only in gray or plum color. Finally, there was the 1916 Buick D6-44 with an innovative rear end which was very similar to the trunks of modern sedans.

34 top Henry Ford with family during the testing of a Model T tourer. This configuration was called a "fore-door" which contrasts with the previous custom of having the door only at the back. Finally the driver was provided with access ... well, actually, the door was fake.

34 center This Model T tourer (probably from 1912) was traditional, i.e. without a front door.

34 bottom The 5 seat Ford T Tourster, one of many variants thanks to which the Model T sold 15 million units.

35 top This curious cinematic still shows the Model T in one of its many film roles. In this case, with Laurel and Hardy in yet another fine mess.

35 center This Ford T was fitted especially for desert conditions, or rather, for a Maharajah. Note the panel that hides the bay for plates and provisions and which transforms into a picnic table.

35 bottom The picture shows several stages which took place outside in the construction of a car. Here a worker is checking the forecarriage of a Ford Model T 5-seater. Note how the chassis is made from side members and how the absence of coachwork enhances the design of the wheels (known as "artillery wheels").

Meanwhile in Europe there were the clumsy baquets (touring cars), near relations of the runabouts and those horrible machines - sometimes called "breaks", sometimes "tonneaux" - which provided a high canopy as a cover. A single example is enough - the Horch 10/12 HP Tonneau from 1903.

On the subject of touring cars, reference must be made to the first Daimler to be called Mercedes (after the daughter of the brilliant Austrian consul in Nice, Emil Jellinek, whose contribution to the growth of the car market was greater than most); it was the 18/22 PS Simplex made in 1902. The top protected only the passengers behind and, although quite short, the car had a footboard which was separate from the front and rear fenders. There was also a landau version of this model with a closed body. The 5900cc engine supplied a maximum power of 35 HP. The same year saw the Benz Phaéton Tonneau

and the Parsifal (engine power varying between 8-14 HP). Both were furnished with a rear end unfortunately similar to a bath tub and certainly neither of them could escape the label "baquet". Meanwhile the American Model K from 1906 did better as a tourer than as a roadster. In 1907, Rambler presented the Model 24 and Buick the Model H; in 1908 came the Oldsmobile Series M Touring. The Opel-Darracq 9 PS from 1909 offered only two points of access and a single sofa for passengers. The top was very wide with two metal support rods, four ribs and two tie-rods which hooked onto the forecarriage, a similar system to the torpedoes. The result was similar to a camping tent with the sides open and exposed to the wind. Due to the very short wheelbase, the footboard was no more than a curve between the front and rear fenders. There was no door. The nose of the vehicle was ugly with the radiator heavily inclined backwards.

The starting handle was very obvious. The driver's posture was still very upright as became a gentleman of the period. Just as a curiosity, the 1910 steam-driven Stanley should be noted. Then there were two Italian cars: the 20 HP Lancia Beta from 1909 and the 15 HP Alfa from 1910. The Lancia has had a clear influence on the Gamma, Delta and Epsilon lines which have followed and its characteristics should be considered. Despite having no doors, its appearance was refined and its equipment luxurious; the fenders were large but well-proportioned; the headlights were also large and housed next to the vertical, gilded radiator in what was to become the standard position rather than next to the driver's seat. The wheels had tires and ten wooden spokes similar to artillery wheels or contemporary locomotives. The spokes were painted, often red, to reflect the fashionable color of the day.

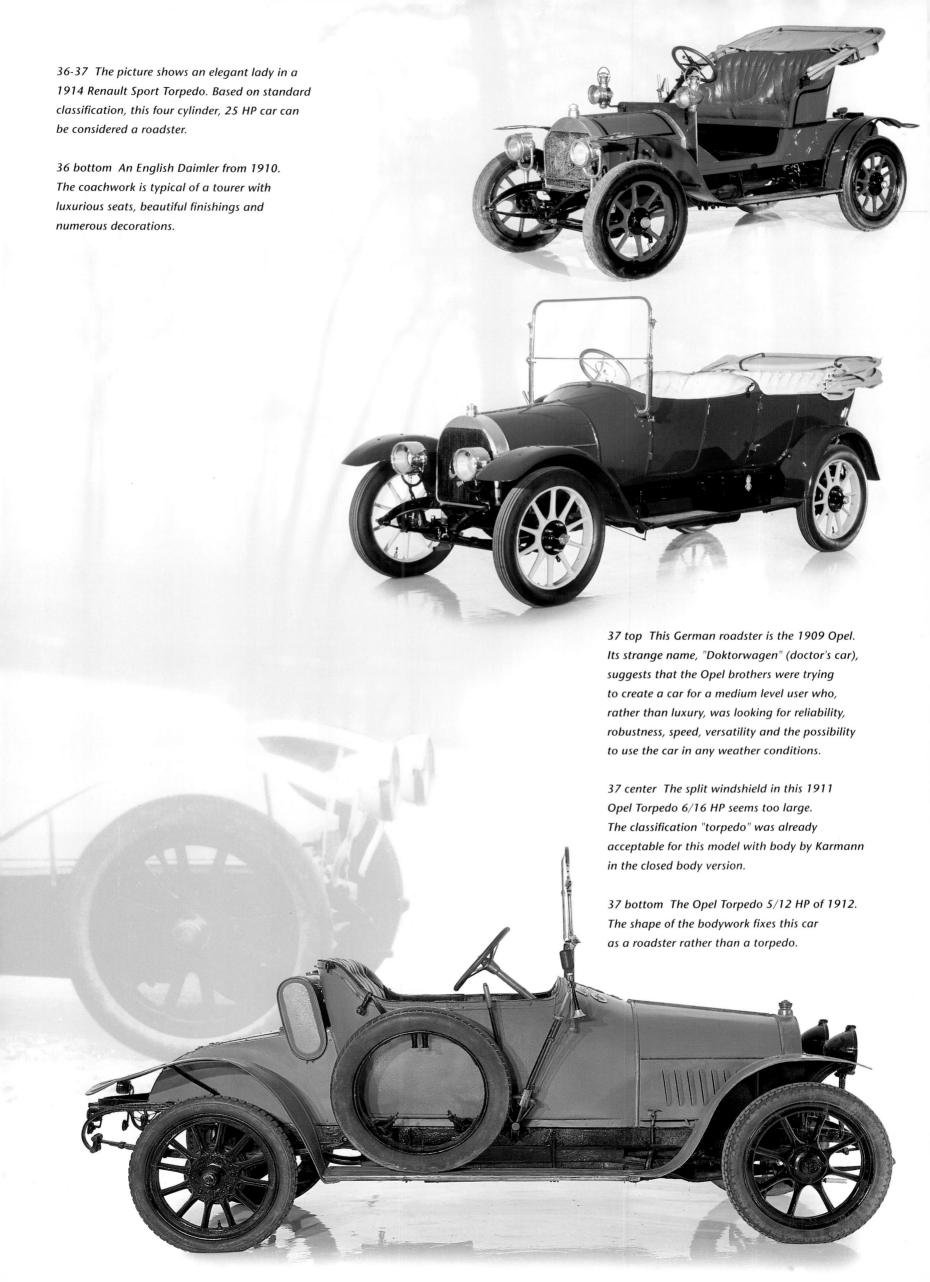

36-37 The picture shows an elegant lady in a 1914 Renault Sport Torpedo. Based on standard classification, this four cylinder, 25 HP car can be considered a roadster.

36 bottom An English Daimler from 1910. The coachwork is typical of a tourer with luxurious seats, beautiful finishings and numerous decorations.

37 top This German roadster is the 1909 Opel. Its strange name, "Doktorwagen" (doctor's car), suggests that the Opel brothers were trying to create a car for a medium level user who, rather than luxury, was looking for reliability, robustness, speed, versatility and the possibility to use the car in any weather conditions.

37 center The split windshield in this 1911 Opel Torpedo 6/16 HP seems too large. The classification "torpedo" was already acceptable for this model with body by Karmann in the closed body version.

37 bottom The Opel Torpedo 5/12 HP of 1912. The shape of the bodywork fixes this car as a roadster rather than a torpedo.

The vehicle was long with the chassis alone reaching 12 feet. Overall width was a shade over 5 feet and the footboard was indispensable for reaching the raised seats. The two front seats were real padded leather armchairs while the two behind were a proper sofa. The frame of the top had four arms.

The car had a 3120cc, four cylinder motor capable of 34 HP at 1500 rpm and for the first time there was a fixed head monobloc engine. It had four gears, a cardan shaft transmission (chain-driven transmission was also used at the time) and mechanical brakes which acted on both the rear wheels and the transmission. Top speed was 56 mph. One hundred and fifty examples of this model were built, one of which can be seen in the Vincenzo Lancia Museum in Turin.

A luxurious touring car was the Rolls Royce Silver Ghost from 1912. It was very long and elegant but had no top. The Chesterfield-style seats were covered with leather; the driving position was central, like horse-drawn carriages, and the cabin had no door. The running boards were connected to the fenders in an unbroken line, creating the dominant theme of the sideview. The headlights were separate from the body as were the wheels, which were not covered by the coachwork; this was to be a feature of Rolls Royce cars for a long time.

Nearly all touring cars mentioned here were produced without front doors, which were only to arrive with the advent of the torpedo.

38 top This is one of the most elegant cars of the period, the Rolls Royce Silver Ghost 40/50 from 1907. It belonged to the Belgian royal family. The top is held taut by tie rods hooked onto the front bumpers and hides the elegance of the large baquet.

38 center The open door of the Silver Ghost shows the richness of the interior, worthy of a monarch. Besides the two jump seats, there is an intermediate windshield making this Roller a dual cowl design.

38 bottom The picture shows the detail of the motor compartment of the Rolls Royce Silver Ghost 40/50.

38-39 A 1911 Rolls Royce Landau. Landau, like landaulette, is a term which generally means very luxurious bodywork and a cab closed on all sides which can be partially or completely opened from the back. Another variable is the covering for the driver, who is sometimes left open to the elements, sometimes included in the closed cab.

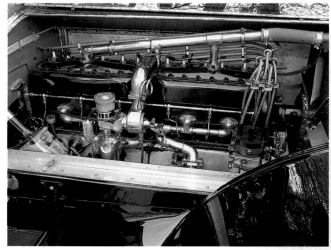

39 top This Rolls Royce was made for
a Maharajah. It has features suitable for royal
parades: The wheelbase is extremely long, the
turret-like cab closed and the rear open. Despite
the luxury of the finishings and the opulence
of the materials used, the shape is awkward and
clumsy.

39 bottom This 1906 Rolls Royce Silver Ghost
has a steel-colored body in a classic baquet
design. The huge tires for the period were
justified by the enormous size of the car.
The footboard hides useful storage
compartments.

HEROES AND THEIR EXPLOITS

A distasteful but probably truthful cliché says that every war generates technological advances that benefit society. The same principle is said to be true about car races: The experiences garnered from the conditions of extreme stress to which the cars are subjected are said to brings benefits to the whole automobile industry.

This is nonsense if we think of the knowledge matured over the past 100 years, but above all

if we bear in mind that the design from scratch of a new car requires hundreds of millions of dollars. For most of the history of road transport, car races have effectively been used as opportunities for experimentation and testing, particularly if the cars being raced are similar to production models as happened with the early open-topped machines.

Leaving aside the useless and ephemeral beauty contests often held in the early days of the industry, the competitive spirit found its outlet in producing a winner over a fixed distance or within a fixed time, in finishing trials of uniform performance without incurring penalties, in overcoming demanding tests of endurance, distance, reliability and consumption, and in beating one's rivals in speed contests whether on racing circuits, paved or unpaved roads.

From 1895 the competitions became valuable for marketing purposes as advertising trumpeted the model and marque of winners. The heroic drivers, whose biographies almost always have a dramatic end, made a powerful impact on the imagination of a public in search of thrills and adventure.

Governments and monarchies considered car racing a political rather than technological fact and did not neglect to support the endeavors of these medieval knights transported into the industrial century.

France was the unrivaled home of car racing: It held the first competitions and instituted the first annual Grand Prix. From 1894 the Automobile Club of France organized demanding intercity competitions for cars that were almost production models.

The list below gives the routes and distances.
1894, Paris-Rouen, 79 miles;
1895, Paris-Bordeaux-Paris, 732 miles;
1896, Paris-Marseilles-Paris, 1063 miles;
1897, Paris-Dieppe, 106 miles;
1898, Paris-Amsterdam-Paris, 889 miles;
1899, Paris-Bordeaux (351 miles) and Tour de France (1350 miles);
1900, Paris-Toulouse-Paris, 837 miles;
1901, Paris-Bordeaux (328 miles) and Paris-Berlin (687 miles);
1902, Paris-Vienna, 615 miles;
1903, Paris-Madrid, 342 miles (cancelled at Bordeaux due to accidents).

41 top right Vittorio Lancia, the famous Fiat engineer and driver, drives the 75 HP successor to the 60 HP at the 1904 Susa-Moncenisio race.

41 bottom right Dan Wurgis, record-breaking racing driver, at grips with a dangerous racing "cart", the Oldsmobile Pirate, with which he beat a Winton Bullet in the first organized racing event held at Daytona Beach.

40 top This picture shows a team passing through city streets in the first Grand Prix, Paris-Rouen in 1894. The passers-by do not seem to be paying attention - probably they are unaware that it is a race, and the streets are still the dominion of the horse-and-carriage. The 79 mile race was won by Count de Dion driving a de Dion, but he was disqualified because he was not accompanied by a mechanic. First place was then awarded to Lemaitre in a Peugeot.

40 bottom Giovanni Agnelli, a founder of Fiat, with Felice Nazzaro during a test run in the 1901 Tour of Italy. The car is a Fiat 8 HP.

41 top left A Fiat 45 HP in action in 1904 with Vittorio Lancia at the wheel. The 60 HP version was better known; its engine was over 10 liters! It was first in its class at the Targa Florio.

41 bottom left Fiat participating at the 1906 Winter Cup. The driver is Salmson, twice winner of this competition, and the car is the 60 HP. Notice the spikes on the spare wheel.

The many accidents during the 1903 race caused the deaths of ten drivers, mechanics and spectators and was halted at Bordeaux. Outright winners of many early contests were the Panhards, driven by Panhard's partner Emile Levassor. The two Frenchmen are also important because they managed to import the technology and motors of Daimler into France from 1890 on. This was due to the intervention of the future wife of Levassor, the enterprising Madame Sarazin, widow of Emile Sarazin the French importer of Deutz products. Peugeot too obtained Daimler motors though was never able to beat the amazing pair. The only cars to manage that feat were Mors and Renault. Mors is generally an unrecognized name today yet it was this company that later nurtured the creative genius of André Citroën. Average speeds for the first races were between 10 and 28 mph

but these soon increased appreciably. In 1899 James Gordon Bennet, editor of the New York Herald's European edition, established a race that bore his name and ran from 1900 to 1905. The French dominated at first, but Briton Selwyn Edge's Napier won in 1902, then Camille Jenatzy's Mercedes 60 PS (1903). Each year, the race moved to the previous victor's country. In addition to the French races and the Gordon Bennet Trophy (which often overlapped), the newspapers reported a large number of events held throughout the industrialized world. Perhaps the list below will give the reader the sensation of competitive tension that existed between 1895 and 1905 before road racing of open-topped touring and racing cars went their separate ways. This happened soon after as countries all over the world instituted their own Grand Prix events, though they were not yet

42 center *The 1903 Simplex 60 HP had baquet coachwork, i.e. with four seats. Note the tub-like rear volume and the fact that there is no front door. The car's overall appearance does not impress, particularly the radiator without decoration of any kind. Several versions of this important model were available including a single-seater, 90 HP racer.*

42 bottom *This photo of a 1903 Mercedes Simplex 60 HP shows the enormous chain-drive crown wheel. Three tires are seen behind the fuel tank which suggests this was to be used on a long journey. This hypothesis is confirmed by the absence of a rear fender and by the trunk fixed to the rear.*

organized into a regular world championship.

1895: Oscar Mueller in a Benz vis-à-vis won the first test of reliability in the US.

1898: The first race on German soil (Berlin-Potsdam-Berlin) with Daimler's racing debut.

1900: The first racing Fiat, a 6 HP model, driven by two future constructors, Felice Nazzaro and Vincenzo Lancia, won the Vicenza-Bassano-Treviso-Padova race at an average speed of 38 mph.

1901: The number of races increased enough to permit division of cars into four classes based on overall weight.

1903: The first victory of a Benz car, at Huy in Belgium, in an acceleration competition. Second was a Daimler-Mercedes. Average speed was 74.9 mph. The 60 HP Fiat tourer won a trial raced on snow, the Winter Cup.

Meanwhile there was an unending series of extraordinary long distance exploits in open-topped cars over dusty, risky courses. Sometimes these were individual undertakings, sometimes

competitions. In 1897, Winton drove from Cleveland to New York in 10 days in a car of his own construction. In 1900 the first long distance trial took place in Great Britain, the "Thousand Miles Trials", and was won by a 4 cylinder English Daimler. In 1902 a two cylinder Autocar Runabout covered the relatively rough and badly surfaced roads between Philadelphia and New York in 6 hours 10 minutes.

Another race version which held great excitement for the public was the challenge between two contestants only. In 1901 the first racing Ford beat a Winton over 10 miles at an average speed of 44 mph. In 1902 the racing circuit at Daytona Beach was inaugurated when Dan Wurgis beat a Winton Bullet driving an extremely dangerous single cylinder machine where the driver more or less clung onto a light cart like a jockey. In the same year a 12 HP Fiat Corsa beat a Panhard in a challenge over 189 miles between Villanova and Bologna at an average speed of 22 mph.

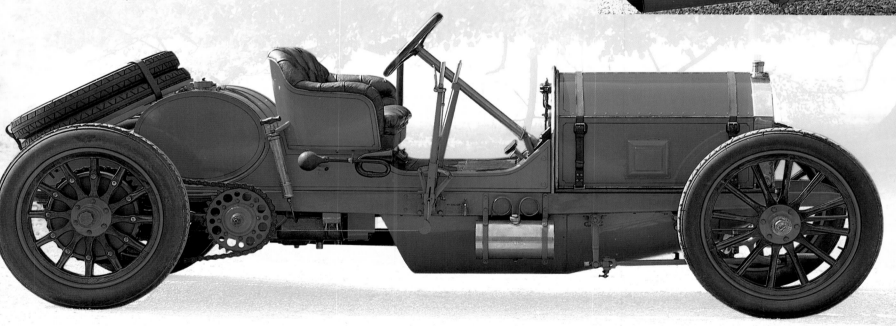

43 top The simplicity of the cockpit of the Fiat Targa Florio 28/40 HP of 1907 was determined by its racing use.

43 center The Fiat Targa Florio 28/40 HP triumphed in a hard fought Targa Florio in 1907. It won first and second places driven by Nazzaro and Lancia.

43 bottom The photograph shows the engine unit of the 1907 Fiat Targa Florio. The size of this 4 cylinder engine was 7363cc. Note the external components of the symmetrical valve timing system but more importantly the

characteristic two block architecture with two cylinders per block. The name 28/40 HP should not fool anyone - the power it produced was actually 60 HP at 1200 rpm, giving a top speed of 59 mph.

44-45 This 2-seater runabout with separate seats is a 1907 Mercedes Simplex. It was produced from 1901 in various body styles and in long and short wheelbase versions. The engine had an unusual structure: the 4 cylinders were grouped in 2 blocks cast separately. Engine size varied from 4.1 to 9.2 liters depending on the version.

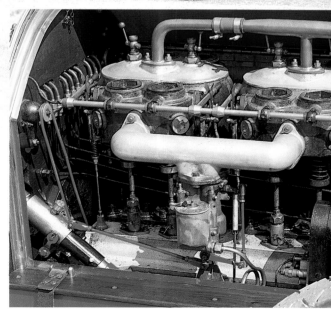

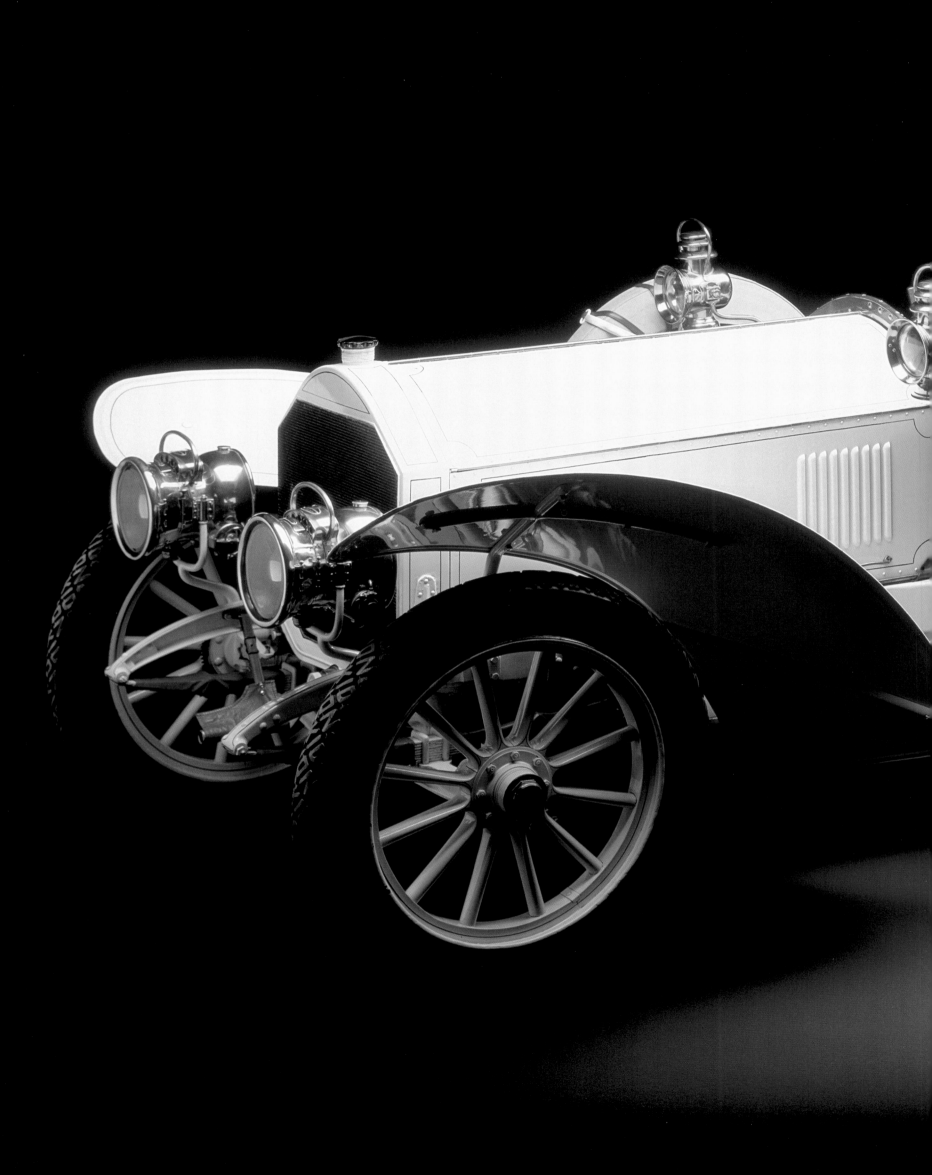

THE CAR "TURNS" OPEN-TOPPED
THE METAMORPHOSIS: THE TORPEDO

46 top Another famous Daimler-Benz owner was Tsar Nicholas II seen here with his daughters while following military maneuvers in 1911. The car was a Daimler Knight 16/40 PS produced from 1910 to the beginning of World War I. The unusual feature of the Knight engine, whose patent was bought by Paul Daimler, was that the timing system used an internal metallic sleeve lining controlled by a lateral camshaft and roller gear. The Knight timing system was silent.

Technical development saw cars become longer, more comfortable and offer more accessories as they moved further and further away from their antecedent, the horse-drawn carriage. It was still too early though for sporting variations on closed bodywork - the forerunner of the coupé was still a long way off - but by 1910 many of the features that would be familiar until the 1940's had appeared.

The link between the "baquet", the touring car from the beginning of the century, and the cabriolet (convertible) and Gran Turismo (GT)

models of the 1920's was the "torpedo". The torpedo was long with bodywork made up mainly of flat, square metal sheets. The doors were low and above them no covering or protection was offered to the passengers. The soft top wrapped around a central rod just behind the driver's seat and was held rigid by three or four ribs; it was either held tight by tie-rods that hooked onto the front leaf springs (a very ugly arrangement) or by slender uprights close to the windshield or thereabouts (windshields were not always

a feature of the torpedo). Seen from the side with the hood down, the top of the car was flat as though it had been planed; with the hood up, the large bay between the central rod and the front fastener becomes apparent.

The Benz 40-45 PS from 1910 is a good example of the transition from baquet to torpedo: The rounded lines have hardened and even the rear fender became a thin flat sheet, but the seats still stand up generously to put their passengers in good view.

46 bottom The Daimler Phaéton 22/40 PS came on the market in 1910. The car in the picture had a slightly more powerful engine and was produced in 1912. Besides the 4-seater 22/40 with the removable top, closed and tracked versions were available, the "Kolonialwagen" and the "Camp".

47 top The steering wheel of the Mercedes 37/90 PS had a pale wooden grip and four undulating steel spokes which were fixed to the steering column.

47 center The Mercedes 37/90 PS was made from the start of 1910. In the foreground the full wheels are clearly seen. Less visible are the straight rear fenders which did not last long as both manufacturers and customers preferred the traditional, curved form.

47 bottom The picture shows the motor compartment of a Mercedes 37/90 PS. Note the timing system, the pushrods and rocker arms (it had three valves, one inlet and two outlets) and the first stages of the curved and welded exhaust pipes which later were to become flexible. The motor had a cooling system for each cylinder which operated via "a welded plate envelope in which cooling water circulates" to quote the technical description of the time. In practice, each cylinder was surrounded by water.

48 top Louis Chevrolet, racing driver, shows off his prototype. The car manufacturing company was actually founded by Billy Durant who wanted to exploit the driver's fame. Louis Chevrolet designed an elegant and luxurious car, as we can see, while Durant needed a cheap model for mass-production, so Louis Chevrolet left the company to work with Frontenac while Durant continued on his way, using the Chevrolet to successfully regain control of General Motors. The black and white photograph does not do justice to the beautiful dark gray of the car which contrasted with the gold on the borders of the door, the radiator grill, the starting handle and the headlights. The wheels were cream-colored.

48 center and bottom This can be considered the first A.L.F.A., predecessor to Alfa Romeo: It is the 24 HP from 1910, here in torpedo form. This car and its early successors were designed by Giuseppe Merosi. The picture below shows the horn: Positioned on the right fender, it could be blown by the driver via a pump outside the door.

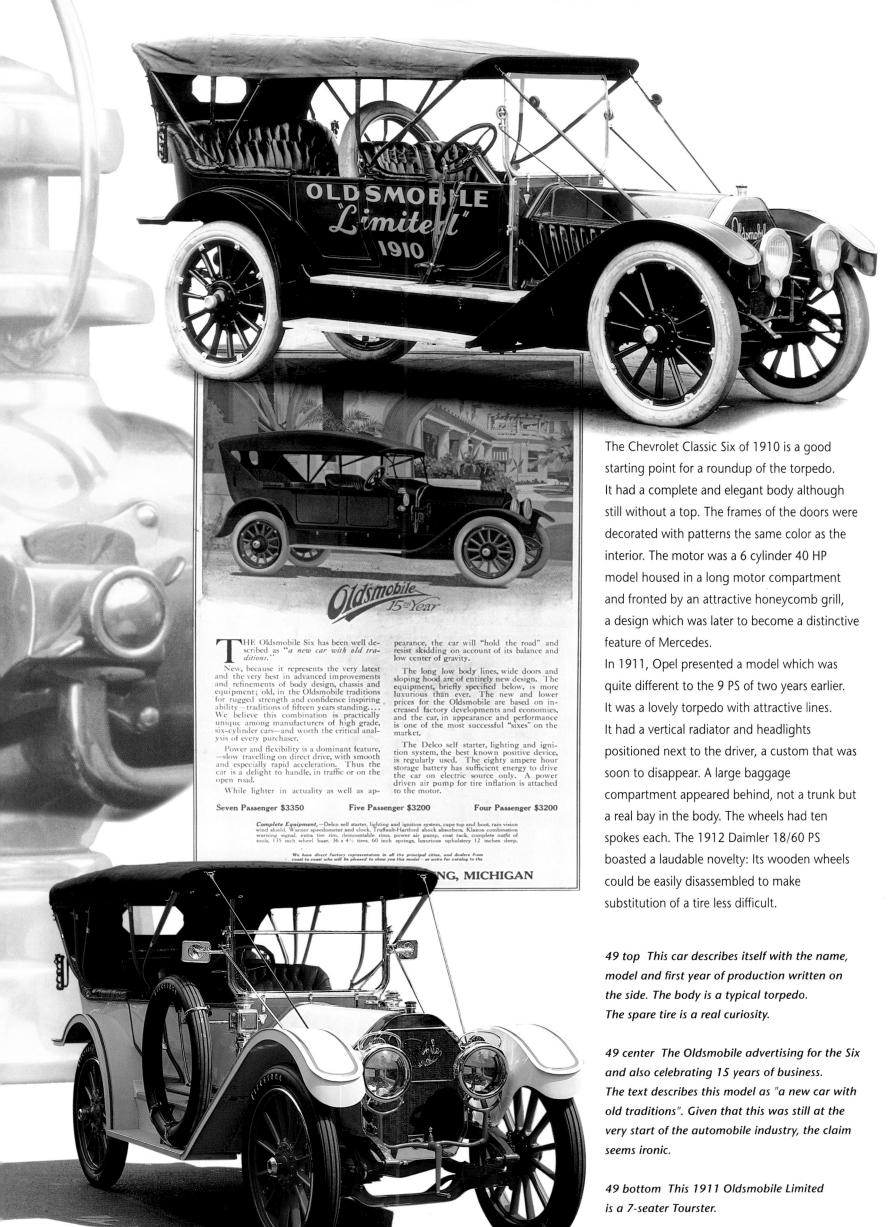

The Chevrolet Classic Six of 1910 is a good starting point for a roundup of the torpedo. It had a complete and elegant body although still without a top. The frames of the doors were decorated with patterns the same color as the interior. The motor was a 6 cylinder 40 HP model housed in a long motor compartment and fronted by an attractive honeycomb grill, a design which was later to become a distinctive feature of Mercedes.

In 1911, Opel presented a model which was quite different to the 9 PS of two years earlier. It was a lovely torpedo with attractive lines. It had a vertical radiator and headlights positioned next to the driver, a custom that was soon to disappear. A large baggage compartment appeared behind, not a trunk but a real bay in the body. The wheels had ten spokes each. The 1912 Daimler 18/60 PS boasted a laudable novelty: Its wooden wheels could be easily disassembled to make substitution of a tire less difficult.

49 top This car describes itself with the name, model and first year of production written on the side. The body is a typical torpedo. The spare tire is a real curiosity.

49 center The Oldsmobile advertising for the Six and also celebrating 15 years of business. The text describes this model as "a new car with old traditions". Given that this was still at the very start of the automobile industry, the claim seems ironic.

49 bottom This 1911 Oldsmobile Limited is a 7-seater Tourster.

49

50 top A Lancia with typical torpedo coachwork. This is the 1913 Theta, a luxurious version which was very successful both in Europe and the US, selling a total of 1,696 units. It was second only to the 1912 Cadillac in having a complete electric plant including starting motor as standard. Note the two halves of the windshield, which could be turned in opposite directions. The front and rear cabs were separate in a configuration known as "dual cowl"; the two rectangular elements by the doors are the backrests of the jump seats.

The term "baquet" had been synonymous with touring car up until this point but now "touring" came to mean a car with four doors, four seats and a long wheelbase; the same in fact as for production model torpedoes. The 1913 Buick Model 25 Touring was an example of the type and enjoyed great success, selling 8,000 units. Cadillac took no chances and decided to call that year's model a Torpedo Touring. Finally, the gearshift and all other controls were placed inside the body.

The Lancia Theta Torpedo (1913-1919) can be considered a standard of this type of car. The body panels were continuous and uniformly square like the door panels. It had a windshield and a less upright driving seat with the steering column and wheel less exposed.

The technological and stylistic progress was clear, particularly compared to the Beta baquet discussed in the previous chapter and the Fiat 20-30 HP Type 3 produced from 1910-12. As a landau version of this Fiat existed, it can be considered a true convertible!

50 bottom Count von Ratibor, president of the Imperial Automobil Club, greets Kaiser Wilhelm II on board a 1913 Mercedes Knight called a "Kardanwagen".

51 top left King Alfonso XIII of Spain on a state parade to Morocco in 1919. The car is a very costly Benz Runabout 22/25 PS.

51 top right The Citroën price list in the 1920's. Besides the torpedo in the center, the top car to the right is interesting - it was the 1923 Caddy Sport used successfully in racing.

51 center This 1913 Lancia Beta Torpedo is distinguished by its long-span hood.

51 bottom This simple torpedo with full wheels is the 1928 Opel Viersitzer Kabriolet.

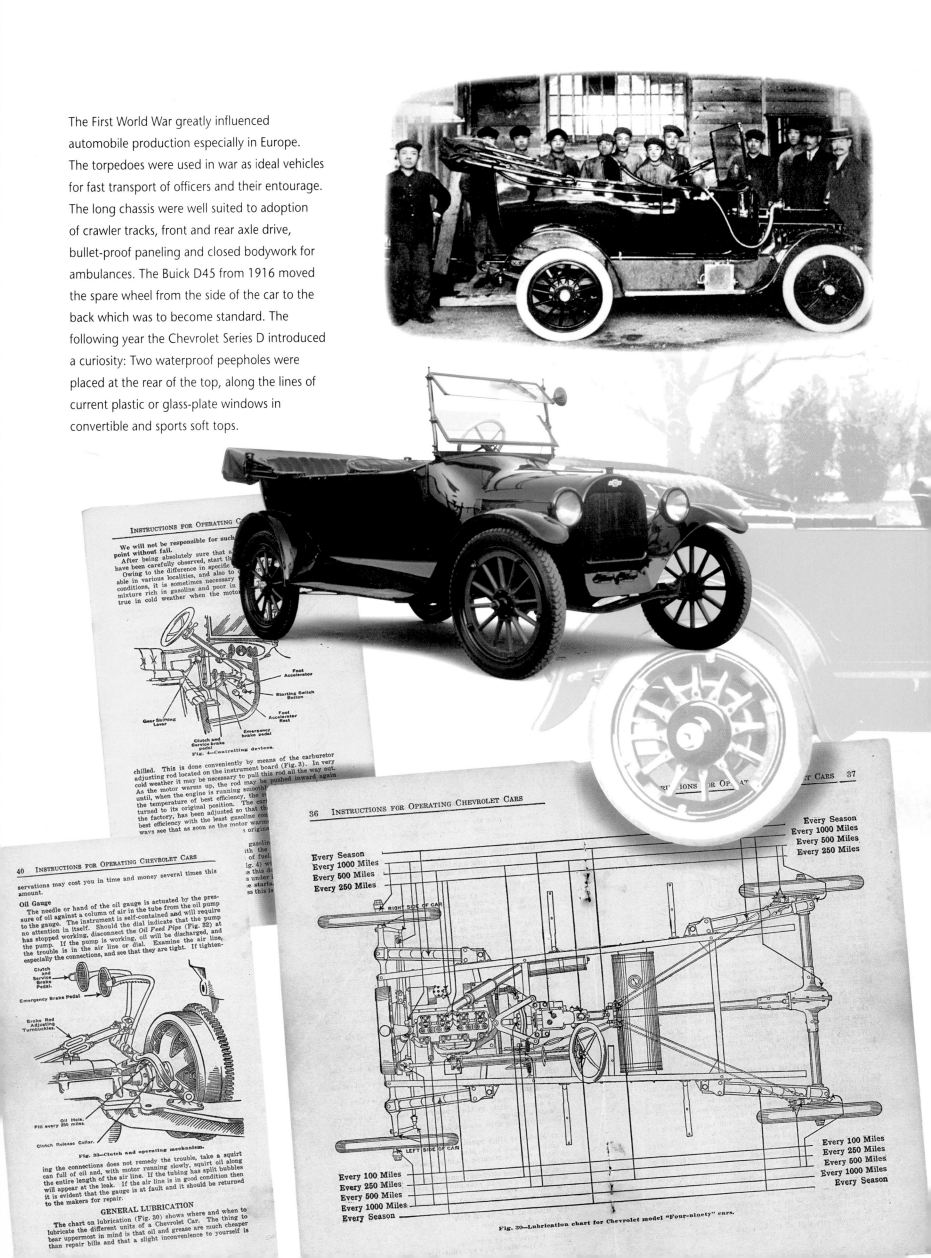

The First World War greatly influenced automobile production especially in Europe. The torpedoes were used in war as ideal vehicles for fast transport of officers and their entourage. The long chassis were well suited to adoption of crawler tracks, front and rear axle drive, bullet-proof paneling and closed bodywork for ambulances. The Buick D45 from 1916 moved the spare wheel from the side of the car to the back which was to become standard. The following year the Chevrolet Series D introduced a curiosity: Two waterproof peepholes were placed at the rear of the top, along the lines of current plastic or glass-plate windows in convertible and sports soft tops.

INSTRUCTIONS FOR OPERATING C...

point without fail.
After being absolutely sure that a... have been carefully observed, start th...
Owing to the difference in specific... able in various localities, and also to c... conditions, it is sometimes necessary... mixture rich in gasoline and poor in... true in cold weather when the motor...

chilled. This is done conveniently by means of the carburetor adjusting rod located on the instrument board (Fig. 3). In very cold weather it may be necessary to pull this rod all the way out. As the motor warms up, the rod may be pushed inward again until, when the engine is running smoothly, the r... the temperature of best efficiency, the r... turned to its original position. The car... best efficiency with the least gasoline con... the factory, has been adjusted so that the... ways see that as soon as the motor warm... original...

Foot Accelerator
Starting Switch Button
Foot Accelerator Rest
Gear Shifting Lever
Emergency brake pedal
Clutch and Service brake pedal
Fig. 4—Controlling devices.

40 INSTRUCTIONS FOR OPERATING CHEVROLET CARS

servations may cost you in time and money several times this amount.

Oil Gauge
The needle or hand of the oil gauge is actuated by the pressure of oil against a column of air in the tube from the oil pump to the gauge. The instrument is self-contained and will require no attention in itself. Should the dial indicate that the pump has stopped working, disconnect the *Oil Feed Pipe* (Fig. 32) at the pump. If the pump is working, oil will be discharged, and the trouble is in the air line or dial. Examine the air line, especially the connections, and see that they are tight. If tighten-

Clutch and Service Brake Pedal.
Emergency Brake Pedal
Brake Rod Adjusting Turnbuckles.
Oil Hole. Fill every 250 miles.
Clutch Release Collar.
Fig. 33—Clutch and operating mechanism.

ing the connections does not remedy the trouble, take a squirt can full of oil and, with motor running slowly, squirt oil along the entire length of the air line. If the tubing has split bubbles will appear at the leak. If the air line is in good condition then it is evident that the gauge is at fault and it should be returned to the makers for repair.

GENERAL LUBRICATION
The chart on lubrication (Fig. 30) shows where and when to lubricate the different units of a Chevrolet Car. The thing to bear uppermost in mind is that oil and grease are much cheaper than repair bills and that a slight inconvenience to yourself is

...gasolin... ...th the... of fuel. ...ig. 4) wi... ...s this do... ...s under i... ...e starts... ...ss this is...

...IONS...OR OP...AT...T CARS 37

36 INSTRUCTIONS FOR OPERATING CHEVROLET CARS

Every Season
Every 1000 Miles
Every 500 Miles
Every 250 Miles

Every Season
Every 1000 Miles
Every 500 Miles
Every 250 Miles

RIGHT SIDE OF CAR

LEFT SIDE OF CAR

Every 100 Miles
Every 250 Miles
Every 500 Miles
Every 1000 Miles
Every Season

Every 100 Miles
Every 250 Miles
Every 500 Miles
Every 1000 Miles
Every Season

Fig. 30—Lubrication chart for Chevrolet model "Four-ninety" cars.

52 top This is a very special car. It is a 1915 Dat 31. Dat was the forerunner of Datsun and therefore of Nissan. For a long time, Japanese car production was almost unknown to the rest of the world, particularly of convertibles which were practically non-existent.

52 center This is a Chevrolet 4 90 Touring from 1919, a low cost and smallish torpedo.

52-53 The picture is of an Oldsmobile Model 53 from 1913. Olds was counting on this model to relaunch sales which had been disappointing with the Limited. The Model 53 had a Delco integrated ignition and lighting unit.

53 top The most popular Buick in 1916 was the Model 45. Almost 74,000 were built.

53 bottom Instead of a rectangular or lozenge rear window, the 1917 Chevrolet Series D had two portholes.

52 bottom Pages from the Chevrolet 4 90 manual. The double page shows the lubrication intervals for each element subject to friction. The motor oil had to be topped up every 100 miles and the suspension was to be checked and tightened at every change of season.

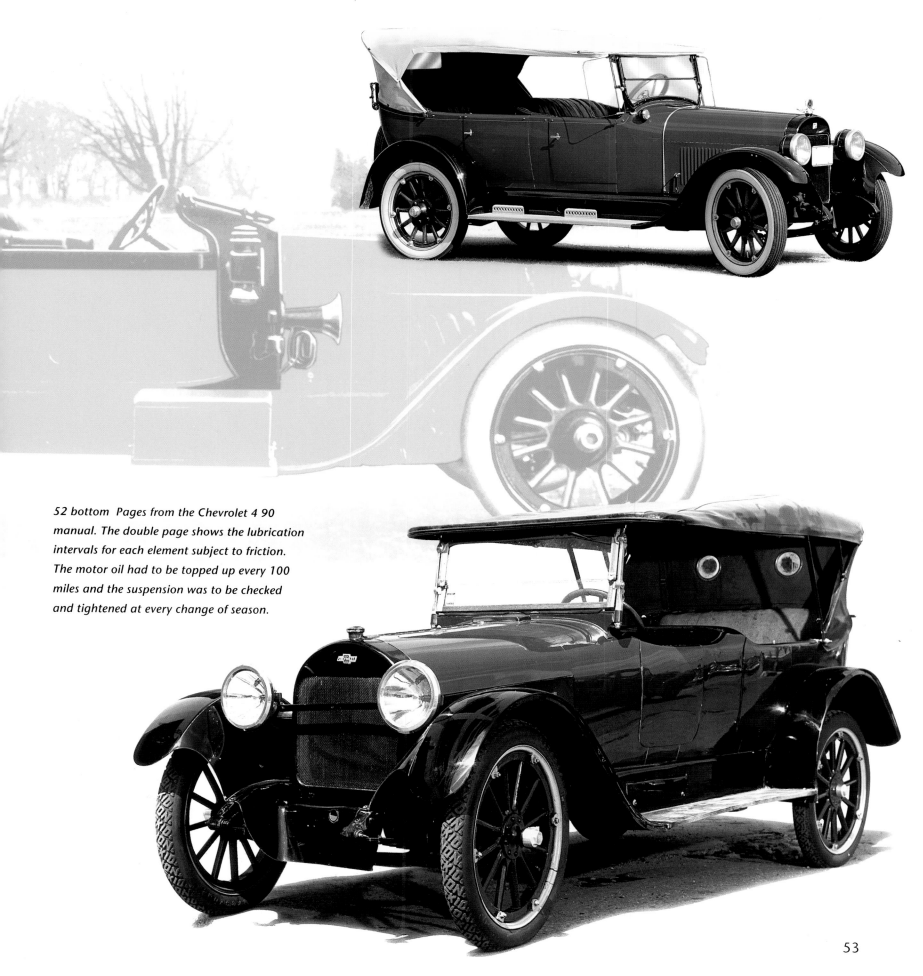

54 and 55 top This is the elegant 1912 Minerva which belonged to the king of Belgium. Note how the top protects only the rear passengers and only partially at that. The detail above shows the hood opening and closing system; the design of the curved, gilded lever depended on the model. It turned almost 180° around a central pin. On the next page at the top,

a detail is shown of the radiator cap, which was often mounted with symbols that identified the car such as birds, cats, mythological or other figures. This one is the goddess Minerva who gave her name to the car. The symbol was also attached to the top of the grill where the goddess was shown in profile with her helmet clearly evident.

55 center The 1914 Rolls Royce Silver Ghost Alpine Eagle was very luxurious. The coachwork was that of a traditional high class torpedo. The touching spoke wheels are very attractive, especially when compared to the more solid "artillery" type design.

The Benz 27/70 PS produced between 1918 and 1923 was also interesting. Like its predecessor it had a concave rear with the body resting on the chassis, and at last here was a top that offered rear passengers side protection with the use of removable panels. The engine was similarly improved; the four cylinders became six in-line in two separately welded blocks. The capacity was 7065cc, and the top speed 59 mph.

The last torpedo in this roundup is the Citroën Type A or 10 HP from 1919. It was special because it was the first European car to be mass produced plus it had electric ignition and was one of the first cars to have left hand drive It had a monobloc engine, four cylinders in-line and a small 1327cc motor which mirrored its low price and popularity: 18,291 units were sold and that was just open-topped versions.

The wheels were particularly interesting for their complete hubcap.

It is just possible to make out a small detail in the bodywork that was to continue for decades in Citroën cars, the large, well-shaped front fender quite separate from the wheel which ends in the footboard at the height of the front door hinges. The top hooks on at the back, one section is held by two spokes, another is suspended and held tight by a rib. Two side uprights pull the top tight at the front. It even resembles a French beret!

Around 1920 it was just possible to see the development appearing of two families of open-topped cars: the cabriolet/convertible, derived from a sedan or created as part of a project for a sedan; and the sports car, designed as an open top, generally a powerful two-seater in which the soft top is as often as not an accessory to be ignored and which has already been mentioned with regard to roadsters.

55 bottom This 1914 Rolls Royce torpedo has many characteristic features. The hood protected only the rear passengers; the driver had a door to himself; the rear passengers had an additional windshield with side vent windows as was to become popular soon after in dual cowl designs; the doors opened in the opposed configuration i.e. front doors as normal but back doors with the hinge at the rear.

THE CAR IN EUROPE DURING THE 1920's

From about 1920 the car took on even more definite shapes. Following the schools of thought and philosophical trends of the day, the secular marriage of form and function took place which is still current today. In the United States basic positive values linked to lightheartedness, fun and well-being came to the fore: Why shouldn't the car be beautiful, too, and a companion to share happy times with?

At the end of the 1990's, a guru of design, Chris Bangle, who works for BMW and is the creator of the modern 3-Series, claims that beauty is functional and not an end in itself as is commonly thought. He says that the ability to "make someone happy", to cheer someone up,

face, Nike of Samothrace, an eagle, a stork, a stylized propeller and a famous jaguar (that would come later). Open bodies were still the most common design and their de luxe variants were no longer the preserve of the aristocracy, VIP's, maharajahs and stars of the silent screen. The middle classes also wanted their elegant and refined status symbols. Now that the carriage had passed out of fashion, how was one to arrive at the Ascot races, Rue Faubourg St. Honoré for a little shopping, Rockefeller Plaza for breakfast, the start of the Targa Florio or the first night of the opera in Berlin? Which vehicle was the best combination of disguised modernism and the need to show off? One just

had to have a torpedo. Industrial production was expanding, and with it the list of potential customers; so too did the range of variants and versions grow. Two events, however, had a major effect on the economic and industrial development of this period (1920-30): the carryover from the First World War and the Wall Street Crash in 1929.

The first affected both ownership structures and production strongly because German industries had made the strategic error of dedicating their efforts to the production of luxury models. The second brought ruin indiscriminately and put paid to the weakest companies or those who had not yet reached large scale production.

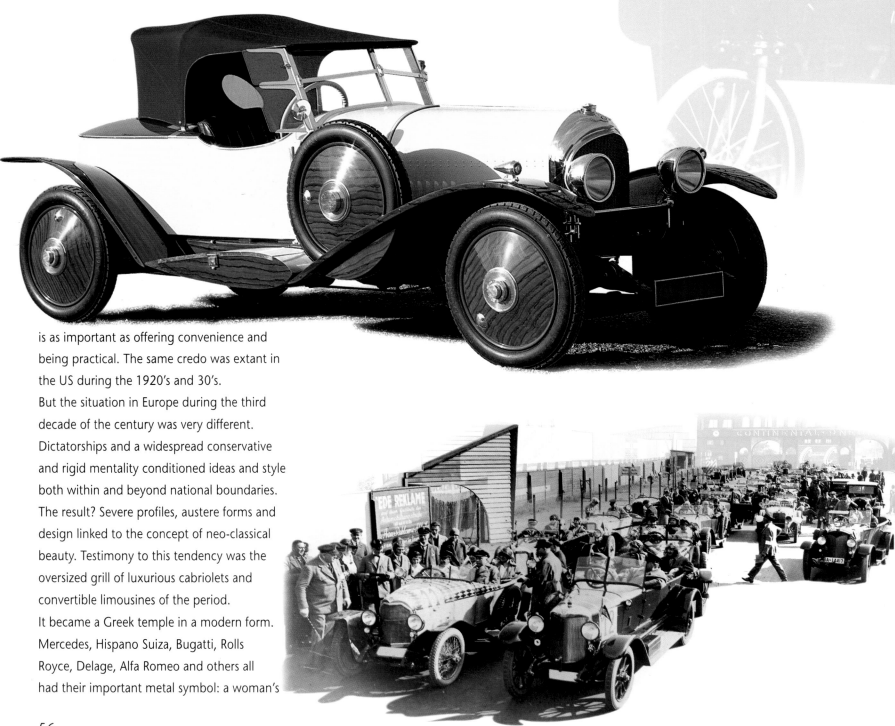

is as important as offering convenience and being practical. The same credo was extant in the US during the 1920's and 30's.

But the situation in Europe during the third decade of the century was very different. Dictatorships and a widespread conservative and rigid mentality conditioned ideas and style both within and beyond national boundaries. The result? Severe profiles, austere forms and design linked to the concept of neo-classical beauty. Testimony to this tendency was the oversized grill of luxurious cabriolets and convertible limousines of the period.

It became a Greek temple in a modern form. Mercedes, Hispano Suiza, Bugatti, Rolls Royce, Delage, Alfa Romeo and others all had their important metal symbol: a woman's

56 top The picture shows a 1926 8 liter Bentley in the long wheelbase version.

56 bottom The Berlin Automobil Club celebrates the anniversary of its founding. It is 1925 and the procession of open tops is preparing to leave the Avus race track.

57 top This Daimler Lancaster 21 dates from 1926. While car design was moving ahead in leaps and bounds in the US, in Europe the trend was towards more austere, classical shapes, particularly in countries governed by dictators like Italy and Germany. This model was fitted with comfortable cantilever suspension.

57 center Henry Royce, one of the founders of Rolls Royce, at the wheel of one of his models with its extra long motor compartment from the 1920's.

57 bottom Rolls Royces evolved too, taking on forms less and less related to the horse-drawn carriage during the 1920's. This 1928 Phantom I Open Tourer boasts a splendid chrome radiator grill topped by the famous Winged Victory. The resemblance of the grill to a Greek temple is quite evident.

56-57 Improved reliability meant that the car increasingly became a means of long-distance family transport. This family in the 1920's seems to be preparing for a long journey to judge by the amount of baggage. Note how the cases are fixed with leather straps to a special flap. Bearing in mind the quality of the roads and suspensions in use at the time, it is easy to imagine the stress imposed on the bags!

The German industrial situation was complex. In 1926 an important financial event took place which affected the balance of the whole motoring industry, the merger of Daimler and Benz. In Germany in 1927 there was only one car per every 171 inhabitants and the total number of cars in circulation was small - 218,000, compared to 585,000 in France and 754,000 in Great Britain. There were also fewer roads, 219,000 miles as compared with 391,000 miles in France; and there were twenty active manufacturers producing forty models. When the government opened its arms to American industry, ruthless competition ensued which saw the less-organized German companies succumb to the enormous economies of scale that the Americans enjoyed. Ford alone produced twice as many cars as all Germany. One of the most important companies was Horch, which had once belonged to August Horch. He had been ousted in 1909 and had since founded another marque, Audi. The name was the Latin version of his own name, meaning "listen". In 1923 the head of the Horch design team was Paul Daimler, son of the great Gottlieb, who had been technical manager of Mercedes from 1907 to 1922. In 1925 Paul Daimler saw his dream come true, a futuristic 8 cylinder motor with double camshafts (later replaced with a single overhead cam due to thermal problems) to power the luxury models of the 300 and later 400 Series. A representative cabriolet of the range was the 375, whose 3-3.9 liter engines produced 80 HP. The pneumatically controlled four-wheel brakes were innovative, but the design was traditional. At the front, two large headlights and the radiator with vertical bars vied for attention. The bumper was composed of three separate chromed parts and was the precursor of a style that was later to be seen on American convertibles of the Machine Age. The wheels had slender "bicycle" spokes and were covered by large fenders on which rested two smaller lights. The spare wheel was close to the driver on a wide footboard. The top was held up by an S-shaped support (as in the majority of such cars) which allowed it to fold down easily. Running along the top of the outside of the windshield was an adjustable fin for keeping the sun off. And Mercedes? It was second in sales volume to Opel and continued to produce beautiful, sophisticated models, especially in the gran turismo niche. Among the cabriolets, the Mannheim series is certainly worthy of note, created by Ferdinand Porsche around a new motor which was supposed to replace the admirable but thirsty supercharged 8 cylinder K Series engine. The first Mannheim was produced in 1926 with a 55 HP, 3 liter, 6 cylinder in-line engine. Soon a new style began to make itself felt based on medium sized American convertibles which had more balance between the front and rear volumes. The passenger cab was a shapeless box created by the semi-hard top. The next version maintained the same overall length but gave more room to the rear passengers and the top returned to the double support design used on the torpedo.

MERCEDES

Fabrikat der
Daimler-Motoren-Gesellschaft
Stuttgart-Untertürkheim

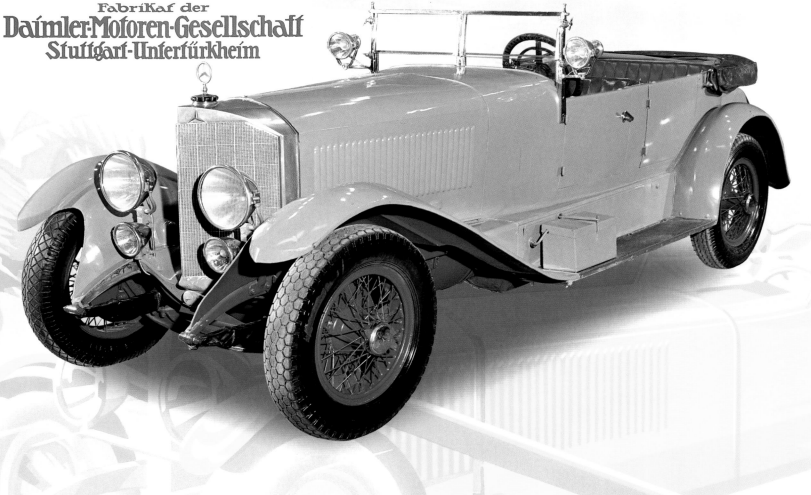

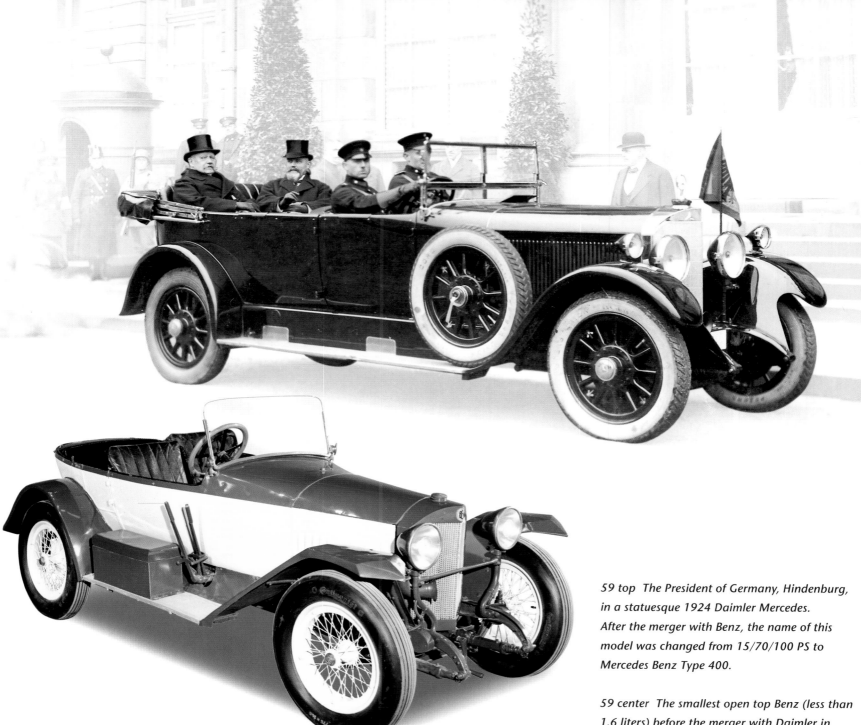

59 top The President of Germany, Hindenburg, in a statuesque 1924 Daimler Mercedes. After the merger with Benz, the name of this model was changed from 15/70/100 PS to Mercedes Benz Type 400.

59 center The smallest open top Benz (less than 1.6 liters) before the merger with Daimler in 1926. This sports model was very popular with the young.

58 top This Mercedes advertisement is set in Egypt. As well as the three pointed star not yet inscribed in a metal circle, note that the official name was still Daimler-Motoren-Gesellschaft.

58 bottom Paul Daimler, son of Gottlieb, brilliant mechanical engineer, brought the experience gained in the first years of Grand Prix racing to bear on the 28/95 PS: overhead camshaft, overhead valves and high voltage magneto ignition (more reliable than coil ignition and long used in airplanes). The grill is not inspired by Greek temples but is a bullnose design. The finishing details, such as the choice of paint, were all of top quality: The wheels, interior, hood cover and underbody were all the same color.

59 bottom These three Mercedes Benz were produced shortly after the Benz merger. On the left is the 15/70/100 PS and on the right two 24/100/140 PS. The K model was part of this series, from which were derived the S, SK and SSK. Production of these models throughout the rest of the 1920's ranged from elegance and absolute luxury to immense power and sportiness.

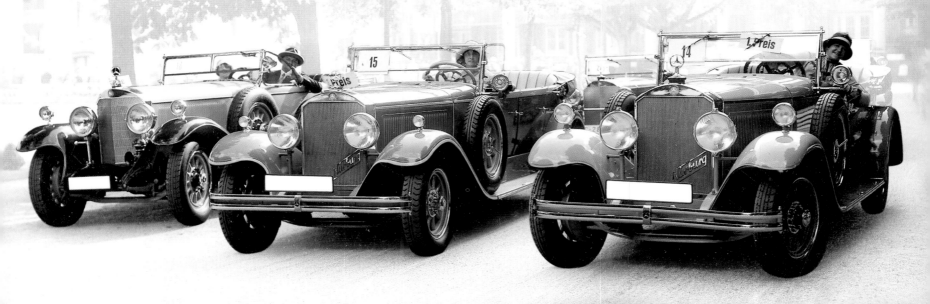

In 1929 a car with an old name, the 3/15, but made by a new company, BMW, went on sale. The Bayerische Motoren Werke was a distinguished company which produced powerful airplane engines. The year before it had bought the company Fahrzeugfabrik Eisenach which already made the Dixi 3/15. The aim of both Dixi and BMW was to assemble and sell small economical cars - and preferably under license, rather than designed and produced from scratch, for the economics of the period discouraged large projects. Their choice was an English car, the 748cc Austin Seven. It was a happy choice and in 1928 alone about 6,000 were sold. This was a perfect example of pragmatism winning over patriotism.

The 3/15 (DA 1 and successive models) differed from the English car by having left hand drive and Bosch electrics. It had a four cylinder engine which produced 15 HP to give a maximum speed of 47 mph. There were cable operated brakes on the rear wheels (later on all four) and bicycle style spokes. The 74 inch wheelbase was that of a small economy car. The shape was square without any attempt at beauty. There were two-seat and four-seat versions.

The Dixi was produced in two open-topped versions, the roadster and the so-called gran turismo, and two closed, the coupé and the RM sedan. The open tops were the more economical of the four. However, there were numerous variants of the cabriolet. The roadster bodywork designed by Ihle displayed the double kidney radiator still dear to BMW designers today. Despite its tiny size, it was called a limousine and had a removable top. As the BMW Wartburg (DA 3), it had no doors and a pointed rear end; as the gran turismo model it had 4 seats, fixed uprights and fixed windows and was very popular; as a cabriolet with bodywork by Buhne, it had windows which could be opened, a sloping windshield and sidelights.

DEUTSCHE KAUFT DEUTSCHE WAGEN

OPEL Der
deutsche Qualitätswagen
VIER- und SECHSZYLINDER

Modernste Konstruktion, größtes Beschleunigungs- und
Bremsvermögen, äußerst bequeme Sitzanordnung. Vereint
Qualität, Leistung, Eleganz, Formenschönheit und bekannte
Preiswürdigkeit. — Der Höchstwert für Ihr Geld.

4 PS Vierzylinder Zyl.-Inh. 1,1 Ltr.
10 „ „ „ „ 2,6 „
8 „ Sechszylinder „ 2,0 „
14 „ „ „ „ 3,7 „
16 „ „ „ „ 4,2 „

Von RM 2500. — ab Werk aufwärts

Auf Wunsch gegen 6, 9, 12 und 18 monatliche Teilzahlung bei
geringster Anzahlung nach dem günstigen Opel-Kredit-System

ADAM OPEL / FILIALE BERLIN
COURBIÈRESTRASSE 14 — UNTER DEN LINDEN 66
Telefon: Sammel-Nummer B 5 Barbarossa 9091

Vergessen Sie bitte nicht, während der Internationalen Automobil-
Ausstellung vom 8. bis 18. November, meine hervorragenden neuen
Modelle in den Ausstellungshallen am Kaiserdamm zu besichtigen.
Alte Halle Stand 13, Neue Halle Stand 205

60-61 This BMW 3/15 took its owner to the Italian city of Pisa at the end of the 1920's. The 3/15 was a small and very successful car under both the Dixi and BMW names but in fact it was a replica of the English Austin Seven. The version shown is the cabrio limousine. At this point it still had not assumed the double kidney grill which was to become the distinguishing feature of most successive BMW cars.

60 top The 1928 Dixi 3/15 was small and cheap and presented in a large number of versions and body types. This was the secret of the mini convertible.

60 bottom This small open top is the Austin Seven that was produced under license in Germany and sold as the Dixi 3/15. The Dixi belonged to the company Fahrzeugfabrik Eisenach which was bought in 1928 by BMW, an airplane-engine manufacturer which wanted to assemble and sell small, cheap cars without much investment.

61 top This 1928 advertisement publicizes "a car of German quality" - quality was what the company founded by Adam Opel wanted to be known for. Opel was going through a golden period thanks to shrewd investments giving it state-of-the-art machine tools and foreign currency in a time of German financial mega-inflation.

61 bottom The small Opel 4/12 HP Laubfrosch ("Frog") from 1924 was built in the most modern German factory of the age. The curious name was given because the 2-seater was only available in green. The engine was a 951cc, four cylinder model which gave 47 mpg and the hood was made of rubberized canvas. Tens of thousands were sold.

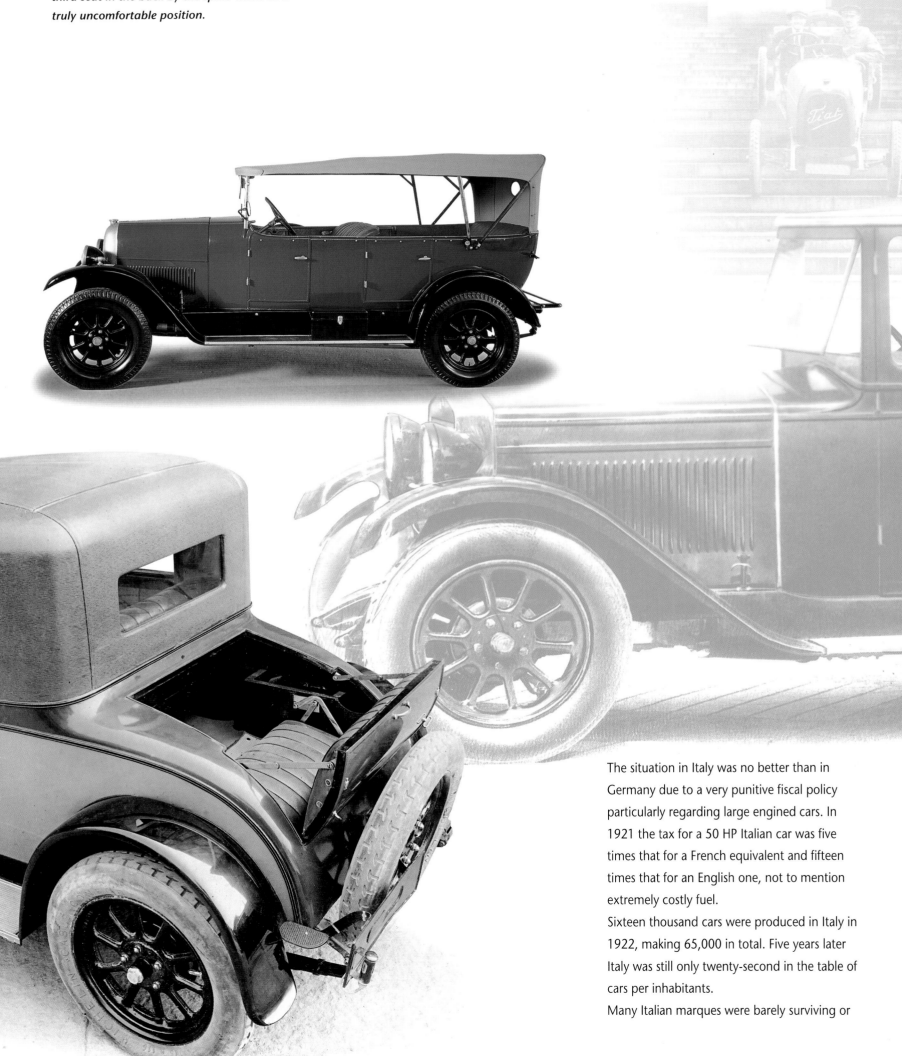

62 top The side view of this Fiat 501 from 1921 shows a perfect example of a mid-class torpedo.

62 bottom and 62-63 center bottom This is the Fiat 509 built from 1927-29. It was called a coupé but it was in fact a convertible. Note the third seat in the back by the spare wheel in a truly uncomfortable position.

62-63 center top A Fiat 501 on the steps of the Reichstag in Berlin. This type of frequent exhibitionism was used for commercial purposes to demonstrate the strength of the car.

The situation in Italy was no better than in Germany due to a very punitive fiscal policy particularly regarding large engined cars. In 1921 the tax for a 50 HP Italian car was five times that for a French equivalent and fifteen times that for an English one, not to mention extremely costly fuel.

Sixteen thousand cars were produced in Italy in 1922, making 65,000 in total. Five years later Italy was still only twenty-second in the table of cars per inhabitants.

Many Italian marques were barely surviving or

had failed or were absorbed by Fiat which in those years controlled 70-80% of the market. Many of these companies had only recently been started up: Om, Ansaldo, Spa, Scat, Diatto, Itala and Bianchi for example. To maintain their position at the top of the production and sales league, Fiat had to renounce any unnecessary feature on their cars, to reduce design to its minimum and leave aside innovation and stylistic flair in favor of pragmatism. And it worked, just as it had for BMW.

A good example is the little 501, a true economy car with a 16 HP engine which sold 45,000 units between 1919 and 1926. It was 12'6" long and had a wheelbase of 8'6". Maximum speed was 44 mph and fuel consumption was claimed to be 22 miles per gallon. An important fact was that the 501 was offered both as a 4-seater torpedo with baggage compartment and as a 2-seater sports car. There is little to say about the bodywork except that it was a set of panels correctly assembled with a minimum of affectation or distinction.

63 right The sequence shows the operations to lay out the Fiat 501's hood. First it was necessary to open the long, horizontal expanse which was then laid out on the Fiat's body.

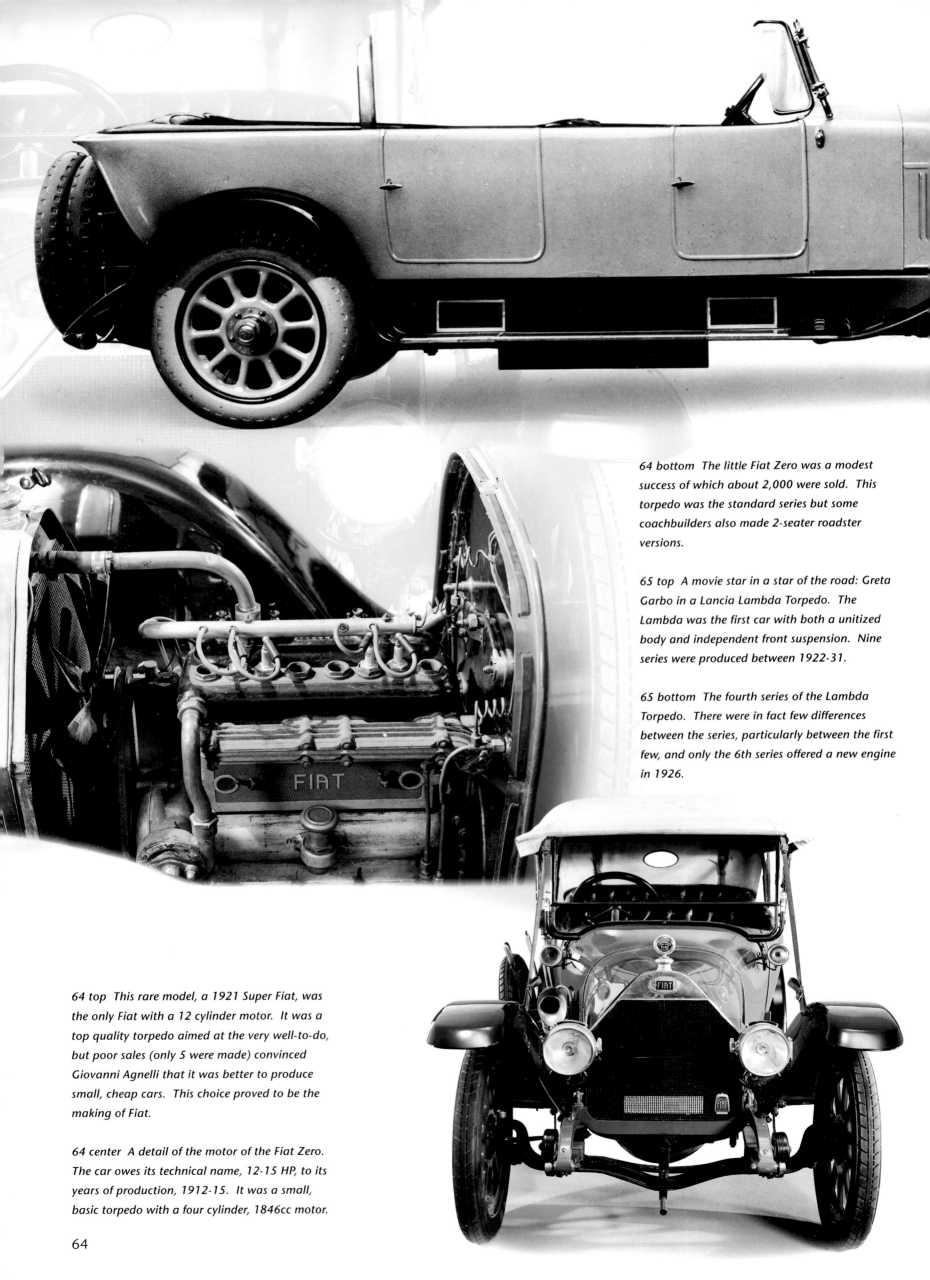

64 bottom The little Fiat Zero was a modest success of which about 2,000 were sold. This torpedo was the standard series but some coachbuilders also made 2-seater roadster versions.

65 top A movie star in a star of the road: Greta Garbo in a Lancia Lambda Torpedo. The Lambda was the first car with both a unitized body and independent front suspension. Nine series were produced between 1922-31.

65 bottom The fourth series of the Lambda Torpedo. There were in fact few differences between the series, particularly between the first few, and only the 6th series offered a new engine in 1926.

64 top This rare model, a 1921 Super Fiat, was the only Fiat with a 12 cylinder motor. It was a top quality torpedo aimed at the very well-to-do, but poor sales (only 5 were made) convinced Giovanni Agnelli that it was better to produce small, cheap cars. This choice proved to be the making of Fiat.

64 center A detail of the motor of the Fiat Zero. The car owes its technical name, 12-15 HP, to its years of production, 1912-15. It was a small, basic torpedo with a four cylinder, 1846cc motor.

The conviction of Fiat boss Agnelli to stick to producing small, economical cars was justified when their only large torpedo, the 520 Super Fiat with V12 engine produced in 1921 for export only, sold 5 units.

Apart from Alfa Romeo which was directing its efforts to producing a magnificent chassis called the RL designed by Merosi, the most active company was Lancia. Their most important car was the Lambda, produced from 1922-31 in 9 series of which, it appears, ten thousand were sold. It had many technical innovations such as a monocoque body with independent front suspension. The motor too was new, a monobloc 2120cc V4 made from aluminum and with three gears. And there were open top models galore, from the traditional Series II torpedo to the two-seater sports version of the Series VII with bodywork by Casaro, and also the lovely Mille Miglia sports.

66 top The 1921 Peugeot Quadrilette had one front seat and one back seat with a door only for the passenger. The length was just 9'5" and the tiny engine just 667cc. 11,575 were sold.

66 center This is not a carousel or a cradle factory but the assembly line for the Peugeot 5 HP cabriolet.

66 bottom The cover of the 1924 Peugeot Revue (in-house magazine) was dedicated to the 5 HP.

66-67 The 1924 Peugeot cabriolet replaced the Quadrilette and repeated its success. The company firmly believed in this 5 HP 172 BC, the first mass-produced Peugeot. It was the smallest model in the 17 series and showed great reliability during the Tour de France. 7,085 were produced.

Peugeot revue

67 top The 1928 Peugeot Cabriolet 183 D had to combine the desire for prestige cars with the need to mass-produce economic models. The design of the coachwork was influenced by what was happening in the US where cars were entering a new phase. Although it was only a small open top, it was elegant, appealing and well-proportioned with a powerful 6 cylinder engine.

67 bottom The Peugeot Cabriolet 174 was built from 1922-28. Peugeot provided the chassis. This example is from 1927 in which the 174 was offered with a small cab and convex wheels. It had a 3828cc engine, top speed was 62 mph and the Peugeot lion pranced on the radiator cap.

Production of cabriolets in France between 1922 and 1926 saw the Peugeot 17-series excel, starting with the successful chassis of the 174 on which many coachbuilders based their creative talents. Various designs were produced but in limited numbers and so were particularly sought after. Curiously, the left hand wheel hubs had a reverse thread with respect to the right hand hubs with the result that two spare wheels were necessary, one for each side.

After the 174 came the 176 and in 1924 the small 172 BC with a 5 HP engine; this car was significant because it was the first cabriolet to be mass produced by Peugeot and because it succeeded in replacing a car that had been very successful, the Quadrilette.

The 174 and 176 followed the contemporary, balanced, three volume design for a cabriolet. The engine was famous because it had sleeve valves; the 174 had a 3800cc version and the 176, 2500cc. The little 172 BC had a tiny engine, 667cc which was increased to 720cc in 1925.

The 1926 "all steel" Citroën B12 Commercial Torpedo was also a novelty. It was designed as an open-topped car but could be converted into a goods van in just a few minutes thanks to its open back and folding flap. It was strong enough to carry up to 1,100 lbs. This was indeed a rare case among European open-topped cars and was an early example of a car with a double use. In all other respects it was a torpedo.

68 top The picture shows the smile of a young woman who has discovered how maneuverable the small 5 HP Citroën Type C is.

68 center Citroën's diminutive 5 HP was also called the Little Lemon because it was colored yellow. It was mostly appreciated by women for its ease of handling and lively spirit. Note the boattail which was also seen on the Caddy Sport.

68 bottom The Renault 10 HP dates from 1923. No great effort was made to make this model look attractive—in fact quite the opposite.

69 top The small red car is the Citroën 5 HP from 1923. It was no longer a cabriolet; its appearance would classify it as a roadster or even a small torpedo. The wheels seem too large for such a small car.

69 bottom This is the Renault 45 HP seen from above. The car had a 6 cylinder, almost 10 liter engine. The body is a dual cowl design with the rear seats well protected from the wind thanks to the windshield. A second result of the rear windshield is to prevent annoying air turbulence from blowing back against the driver's and front passenger's neck and shoulders. In recent times this has been avoided by the placing of a wind-blocker just behind the front seats.

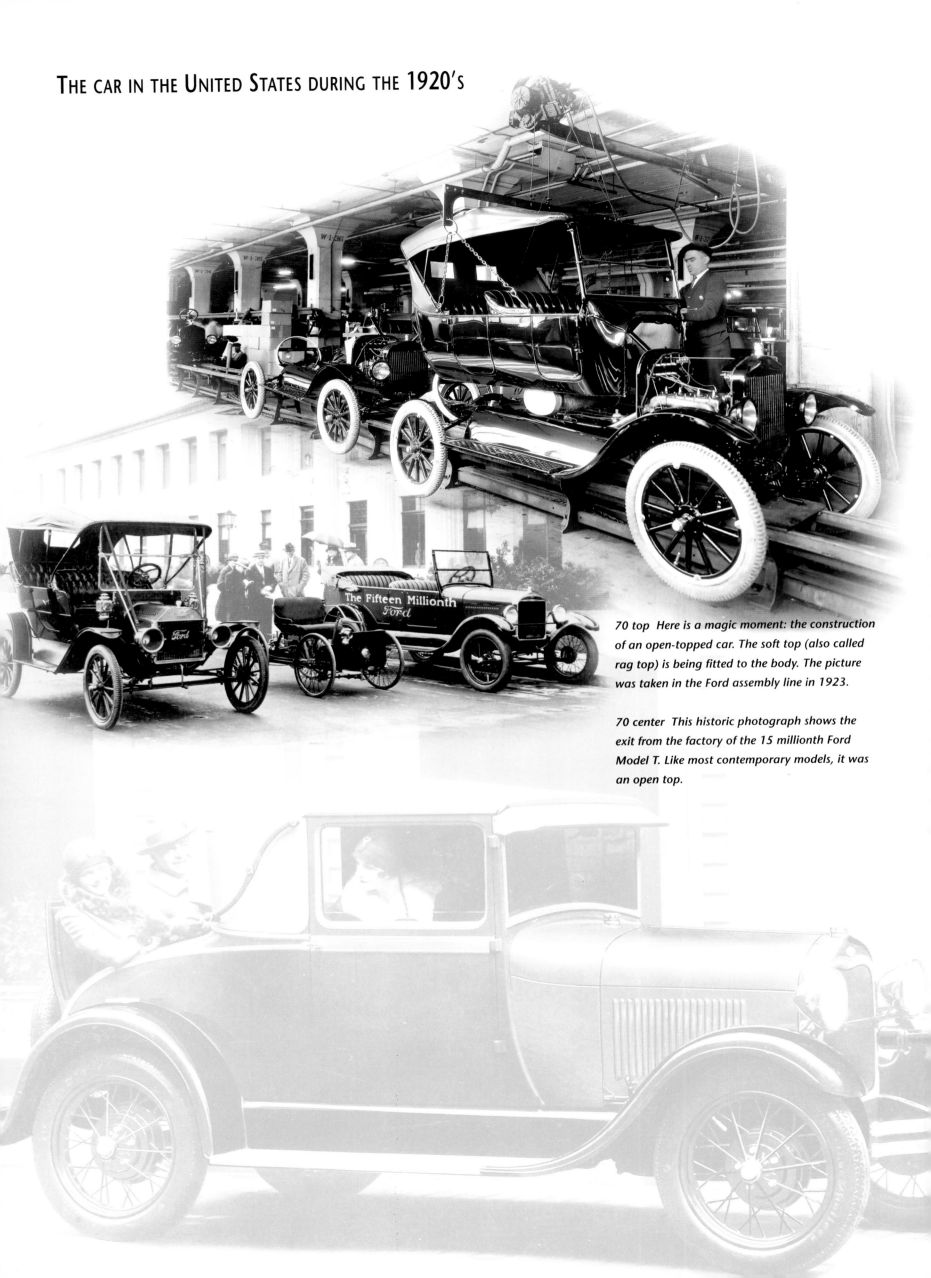

70 top Here is a magic moment: the construction of an open-topped car. The soft top (also called rag top) is being fitted to the body. The picture was taken in the Ford assembly line in 1923.

70 center This historic photograph shows the exit from the factory of the 15 millionth Ford Model T. Like most contemporary models, it was an open top.

Between 1918 and 1926 the United States became increasingly motorized and was only partially hindered by the depression of 1921-22. Industrial development during this period helped to consolidate the positive image and the confidence America had in itself, which would take the country one step too far one Friday in October 1929. The Wall Street crash was to have a strange effect on the car market; it encouraged the design and production of extremely luxurious cars - but this will be discussed later. The open-topped cars from 1927 on were quite different to those that had been available from the end of the First World War until 1926. These were the Roaring Twenties when the desire to have fun was the motivating force behind American consumption. The car was part of the fun thanks to the increasing number of surfaced roads and freeways. It was also noticeable that the car became an outlet for the frustrations created by the 1920 Prohibition law. Consumerism and euphoria encouraged the average American not only to buy his first car but also to consider it old after just a few months. This belief in early obsolescence was cunningly exploited and fostered by marketing genius Alfred P. Sloan, President of General Motors. As regards price, the colossus of the industry, Ford, which alone accounted for more than half of American cars sold, repeatedly cut the cost of its best-seller, the Model T, a fact which could only brace the market. A description of the American car market may help to understand the mood of the public, particularly remembering that 9 out of 10 new cars were still open-topped.

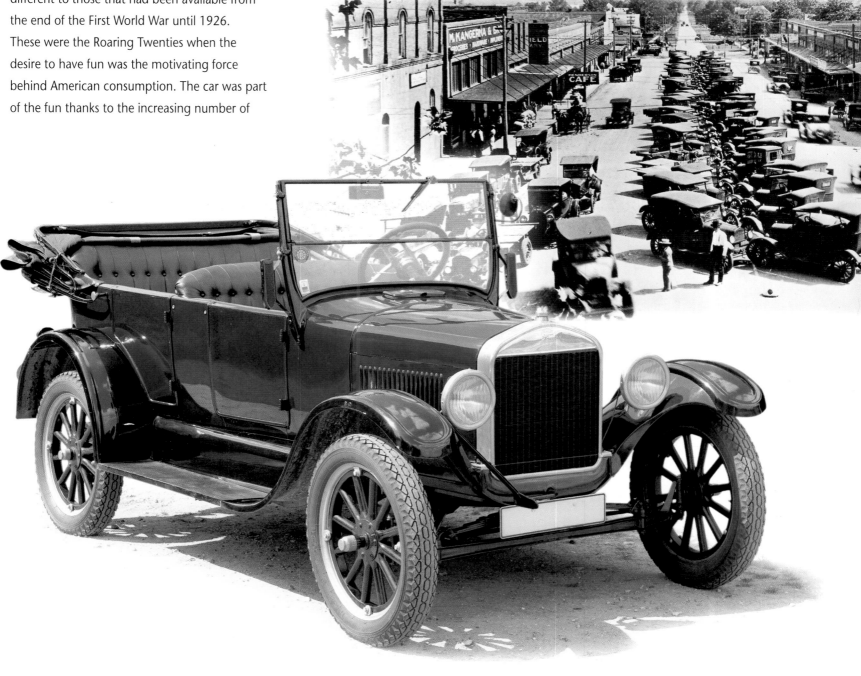

70 bottom This was the convertible coupé that replaced the Model T. It was the Model A, here in roadster guise, which aroused enormous interest when, in 1928, it went on sale. In the first 36 hours, it was visited by roughly 10 million people.

71 top An ordinary day during the Roaring Twenties when consumerism and fun were the order of the day. This is Main Street in Hardesan, Texas. What is special about this picture? The majority of cars parked or passing are Model T's.

71 bottom The picture shows the tourer version of the Model T. Tourer meant a small torpedo without expensive fittings or a powerful motor. Unusually this one was blue.

In 1918 the number of cars the US produced was approximately 943,000 which rose to 1,650,000 the following year - and still the manufacturers were unable to satisfy the demand from desperate dealers due to the influence of strikes, salary increase demands and lack of components.

In 1920 the growth continued to 1,900,000 vehicles, a total which countries like Great Britain, France and Italy only reached in the 1990's, but the depression of 1920-21 reduced the market to 1.5 million. In Dallas the first drive-in appeared and in Detroit the first 3 color traffic light. After the depression, demand soared to 3.6 million in 1923, and in 1925 the 25 millionth US car was built. The volubility of users remained high, typical of immature markets, until 1929, when the record figure of 4.5 million cars were produced. Then the Great Depression smothered the consumerism of the working and lower middle classes.

To return to what happened in the world of open-topped touring vehicles during the 1920's, technological innovations made giant strides both in quantity and quality. Cars became safer, easier to drive, more comfortable, more practical and longer lasting. Safety was increased through the use of steel which progressively replaced wood; hydraulic brakes replaced mechanical brakes (and on all four wheels rather than two); wheels became stronger and more robust; and new, laminated sloping windshields were introduced. Functionality and practicality took a step forward with synchronized gears, automatic spark control, and more instrumentation on the dashboard, including the speedometer and a fuel level indicator; the horn disappeared below the hood and the radiator cap often included a thermometer for measuring water temperature. Comfort was increased by the introduction of rubber supports to reduce vibration; passengers were warmed by the underfloor passage of air from the motor; and radios became a common accessory. Mechanical functionality was improved with the universal adoption of a water pump, oil and water filters, and battery operated ignition rather than a magneto; carburetors were perfected and compression

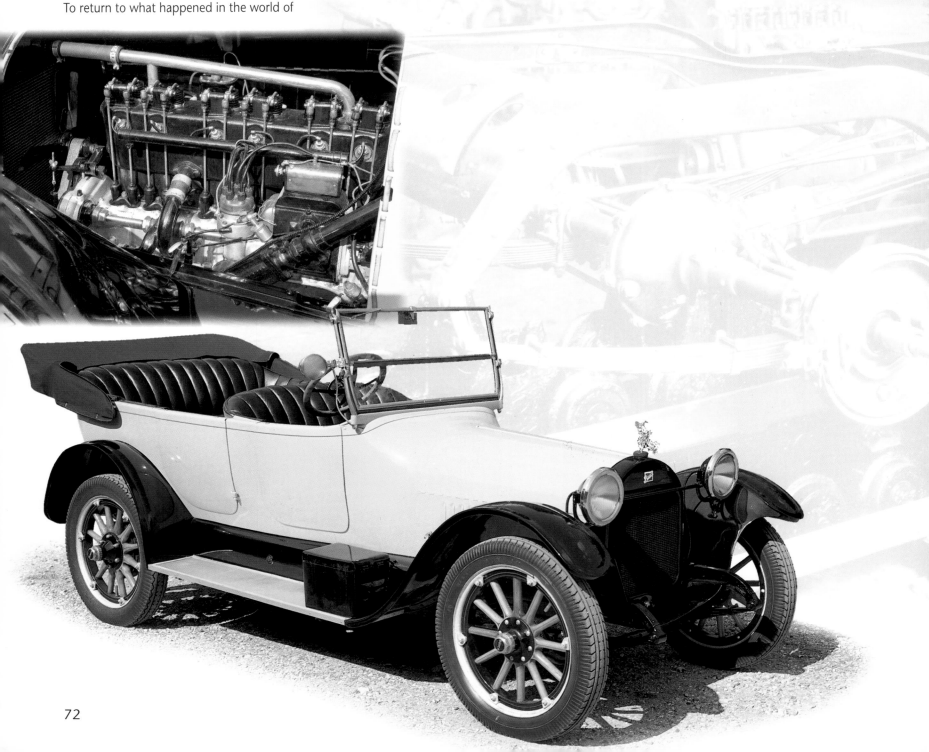

72-73 The picture seems to be taken from Charlie Chaplin's "Modern Times". This is Buick's assembly line in 1923. The workers are fitting the engine unit to the chassis.

72 top Note the 6 cylinder in-line of this 4 liter Buick E/645 from 1918. The distributor cap is identical to those on modern cars.

72 bottom The official name of the 1918 Buick E/645 was Tourer according to the terminology of the period but it might be classified as one of the small torpedoes that were popular in the US among the less well-off. This type of bodywork was known in Germany as a Fetonte after the name of the son (Phaeton) of the Sun God.

73 top This was one of the cheapest cars sold at the start of the 1920's, the Chevrolet 490 which was available in 1918 for 685 dollars.

73 center Mary Pickford at the wheel of a Maxwell, a car manufacturer which did not survive the era.

73 bottom Cadillac called this model the "Standard of the World", not a modest title for this 1922 Type 61. The horn is no longer visible, being hidden under the hood.

ratios improved for greater efficiency and power. Considering the boiling market and enormous speed of technological development, car design was really short of imagination, although there was no lack of great designers (Harley Earl, Ray Dietrich, etc.) and important private coachbuilders (Derham, LeBaron, etc.). Perhaps this is why the best-selling European car in the US between 1923-25 was the beautiful Isotta Fraschini Type 8.

There were still two types of open-topped car: the tourer (like a European torpedo but shorter and less elegant and well-finished) and the roadster with a short wheelbase, practically a small two-seater convertible. The touring car was the star of the market as it represented the largest percentage of open-topped cars sold - and open tops accounted for 90% of all cars. Examples of touring cars are the 1918 Chevrolet 490 and Overland Light Four; the 1919 Buick H-45, of which 44,589 were sold; the 1921 Willys-Knight (provisionally owned by Walter Chrysler) Model 20; the 1922 Cadillac Type 61 which was rather presumptuously called the "Standard of the World"; the 1924 high-compression Chrysler 6V and the Series 60 touring phaéton of 1927. Among smaller roadsters was the Dodge Model 30 Roadster of 1918,

which had six diamond-shaped holes in the back of its top by way of a window. There was also the omnipresent Model T, in every kind of guise but always very cheap; the 1923 Buick Roadster; the 1924 Oakland "True Blue" (the first car to use fast-drying synthetic paint); and the 1927 Nash Light Six.

A novelty which was to have lasting appeal was

74 top Inexpensive Dodge cars being tested after leaving the assembly line and before being delivered to their customers.

74 center Walter P. Chrysler presents the first car bearing his name: the Chrysler Six from 1924.

74 bottom A 1926 Roadster with the "mother-in-law's" seat in position at the mercy of the elements. This bright yellow car is a Chrysler G70.

75 top As proclaimed by the writing on the windshield, this is the first Dodge in the city of Boston.

75 bottom The photograph shows an elegant 1915 Dodge cabriolet.

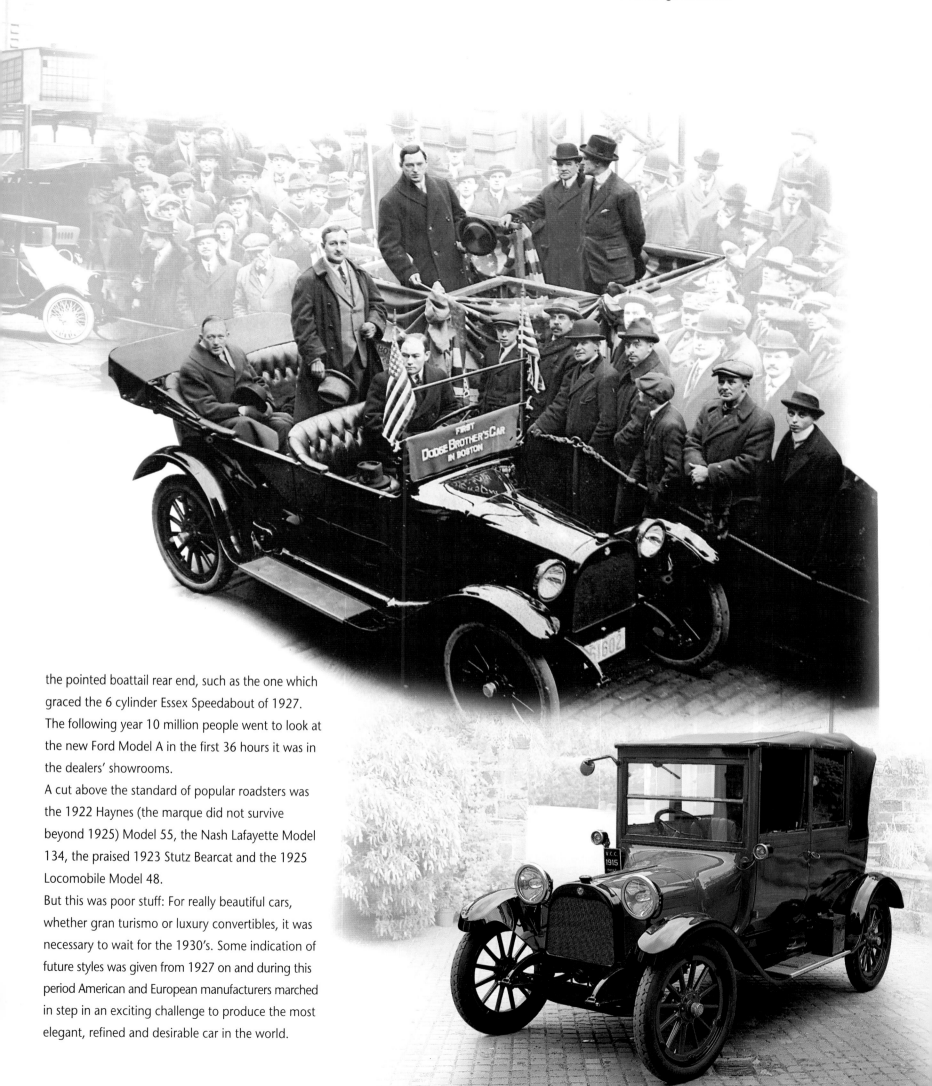

the pointed boattail rear end, such as the one which graced the 6 cylinder Essex Speedabout of 1927. The following year 10 million people went to look at the new Ford Model A in the first 36 hours it was in the dealers' showrooms.

A cut above the standard of popular roadsters was the 1922 Haynes (the marque did not survive beyond 1925) Model 55, the Nash Lafayette Model 134, the praised 1923 Stutz Bearcat and the 1925 Locomobile Model 48.

But this was poor stuff: For really beautiful cars, whether gran turismo or luxury convertibles, it was necessary to wait for the 1930's. Some indication of future styles was given from 1927 on and during this period American and European manufacturers marched in step in an exciting challenge to produce the most elegant, refined and desirable car in the world.

OPEN-TOPPED RACING

The races that held the fans in thrall all over the world had convinced supporters like Henry Ford, Giuseppe Merosi (first designer at Alfa Romeo) and August Horch (founder of Audi) of their worth, but had equally convinced their detractors, like Gottlieb Daimler and Karl Benz, of their worthlessness. Benz had always considered racing a distraction - simple fun for time wasters and the bored sons of the well-to-do - and he strenuously but vainly opposed the pressure to race imposed by company management. As for Daimler, nobody could refuse the rich diplomat Jellinek and his profitable orders for more powerful and competitive engines. More than anyone, it was he who instilled the competitive spirit in Mercedes.

Paradoxically, even a champion driver like Vincenzo Lancia thumbed his nose at the idea of using his cars for racing, especially if it meant making modifications to the basic model. But the commercial value of racing was confirmed, just to give one example, by the history of Alfa Romeo, which probably owed its survival to the successes of the RLs and 1750s driven by such greats as Ascari, Brilli-Peri, Nuvolari, Campari and Sivocci, in a cutthroat market that saw other glorious marques fail. After a difficult initial period, racing began to specialize. Road racing became more competitive and interesting and the number of cross country time trials (later to develop into rallying) increased. There were two important events in road and track racing in 1906: It was the first time the now-legendary Targa Florio in Sicily was held (the last would be 1977), and the first year of the French Grand Prix - the first Grand Prix to be held on an annual basis. Cagno in an Itala won the Targa Florio and a Renault won the French Grand Prix. The second time each was held Fiat won both, while at the 1908 French GP a Mercedes won with a 9 minute advantage over the second place Benz. At

Brooklands in Great Britain, Felice Nazzaro in a Fiat SB 4 came home in front of Napier at an average speed of 120 mph.

In 1910 a Buick Bugs inaugurated the most famous track in the world, the Indianapolis ring at over 106 mph. The rounded and aerodynamic shape of the car reminds one of the racing cars to come. 1912 saw the first of a hat-trick of victories by Ralph de Palma in the Vanderbilt Cup in New York. An important detail was that the three pointed star made its first appearance on the radiator of a Daimler Mercedes. At the same time Alfa made its racing debut in a 12 HP car at the Modena time trials which it finished without incurring a penalty.

Hill trials were also popular, with the thrilling ascent of Mont Ventoux near Marseilles being a classic. Today designers use this course to test the equipment and roadholding of production cars; in 1905 the racing Fiat 100 HP with a 16 liter engine won; it was driven by Cagno who finished the 13 mile race in just 19.5 minutes. The Alps were also ideal for racing: August Horch won the Alpine Cup in 1912 in an Audi C Type 14/35 HP, a success he was to repeat the following year.

A true precursor of modern day rallying was the

76 top A historical photograph showing the brilliant Felice Nazzaro at the 1907 Targa Florio with a Fiat 28-40 HP. Nazzaro drove car number 20B while Vincenzo Lancia, second in a similar car, drove 20A.

76 center Car racing and long distance journeys created great excitement in the western world. This is the front page of the Seattle Daily Times for 23 June 1909 which reports the victory of a Ford in the New York-Seattle race which took participants 23 days to complete.

76 bottom One of the greatest racing drivers of all time, Antonio Ascari, at the wheel of a Fiat S 57/14 B Corsa. This Grand Prix car could reach 94 mph thanks to its 135 HP engine. It was fitted with servo-assisted braking and Hartford mechanical shock absorbers. Together with Tazio Nuvolari, Rudolf Caracciola, Gastone Brilli-Peri, Louis Chiron and Giuseppe Campari among other great early drivers, Ascari brought the highly popular races to life after the end of the First World War. Ascari died at the wheel of an Alfa Romeo in the 1925 French Grand Prix.

77 top Manufacturers soon learned to exploit their racing triumphs to boost sales. Here Bugatti, which produced fast racing cars as well as glorious and luxurious road cars which still amaze for their quality even today, takes advantage of its win in the famous hill-climb of Mont Ventoux (France) as well as its successes in 1911, 1912 and 1913.

77 center The Bugatti Type 35 has been considered by many to be the most beautiful racing car of all time.

77 bottom In the foreground, Alessandro Cagno, driving an Itala, won the first round of the world-famous Targa Florio, held near Palermo, Sicily. The picture brings home the courage of these early drivers, who often died while racing. The fortunate Cagno was an exception, and he lived to a pleasant 78.

78 top Doctor Stoss at the wheel of a 1906 Horch in which he won the Herkomer race (as he also did the following year). August Horch, founder of the company of the same name and then Audi, is standing beside him. This model was one of the first to be shaft driven rather than have chain drive.

78 center Refueling during the 1907 French Grand Prix. The car is a Fiat and the driver, Vincenzo Lancia. His teammate, Felice Nazzaro, won the race at an average of 70.6 mph.

78 bottom The picture shows a moment from one of the most outstanding achievements in the automobile world of the period: Prince Borghese, journalist Luigi Barzini and mechanic Guizzardi are passing through Berlin in an Itala during the Paris-Peking race. This team later won the exhausting event.

Herkomer Race which was instituted by the Anglo-German painter Sir Hubert von Herkomer. It was held from 1905-07 on a course that started and ended in Munich taking in Baden-Baden, Stuttgart and Nuremberg. In 1906 the German driver Stoss won in a 18-22 HP Horch; the next year Erle won in a 50 HP Benz. More difficult were the endurance trials. Sometimes these took place as a point-to-point journey, and sometimes in the form of the modern endurance trials circling the same track repeatedly. In the latter case the aim was to demonstrate the reliability and superiority of one's car. In 1905 a Curved Dash Oldsmobile, "Old Scout", won the first transcontinental race, from New York to Portland, taking 44 days to travel 4,000 miles. The following year at Ormond Beach, a Ford K covered 1,135 miles in 24 hours at an average speed of 47.2 mph. In 1907, an Itala driven by Prince Borghese, Luigi Barzini and their mechanic Guizzardi completed the exhausting run from Peking to Paris (10,000 miles). And in 1909, an undertaking worthy of note - Mrs John R. Ramsey was the first woman to cross the United States, in a Maxwell.

To give an idea of the speed at which engines were evolving, here is a list of some records set with fairly standard technology. All were performed in open vehicles, but as some were competition cars, single seaters, prototypes or specially made record breakers, they do not all belong to the world of the convertible and sports car.

1897 - In the US, a Winton covered the mile in 1:48 at an average of 33.8 mph.

1900 - A 35 HP Daimler set a new speed record for the flying kilometer at 54 mph.

1902 - Henry Ford's "999" racer beat the record for the flying five miles, taking 5:28 for an average speed of 55.5 mph.

1903 - At Daytona Beach, Dan Wurgis' Olds Flyer does the mile in 42 seconds at 86.25 mph.

1904 - Henry Ford himself reached 91.5 mph in the Ford 999.

1909 - Fred Marriott established a new speed record of 128.4 mph in his own steam driven car. The same year, a 21.5 liter Benz capable of producing 200 HP broke the 125 mph barrier in Europe for the first time with a speed of 126.7 mph.

1911: at Daytona, ex-Buick racing driver Bob Burman raised the record to 142 mph in a Benz with a modified body. This car and other record breaking machines came to be called "Blitzen Benz".

1919: Ralph de Palma reached 149 mph in a Packard, but at Daytona Beach a racing Duesenberg touched 165 mph.

79 top The start of the 1908 Targa Florio from Cerda in Sicily. Vincenzo Lancia's Fiat 130 HP is about to race away. The race was won by Vittorio Trucco in an Isotta Fraschini.

79 bottom The start of a race at one of the most exciting and dangerous tracks in the world, Indianapolis. This was a 1909 event (the Indy 500 began in 1911). The light colored cars are all Buicks and the dark ones all Marmons. Bob Burman won in the Buick number 34.

80-81 This flame-red Fiat 501 SS is a sports version. The basic model was a small but important car that sold 45,000 units. It allowed Fiat to start up postwar production in the best possible way. The 1922 sports version shown here was fitted with a 1.5 liter, double camshaft engine. It won its class in several races, one of which was the 13th Targa Florio.

STYLING REVOLUTIONIZES THE CAR
DESIGN STUDIOS ARE BORN IN THE UNITED STATES

82 top This car belonged to Greta Garbo and can be considered a milestone in the history of the automobile. It is the Duesenberg J, loved by the wealthy for its elegance, power and uniqueness. It was produced in numerous variations and built by the best coachbuilders.

Note the survival of traditional features in the J such as the shape of the radiator and the large fenders separate from the motor compartment, together with the first streamlined innovations like the drop-shaped front and rear fenders.

In previous chapters the adjective "beautiful" and its synonyms have been used with economy. Without wishing to discuss what beauty involves - whether it is intimately linked to harmony or transgression, if it is objective or subjective, or if it owes its existence to its own organic nature or man's faculty of reason - now is the time to use with greater freedom the adjectives that express the breathtaking splendor of lines and forms that stylists and coachbuilders of open-topped cars used in the 1930's.

Why was it that this refined development did not flower during the 1920's, the decade that

was so full of intellectual and artistic fervor? Why was it that even top-of-the-range torpedoes were generally more interested in demonstrating "luxury" than "beauty"?

It is the authors' belief that the need on both sides of the Atlantic to respond to a strong requirement for motorization was responsible. Commitment to technological research, huge steps forward in reliability and functionality and a reduction in purchase price were all factors that contributed to the diffusion of the car among the public.

Beauty, too, is rarely a definable asset.

Paradoxically, the best in terms of harmony, affectation and fluidity of lines and forms became prevalent in the models that immediately followed the Wall Street Crash. Fewer cars were sold, but the public admired cars in which luxury (as a byproduct of beauty) was implicit - luxury that might exorcise their underlying fear of financial suffering. Before even worse miseries were to devolve on Europe, there was a brief period in which cars were created whose "beauty" was clearly contrived as a totem against poverty and distress.

The creation of objectively "beautiful" cars was

82 bottom The 1930 Cadillac Fleetwood was fitted with an enormous V16 engine. A more "economic" version was produced the following year with a "simple" V8.

83 top The 1932 Pierce-Arrow Roadster, an example of a convertible coupé.

83 bottom The Duesenberg J Convertible Coupé was an extraordinary car. Unique versions were owned by Gary Cooper, Clark Gable and Mae West, generally in a roadster design. The most popular version was produced by coachbuilders Bohman & Schwartz.

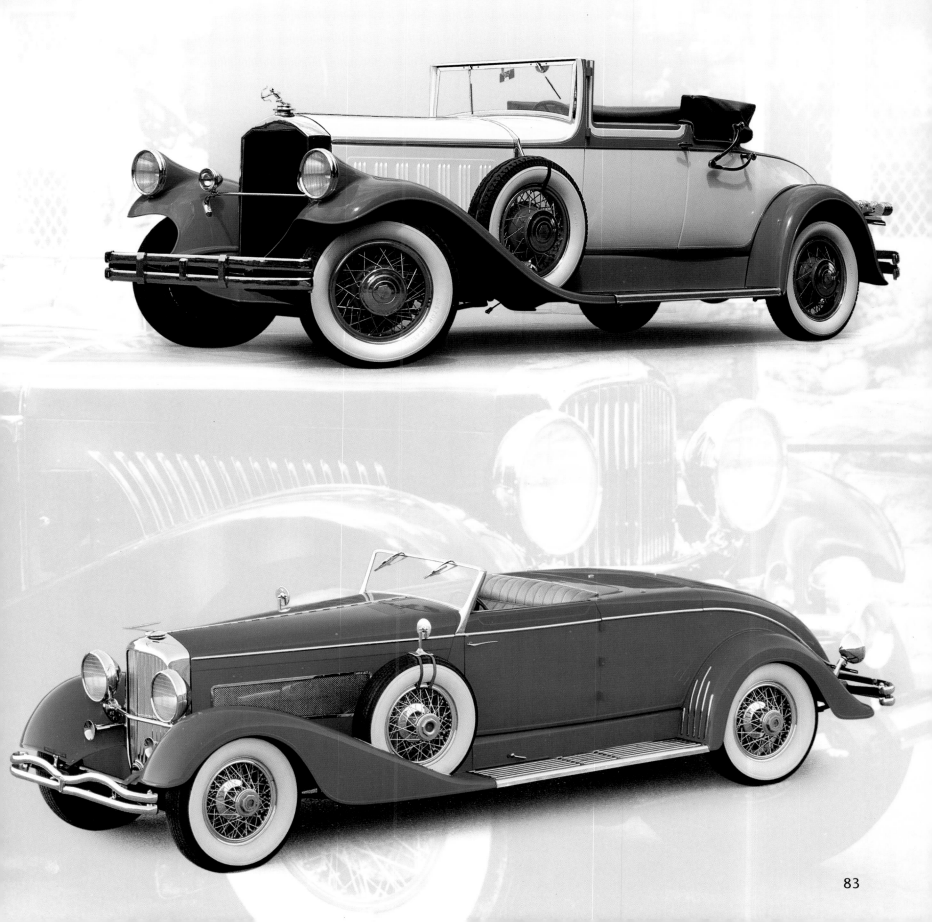

not casual. It coincided with the birth of design studios inside the large carmakers, with the maturing of new, fresh ideas spread by young architects, and with the rising sophistication of specialized coachbuilders. Often these three approaches crossed and intermingled. In general the style centers were responsible for the diffusion of new, long-lasting trends, the designers for surprising, imaginative and provocative ideas and the coachbuilders, often manual workers of humble origin, for the creation of moving sculptures that represent

beauty in the classic sense. This chapter will examine, as far as possible, the output from these three schools of thought.

The starting point came when a large auto manufacturer assigned a car body's design (and often production) to a specialized company. The difference in this respect between the Old and New Worlds was that in Europe, the coachbuilders' work was inevitably aimed at luxury sedans and tourers; in the US, it was often spread over the whole production range. The requirement was therefore stronger in America

for the creation of internal design studios which would produce a "company brand" or a corporate style, an image which the public could identify with. Furthermore, it was in the United States that young designers, including Europeans, could best express themselves. Credit for developing the concept of a "style center" is universally attributed to the boss of General Motors, Alfred P. Sloan Jr., who was among the first to understand that the interest of the public was moving away from the chassis towards the body.

84 The picture shows the glamorous lines of the Duesenberg J Dual Cowl Phaéton of 1934. The design displays the full maturity of the type of design known as the torpedo that by this stage was not far from decline, though remember this model was at the top of the market as regards power and quality of equipment, fittings and *materials. There is no modern design feature to be seen in this magisterial interpretation of the classical style. Only the very best from Cadillac and Packard (in the USA) and Rolls Royce and Mercedes (in Europe) can be compared to this sculpture in movement as Bugatti and Hispano Suiza were already out of business.*

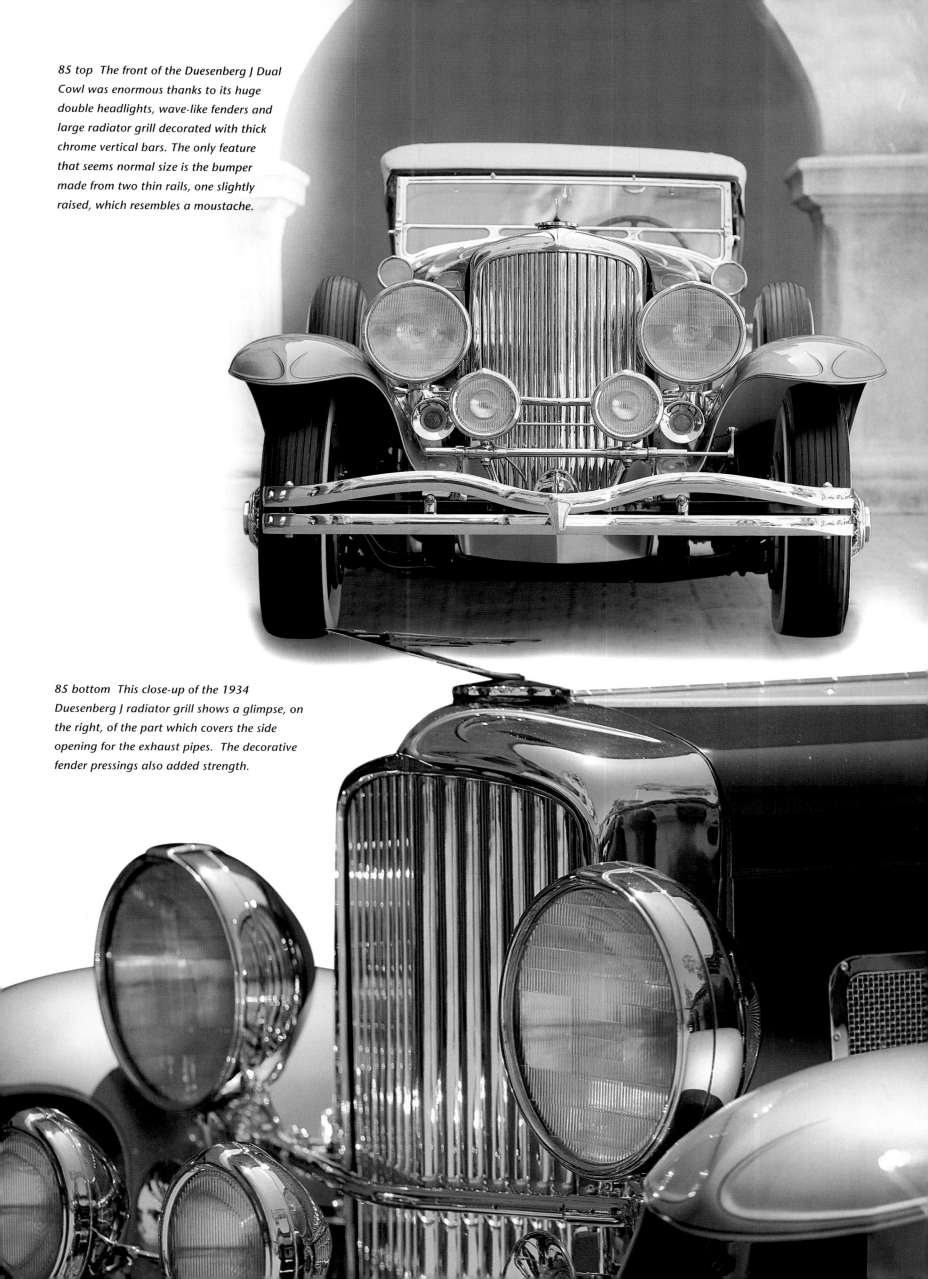

85 top   The front of the Duesenberg J Dual Cowl was enormous thanks to its huge double headlights, wave-like fenders and large radiator grill decorated with thick chrome vertical bars. The only feature that seems normal size is the bumper made from two thin rails, one slightly raised, which resembles a moustache.

85 bottom   This close-up of the 1934 Duesenberg J radiator grill shows a glimpse, on the right, of the part which covers the side opening for the exhaust pipes. The decorative fender pressings also added strength.

86 top Alfred P. Sloan Jr., President of General Motors, was responsible for creating the Art & Colour department, where the work of dozens of designers was coordinated by Harley Earl.

86 center The 1927 LaSalle Convertible Sedan. Designed by Harley Earl, its importance lay in the fact that it marked a transition between styles. With this LaSalle, Earl started to work on the details of body shapes, rounding off edges and attenuating curves.

86 bottom The Two Passenger Coupé was the last version of the 1927 LaSalle. The difference between the coupé and sedan was the number of doors, two and four respectively. The LaSalle was positioned between Cadillac and Buick in the marketplace.

This was partly due to an increasing interest in cars among women who were more aware of aesthetic details and color. Sloan created the GM Art & Colour Department and put a designer of giant talent and physique in charge of it, Harley J. Earl. With the help of his managing director, Howard O'Leary, Earl formed a formidable team around him which included Vincent D. Kaptur (who had already worked for Cadillac and Packard), Thomas L. Hibbard and Howard "Dutch" Darrin. It is not possible to list all the names of the designers and coachbuilders because by January 1928, having plundered the design teams of the competition, Earl had 50 specialists on his pay book. He was talented in coaxing the creativity out of individuals so he limited himself to outlining a project and then handing over responsibility for it to a team. Each team worked exclusively for one GM division and by keeping the teams separate, Earl created competition between them. Earl's debut model was the 1927 LaSalle. It was a medium-high class, open-topped model which was positioned between the luxurious Cadillacs and the average Buicks in the GM price catalog. It preserved several dominant features of the 1920's but was already softer in its lines with a new curvaceousness in the waist. It is possible to generalize that from 1927 on it was the rear end of the car body that evolved more rapidly than the front. Roadster tails were stretched into more aerodynamic forms like the boattail and sloping backs, while the front end was still dominated by a long hood, large circular headlights on the fenders, the fenders themselves, the radiator grill and sometimes visible exhaust pipes. The round headlights of the LaSalle were positioned in front of the vertical, traditional radiator grill. The fenders did not reflect the aeronautic fashion of the period but were discreet and of a different color to the rest of the car, which sported gilded door-handles and decoration. The roof panel sloped sharply down at the back and although the top was soft, it gave the car a sense of rigidity. The windshield could be inclined forwards. This car was considered one of the first convertibles in the US, almost a standard, thanks to its vertically opening side windows and the absence of midpoint uprights. The exact term is "convertible coupé" as there were two doors rather than four (in which case it would have been a "convertible sedan"). Earl later admitted frankly that he had been inspired by one of the most luxurious European gran turismo cars, the Hispano-Suiza. Another innovative American convertible was the Cadillac V-16 of 1931.

March 12, 1927   THE SATURDAY EVENING POST

welcomes LaSalle

Six models of rare beauty, powered by a 90-degree, V-type engine of great power, dependability, speed and stamina: Five-Passenger Sedan; Four-Passenger Phaeton; Four-Passenger Victoria; Two-Passenger Convertible Coupe (with dickey seat); Two-Passenger Roadster (with dickey seat); Two-Passenger Coupe.

87 top left The LaSalle advertising describes the full 1927 range of six models.

87 top right The guru of American car design from the 1920's on was Harley Earl, shown here in a prototype of a "personal car" called the Y-Job. The differences in style between this model and others on this page are clear, as this model dates from 1937.

87 bottom The similarities between airplane design and car design were to be much greater than the photographer of this historic picture could ever have guessed. The effect on the collective imagination of Charles Lindbergh's crossing of the Atlantic from New York to Paris in this ugly but strong plane, the Spirit of St. Louis, was to have long repercussions on car design on both sides of the Atlantic.

88 top This 1937 two-tone Buick Eight Drophead displays several design features that profoundly changed in the 1930's. Despite still having separate fenders and a footboard, it looks slimmer than its predecessors thanks to the new frameless "fencing mask" grill and is rounder. Note also the drop-shaped fenders, signs of the aerodynamic styling influence.

88-89 and 89 This 1931 Cadillac V16 is a typical torpedo dual cowl. This elegant model has circular instrument dials in an engine-turned panel. Note the floor type gearshift and the side-light lever clamps.

At Ford the situation was similar. Edsel Ford, Henry Ford's son, spent most of his efforts having to mediate between the unwavering traditionalism of the founder (Henry Ford's famous dictum "You can buy a Ford of any color as long as it's black" showed how interested he was in aesthetics) and his own knowledge of the necessity of moving with the times. He asked one of the first and most brilliant independent coachbuilders to Detroit, Raymond Dietrich, to create a package to rationalize prices, times and components for a design center capable of styling cars intended for series production.

Edsel used the Lincoln marque, of which he had been president since 1922, to experiment on the innovations that he wanted to see on the company's principal marque, Ford. He immediately demonstrated his qualities as a strategist and designer: the Ford Model A, which replaced the obsolete Model T, showed stylistic touches that were evident at Lincoln, while the bodies that were made for Ford by the Murray Body Corporation of America and the Briggs Manufacturing Company were examples of the general style and details prevalent at Lincoln.

90 top and center Chrysler's 1931 advertising shows some of the most popular body designs of the time: the roadster, convertible coupé (also seen in the center picture) and the limousine. The technical boasts of the 1931 Chrysler range included an 8 cylinder motor along with the existing 6 cylinder and Floating Power, a rubber support system for the engine.

90 bottom The 1930 Chrysler roadster was one of the first models to truly fulfill Chrysler's dream of luxury and speed at a reasonable price.

91 The 1940 Lincoln Continental had a grill that was reminiscent of some earlier Independents'. The Continental was in effect a rehash of the famous and important Ford Zephyr designed by Bob Gregorie and championed by Edsel Ford. The butterfly wing grill was the cause of a long dispute between Gregorie and Ford's head of engineering, who argued that the air intake would not be efficient. The picture above shows a happy Mickey Rooney taking the keys of his new Lincoln Continental.

C H R Y S L E R

CHRYSLER SIX ROADSTER $885

CHRYSLER EIGHT DE LUXE COUPE $1525

CHRYSLER IMPERIAL SEDAN (7-PASS.) $2945

Only Chrysler Engineering Gets Chrysler Results

CHRYSLERS at every price are *Chryslers*—and therefore joyously different from other cars. More alive, more responsive, smoother in action. All Chrysler cars are definitely related to each other by the same general design, by the same general basis of quality, by the same general excellence of engineering, by the same general spirit ... ler for practically every ...value. ... big Six of sterling abil... 78-horsepower en... unch, rigid double-... bodies

Or the new Chrysler Eight De Luxe—*de luxe* in everything, inside and outside. Divided windshield. Unusually roomy bodies. Unusually deep, soft cushions. An easy-riding 124-inch wheelbase. Unusually long springs. A smooth 95-horsepower straight eight engine that gives you eighty miles an hour if you want it — with the safety of low-swung balance of weight and the positive, easy control of internal hydraulic brakes . . .

CHRYSLER SIX . . . . . . $885 to $935
CHRYSLER EIGHT DE LUXE $1525 to $1585
(Five wire wheels standard; six wire wheels $35 extra)
CHRYSLER IMPERIAL EIGHT $2745 to $3745

Or the magnificent Chrysler Imperial Eight — Chrysler's very finest—a motor car for connoisseurs of motor cars. An ultra-fine car of 145-inch wheelbase and 125-horsepower — winner of 12 official A. A. A. Contest Board stock car speed records.

Both the De Luxe Eight and the Imperial Eight have the exclusive Chrysler Dual High gear transmission. TWO high gears, and you can shift from either to the other *instantly* — at any car speed — without clashing. One high gear is for flashing action in traffic. Another still higher gear gives faster car speeds at *slower* engine speeds.

Drive a Chrysler — any Chrysler — and enjoy ...

In 1932 Ford employed a young architect, Bob Gregorie. He and Edsel designed and proposed to car body suppliers a series of ideas that were full of distinctive personality. Examples might be the 1939 Lincoln Zephyr, first designed in 1933 by John Tjaarda, a designer of Dutch origin working at Briggs, or the 1940 Ford De Luxe, a low-budget compact convertible (or convertible coupé - call it what you will). The Zephyr's story started in 1933 when it was designed as a dreamcar by Briggs in the most difficult year of the Depression. There was a battle of wills between Gregorie and Chief Engineer Frank

Johnson, who strongly opposed the idea of moving the radiator fan lower down. His reason was that during summer months and in the hot states of the southwest, the engine would soon become excessively overheated. In response Gregorie proposed that the entire grill should be flattened. Edsel Ford approved the idea which was tested in the wind tunnel. It was successful, and so a new grill design ensued from a technical requirement; instead of being tall and narrow, it became low and wide. This was completely different from the Zephyr of that year with its body by LeBaron, where the grill was similar to a

fencer's mask. The last of the American Big Three, Chrysler, was undergoing a similar process. Its own design department, also called Art and Color, was instituted in 1928 and put under the management of Herbert V. Henderson who had experience in industrial as well as interior design. He only had a small team, 5-6 people, which was responsible for the entire group with all its different marques: Imperial, Chrysler, De Soto, Dodge and Plymouth. Amusingly, it seems that Walter Chrysler was unable to restrain his curiosity and often liked to glance through the unfinished sketches of his (no doubt annoyed) designers.

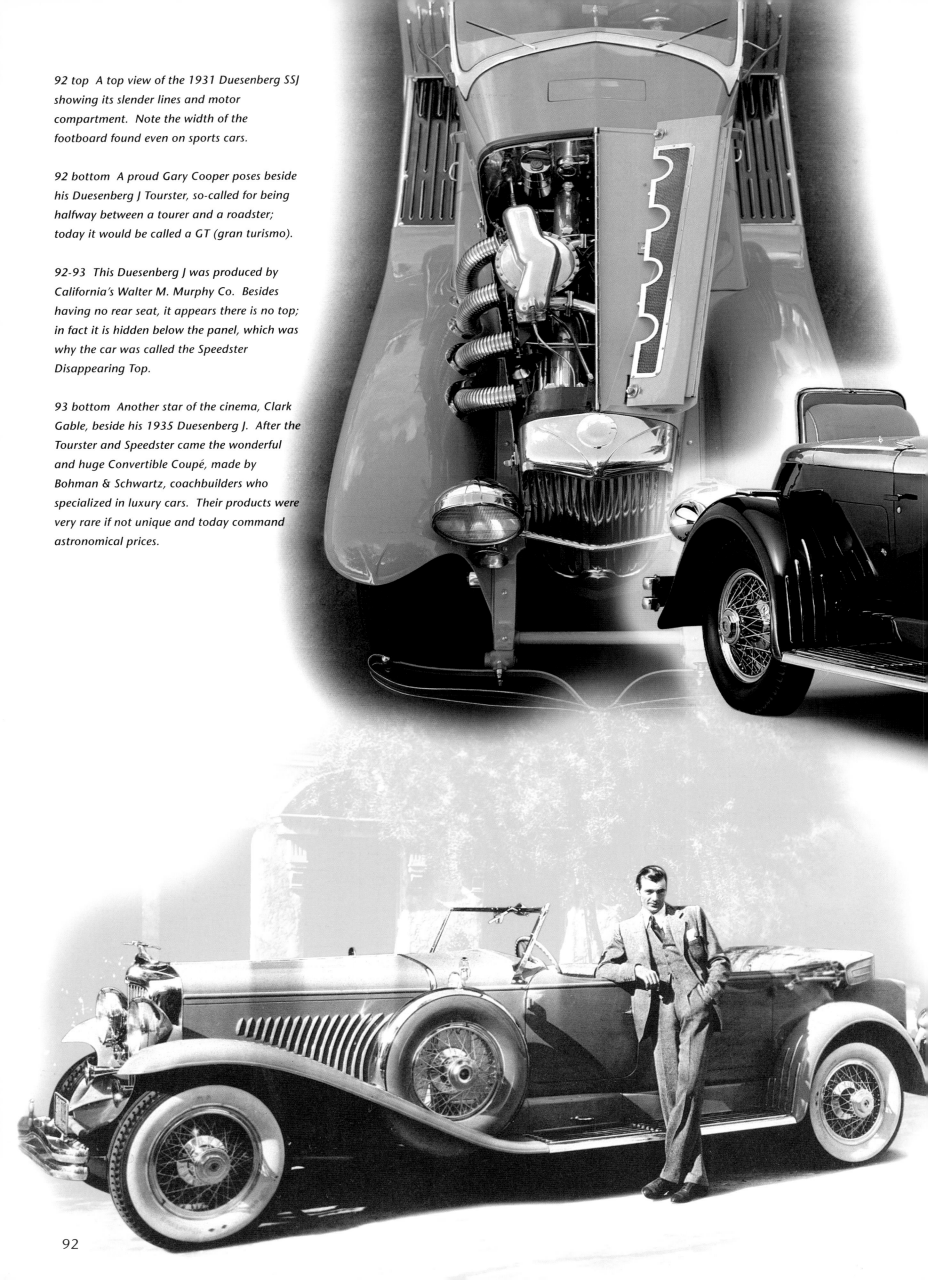

92 top A top view of the 1931 Duesenberg SSJ showing its slender lines and motor compartment. Note the width of the footboard found even on sports cars.

92 bottom A proud Gary Cooper poses beside his Duesenberg J Tourster, so-called for being halfway between a tourer and a roadster; today it would be called a GT (gran turismo).

92-93 This Duesenberg J was produced by California's Walter M. Murphy Co. Besides having no rear seat, it appears there is no top; in fact it is hidden below the panel, which was why the car was called the Speedster Disappearing Top.

93 bottom Another star of the cinema, Clark Gable, beside his 1935 Duesenberg J. After the Tourster and Speedster came the wonderful and huge Convertible Coupé, made by Bohman & Schwartz, coachbuilders who specialized in luxury cars. Their products were very rare if not unique and today command astronomical prices.

A special mention should be given to Errett Lobban Cord, the owner of Auburn, Cord and Duesenberg. His models were designed by the best stylists and designers of the age. They merit great respect and a picture in this volume. When E.L. Cord took over Duesenberg in 1926, he asked the previous owner, Fred Duesenberg, to design him a gran turismo car. In 1928 the Model J appeared; it was produced between 1934-36 and in some special versions (SJ, SSJ Speedster, SJ Speedster-Roadster) for actors Clark Gable, Gary Cooper and Mae West and VIP's like Howard Hughes, the Maharajah of Indore and Prince Nicholas of Romania, who raced his at Le Mans twice without success. The J had a pointed tail like a traditional roadster. The SJ was largely influenced by top stylist Gordon Buehrig who had a hand in the design stage. It had a very curvaceous waist which was emphasized with a reddish-brown line of paint and a beautifully styled rear end. This car makes up a trio with the 1931 Alfa Romeo 6C 1750 S Flying Star by Italy's Carrozzeria Touring and the 1939 Mercedes 540K; all were unique in their static beauty and can only be compared to the very best customized models where no expense has been spared. The Duesenberg SJ had the most powerful engine in the world, a supercharged 6876cc Lycoming with 8 cylinders in-line capable of producing 320 HP and moving the car in excess of 125 mph (Lycoming still produces airplane engines). The motor of the Model J, if not supercharged, "only" produced 250 HP!

In 1929 another Cord model, the L-29, provoked interest mainly for its front end, which emphasized its front-wheel drive to such an extent that this styling was taken up by Chrysler in 1931. The design had come from the pen of Al Leamy, head of the Auburn design team. In addition to the very small convertible coupé there existed a long wheelbase, dual cowl version with body designed by Murphy, while Sakhnoffsky designed an elegant "short" version much loved by celebrities. The talented Ralph Roberts also worked for Duesenberg (and therefore for the whole Cord group); unfortunately, 1937 brought the final closure of the company.

94 top The Cord L-29 was very successful in its different guises from 1929 on. The picture is taken from an advertising brochure which rightly states that Cords occupied a unique place in the automobile industry. Auburn, Cord and Duesenberg were all part of the same group, founded and run by Errett Lobban Cord. Many brilliant designers produced innovative and avant-garde models for this company that unfortunately went out of business in 1937. The Cord L-29 was very popular with coachbuilders, especially in the convertible coupé version shown here.

94 bottom These two Auburn Speedsters date from 1935. The model was the result of the combined work of Gordon Buehrig and August Duesenberg who wanted to design a new version of the 1930 Auburn with supercharger at a limited price. They came up with this solid but fluid design with a deep-set grill. The extra-large fenders were so wide they seemed like a flat surface; it seems unlikely they were aerodynamically effective.

95 top left Errett Lobban Cord, founder of the Auburn-Cord-Duesenberg group.

95 top right A good example of the boattail back end that made large, powerful cars seem lighter and more slippery. This particular model is an Auburn 851 Speedster from 1935.

95 bottom A version of the Cord L-29 convertible coupé by designer Sakhnoffsky.

96 top and center Packard was probably the most conservative car manufacturer during the 1930's. This model is the 236 Touring R from 1925. The picture (center) shows inside the motor compartment with the spark plugs in view on the head. The sparking sequence of the 8 cylinder in-line is shown on the block below.

96 bottom This 1930 Packard 7-34 rivaled the Cadillac V16 and Duesenberg J as a large roadster. They were three beautiful and powerful models with similar lines and boattail rear ends.

The 1930's saw emphasis move to the appearance and the shape of the car, at least for top-of-the-range models which of course included convertibles and roadsters. Consequently, the factories welcomed a new breed of employee - painters, artists, designers, illustrators, and craftsmen who worked in wood and iron - who created a strange contrast with the workers in blue overalls of the production line. It is easy to imagine the skepticism with which they were viewed. How is it possible to design a car without knowing the mechanical components? That was the reasoning behind the reluctance of some companies (like the conservative Packard) to use designers' ideas for more than decoration or less important features. However Packard in particular made a complete turnaround where styling was concerned, passing from the highly luxurious 1929 post-torpedo 645 De Luxe Eight to the ultra-elegant, fluid curves of the 1940 Super Eight-One-Eighty Victoria designed by Howard "Dutch" Darrin.

General Motors, Ford and Chrysler continued to revolutionize the appearance of the car. The coachwork was to assume elastic and slender shapes influenced by aeronautic design and the freshness of ideas blowing in from modern graphic design centers.

97 The car at the top is yet another luxury interpretation of the convertible coupé. This is the 1933 Packard V12 designed by coachbuilder Dietrich. Compare it to the Super Eight below from the year after with its strongly emphasized and curved fenders: The tire is almost invisible.

ORIGINALITY, TRANSGRESSION AND "AESTHETIC STREAMLINING"

The Great Depression of the 1930's which followed the collapse of Wall Street shook not only the economy of the whole world but also the tranquility of the American people. It was a lesson in humility that the consumer society had inflicted on itself. Poverty visited the homes of many American families while mechanical industry, until recently geared up to simply produce, produce, produce, was now running down.

In 1932 Franklin Delano Roosevelt was elected President and launched plans aimed at rousing the stunned economy. His New Deal contained the ingredients of hope and trust.
Intense intellectual activity animated the cultural debate, particularly with regard to the figurative arts, architecture, town planning and design. Intellectual energy was channeled into currents of thought that were often contradictory. They

generated peculiar trends that trod the limits of transgression (which someone claimed was a close relation of beauty) or appeared as malicious provocation.
Cars were relatively fertile ground for application of the new styles but objective limitations like functionality and fitness for use checked extravagance so that designers were forced to restrain themselves if they wanted their ideas to

take material form; function took priority over looks. The car united art and technology, form and function, and the architect Le Corbusier published a report in 1928 on the criteria on which design of comfortable passenger compartments should be based.
During the 1930's public interest in everything mechanical was strong both in the United States and Europe. The Futurist cultural

98 top and center Two interesting advertising brochures: The upper diagram summarizes the technical data of the two emerging methods of transport, the car and the airplane (the car in this case is a Studebaker). The picture (center) is taken from a brochure for the German manufacturer Adler. The American brochure offers images of the Machine Age while the continental European advertisement is based on the theme of liberty with an elegant, sporty car and a beautiful smiling woman wearing racing goggles.

98 bottom A 1928 Packard sports roadster painted bright orange - including the wheels!

99 top This advertisement photograph was taken in 1925 on the island of Malta to launch the Fiat 509.

movement started in 1909 by Marinetti exalted speed and the car as the ideal messenger of liberty and independence (concepts which are still partly valid, given that progress in the fields of transport and communications have turned the global village dream into reality) but shortly afterwards four wheels had to give way an almost unbeatable rival - the airplane.

The event which gave impetus to "air frenzy" was perhaps exaggerated by the newspapers of the time, who were always in search of new heroes: Charles Lindbergh flew non-stop from New York to Paris in May 1927 on board the Spirit of St. Louis. All over the world records and air crossings followed one after another and fashions and styles were influenced by the search for streamlined, aerodynamic shapes.

99 bottom This is a curious experimental car, the Mercedes 500 from 1933. The aerodynamic design theme is used across the whole body. It is a pity that the designers stayed within the accepted forms of the day, for example with the front fenders that almost hide the wheels; in an experimental model they could at least have been more ambitious.

100-101 Here is a synthesis of the breaks with accepted form by emerging designers during the 1930's. The picture in the center is an Auburn Custom Twelve Speedster from 1932. Apart from the standard roadster boattail rear end, note the subtlety of the fenders made to look more streamlined by the long wheelbase and extremely long front volume and accentuated by the low, inclined windshield. In the top right there is a 1936 852 Supercharged Convertible Phaéton. A revolution in design seems to have taken place between the two Auburns: despite being less attractive, the second is smaller and has fewer parts that stick out of the overall body shape. It almost seems possible to guess what the shape of cars will be during the 1940's. The picture in the bottom left shows a car from the same group, a Cord, certainly one of the more revolutionary marques compared to other contemporary models. This is the convertible version of the Cord 810 designed by Gordon Buehrig in 1936. It is remembered as the car with the "coffin hood". Also worth noting are the headlights which disappear in the fenders.

profile is the one that presents an ogival, hemispherical section at the point where the flow is met. It should also be biconvex, i.e. convex in the central part both above and below, and taper at the tail. In other words, like a waterdrop. In "Towards a New Architecture" Le Corbusier invokes aerodynamic lines and abolishes the rigid canons of the past. He recommends removal of everything outside the car body such as oversized headlights, elaborate fenders and side-mounted spare wheels in order to reduce the car to an outline over which the air could pass without meeting resistance. But to do so seemed to most people impractical and unthinkable. The traditionalists were not altogether wrong, certainly; long, uniform profiles without obstructions improve the coefficient of aerodynamic penetration, and therefore performance and fuel consumption, but for the cars of the 1930's that were not designed for high speeds, it was of negligible importance.

So it was not function that prompted designers to adopt rounded, sinuous forms, it was aesthetics, a little like what happened to the sports versions of compact cars during the 1980's which were dressed up in completely ineffective spoilers and miniskirts but which gave the driver the sensation of being at the wheel of a powerful sports car. This kind of decoration is applied more by the marketing department than the designer and is known as "patches". Research into streamlined profiles continued apace, and for those without expensive equipment like wind tunnels, knowledge was gained through racing.

Beautiful cars immediately attempted to adopt the slimness, fluidity and smoothness of the airplane, and what better models than sports cars and convertibles, open-topped glories, born to fly? In order to distinguish in broad outline between aesthetics and function, it is necessary to discuss briefly the basic concepts of fluid dynamics. The most efficient shape of a wing

As far as this book is concerned, the term "aeronautic" refers to shapes inspired by the passion for flight and "aerodynamic" to those involved in improving the coefficient of aerodynamic penetration and performance. Alternatively, a division between aesthetic streamlining and functional streamlining might be considered although often the line between the two gets blurred.

The 1931 Lancia Astura Cabriolet was a good example of balanced streamlining which contributed to the car's beautiful appearance to such an extent that it appeared modernized. Thanks to its length of over 14'8", the tapered fenders were absorbed into the body of the car without problem. Although classically elegant and keeping a large front end, it seemed new, slender and in a certain sense "dynamic". The cream of Italy's special-body designers and constructors, all of whom had a cautious interest in the new shapes, became involved in the design of top level models like the Astura. Even the cab of a car could become a reproduction of a pilot's cockpit as happened to the 1931 Lincoln Aero Phaéton with body design by LeBaron. It was a dual cowl model with rear seats separated from the front ones, not by a windshield as in the production series of 1929, but by a small spoiler and, cherry on the cake, a fake ornamental rudder. Naturally there was a small fuselage on the radiator cap.

The 1932 Chrysler Imperial CH claimed to be a speedster and with good reason. Much could be written about this car which summarized the characteristic features of the gran turismo, perhaps the most important class of vehicle during the 1930's. The headlights were the complete antithesis of Le Corbusier's recommendations, being larger than ever. The fenders were still wide and rounded but behind, despite being large, the Imperial Speedster was smooth and slim. The rear volume and fenders were distinct, but in perfect harmony.

103 top The austere forms and imposing dimensions belong to a 1938 Packard Super 8, dual cowl version. The picture shows the side windows to good effect but above all the coherence of the curves; perhaps the only fault in the Super 8 is the excessive length of the wheelbase.

103 bottom The chassis of this open top crossed the ocean to be built. It is the 1939 Buick Special Albemarle designed by the English master craftsman, Carlton.

102 top One of Pinin Farina's many interpretations of the Lancia Astura. Vincenzo Lancia, ex-Fiat official racing driver, was known for the care he expended on the details of his cars and his stylistic intuition. Study of this Farina design shows that this came from the end of the 1940's: the vertical seams, previously horizontal, on the hood are the clue.

102-103 The car below is the cheaper, 1934, version of the two LaSalle roadsters available during the mid-1930's.

102 bottom Jack Dempsey, world heavyweight boxing champion, is sitting at the wheel of the Chrysler Imperial Custom Roadster.

104 top This little open top is the Frazer-Nash Tourer of 1927 which three people could squeeze into. Note the two-tone coloring which highlights the motor compartment.

104 center The picture represents a step towards the past: this is the Isotta Fraschini, one of the motoring symbols of the Belle Epoque together with Bugatti and Hispano Suiza. The car in the picture was designed by the Italian coachbuilder Castagna, known for its interpretations of Alfa Romeo GT's and the Isotta Fraschini Type 8A, the best-selling European car in the US during the late 1920's.

With regard to new, fluid shapes, a figure worthy of note was the Italian Count Mario Revelli of Beaumont. Considering that coachbuilders are usually manual workers who have opened their own workshop, the presence of an aristocrat in the lineup is a trifle odd. Actually the Count liked nothing better than to design one-off machines for his friends and produce them with the help of his colleagues Giacinto Ghia and Vittorino Viotti, two professional coachbuilders. He loved mechanical things and especially motorcycles (he was World Champion in 1925 on a motorbike of his own devising). He was a friend of Vincenzo Lancia and Battista "Pinin" Farina and he created, among others, splendid variants of the Isotta Fraschini (for the Duke of Bergamo), the Fiat 525 (for the Princess of Pistoia-Aremberg), the Lancia Aprilia Viotti (for

Mussolini) and the Lancia Lambda VIII sports, the Itala 65 torpedo, and the two-tone Chrysler 75 coupé de ville. Revelli was one of the most acute designers of the streamlining trend and took a hand in the design of the production Fiat 1500 of 1936. Analogies with aerodynamic research were even more evident in the 1941 convertible presented by Lincoln designers. This was the monumental Continental, one of the links between research, the introduction of aeronautic concepts and the rounded shapes of convertibles from the 1940's and 50's. Streamlining, future gazing, new trends: The aesthetics of the luxury cars of the 1930's became a melting pot of Art Deco, the wish to fly, novelty and daring. What a tangle of styles, ideas and shapes! In these years there was a

little bit of everything present and to classify them would be impossible. The stylistic earthquake did not influence just design of the car; even Coco Chanel was struck by Art Deco and its development. The car was more practical and widespread than the airplane and it was a splendid subject for the experimental whims of young designers and the avant-garde filled with inspiration from the Bauhaus and the daring of Art Deco.

One of the most brilliant designers was Raymond Loewy, a Frenchman who had moved to the US in the 1920's. He was the creator of the Esso and Shell trademarks and the Coca Cola bottle. When it came to cars, he threw off two quick sketches, one a Hupmobile and the other a Studebaker. One of these, maybe a 1947 Studebaker Champion, appeared like a vision to a child along the streets of Tarvisio in Italy who was so awestruck that he dedicated his life to car design and became the head of the Mercedes design team: Bruno Sacco. The new designers embraced functional objects, too, provided they made life easier, more fun or slightly outré; objects like these were a tangible demonstration of re-found material optimism. The US had been starved of this and welcomed the new ideas with open arms. In Europe the increasingly dictatorial political situation made it difficult for those unwilling to tread the approved paths, with the result that many American design projects were created by European architects, engineers and stylists who had emigrated if not fled their homelands. Loewy was only one example of those who helped to change the shape of consumer items like wardrobes, bicycles, glasses, houses, bridges or cars, etc.

104-105 and 105 top This Frazer-Nash TT from 1933 is a typical European roadster with its barrel-type rear end (in the US, the boattail was all the rage). The front end was aggressive but attractive and could be thought to resemble a customized motorbike with a little imagination; it almost looks as though it is about to rear up. The Frazer is in fact very "American" being mid-sized with a sloping tail and square cab, characteristic features of convertible coupés.

Among those cars which created a real sensation was the 1936 Cord 810, a classic of the new style. It was designed by Gordon Buehrig and the staff of the Auburn motor company. The brilliant design reduced the car to its fundamentals and then developed each element separately. The most obvious result is the nose which worryingly resembles the giant statues on Easter Island. "Coffin" was the name many maliciously gave to the engine compartment, a huge uniform nose in which the grill was replaced by thick, striking chrome horizontal frames. The headlights, apart from two foglights, were housed inside bays in the fenders while the exhaust pipes, often more ornamental than functional, became flexible tubes, though this was not an original idea. The lower part of the front half of the rear fenders was chromed, a detail which would be repeated often in the future.

106-107 The open-topped version of an important and revolutionary car from the 1930's, the 1936 Cord 810. The designer, Gordon Buehrig, was one of the most famous of his time and he surprised the world with this model that altered the accepted vision of car design on several points. For example, the lights had almost always been an important element attached externally to the car body; in the Cord they were hidden in the fenders and introduced the streamlining concept of pop-up headlights (the idea was reintroduced in sports cars during the 1960's & 70's). But the Cord will be remembered more for its very unusual nose, blown up in the picture to the left, which maligners likened to a coffin and that anticipated the themes of anthropomorphism and zoomorphism. Grills and front end design of convertibles from the end of the 1940's and the 1950's sometimes explicitly resembled faces.

107 bottom One of the countless configurations of the Cord L-29. This is an elegant two-seat, two-tone roadster, but the dual cowl and phaeton were also very successful with VIP's and movie stars.

The car was unusual for its time and for what was to follow but it represented the maturity of the work that had been carried out over the years with greater or lesser success by open-minded coachbuilders.

For example, the Auburn 8-100A Custom Eight from four years earlier had a split personality. The production model could happily be considered a convertible coupé but the Speedster version showed influences of the style to come: angular shapes in the radiator and the grill, which drops at a strange angle towards the protruding crosspiece. The headlights resemble lanterns while the chromed fender follows the angle of the radiator and takes the shape of an arrow in the center. The fenders are very obvious, designed to look like the shoulder-pieces of a suit of armor and are, as much as possible, placed further from the wheels.

Studebaker brought out 3 models in 1935 with names as worrying as the shapes: the Dictator Six, Commander Eight and President Eight. It is interesting to note how in this case, as in others, and particularly with regard to four door convertibles, the new ideas tended to give a slightly rigid appearance to the car rather than create imaginative curves and shapes. This was the opposite effect to that hoped for by the standard-bearers of Futurism. As usual, the character of 1930's cars was most defined by the radiator grill and the huge fenders which tended to fold inward. Other industrial designers who distinguished themselves in American car styling in the 1930's were Norman Bel Geddes, who worked with the short-lived firm Graham-Paige and whose ideas for the Chrysler Airflow will be seen later, and Walter Dorwin Teague, designer of the 1933 Marmon Sixteen, halfway between a convertible coupé and a roadster. This design found no success either; Marmon was absorbed by the American Automotive Corporation and closed down in 1937. In Europe too models with streamlining and Art Deco designs found an enthusiastic following. There were Voisins, Bugattis (from both Ettore and Jean Bugatti) and the rare and elite Delage, which sported a Lalique figure in glass paste on the radiator (Lalique was a famous artist noted for his glass crystal figures but he was also responsible for designing the large bronze plate presented to the winner of the Targa Florio in Sicily). Before discussing the model that more than any other represented the synthesis of Art Deco design in the car world, the Bugatti Type 57, it is worth remembering some open-topped cars that led up to it. Combining some of their elements with those of the Coupé Type 50, designed in 1932 by Ettore's son Jean, gave us the Type 57.

108 top and bottom The pictures effectively demonstrate why Bugattis have always attracted such attention. The roadster in question shows great plasticity of form both from the side and from above. The side view in particular shows the beauty of the fender-footboard-fender feature which may be the most beautiful of all time: There is no interruption between the front and rear fender, and the whole forms a soft, undulating double curve. Such dynamism of design reached its culmination in the Bugatti Type 57, a perfect interpretation of the Art Deco style.

108-109 A unique means of advertising was used to present the Studebaker President Eight. The figures in the picture give an idea of the size of the wooden silhouette used to launch this important model, which made up a trio with the Commander Six and Dictator at the start of the 1930's.

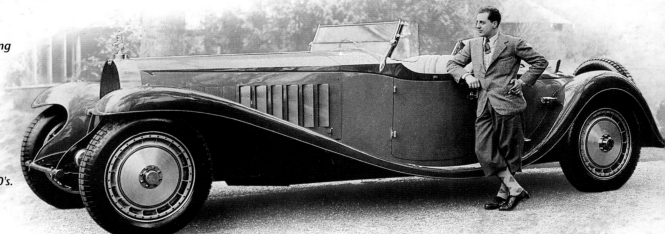

*109 top and bottom The small Type 55 Roadster
has all the characteristic style of a Bugatti. The
picture below shows a Type 50 with coachwork of a
three-seater convertible coupé. The supercharged
engine could be as large as 4.9 liters.*

*109 center A model from another important
marque from the early days of the automobile
industry, the Studebaker President Roadster of 1932.*

A strange car appeared in France in 1934, the Peugeot Cabriolet 301 Eclipse; its astronomical name was continued with the 402 in 1937. The two cars had in common a patent by dentist Georges Paulin who used to work on chassis sheets in his spare time in the workshop of his friend Marcel Pourtout. Paulin had invented a metal roof which slid into the baggage compartment electrically and which came to be used on the Peugeot. (In 1930, however, B.B. Ellerbach had already patented a retractable hard top in the US).

The Peugeot's body represented the best amalgamation so far of the various characteristics of the new trends. The sinuous forms were most clearly seen in the fender and along the car's waistline which both reflected the contemporary fascination with aeronautic design. The radiator was not flat like the austere, luxurious Rolls-Royces, Hispano-Suizas and Mercedes but more resembled that of the Auburn A100 being concave, tall and narrow. Another aeronautic touch was the closed case that held the spare wheel. The door was wide with a slight curve along the edge towards the bottom, a form that would be repeated time after time in English old-fashioneds.

The 402 was much more interesting. Five years of experiments had allowed Paulin to improve

the roof mechanism so that it was not just reliable but also more in harmony with the car body. What had been an experiment in 1932 was now a reality as long as the owner did not mind having to open and shut the roof manually - there was no battery powerful enough to do it electrically! With the hard top up the central volume of the car balanced the front and back ends perfectly; the nose on the 402 was shorter and the tail longer. The wheels were almost enclosed in the body with the rear wheels protected by side panels very much influenced by undercarriage fairings on airplanes. The front had a backwards sloping grill which was an intuitive foretaste of the designs to come. The door had been straightened. Other important reference points in the history of style in the 1930's were the BMW 315/1 and 319/1 roadsters made in 1935-36 and used successfully in racing. Both models had 6 cylinder engines,

respectively 1490cc and 1911cc, which produced 40 and 55 HP. Maximum speed did not exceed 81 mph. The next year, 1937, saw the arrival of the Bugatti Type 57. It was compact, completely rounded, with a two-tone livery that helped to create the impression that

this little sports car was nothing but a combination of curves and ellipses with filled and empty spaces. The prominence of the front of the fenders was typical and their length towards the central section of the car made use of a footboard impossible. The Type 57 was not confined to the 1930's: in 1980 a replica called L'Atalante was produced and sold to enthusiasts by a Frenchman called de la Chappelle. Shapes like this were to return in numbers after the Second World War and remain popular until the 1960's, then to return once more during the late 20th century.

110 top and bottom The 1934 Peugeot Cabriolet 301 was called the "Eclipse" for its mechanism designed by Georges Paulin, a dentist who tinkered in his spare time, for electrically raising and lowering a hard top. His efforts were long from meeting with success because of the lack of a small battery strong enough to do the job. Paulin's dream was realized in 1937 as shown by the car below - the Peugeot 402 Eclipse - though the electrical operation was abandoned. Note the stylistic feature used by all design schools - the rear wheel almost completely covered like on airplane fairings.

110-111 This 1938 Peugeot was slightly modified with respect to the standard production version. The most evident feature is the convex radiator cover with a grill made up of thin, closely placed strips. On some models of the time, the headlights were placed inside the grill for protection but the Peugeot has them located between the fender and the hood.

111 top The rear outline of a huge 1934 cabriolet, the Hispano Suiza Type 68 which was famed for its V12 engine.

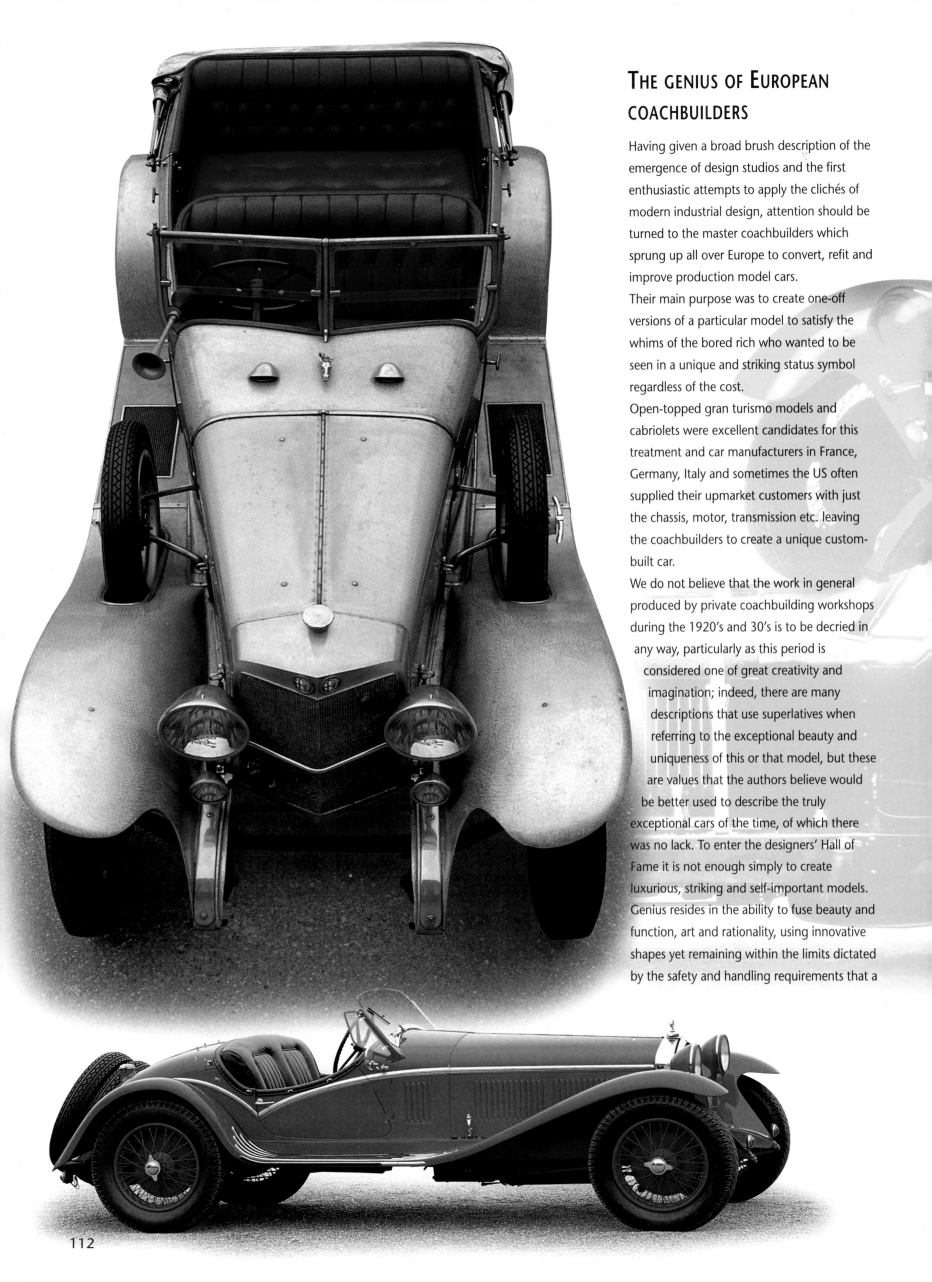

THE GENIUS OF EUROPEAN COACHBUILDERS

Having given a broad brush description of the emergence of design studios and the first enthusiastic attempts to apply the clichés of modern industrial design, attention should be turned to the master coachbuilders which sprung up all over Europe to convert, refit and improve production model cars.

Their main purpose was to create one-off versions of a particular model to satisfy the whims of the bored rich who wanted to be seen in a unique and striking status symbol regardless of the cost.

Open-topped gran turismo models and cabriolets were excellent candidates for this treatment and car manufacturers in France, Germany, Italy and sometimes the US often supplied their upmarket customers with just the chassis, motor, transmission etc. leaving the coachbuilders to create a unique custom-built car.

We do not believe that the work in general produced by private coachbuilding workshops during the 1920's and 30's is to be decried in any way, particularly as this period is considered one of great creativity and imagination; indeed, there are many descriptions that use superlatives when referring to the exceptional beauty and uniqueness of this or that model, but these are values that the authors believe would be better used to describe the truly exceptional cars of the time, of which there was no lack. To enter the designers' Hall of Fame it is not enough simply to create luxurious, striking and self-important models. Genius resides in the ability to fuse beauty and function, art and rationality, using innovative shapes yet remaining within the limits dictated by the safety and handling requirements that a

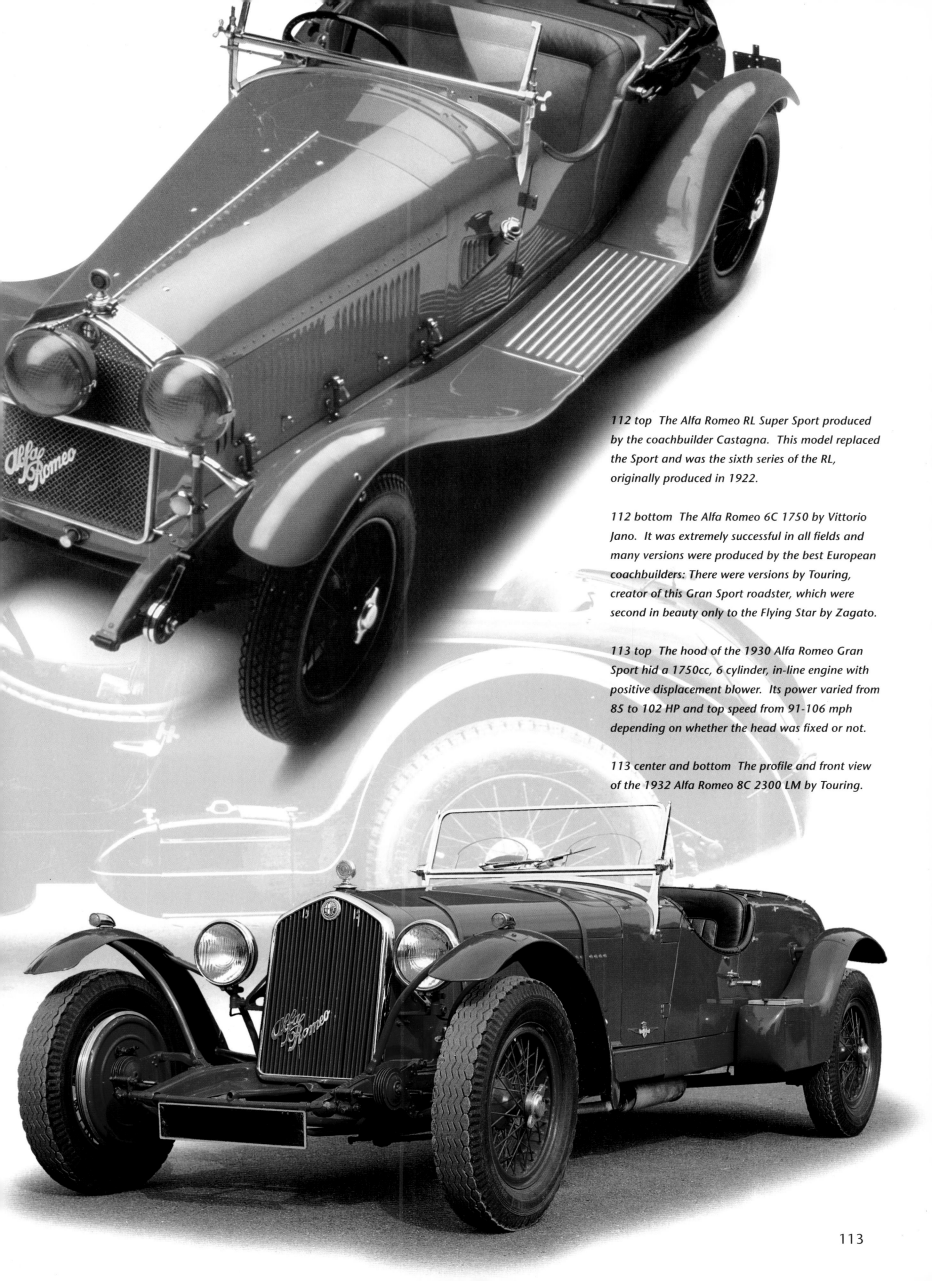

112 top The Alfa Romeo RL Super Sport produced by the coachbuilder Castagna. This model replaced the Sport and was the sixth series of the RL, originally produced in 1922.

112 bottom The Alfa Romeo 6C 1750 by Vittorio Jano. It was extremely successful in all fields and many versions were produced by the best European coachbuilders: There were versions by Touring, creator of this Gran Sport roadster, which were second in beauty only to the Flying Star by Zagato.

113 top The hood of the 1930 Alfa Romeo Gran Sport hid a 1750cc, 6 cylinder, in-line engine with positive displacement blower. Its power varied from 85 to 102 HP and top speed from 91-106 mph depending on whether the head was fixed or not.

113 center and bottom The profile and front view of the 1932 Alfa Romeo 8C 2300 LM by Touring.

114 and 115 bottom The Alfa Romeo 6C 1750 Gran Turismo with bodywork by Castagna. The aerial view of the rear (left) clearly shows the dual cowl design elements in which configuration of the cab is divided into two compartments with a mobile windshield to protect the rear passengers. Note how the doors opened: the front doors opened from the front while the rear doors opened normally so that they are hinged at a single point. Very attractive were the layout of the pedals and the gated shifter, which Ferrari lovers now consider a characteristic of the cars from Maranello.

115 top A 1933 Alfa Romeo 8C 2300 (the prestigious GT was built from 1931-34). In the fashion of the time, it was a bigger version of an earlier car, the 6C 1750. The company produced eight chassis types - short and long wheelbase (each in three series) and Spider Corsa short wheelbase (in two series) - but there were countless different bodies.

car must possess. Thoughtlessly following the fashions of the time and embellishing the exterior and interior as though it were the drawing room of a home was often a temptation that even top-class coachbuilders fell victim to. Having said that, it should not be thought that the work of master coachbuilders in those contradictory years (characterized by widespread poverty side by side with an opulence that went beyond the boundary of simple riches) was negligible. On the contrary, they were responsible for shaping the world's most exciting automobiles and it is worth considering what they might have achieved with modern materials and technologies. Generally of humble background, their success was not due to particular artistic or aesthetic gifts, which of course have their own importance, but to their ability to stamp metal sheets and panels into

fluent, homogeneous and accurately gauged forms and to resolve tedious technical problems linked to comfort. The most bothersome of these was probably the system required for joining the body onto the chassis in order to ensure the bodywork the maximum flexibility and tolerance to the stresses generated by the unevenness of the roads. A widespread system was that employed by French pilot Charles T. Weymann. He used a wooden framework positioned on rubber supports and lined with a special type of fake leather, a system often copied by the Italian coachbuilder Touring. Other experimental techniques used with success were the French Clairalpax (used by Viotti), the German Kellener, the Italian Plumelastica used by Eusebio Garavini who was associated with the manufacturer Diatto for a time, and Triplex by Ghia, which could be recognized by its lining of fake crocodile skin. Later, the increasing number of design studios, the ever-more urgent requirement for technology in the design of the exterior (especially for finding a lower coefficient of aerodynamic penetration) and more and more restrictive safety standards slowly reduced the creative margin for coachbuilders.

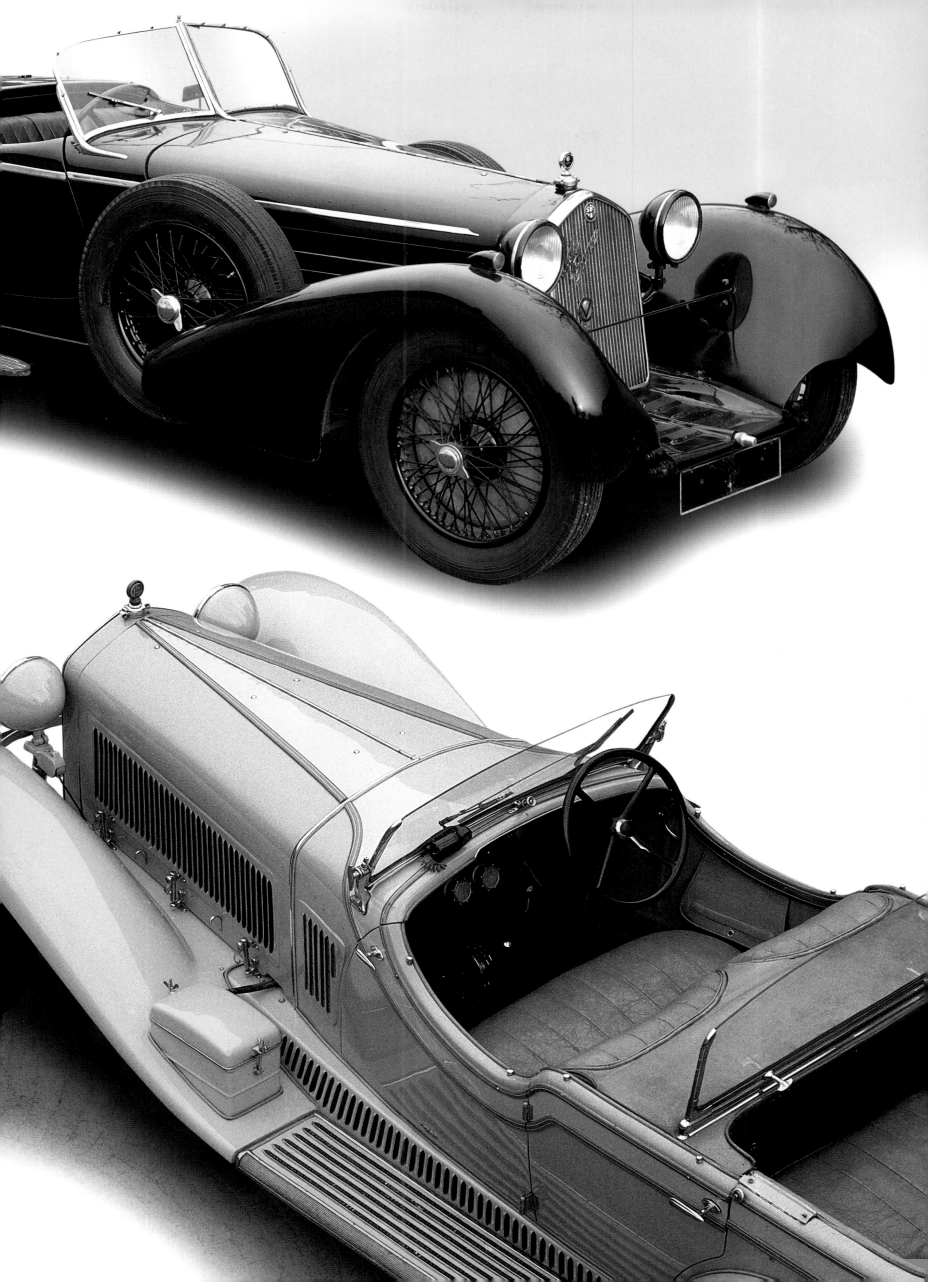

Some of them owed their fortune (or survival) by specializing in the open-top sector, others managed to transform themselves into industrial companies by following the moods of the market. The majority however went under for lack of ideas, of genius or of capital.

For reasons of chronology, this chapter will not deal with coachbuilders who came later like Michelotti, Vignale or the great Giorgetto Giugiaro, and for reasons of space it is obliged to pass over those workshops which are considered to be only medium-sized stars in the galaxy of coachbuilders of this period. It is hoped the reader will understand and make allowances. Many of the coachbuilding practitioners of the 1930's had started as carriage builders for horsedrawn vehicles such as Giovanni Bertone, Carlo Castagna, Cesare Sala and Alessio, Assmann, Belloni, Fontana, Studebaker, Young and Vereinigte Werkstätten.

116 top The side view of this small Fiat 1500 convertible is a good example of how the aeronautic theme was applied to car design in the second half of the 1930's. This 1937 version by Viotti has streamlined fenders and a flat, inclined rear end which together suggest, correctly, that the car also has a heavily inclined front end for a low coefficient of aerodynamic penetration, or Cx.

116 center The front end of a 1934 Renault Straight 8. Note the attractive windshield and vent windows.

116 bottom The name of this 1933 Fiat, the Ardita, was an obvious tribute to the Fascist regime in power in Italy; the car was more prosaically known as the 518. The version in the picture is a Double Phaéton by Pinin Farina following the American fashion.

116-117 This 6 cylinder 1938 Fiat 1500 was designed by Balbo in an aeronautical style. Most evident are the exaggerated, quite overly rounded fenders.

117 The rear end of the 1938, 6 cylinder Fiat 1500 by Balbo. Observe the splendid roadster back end with a nod in the direction of the boattail.

Today Bertone is still one of the world's most well-known design centers despite the death of Nuccio Bertone, never a designer but a genius at talent spotting. Giovanni Bertone, father of Nuccio, was building carriage bodies in 1912 but from 1921 moved into assembling bodies for Lancia. It was anonymous, boring work. Bertone put up with it for too long and it was only in the mid-30's that he transformed his workshop into a coachbuilder for production of custom-built cars. He worked mostly on the Alfa Romeo 6C 2300 and 2500 as did many of his colleagues like Castagna, Pinin Farina, Touring and Viotti. Castagna is also a celebrated name in the history of coachbuilding for his work on Alfas. One in particular must be mentioned but at the expense of others equally praiseworthy: The 6C 1500 was deserving of comparison both as a cabriolet and roadster with the works of Pinin Farina, Touring and Zagato. Castagna was guilty of one excusable error: In 1937 he produced the 6C 2300B Pescara Cabriolet which was a shameless copy of the previous year's Cord 810 by Gordon Buehrig. Castagna shut up shop in 1954. Sala was to close down in 1933 but his Isotta Fraschini 8A Super Sport torpedo of 1927 was a car to remember. Cesare Sala spent most of his time on large and luxurious models but on

this occasion he turned his attention to a sports car. It was not an easy task as the starting model weighed three tons. The result he came up with was a torpedo without a top. The rear passenger section was separate from the front one and so it was necessary to incorporate two small, hidden doors so that the design might more correctly be called a bateau than a torpedo. The door frames and cab were made from treated wood. The engine was a powerful 8 cylinder, larger than the 8A, and supposedly capable of pushing the car to 100 mph.

Mention has been made of coachbuilders who specialized in cabriolets and sports cars. Many are still in business and keep their handbuilt tradition alive like, for example, the Swiss Worblaufen, while others have disappeared from the scene, such as the Italian Montescani and the German Reutter. During the 1930's some companies were already in existence that have since become famous for sports car designs: for instance, there is the German Karmann, the American LeBaron and the French Chapron. Wilhelm Karmann was producing car bodies made entirely from steel as early as the 1920's. Two of his projects were the 1939 Ford Eiffel, made by the American

company's European subsidiary, and the Adler Trumpf Junior, which had a strong aeronautical influence. Later the company was to design the Beetle cabriolet and the Golf Cabrio as well as other models in which there were often two swellings on the body similar to a hunchback. Of all coachbuilders, Karmann can be considered as one which has produced the best selling models. No less important has been the American LeBaron, which was referred to in the previous chapter with regard to the curious Lincoln dual cowl "Aero Phaéton". The LeBaron studio was part of the Briggs industrial group which supplied bodies to companies such as Chrysler and Ford during this period. In 1932 the company produced the Chrysler CH Imperial dual cowl phaéton which was identical in the front to the speedster version whose aerodynamic appearance has previously been discussed. This version was less engaging but also less extreme. Similar to versions produced by Murphy and Derham, it was particularly luxurious and sophisticated. The name of the already-defunct LeBaron concern was sold to Chrysler in 1953; embarrassingly, it was post-humously applied to a line of plebian production cars and is now most associated with the small Chrysler LeBaron convertibles of the 1980's.

The obstinate but quick-witted Chapron was to become famous for the cabriolet of the Citroën DS, but other of their notable designs were the 1938 Talbot-Lago and the 1947 Delahaye 135M which, despite its postwar production date, displayed prewar styling.

A compulsory mention must be given to Touring, one of the few companies not to be called by the name of its founders, Felice Bianchi Anderloni and Gaetano Ponzoni. Touring was active between 1926 and 1966 and from 1930 produced steel bodies for Alfa Romeo, BMW, Lancia and Talbot. Among their very many excellent designs, the one that most deserves close attention is their interpretation, the umpteenth, of the Alfa Romeo 6C 1750, which they called the Flying Star after the decorations in the shape of a comet on the sides of the motor compartment. Another feature of this design, which might well be considered one of the most beautiful cars of all time, was the absence of join between the front and rear fenders which in general created the footboard in cars of the period. On the Flying Star, the front fender tapered inward and downward to end somewhere on the same line as the windshield while the rear fender was similarly designed but tapered upwards, creating a convenient step. The car's back end is pro-portionally small and constrained by the two spare wheels. The wheels with touching spokes and chrome wheel guards give the car the air of a competition vehicle while underlining its dynamic and elegant lines at the same time. Touring was to repeat the excellence of the

Flying Star on the large Hispano Suiza and another Alfa, the rare and costly 1938 8C 2900B Spider. Although seven years later than the 6C 1750, Touring kept the same front to rear proportions but the curves followed the aeronautical fashion much more. The radiator grill again resembles a fencer's mask while the headlights are similar to, but slightly higher than, those of the version prepared by Pinin Farina. Farina's version also had concentric disk hubcaps which were more modern but less sporty than Touring's spokes.

Another company that flourished belonged to the young and enterprising mechanic Giacinto Ghia. The story of Ghia has followed the events of the history of the car like no other and would merit its own television series. The company worked with and for Alfa, Lancia, Fiat, Chrysler (together with two famous stylists, Virgil Exner Sr. and Jr.), Karmann, Duesenberg, Bugatti and De Tomaso. Those who worked for Ghia included Rovelli, Boano Sr. and Jr. (who once owned it but who were ousted by Luigi Segre), Frua, Michelotti, Savonuzzi, Sartorelli, Coggiola, Tjaarda, Sapino, Giugiaro etc. - indeed, most of the coachbuilders' Hall of Fame. In the 1970's Ghia ended up as part of Ford, for which it designed prototypes and special production series. During the 1930's it produced the Itala 65 and the 1933 Fiat Balilla sports.

Another famous name is Ugo Zagato. He founded his workshop in 1919 and became the official coachbuilder for Alfa Romeo particularly for sports models.

In 1927 he produced the Spider Super Sport based on the RL chassis which was as

exceptional as that of the 6C 1750. While Montescani envisioned the RL as a dual cowl model, Zagato saw it as a roadster with a highly profiled tail. Comparing Zagato's sports version, Montescani's elite dual cowl model, Castagna's luxury interpretation and Weymann's official landaulet, it is possible to understand the freedom of maneuver the chassis of the 1920's and 30's offered to coachbuilders. Still based on the RL chassis, Zagato had designed a classic torpedo, the Coloniale, some years before.

118 top The characteristic emblem of Pinin Farina, a blue "f" on a white background, has remained the mark of the firm's designs.

118-119 top This model is an example of how well Pinin Farina was able to combine sculptural

forms with the aeronautic style. This is a 1937 Alfa Romeo 2900B Convertible, a balanced, versatile car which was popular with coachbuilders for its choice of long or short wheelbase. The flat, uniform rear end absorbs the curves of the wheelhouses.

118-119 bottom The nose and tail of the 1935 Lancia Astura Roadster Pininfarina. Note the decoration on the side in the style of a flying star (also used by Touring), the shield-shaped radiator, the split windshield and the visible sills, though without a footboard. The doors open from the front.

A praiseworthy company of the same period was Autenrieth Darmstadt which designed numerous open-topped cars. With the collaboration of Baur Stuttgart they produced the 320, 326 and 327 models using BMW chassis. Erdmann & Rossi, founded in 1898, produced a version of the Audi 225 reminiscent of the Art Deco style of the Bugatti Atalante, and also a highly profiled roadster based on a BMW 326 chassis. All Erdmann & Rossi productions were slightly extravagant but their uniqueness was well received by their customers of Bugatti, Cadillac, Horch, Mercedes Benz, Packard and Rolls Royce chassis. Lack of space makes further description

impossible but here are the names of some famous coachbuilders linked with the marque they are most associated with: Mulliner with Bentley, Boneschi with Alfa Romeo, Guilloré with Delage, Pourtout and Pennock with Delahaye, Figoni and Falaschi with Talbot, Viotti with Lancia, Kellener with Hispano-Suiza, Letourneur and Marchand with Delage. One name, the most famous of all coachbuilders, has not been discussed: Pinin Farina, the dynasty of designers that more than any other has left its mark on car designs. The dynasty began when Battista Farina, nicknamed "Pinin" (Piedmontese for "small"), began to work at the age of 12 for his

coachbuilder brother Giovanni. Giovanni produced fine cars until his company, Stabilimenti Farina, was forced to close in 1953. Pinin Farina had meanwhile started up on his own in 1930 and began to make progress in a business sector already filled with legendary names. In 1961, the office of the Italian President decreed that "Pinin" Farina might be unified to a single surname, Pininfarina, which would now be valid for Battista's son Sergio and the firm at large. Sergio, in turn, did not know how to design at first, but this only served to increase his applications. Fortunately for Sergio, the esteem he was held in by Enzo Ferrari was his road to greatness; it was

120

the Ferrari marque for which he created true masterpieces, both sports cars and GT coupes. Designs from Pinin Farina include the 1931 topless Cadillac two-seater sports in the bateau style thanks to the tapered rear end. The surprising shape of the rear fender, curved in the front, was an illusion designed to give length to the back. The front fender was also short which seemed to leave the spare wheel hanging in midair. The sill panel was a striking, engraved metal strip. The following year brought the Fiat 518 A Ardita which showed Pinin's interest for aerodynamics, or anyway for sinuous curves later associated by historians with the shape of the female body. The same year saw a typical cabriolet, a powerful Mercedes 500 SS in which references to the mother of all convertible coupés, the 1927 LaSalle, could be seen. There were also numerous versions of the Lancia Astura and Alfa Romeo 8C 2300 characterized by a classical, sculptural design. In the following years the streamlining of his designs for the Astura became sharper including the fairing for the rear wheelhouses, which was a feature of French cabriolets and based on airplane undercarriage fairings. Work from the Pininfarina studio has continued uninterrupted throughout the century. Finally, attention is passed back to the US to admire the work of Bohman & Schwartz, designers of the 1940 Cadillac Series Sixty-Two. A chromed line ran along the length of the side, dropping slightly along the doors and clipping the rear fender. It creates a mirror surface that was to become common in this position, almost a signature of the period. The front end was not raised as was common in other cars at this time but fluid with a low, narrow grill that had an abundant covering of horizontal chromework. The bumper had similar decoration, was flat on top and did not end in a point like the contemporary aerodynamic styles. The engine was a traditional 135 HP, 5.7 liter V8.

120 top This luxurious cabriolet is the 1934 Bentley with coachwork by Vanden Plas. Despite a 6 cylinder, 3.7 liter engine, top speed was only 91 mph.

120-121 bottom A Mercedes Benz 500K with bodywork by Windover. A Mercedes tradition, often annoying, was to use abbreviations in the name. In the 1930's the letter K stood for "Kurz", meaning short wheelbase, but it was changed to "Kompressor" (supercharged) as in this model.

120-121 top and 121 A Bohman & Schwartz Cadillac produced on a Series Sixty-Two chassis from 1940. Apart from the quality of materials and finishing, note the wheels with their 3 colors (black tread, white walls and red shoulders) not to mention the chrome hubcaps. Chrome was used everywhere including in the Cadillac name on the fender. This trend was to be taken to the limit in 1950's convertibles.

121

122 top Although they both resisted pressure to take part in racing and to build record-breaking speed cars, both Daimler and Benz were forced to give in eventually to the demands of customers and management. The results were prototypes such as the Tropfenwagen (in the picture) used to study aerodynamic effects, speed machines like the Blitzen, and production cars like the Daimler 16/45 PS Knight and Benz 6/18 PS.

122 center The photograph immortalized a frantic refueling stop for a DKW P600 Sport of 1930.

Having acknowledged the importance of style and design, attention should be paid to other directions in which the evolution of the car, whose sports models both with and without a top traditionally represent the state of the art, produced technically connected advances:
 1) Improvement of mechanical performance as measured by the power-to-weight ratio (the weight one horsepower must move).
2) Optimization of body design so that the coefficient of aerodynamic penetration is minimized, giving better performance for the same power and a reduction in noise, vibration and fuel consumption plus increased comfort. So let technology measure the development of a car as long as it is not forgotten that aesthetics,

especially in roadsters and convertibles, plays a functional role which is fundamental to successful sales. A small sedan may be able to get away with sacrificing form for exciting performance but an open-topped car must satisfy aesthetic requirements in order to balance its simpler functionality and lack of creature comforts. Nor should it be forgotten that an open-topped car with its roof up or down will never have a Cd (coefficient of aerodynamic drag) less than or equal to a similar car with a hard top. Extremely common, open-topped cars were still the protagonists in racing and it was logical that they should be the basis for fluid dynamics experimentation. This was serious research carried out in the first wind tunnels and

supported by competition results, and it was the racing circuit, tinged with political implications that were particularly strong in Europe during the 1920's and 30's, that became the test bed for innovations.

The distinction must be born in mind, however, between these mobile laboratories and the stylistic exaggerations based on the fashion for flying - the "false aeronautics" also prevalent in racing, though road-based rather than track. Road racers were often enormous, heavy machines that were rigid, very dangerous and extremely difficult to drive in which tapered profiles and slim shapes were as pleasing to the eye as they were useless. One example was the highly admired Delage D8 S driven by Renée Friedrich, daughter of the Bugatti driver of the same name. In a women-only race from Paris - St. Raphael in 1932, the young and beautiful driver smashed into a tree and died when she lost control of her four-wheeled dinosaur.

122-123 Unlike nearly all racing cars, this 1930's racing Mercedes has fenders.

123 The rear and front ends of one of the Benz Tropfenwagen prototypes, almost a single seater. Note the large central headlight and visible suspension.

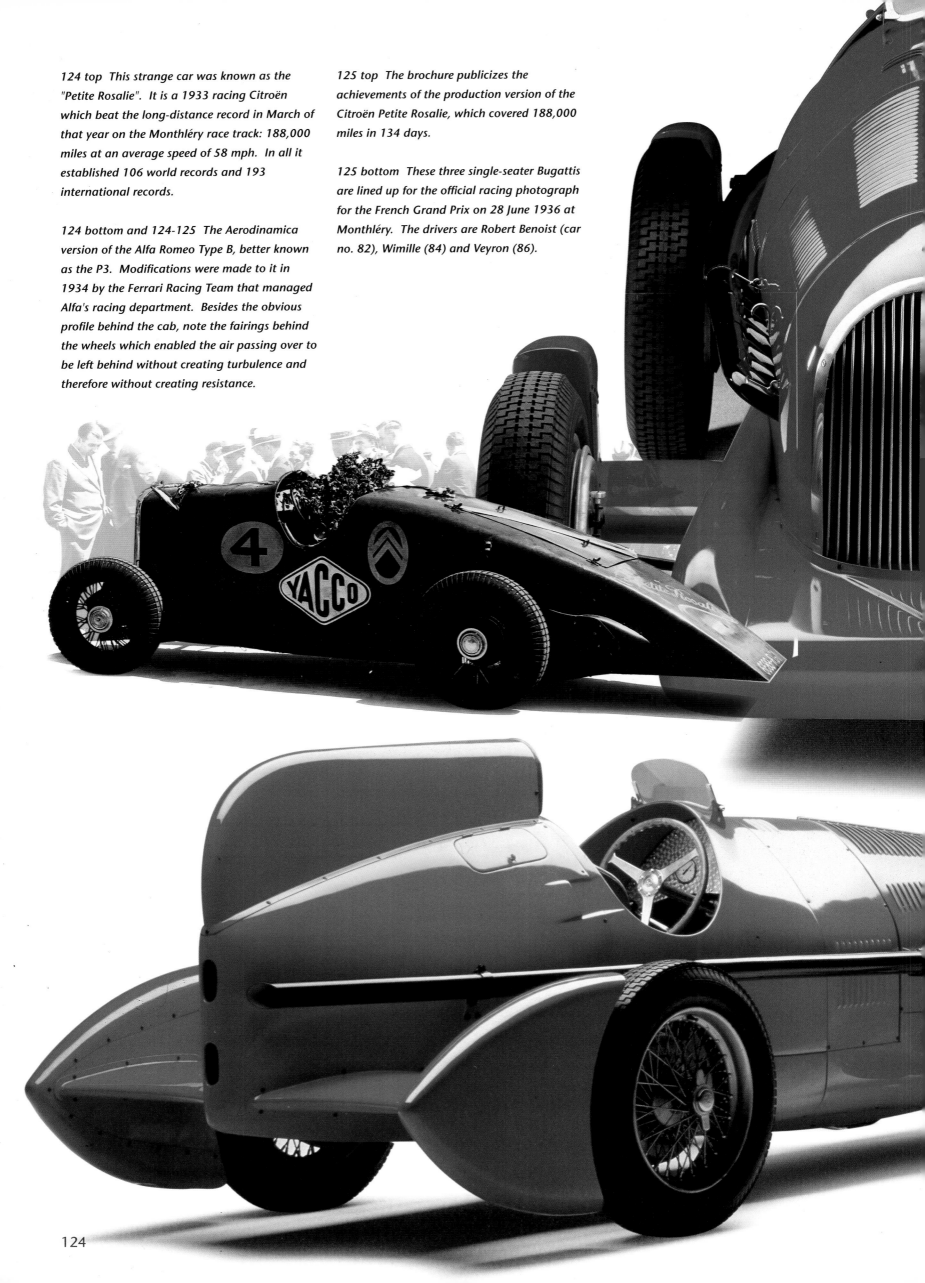

124 top This strange car was known as the "Petite Rosalie". It is a 1933 racing Citroën which beat the long-distance record in March of that year on the Monthléry race track: 188,000 miles at an average speed of 58 mph. In all it established 106 world records and 193 international records.

124 bottom and 124-125 The Aerodinamica version of the Alfa Romeo Type B, better known as the P3. Modifications were made to it in 1934 by the Ferrari Racing Team that managed Alfa's racing department. Besides the obvious profile behind the cab, note the fairings behind the wheels which enabled the air passing over to be left behind without creating turbulence and therefore without creating resistance.

125 top The brochure publicizes the achievements of the production version of the Citroën Petite Rosalie, which covered 188,000 miles in 134 days.

125 bottom These three single-seater Bugattis are lined up for the official racing photograph for the French Grand Prix on 28 June 1936 at Monthléry. The drivers are Robert Benoist (car no. 82), Wimille (84) and Veyron (86).

Manufacturers most involved in advanced research were, unsurprisingly, those most heavily involved in racing: Alfa Romeo (whose survival as a company probably depended on the successes of its gran turismo cars like the RL and 6C driven by exceptional talents like Ascari, Brilli-Peri, Nuvolari and Sivocci), Auto Union (created by the merger in 1932 of Audi, DKW, Horch and Wanderer, the four companies represented by the four ring Audi symbol today) and, most important, Daimler-Benz.

As early as 1914 Daimler had presented a

UNE **8** CV
CITROËN
DE SERIE "PETITE ROSALIE"
A PARCOURU
300000 KMS
EN 134 JOURS A 93 DE MOYENNE
AVEC UTILISATION CONSTANTE D'HUILE YACCO DU COMMERCE
LE CHASSIS DE PETITE ROSALIE EST STRICTEMENT IDENTIQUE
A CELUI DES VOITURES LIVREES QUOTIDIENNEMENT A LA CLIENTELE

development of the 28/95 which anticipated the boattail forms of a decade later, for example, in the 1923 Citroën Caddy Sport. The 28/95, which in all other versions had a racing streak running through it, was completely lined with strips of mahogany; the tail was tapered like the nose of a rocket, an indication of things to come, and the wheel coverings were full and convex. Benz cars were similar in vein, like the 1921 10/30 - as Futurist and ugly as it was longed-for by enthusiasts. Descendant of the Blitzen Benzes, the record-breaking tapered cars of the second decade of the century, the 10/30 opened the way for the Tropfenwagen. The Tropfenwagen is not relevant so much for being a streamlined, open-topped car but because it was an obligatory passage on the evolution of the car shape although it was

never sold. It was produced from 1923 in different versions having originally appeared as a single-seater torpedo able to reach 100 mph (the 6 cylinder engine was capable of producing 80 HP with short bursts of 90 HP). It then became a two-seater in which the fenders were turned into fins which gave the car a rather comical appearance.

The "Tropfel" was raced on several occasions with reasonably successful results. Mention should also be made in passing of the 1933 Citroën "Petite Rosalie", the 1934 Alfa Romeo Type B Aerodinamica and the 1937 Fiat 508 C MM, but the list could be extended at length. Chrysler's determined efforts in the "airstream" category of car designs were of no relevance to racing but influenced road cars for years to come.

126 top These photos demonstrate either courage or folly depending on your point of view. The photo was taken in 1937, when Auto Union and Mercedes battled to show Hitler their technological superiority. What better demonstration of power and invincibility was there than to beat speed records in front of their Italian allies and continental enemies? This aerodynamic Auto Union driven by Bernd Rosemeyer reached 253.7 mph. Above, we see it on the banking of the Avus circuit near Berlin, which was finally bisected by the construction of the Berlin Wall. Rudi Caracciola broke the record again in 1938: 273 mph (one way) which worked out at an average of 270.5 mph (both ways). A few hours later the famous driver Rosemeyer tried to beat the new record, but his car literally took off and the driver was flung into the woods where he died. As for the shape of the cars, in 1937 ideas regarding streamlining and low coefficients of drag, known as Cd, were already clear.

126 bottom This enormous French "boat", with bodywork by Figoni et Falaschi based on the Delahaye 135 chassis, was first shown at the end of the 1930's. Despite its originality, this production was one of the French coachbuilders' more sober designs.

127 A model as revolutionary as it was unsuccessful: the 1940 Chrysler Newport. The company presented the Newport as the car of the future for its total dedication to streamlined styling, which meant every part sticking out beyond the car body was removed. Unfortunately the public did not generally accept Chrysler's courageous effort.

The 1935 Airflow was too futuristic for its time and nor did its convertible version, the C7 Airstream Six, do any better despite the six years of experimentation that went into its production. Finally Chrysler hit the jackpot with the 1941 Newport and Thunderbolt Convertible models. In the authors' opinion, the Newport merits the designer, Ralph Roberts, a place in the Hall of Fame for creative car designers. The line was definitely aerodynamic or "airstream". All the elements which stuck out further than necessary on contemporary cars were absorbed into the body, so that it appeared almost like a boat. The shape was rectangular and the central section of the front end resembled the loudspeaker of an old radio. The car was certainly very striking, even excessive, but no single part of it seemed disproportionate to the rest, which was pure

emotion. The actress Lana Turner had a flame-red dual cowl Newport. As a true dual cowl model, the front and back seats were separated not just by a metal structure but also by an elegant windshield. The doors opened from the inside and were almost invisible as they had no exterior handles. The rear of the car was an example of how convertibles were to appear in the years to follow. It seems incredible that car design was able to undergo such a radical transformation and look to the future in such a short space of time. With regard to the years to come, the publicity for the Thunderbolt Convertible concept car called it the "car of the future". Its shape seemed smoothed by the wind, the aluminum body was uniform in every detail and without edges. The hard top looked like a turret and was electrically controlled.

This chapter, which links open-topped cars to aerodynamic design, ends with mentions of two record-breaking cars, both totally streamlined. The first is the 616 HP Mercedes used by Rudi Caracciola to break the 228 mph speed record in October 1936. The driver was seated centrally and the body was completely smooth with a single shark's mouth aperture at the front. The second is the Auto Union Aerodinamica, in which Bernd Rosemeyer was killed trying to increase his own 253.7 mph record. The same Caracciola took up the challenge the following year, reaching the incredible speed of 270 mph. But these cars are not truly relevant to the history of open-tops, being no more than Grand Prix-based record rockets designed for maximum speed. Still, one wonders what it must feel like to have one's head enveloped in a rush of 270-mph air....

THE ERA OF THE CONVERTIBLES BEGINS
GRAN TURISMO: FROM ROAD TO RACING AND BACK

The preceding chapter explained how the appearance of open-topped cars in the 1930's was characterized by the emergence of design for design's sake, or at least closer attention to shape. However the case was actually wider ranging than that; there was another element which had a greater influence on the personality, appearance and social symbolism of the open tops - the percentage they represented of the total number of cars sold. During the 1920's, 90% of cars on the roads were open-topped because of their lower design and production costs. Ten years later they were only 10% of the total and falling until, at the end of the 20th century, they represent between 1-5% depending on the relative wealth of the country. This inversion has turned the open-topped car into a luxury item more dependent for success on the fact that it is unusual than on its design.

At the end of the 1930's the car had conquered people's hearts. Although still not widely diffuse, it could be considered as a social macro-phenomenon, crisis or no crisis. The total number of cars in the US was approximately 25 million, in Great Britain and France 2 million each, in Germany 1.3 million while in Italy it was only 291 thousand. These figures represented a density of roughly 115 cars per thousand inhabitants in the US, 45 in Britain, 44 in France, 18 in Germany and 7 in Italy.

It is worth remembering that the large motoring corporations had been consolidated for some time: in 1929 in America, General Motors, Ford and Chrysler accounted for 90% of the market; in France, Citroën, Renault and Peugeot had tied up 68% of sales; in Great Britain where Bentley had been taken over by Rolls Royce, Austin, Singer and Morris represented 76% of the total; in Germany, Opel was top of the sales list; and in Italy Fiat produced 75% of all new models sold.

Despite the change in market positioning of open tops both in terms of quantity and price, their traditional classification had not altered much and now they could be categorized into three rather than two types. Previously they

had been either mainly sports or mainly luxury cars, on the one hand in the form of runabout, speedster or roadster and on the other, touring car, phaéton or torpedo. This categorization excludes hybrids or customized cars. Development of the runabout and roadster produced what shall be referred to here as gran turismo (GT) models which were the link between the dynasty of English sporting open-tops and European sports cars in general. A link also exists between the gran turismo models and the American convertibles of the 1960's,

although these latter cars inherited a great deal from the convertible coupés of the 1930's, 40's and 50's, and it is these (described below) which form the second of the three classifications. The third is the convertible sedan, which differs from the convertible coupé in having four doors rather than two. Of the three categories, the last two (convertible coupés and convertible sedans) are prevalently American while the GT's, thanks to their frequent participation in sports car races and smaller size, were European.

128 top This photograph demonstrates better than any other the clarity of Bugatti's design philosophy. The harmonious whole of this cabriolet show Bugatti to have been a car manufacturer without equal, even greater perhaps in design of individual details than the Rolls Royce grill topped by the graceful winged Victory. From this perspective, the fenders, which enclose double headlights and two-tone horns, seem like enormous folded leaves. The cab seems small, indistinct and far away.

128 bottom The race has just finished and the winner, Meo Costantini, is being feted. The track is Monthléry where the French Grand Prix were held. The car is a Bugatti T39 1.5 in a torpedo or touring design. The man in the colonial hat behind the car is Ettore Bugatti.

129 top Adolf Hitler in one of the most beautiful and luxurious cabriolets of the 1930's, the Mercedes 770K. Dictators of the period did not hesitate to display themselves in convertibles which were ideal for parades.

129 bottom This little car with the racing appearance is the Fiat 508 Balilla built from 1933-37. Many variants of this model were produced including racing and street roadsters, torpedoes and closed body versions. This is the famous Balilla Sport Coppa d'Oro which can be recognized by its fenders that continue behind the wheel to meet the footboard.

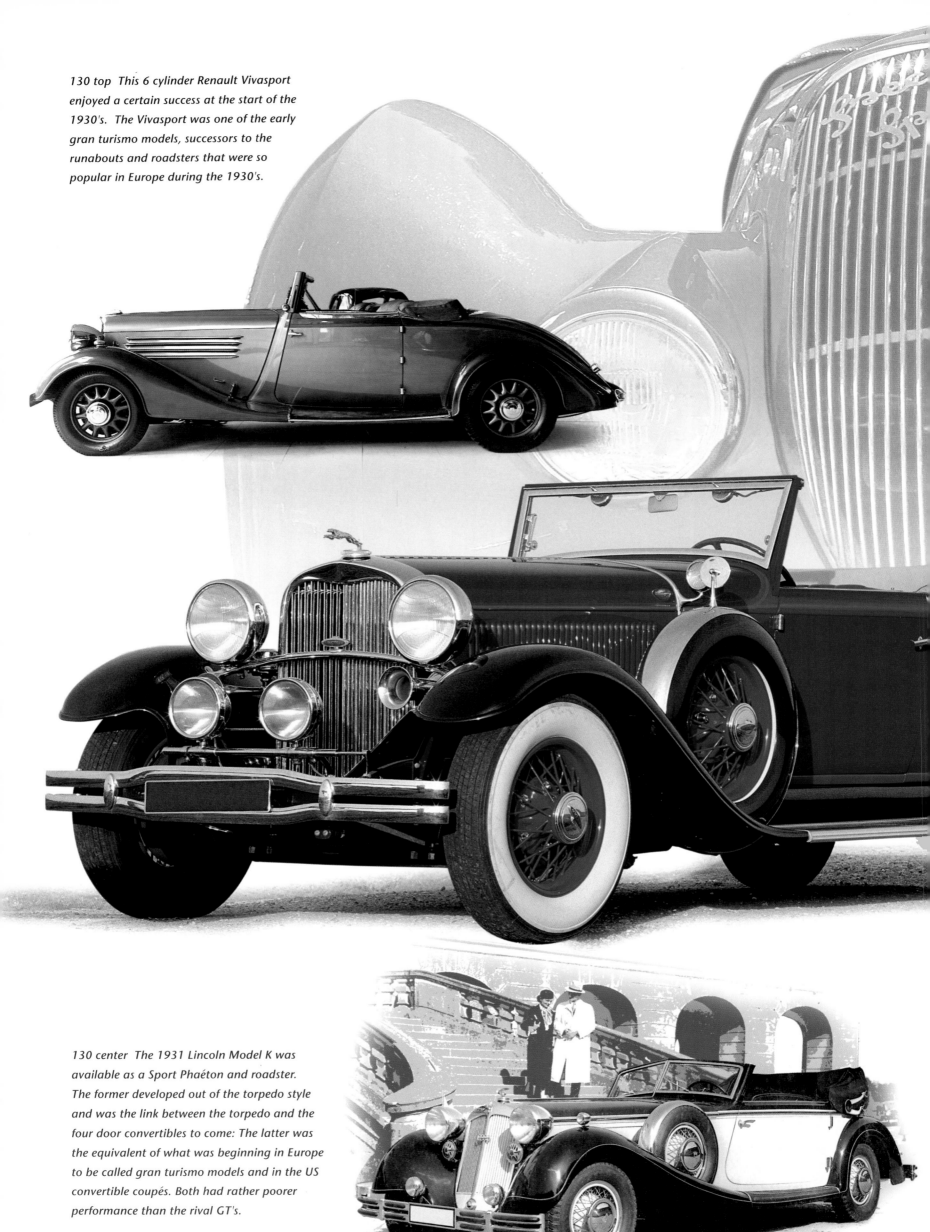

130 top This 6 cylinder Renault Vivasport enjoyed a certain success at the start of the 1930's. The Vivasport was one of the early gran turismo models, successors to the runabouts and roadsters that were so popular in Europe during the 1930's.

130 center The 1931 Lincoln Model K was available as a Sport Phaéton and roadster. The former developed out of the torpedo style and was the link between the torpedo and the four door convertibles to come: The latter was the equivalent of what was beginning in Europe to be called gran turismo models and in the US convertible coupés. Both had rather poorer performance than the rival GT's.

The European GT's are a good example of the interchange of experience and applications between racing and production cars. In general, the most common version of their outline was similar. They were for the most part two-door cars but four doors were not unusual. The road versions had four seats but the racers only two. The upper line of the doors was straight and horizontal (although the English sports cars were different in having a wide ridge) and a footboard was standard. The fenders were wide and very obvious, and often supported the headlights between the fender and radiator. The grill was either classically flat or bullnose and had a vertical or grid design, though occasionally honeycombed. With the top up the vehicle was less interesting and resembled the old torpedoes. Besides being known as GT's, sports or super sports models, the term Fetonte (from the name Phaetone, the son of the Greek sun god) was sometimes used in Germany.

The term "gran turismo" signified a car that was powerful, costly, sometimes customized, with a Spartan if not frugal and uncomfortable interior, and a sporting temperament. This rather formidable nature was to undergo a happy transformation during the 1940's. Streamlining seemed to absorb the headlights into the fenders which at times became a single unit with the car body; the radiator sloped, became narrower and lower.

At the beginning of the 1930's the various elements of a car body had been quite distinct, austere and oversized as in the case of Daimler Benz. Perhaps as a result of the background of the people in charge it was the engineers' designs rather than the architects' designs that were adopted (as opposed to what was happening in the US). Remember that the design head of Daimler Benz in the early 1920's was mechanic Paul Daimler, who was succeeded by another true genius, Ferdinand Porsche, from 1923-28 (later to design the extraordinary Volkswagen Beetle and Porsche 356).

130 bottom The Horch 853 was sold from 1937-40. Auto Union, the group made up of four important German companies including the one started by August Horch, called this two-door model the Cabriolet Sport to distinguish it from the more aggressive 855 Spider.

130-131 top and 131 bottom Another interpretation of a roadster on a 1938 Peugeot chassis. The car's profile seems very influenced by the English trends with a low driving position and inclined waist.

131 top Only two examples of this French gran turismo, the Citroën 15 Cabriolet, were built, one of which was destined to be owned by the Michelin family.

132 top The front of the 1930 Mercedes Benz
38/250 SS. The 'SS' was used to distinguish
particularly powerful, sporting models but the
whole series of S, SS and SSK versions at the
beginning of the 1930's was impressive and
important in terms of engines, racing and design.

132

An example of a typical top-of-the-range gran turismo model was the Daimler Benz SSK which was very successful in terms of sales as well as racing.

The SSK was one of the very powerful sports cars produced by Daimler Benz during the second half of the 1920's. In principle there was the 600 K series from 1924, six cylinders in-line with a total of 6240cc producing 140 HP with a supercharger (100 without) and popular among private individuals who used it for racing. Then came the 'S' series in 1926, even more powerful and more sporty looking. For example, the 680 version had a 6720cc motor which produced 180 HP to reach a maximum speed of 111 mph. The 'SS' was the sports version of the 'S': the footboard was replaced by a drop-shaped silhouette which was mirrored in the design of the front and rear fenders. There were two large headlights next to the radiator and two more by the windshield. The 1928 'SSK' was a synthesis of the two previous models though lighter and better finished. The footboard was reintroduced

for both the sports and road version. The latter had a tapered rear end and the spare wheel was moved into the space between the front fender and motor compartment. The wheelcovers were full and very elegant (if it was possible to keep them clean and shiny). The sports version hid the three large exhaust pipes under the hood and the door faded into a grooving in the side panel. The rear end was flat to allow the spare wheels to be attached.

The engine size was increased to 7065cc so that the car could take part in the 7 liter category races. The result was 225 HP giving a maximum speed of 119 mph. Yet this was not the most powerful version of all; there was the 'SSKL' which developed 300 HP and reached 147 mph! The supercharging on this model was by Ferdinand Porsche and the most powerful that he achieved during his time with Daimler Benz. The K, S and SSK racked up many victories in endurance races and hill climbs. Rudolf Caracciola's win in the 1931 Mille Miglia was the car's most celebrated result.

132 bottom The legendary Mercedes SSK racing around a bend with the famous and fearless Rudolf Caracciola at the wheel.

133 top This unusual picture shows a version of the SSK chassis shortened by 18" to make it more manageable.

132-133 This three-quarters shot of the 680 SS shows the splendor of Mercedes production between 1927 and 1935. Remember that the technical director during this period was Ferdinand Porsche. It is easy to imagine the attraction that this powerful car exerted on "gentleman drivers" of the period. The SSK was the best synthesis of top-of-the-market gran turismo cars, i.e. cars with large engines. It is difficult to explain the range of motors and car versions briefly but the road versions of the S and SS were produced from 1926-30 with 6.8, 7.0 and 7.1 liter engines, while the sports versions of the S, SS and SSK were produced from 1927-34 (including the SSKL) with 6.8, 7.0 and 7.2 liter engines. All could be supercharged, and power ranged from 180-300 HP.

134 top The stupendous lines of the Alfa Romeo 6C 1750 Super Sport. If the S, SS and SSK Mercedes represent the most significant large-engined GT's, the various versions of the 6C 1500 and 1750 at the start of the 1930's guaranteed the survival of Alfa Romeo. It is widely thought that the racing successes of Nuvolari and Campari kept the Milan company's prestige high.

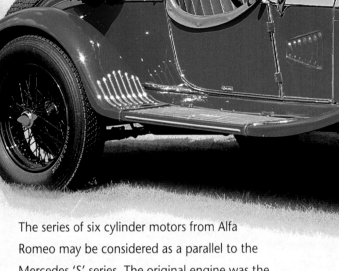

The series of six cylinder motors from Alfa Romeo may be considered as a parallel to the Mercedes 'S' series. The original engine was the rather rough RL produced as early as 1922 for a torpedo body. Six other series in innumerable versions followed up until 1927. The sports versions were very successful on the track and even the Italian leader, Benito Mussolini, liked to ride around in an RL SS.

Alfa Romeo's jewel in the crown was the 6C, the 1500 and later the 1750. Maybe the Arese (next to Milan) based company owes its very survival to the successes of this car during a period when many manufacturers of large, luxurious sports cars were suffering seriously from the economic crisis. The first 6C was produced in 1927 from a design from the genius of Vittorio Jano. The engine size was 1487cc and so it was called the 1500. The car was certainly Spartan if compared to the Mercedes S but versatile and reliable. A simple cabriolet version from Carrozzeria Touring can be considered the European equivalent of the American convertible coupés like the 1927 LaSalle.

1929 saw the arrival of the first 6C 1750's. They were beautiful, balanced and dazzling. Of this model, too - understated because it was considered the evolution of the 1500 - there were six series and countless versions (Touring's Flying Star has already been discussed in the chapter on European coachbuilders). Racing versions were driven to success by many, including Nuvolari, Campari and Benoist. Some of its major triumphs were two Mille Miglias, two 24 hour races at Spa and a Tourist Trophy.

The 6C evolved in 1931 into the 8C (8 cylinders) 2300 in the road version, and the 2300 Le Mans, 2300 Monza and 2600 Monza. The traditional shape was dominated by the design of the fenders and a front grill like a Greek temple.

134 center Zagato's interpretation of the Alfa Romeo 6C 1750 Sport chassis. The waistline was straight and the forms basic without concessions to the aeronautical trend of the period. The sinuous line of the front fender merged into the footboard which lay at the feet of the rear fender. The front end was still dominated by the upright chrome grill. The headlights, sometimes three in line, were held by supports fixed to the fenders.

134 bottom The Alfa Romeo 6C 1750 engine was developed into the 8C 2300 and produced in two versions, the Le Mans (shown) and the Monza. It was one of the most successful prewar racing GT's.

135 top The Alfa Romeo 6C 1750 Tourer from 1932; the name indicates that the version was more docile than the Sport or Super Sport.

135 bottom left An important person who does not hide his admiration for the 6 cylinder Alfa Romeo: Benito Mussolini. The photograph was taken in 1934.

135 bottom right The back of the 1932 Alfa Romeo Tourer.

136 top The 328 was the model which brought most European public attention to BMW. It was introduced to racing in 1936 and achieved so much notoriety that the Munich company decided to market it the following year. The 328 was built from 1936-40. Note the double kidney grill, vestiges of which are still seen on today's BMW's, and the absence of door handles.

136 bottom The 328 Mille Miglia at the beginning of a race. This excellent BMW dominated the 2 liter class in all races during the second half of the 1930's. Among its more important victories were the Mille Miglia of 1938 and 1940, the first won at an average speed of 75 mph and the second, 104 mph.

137 The front and rear of the BMW 328 Mille Miglia Touring. Although it was a racing car, it should be noted that the motor compartment and fenders had finally been joined. The lights were now housed in the new, more compact, single volume and the gap that previously separated the wheels from the body was now a shallow hollow. The BMW double kidney grill is clearly seen.

Similar in shape and sporting success, though at a lesser level, was the DKW Sport which collected 12 consecutive class records in 1930 on the Monthléry race track where the French Grand Prix was held. Horch (which merged with Audi, DKW and Wanderer in 1932 as the Auto Union Group) offered an elegant and refined machine, the Sport 670 produced between 1931-34. Given its design, it might better have been considered a convertible coupé but its 12 cylinder engine gave it outstanding performance. There were very many open-topped racing cars: to name just a few, from the United States there were the 1929 Stutz Model M, the 1929 Chrysler 75, and the 1930 Cadillac 8 while from Britain came the 1934 Jaguar SS2 Tourer. But it is better to look further ahead in time to see the final European car developments before the start of the Second World War canceled all traces of pleasure in design.

A German classic from 1935 was the 1.5 liter BMW 315/1 also available in a 2 liter version named the 319/1. It evolved from the production 315 but it was a smaller, sensitive machine. The headlights and fenders were still separate from the car body but there was a slight move in the direction of streamlining with the flat rear volume which hid the spare wheel. The rear wheels were half covered, like many French cabriolets. The grill had a distinctive double bean (also called double kidney) design. The 315/1 was the testing ground for a great success, the 328. This car was produced from 1936 for sports use but was also manufactured for the road after receiving general approbation despite being uncomfortable and having little baggage space. The 328 was lined with leather, was well-finished and had a functional glove box. The lines of the car were very modern with the lights housed inside the compact form produced by the fenders and radiator (beginning to become a single unit). The BMW beans on the radiator grill were long and narrow and belts appeared over the hood to prevent the panels from rattling. The doors were tiny and useless and the rear wheels were hidden under a wheelhouse. Being a sports model, the spare wheel was brought back into view though half hidden in a cavity. The chassis was tubular with box cross-members. The six cylinder, 2 liter engine could produce 80 HP to give a maximum speed of 94 mph.

138 top left This car certainly experienced a slice of history and not because Rock Hudson is at the wheel, nor because it was used in the shooting of the film "The Earth is Mine". This beautiful 8 cylinder Horch, one of the best expressions of luxury roadsters during the 1930's, belonged to Adolf Hitler's lover, Eva Braun.

138 top right One of the models which contests the pinnacle of open-topped car design of all time; this is the Mercedes 540 K, the successor to the 500 K, which first appeared in 1936. It differs from the 500 K by its longer, flat rear end. All external and internal details are perfectly in harmony. The car had a supercharged, 5401cc, 8 cylinder in-line engine capable of producing 180 HP.

This was the era of the Third Reich when Hitler wanted a return to classical, imperial, sculptural forms and Daimler Benz obliged with two austere models: the 500 K Spezial Roadster of 1934 and the 540 K of 1936. Both had a supercharged 8 cylinder motor but differed in length, the 500 roadster had a wheelbase of 9'8" as opposed the 540's 10'8" and an overall length of 16'11" against 17'1". The shorter length of the 500 affected the design of the side of the car and made it appear more contained than its brother. The Spezial Roadster version however was given a much more luxurious appearance by the different curvature of the fenders which seemed like two waves. The door was wonderfully concave while the 540's was convex, making both a playful series of wide, sinuous curves.

Another distinctive element of the 540 K, one of the most beautiful automobiles ever produced, was the extra long rear end which was made less heavy by a light chromed fin running around the hood dock and spare wheel cover. Everything in this car gives the sensation of movement, especially the inclined windshield and side windows, both with a chromed frame. What was happening across the ocean? The open-topped cars of the period had quieter lines and those of the true convertibles and the roadsters were less and less in evidence. American design was in a sense more advanced with more uniform lines, perhaps to the detriment of the sporting style. One independent example was the wonderful Duesenberg SJ roadster which was similar to the 540 K and a favorite of the rich and important of the time.

138-139 and 139 A unique gran turismo model, the Mercedes 500 K. It was one of the last examples produced and dates from 1936. These pictures are a perfect example of what the term "gran turismo" signifies in this book which crosses the boundaries that separate the definitions of roadster, sports car and convertible. Gran turismo models were elegant and luxurious but maintained all the power and performance of a roadster. It is as if the manufacturer wanted to state clearly that the dignity of a convertible could reside equally well in its sporting temperament.

CONVERTIBLE COUPES

Convention has it that American open-topped cars (and the European models they inspired) from 1927 on are called convertibles, though the authors follow this convention with reserve. These convertibles may be described as cars with a soft, folding top permanently attached at many points around the car body. The windows opened and closed vertically and in general there were no uprights or similar structures which rose above the waistline except of course for the windshield. The commonest version was the two-door, called a "convertible coupé", while the four-door version is known as a "convertible sedan". Both designs seat four or five people. Without wishing to lay down semantic rules, the terminology may be defined further: The European equivalent of the convertible was "cabriolet", especially when referring to an open-topped model of a closed body car, but not everywhere. The term "drophead coupé" was used in Great Britain for two-door versions and "cabriolet" was used for the four-door ones.

The cabriolet was curvaceous, sleek and had a striking profile. The cab, if covered, was like a turret placed in the center of the body. In Europe the open-topped car was endowed with the dignity of an elite car not just because of its superior performance and fittings, but also because of the growing number of hard top sedans which took the place of the open-tops as the car of the masses. Although there was no shortage of design ideas, throughout the 1930's and 40's the European public preferred the traditional styles with the car body components well separated from one another. The formal variables that differentiated the marques were minimal, aesthetic and non-structural. Combined with the heavy and powerful influence of Nazi

140 top A German interpretation of the cabriolet, or even convertible coupé. This is a 1932 Horch 670 V12 - an atypical example from the company (which became a partner in the Auto Union group), as Horch specialized in 8 cylinder engines during this period.

140 bottom The 1936 Bentley 4-1/4 liters. In Great Britain the expression "drophead coupé" was used instead of "convertible coupé," while "cabriolet" meant 4-door open tops.

141 top This elegant BMW was a typical example of a convertible sedan though the term cabriolet was preferred in continental Europe. The position of the raised glass side windows shows off the configuration of the doors; the front doors open from the front and the rear doors from the back.

141 bottom The 1932 Peugeot 301, here shown in one of countless interpretations by French coachbuilders, was characterized by an unusual, slightly concave nose bearing a shield. Note the lack of a footboard which highlights the sill. Traditionally French, the car's dimensions and engine size were limited.

and Fascist architectural principles, allusions to the Machine Age, Art Deco and airstream designs remained sadly just that.
The recommendations by Le Corbusier on the need to integrate the car's projecting elements into the body (radiator grill, headlights, rear lights, secondary lights, fenders, bumpers, exhaust pipes, footboard, spare wheel, license plate holder, etc.) were ignored. The European equivalents of the convertible coupés were the cabriolets. Their shapes differed from those of GT's but were still very much tied to neo-classical styles.

141

Models like the 1934 Mercedes 500 K Cabriolet B and 1940 Lancia Aprilia Cabriolet Aerodinamica Pininfarina were objectively much more beautiful than their American counterparts but added little to what had already been tried and tested by coachbuilders and designers. In the United States the story was quite different. The stylistic hangover from the age of the carriage was still in evidence but open-topped cars took on forms and characteristics that were more typical of modern design (though certainly not typical of modern functionality). From 1930 on, the shape that was so redolent of the carriage was left behind and the car began to assume its own distinct character. This was very evident among the open tops which displayed a functional compromise between artistic expression and industrial design. The resulting style was adaptable and was variously interpreted, as can be seen by leafing through any book on the history of the convertible. All of a sudden it became obvious that the car was somehow different. When did it lose the resemblance to the carriage? When did it assume the compact, all-of-a-piece shape that is still common today? It is difficult to give an exact date, as the transition was gradual and its application to either prototypes or production models could be cited.

Around 1934 the fencer's mask style began to replace vertical radiator grills, as was seen on the Buick Series 60 or the Ford De Luxe. This one variation freed the front end of static, imposing and often inadequate forms. But for the development to be more evident it was necessary to wait for the fenders to be sacrificed on the altar of modernity. This process began with their streamlining even at the sides like on the LaSalle, Pontiac and Cadillac of 1935. Even the design of the lights helped to give a sleeker, smoother appearance thanks to the streamlining at the rear. Car length increased with respect to the wheelbase and so, therefore, did the overhangs, the distance between the wheel axles and the ends of the body. Height was reduced and the coefficient of aerodynamic penetration began to take on some significance, as in the 1937 LaSalle.

Mention has already been made of the 1938 Ford Zephyr which showed startling stylistic innovations that might be considered to herald the birth of the New Car, enclosed or open top. The Zephyr had front lights integrated in the bumper (like the 1936 Cord but without the peak) and therefore right at the end of the car, no longer in the central mass. The gap between the bumper and engine compartment became a shallow cavity and was later to disappear altogether. The radiator was lowered and the hood flourished a comet which was considered a sexual reference or at least biomorphic, and at the rear end the wheelhouses were less apparent, hardly protruding from the body. One aspect of the past remained, the footboard; but that too was destined to disappear.

142 top This picture shows how modernization of the front volume made it flatter. This example is a Packard Darrin Coupé, Darrin being the name of the designer. The model was first produced in 1940, but still shows partial separation of the fenders from the hood plus a temple-like radiator that resembled those of Rolls Royce and Mercedes. On the other hand, Packard was one of the most conservative and traditionalist American manufacturers.

142 bottom A Buick 2-door convertible. Note the straight hood and narrow, curved nose. It was not unusual for cars from the 1940's and 50's to have anthropomorphic, zoomorphic or sexual connotations in the design of their front ends. This 1938 model is a Special Albemarle with bodywork by Carlton.

143 top This convertible coupé belonged to the Chrysler group; it is a 1940 DeSoto Custom S7. The low grill resembles that of the Ford Zephyr. Similarity can be seen between the rounded, pronounced hood and a nose, while the radiator grill resembles a mouth; the headlights are moved right away from the center to give the overall impression of a face.

143 bottom This photo depicts the 1938 Oldsmobile which features a curved grill and two shiny meshes at either end.

144-145 This 1939 Cadillac clearly shows the typical design features of a convertible coupé but also the renewal that open-topped cars underwent from the mid-1930's. The fenders are more wrapped around and less extreme; now they are integrated into the sides and front. A fencing-mask grill has replaced the vertical radiator shell. The lights with streamlined houses make the lines of the car lighter, while the spare wheels between the door and fender are no longer visible but hidden in what seems a more rounded third fender.

146 top This large Cadillac, the Series 62, can boast a prestigious line of classic, luxury convertibles as descendants, including the Eldorado. The nose was characteristic with the grill crossed with thick, chrome horizontal strips and the bulbous hood topped by more chrome. The aeronautic theme was still popular.

146 bottom The 1952 Muntz Jet Convertible R was free from any type of extraneous decoration or parts that stick out from the main body. An inspiration was the Chrysler Thunderbolt of 1941, a convertible presented as the car of the future but which unfortunately was short-lived.

146-147 Gary Cooper in tennis clothes poses beside his Buick Convertible Cabriolet.

Other examples from the same period and of the same ilk were the Ford De Luxe and the Mercury. Both had an 8 cylinder engine though the Mercury had 10 HP more to offer (95 vs. 85). Further examples are the sedan and coupé versions of the Plymouth Convertible.

From the 1940's on it was no longer unusual to find lowered motor compartments with the car sides only slightly lower than the central mass. The design studios led, and the manufacturers followed, towards final liberation from the structure of the carriage.

But what was received in return? Modernity, yes. Streamlining too. But the result was disappointing. The elegant, nervous stallion that was difficult to master had been transformed into a massive ox! The power was certainly there but the brute was heavy and somnolent. It seems incredible, but

again it was the Ford Zephyr which offered a step forward. The 1940 version removed the footboard and replaced it with a light ribbing which was only a reminder of the original part. The economic crisis was now almost past (the worst year had been 1933) but other dark clouds were massing on the horizon. The bombs that were exploding in Europe began to echo louder in the United States and only a short time was to pass before heavy industry turned its attention to the production of weapons, airplanes and munitions. For the moment however, the war was distant and life in America went on almost as normal. New cars were built like the 1942 Buick Roadmaster with its elegant chromework down the side which somehow connected with the bumpers. The design of the front wheelhouse was attractive; it ran like an elegant pleat from the front lights to the edge of the rear fender. Despite construction being interrupted by the

war, the Roadmaster returned with a motor capable of developing 165 HP. In the meantime, the young marque Mercury seemed to take a step backwards when it reintroduced the footboard and, alas, a horrendous front end which was very wide and covered with heavy, ugly and useless chromework (especially when compared to the new Chryslers which had eliminated everything unnecessary to give the Newport and Thunderbolt the maximum in terms of modernity and streamlining). Chrysler went on to produce the New Yorker the next year, which was still heavy with chrome but at least more fluid in shape. The war intervened until 1946 when the manufacturers had to gear themselves up to produce something new, fresh and innovative to make the public forget the horrors just lived through. The wheel had come full circle and the car was once again the means to enjoyment and fun

as it had been in the 1920's. While the manufacturers were emptying the stores of the old hand-beaten metal panels, car shapes became more tapered and flat panels slowly returned to fashion; in turn this led to the immense horizontal and vertical expanses of the 1950's and 60's convertibles covered in lights, fins and chrome. Indications of the road that was being trod were given by the 1947 Fords and Mercury Sportsman, the Cadillac Series 62, the Studebaker Commander Regal De Luxe and the 1948 Pontiac (with its trademark Silver-Streak hood trim). Finally came the 1949 Buick, which introduced four small, rather curious-looking portholes on the side of the car - from the aeronautic to the marine!

147 top The grill of this Cadillac Series 62 seems lighter than those of previous models.

147 bottom The motif is taken from contemporary jet engine air intakes - a stylistic fillip also toyed with by the Italian Pinin Farina. The famous car in the picture is the 1947 Studebaker Regal De Luxe designed by Raymond Loewy, creator of the Coca Cola bottle.

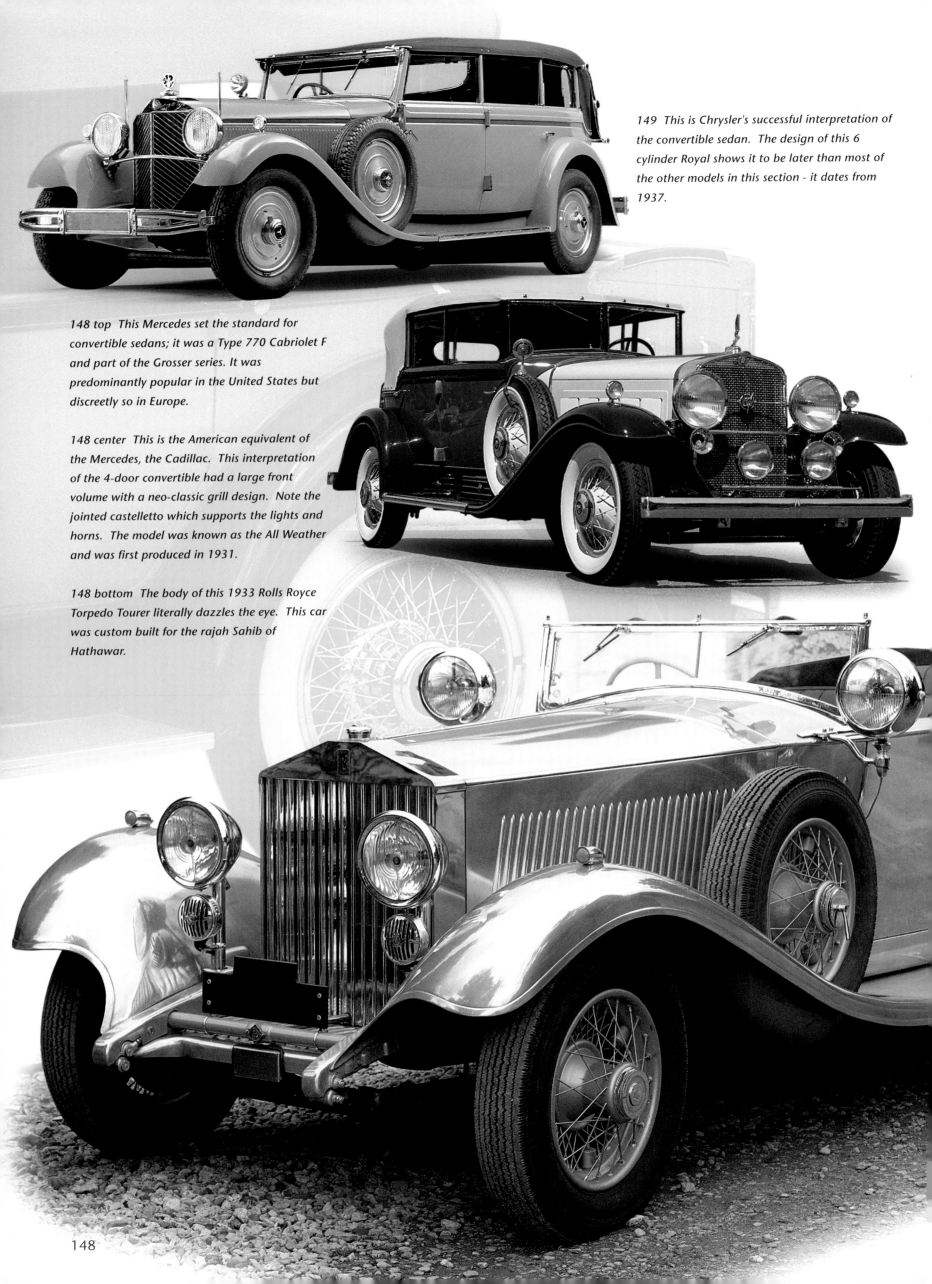

149 This is Chrysler's successful interpretation of the convertible sedan. The design of this 6 cylinder Royal shows it to be later than most of the other models in this section - it dates from 1937.

148 top This Mercedes set the standard for convertible sedans; it was a Type 770 Cabriolet F and part of the Grosser series. It was predominantly popular in the United States but discreetly so in Europe.

148 center This is the American equivalent of the Mercedes, the Cadillac. This interpretation of the 4-door convertible had a large front volume with a neo-classic grill design. Note the jointed castelletto which supports the lights and horns. The model was known as the All Weather and was first produced in 1931.

148 bottom The body of this 1933 Rolls Royce Torpedo Tourer literally dazzles the eye. This car was custom built for the rajah Sahib of Hathawar.

148

CONVERTIBLE SEDANS

Before the advent of the enormous, finned and brilliantly shiny open-topped cars of the 1950's, American car manufacturers offered not only two-door convertible coupés but four-door convertible sedans (sometimes called a convertible phaéton). Sales of these latter models were modest, partly because open tops had an increasingly small share of the market but, in addition, because they were ugly.

For this reason, little space will be devoted to them here, enough to understand that their relationship with convertible coupés was very close, and that they were if anything even more "middle-class".

They had no particular stylistic feature except the variable layout of the doors. There were three variations: The traditional one where both front and rear doors opened normally with the hinge placed at the front; opposing, where the front door opens as normal but the rear door has the hinge at the back; and butterfly, where the rear door opens as normal but the front one has the hinge at the back. With both doors open in the "opposing" configuration, the car seems cut open lengthwise and entry and exit are certainly easy. The butterfly option though makes access more uncomfortable and awkward.

Examples of cars with the traditional door layout were the Ford Flathead V8, De Soto Convertible Sedan and Cadillac Series 70 from 1936, the 1939 Packard 120, Cadillac Series 62, Oldsmobile Custom Cruiser 8 and Buick Roadmaster from 1941 and the Frazer Manhattan from 1949.

Cars with opposing doors were the 1937 Pontiac Deluxe Eight and the Cadillac Series 75 and 90 from 1938 and 1939.

As for the butterfly variation, there was the 1931 Cadillac All Weather Phaéton, the 1932 Packard Model 32 and the Cadillac V8 and Buick Series 60 from 1934. It can be seen that the models produced with the unusual butterfly door layout were prevalent in the early 1930's when cars were still linked to the design of the carriage, whereas the layout that we find normal today became standardized during the 1940's.

Four door convertibles have played an important role in history, however. They are ideal for parades, being used by US Presidents including Roosevelt, Truman, and certainly John Fitzgerald Kennedy, who died while traveling in a presidential Lincoln convertible. They were just as popular with European leaders such as Hitler and Mussolini, and with many royal families around the world - except those who, for reasons of ceremony, may not have anyone show his back to the monarch!

In Europe development of four door cabriolets was parallel but not similar to those of the United States, as cabriolet design during the 1940's was still traditional. Mercedes and Rolls Royces were classic examples of luxury open-topped cars reserved for VIP's and parades.

There is little else to say about four door convertibles and novelty in terms of design, but it should be noted that, despite the lack of change, the period they covered lasted from the beautiful torpedoes right up to the sparkling convertibles of the 1950's and 60's.

THE ENGLISH OLD-FASHIONED ROADSTERS

So far the story of automobile development in terms of creativity and design seems to have centered on the French, Germans, Americans and Italians. To attempt to grade their contributions would be both meaningless and impertinent.

And the British? They were no less involved - on the contrary. Britain can claim the parentage of a small sports roadster which uniquely has remained almost the same for sixty years or more. Unfortunately the British perhaps claim a

cars were influenced by the experiences accumulated in Europe and the US in the design of runabouts, roadsters and racing GT's. What was special in Britain, however, was the cultural stew in which ideas surrounding open tops fertilized and prospered. A great love of nature and outdoor pursuits, an irresistible attraction to a unique, exclusive and handmade product and a touch of exhibitionism mixed with humor all combined to create the cult of small, glamorous, lovable MG's,

little too much when they say that the two seater sports cars from the 1960's on are the direct descendants of the old-fashioned models designed in Great Britain from as far back as the 1930's. The authors do not share this opinion as sports cars, like all other types of automobiles, are developed from constant evolution and crossover that has no geographical boundary. It is also just as clear that the classic English sports

Morgans, Triumphs, Jaguars, Bentleys, Aston Martins, Lagondas, Alvis', Lotus' and all the other copies and similar makes of the past and present. This English style had an infallible effect on the American pilots stationed in Britain during the Second World War.

There can be no doubt that they were in serious need of fun and distraction when off duty. What better than an open-topped MG? On returning

to the States, the young pilots took their cars with them so helping to spread a contagious passion; a passion not just for the beauty of the designs but also for the fun of driving. Low and with the driving position set back, these cars imparted strong sensations to the driver. The response of the cars to longitudinal and lateral acceleration was immediate and tangible and the driver might feel he was at the wheel of a

single seater. And what fun when the back-end started to slide out on a bend - as long as it could be controlled, of course! When sitting in an English roadster with the top down, the driver is low to the ground and everything seems immediate: the rumble of the motor, the road rushing past to the side and the heavily sloping windshield to give the effect of being on a motorcycle.

150 top Rolls Royce contributed significantly to English design styles in the 1930's. This Springfield Roadster was designed in 1925 and shows the first hints of the old-fashioned style to come.

150 bottom A page from an advertising brochure for the MG Midget, not the most attractive but certainly the most popular of the English cars. The slogan tells us that the Midget has sporting blood in its veins and that it is the first car with a 750cc engine to exceed 100 mph.

150-151 The rear end of a 1939 Alvis with coachwork by Vanden Plas. It was in fact similar to other continental roadsters and it can be compared to the 1936 Mercedes 540 K. Another point to be noticed that was borrowed from French cabriolets is the drop-shaped front fender.

151 top The MG Model VA from 1937. Morris Garages (MG) was one of the most faithful interpreters of the old-fashioned style and offered traditional convertibles like this one, large and heavy.

152 top The MG 15/100 MK III Tigress had bodywork typical of small racing GT's, including the boattail. The fenders seem to have been taken from a motorcycle.

152 center Workers on the MG 18/80 assembly line at the Abingdon factory in 1930. MG had transferred here just one year before.

152 bottom and 153 bottom Square lines for the MG 18/100 MK III Tigress with its lights pushed forward of the radiator grill. Note the "U"-shaped access to the seats. The steering wheel had four crossed spokes and the dials were set on a white background - a pure sporting thoroughbred. Note the concave, rectangular shape of the outside mirror.

No wonder the drivers had such fun as they whizzed around semi-deserted country roads. In such conditions the old-fashioned English sports cars are irresistible and unbeatable in the picture they offer of the car as fun (the very reason that young Americans were so taken by them). It was this excitement and driving experience that was continued (and not just in Britain) in the development of sports cars to come by making them low, compact and basic.

The history of the English sports cars generally began in workshops and garages out in the country or suburbs. Perfect examples of this genre of car are MG and Morgan, and although there are many other marques with similar stories, these two may be the most significant.

MG came into existence in 1922 when Cecil Kimber wanted to put together a racing car based on a Morris Cowley. His success encouraged the creation of the MG company (which stood for Morris Garages, owned by William Morris, Lord Nuffield, who provided sales outlets and assistance). In 1929 the two-seater

MG Midget was produced based on a Morris Minor which had an 847cc motor developing 8 HP. This was not yet a typical English open-topped sports car but it provided a chassis for the Midget J2 which is considered the originator of all MG models built up until the 1960's and an archetype of the old-fashioned English sports car. It was presented in 1932 with the same engine as the original Midget but power had been increased to 36 HP which gave it a top speed of 69 mph.

The Midget's external appearance was truly interesting in its lack of embellishment. The fenders were beautiful in their simplicity, taken literally from a motorcycle. The driving position was set well back to give space to the disproportionately long motor compartment for the small four cylinder engine it housed. Overall length was extremely short, 7 feet, and the width just over 3 feet. The door was characteristic with the oblique angle of the top of the door similar to the F1 Magna of the preceding year.

152-153 A parade of MG's ready for delivery exits the Abingdon plant. Abingdon was the home of MG from 1929-1980.

153 top right Note the spectacles-type windows that functioned as windshield in this MG J2 from 1932. This model was an important roadster in the creation of the English old-fashioned style. In particular, note the irregularity of the waistline which cuts the door to follow the slope of the wheelhouse.

154 top The picture shows one of the best-selling MG's, the TF, which went on sale in 1953. Although presented decades later than Morris Garages' first models, the TF maintained all the features of typical English roadsters and even emphasized them, for example, the front fender-footboard combination.

154 center A parade of MG J2's crossing a ford during an outing in the English countryside.

154 bottom and 155 The pictures show the backs of the MG PA and ND. Note the curious design of the dash on both cars. Like other, similar small roadsters, the PA had a small 4 cylinder engine, 847cc, capable of producing 36 HP. The ND was produced on an "N"-type chassis and was known as the Magnette.

The body panels were rather crudely manufactured with slits in the side to cool the motor. The radiator was covered by a rectangular bullnose grill and the headlights sat alongside on horizontal pins. On the J2, this grill seemed an ironic comment on the imposing Greek temple design grills of the gran turismo and torpedo models of the day.

The evolution of this early sports car was seen in the similar but better finished models which followed: the 6 cylinder L-Type Magna and the PA of 1934; the '35 PB which was very successful and one of the most representative cars of the English genre; the 1936 TA, the 1939 TB and the 1945 TC, the first postwar model.

To end this glorious series was the compliant TF 1250 sold in 1953-54. In twenty two years almost nothing had been altered; the length had increased by 9 inches to give a more shapely look, top speed had increased by only 12 mph though this was significant for these cars, and engine power had been raised from 36 to 58 HP in the now 1250cc engine (which gave the car its name). In line with the fashion of the time, the hood sported two chromed grooves. Then the shape of the open-topped MG's changed radically with the MGA and MGB, adopting the design that was typical of 1960 sports cars. Both models were very successful commercially.

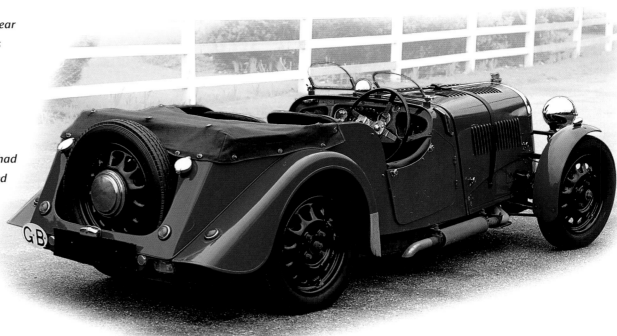

156 top The 1948 Morgan 4/4; it is very difficult to identify from pictures exactly the year any Morgan was produced as the company is the most faithful of all English roadster manufacturers to the traditional style established at the end of the 1920's.

156 center A very elegant and elite 1953 Lagonda from Aston Martin. The retro style had been superseded by the more modern one used by Italian and French producers.

156 bottom One of the most celebrated actors of the time: Clark Gable in a beautiful Jaguar XK 120.

157 top Only 15 examples were ever produced of this refined car: it is the first model of Aston Martin's DB series and it is interesting because it marries the traditional style of the English GT's with that of sports cars of the 1950's. It was brought out in 1948.

Morgan was founded by H.F.M. Morgan who began to assemble three wheeled vehicles back in 1909. The first four wheeler was produced in 1936 with a waterproofed ashwood frame attached to steel side struts, a structure which has hardly changed even now. The model was called the 4/4 (four wheels, four cylinders) and is still in production today. In 1950 it was joined by the Plus 4 and in 1968 by the Plus 8. As representations of English style, the Plus 4 is more indicative with its diagonally cut door as opposed to the vertical edge of the 4/4. Construction was and still is by hand and consequently slow, meaning production is limited. This is the great difference between Morgan and the other English sports car manufacturers which have developed into semi-industrial companies that adapt their car designs as the market develops.
But Morgan has remained faithful to the form, construction and driving techniques of the classic English sports cars. This has been the key to their success, particularly during periods when

157 bottom The enormous front of the Jaguar SS 100 in a splendid interpretation of the roadster theme that disregarded both the size and power attributes of small old-fashioned models and the lines that were strictly linked to the neo-classical style seen on contemporary Mercedes. This Jaguar dates from 1936.

the desire to travel with the top down without fear of being thought to show off was strongest. During the 1970's, when youthful dissent was loud and appearance was strongly criticized, companies such as Morgan suffered badly but made a strong comeback in the 1990's thanks to a return to fashion of old-styled roadsters in modern makeup. A point of interest regarding Morgan was that when the British air force, the RAF, wanted to test their first inflight refueling system during the Second World War, they asked Morgan to be the prime contractor.

Returning to English roadsters, it is impossible not to mention Triumph, which produced the lovely prewar Southern Cross and Dolomite, the TR 1800 from 1945, and then the snappy TR2 in 1953 and perfected TR3 in 1955. The latter were very aerodynamic and represented a distinct technological evolution of the old-fashioned English sports car - if such a thing was allowed. The hoods were wider and the lights were almost integrated. The fenders were long and shaped into a single unit with the body; there was no footboard. The list could go on and on and we have not even mentioned Jaguar (the 1935 SS 100 and the 1948 XK120) or Aston Martin, nor, and why not, even some continental marque such as Fiat and BMW.

POSTWAR EUROPE
CABRIOLETS, A LOT OF SHOW BUT LITTLE SUBSTANCE

After the war, the European car industry had one main objective: to reconvert itself. More or less all the large scale manufacturers had had the production of military vehicles and munitions as their main activity and frequently their factories, especially the Italian and German ones, had been bombed. In addition, there was a strong need for cheap, functional cars to move people and goods. Large scale motorization was required to put the destroyed industrial, commercial and social systems back in operation. Naturally the need for functionality meant that the more elite vehicles suffered. That said, there was still no lack of interesting and attractive cabriolets or sports models.

The term cabriolet will be used more often so it is best to define it. In current terms it means a topless sedan or, more rarely, a two-seater sports car. From a design point of view and to ensure the continuity of terminology that has been used up to now, the authors believe a cabriolet should be defined as a convertible devoted to comfort and even luxury (though not always), sometimes with four doors but always with four or five

seats. The ride is soft and performance dignified. Often there is a roll-bar behind the main seats and a reinforced windshield frame to protect the passengers in case the car turns over.

On the other hand, sports cars are generally open-topped, low two-seaters or maybe 2+2's. From a formal viewpoint, cabriolets are descendants of the torpedo, touring car and baquet and of the American convertible coupé and convertible sedan of the 1940's. Sports cars continue the genealogical line of the roadster, speedster, runabout and GT.

Production of cabriolets immediately after the war was limited although all the motorized countries, Britain, France, Germany and Italy, had interesting cars on offer both for their intrinsic quality and because they ensured continuation of the line of open-topped cars. More generally, it can be stated that the generational leap from wheels in view to fenders as part of the motor compartment took place slowly thanks to the black-out during the war. European cabriolets very much resembled American convertible sedans and coupés but

they were more elegant and balanced being slightly smaller and having less swollen, more linear profiles. This might have been translated into austere, rigorous, unexciting shapes but it did not happen that way - quite the opposite. The wish for fun was strong too in Europe and this took form in "La Dolce Vita" by Fellini. There was a curious parallel at this time between the American passion for glitter and European flamboyance, not in the sense of color or use of chrome but in the design of form itself rather than additions to it. This phenomenon was less intense, evident or widespread than American glitter but it did not lack attractiveness as interpreted by European coachbuilders. Take for example some French cabriolets. There were very many interesting versions based on the Delahaye Type 135 chassis: by Antem, Chapron, De Levallois, Ghia, Faget-Varnet, Figoni & Falaschi, Franay, Graber, Guilloré, Letourneur & Marchand, Pininfarina, Pennock, Pourtout, Saoutchik and Worblaufen. This long list gives an idea of how much this car, from a now non-existent manufacturer, was suitable for

participation in the numerous beauty competitions during this period, but it also confirms the renaissance of the coachbuilders' craft which was, however, to show itself to greater effect on sports cars.

The Delahaye 135 was a large cabriolet which had been presented at the 1934 French Motor Show. In 1936 it won the Monte Carlo Rally and even after the war it kept the same 3.5 liter, 6 cylinder engine. Despite not having a high profile in the history of the car, it is worth describing some of the interpretations of the Delahaye created by the great coachbuilders' between 1946-51.

Antem's 1946 version retained the footboard and the headlights low down near the tall, narrow radiator.

158-159 and 159 top The elegance of the 1954 Jaguar XK 140. The XK series started with the 120 and was one of the most outstanding achievements of the 1950's; it took up the Art Deco stylistic themes expressed in cars like the Bugatti Type 57, particularly in the closed body version. This example, the Drophead Coupé, had softer lines. The roadster version was an original and glamorous interpretation of the postwar desire for speed, luxury and fun. Note the folded, split windshield.

158 bottom This is a luxury convertible, the Bentley MK6 from 1951. The classic version had enormous drop-shaped fenders; the front ones were painted a different color to the rest of the body and slowly faded away towards the rear axle. In this version, the features are more discreet.

159 bottom A moment from the most glamorous wedding of the 20th century: Prince Rainier of Monaco and the actress Grace Kelly pass through the streets in an enormous Rolls Royce after the wedding ceremony on 19 April 1956.

It did not use chromework heavily but brought attention to the car through the soft curves of the wheelhouses; on the other hand, the wheelhouses were less obvious in the 1947 versions by Chapron and De Levallois. Three extraordinary versions were created in 1950. The first was by Franay which replaced the grill with horizontal chromework and inflated the curves of the fenders, though not as much as Saoutchik, and certainly not as much as the

bodywork like the Chrysler Thunderbolt. In comparison with the profusion of sheet metal used on the hood, the grill and lights seem small. It was very similar to the cabriolet version of the Bugatti 101 of which only 2 examples were ever made, so similar in fact that it produced open comments. Versions of the Delahaye by Ghia and Pininfarina were very similar to Pourtout's ideas. At the other end of the scale from all points of view was the

version, meaner looking but less powerful, brings it within the bounds of a cabriolet. In Germany and Italy, the two countries that lost the war, starting up again was a slow process. Whereas both were to sparkle in the design of sports cars in the years to come, the production of cabriolets was sparse and uninspired. In Germany the only cabriolet worthy of inclusion was the 1949 Mercedes 170 S, one of the first German postwar cabriolets. In Italy Ghia and

Pininfarina designed many models, for example, the Alfa Romeo 6C 2500, the Lancia Aprilia and Aurelia, and the Fiat 6C 1500. These designs shared points in common: the desire to join the front and rear wheelhouses and fill the space between, elimination of the footboard, the occasional enhancement of the sill (the element under the door often lined with chrome), and the addition of features to enliven the expanse of the sides of the car. Many comments were made in northern Europe about the wheelhouse "gaiters" which still resembled undercarriage fairings. Ghia and Pininfarina's design studios had one other point in common: The "flamboyant" style produced by the Ghia workshop. This style was propounded by their designer Capalbi, who had formerly worked for the Farina brothers and it was while working for them that the basis of the style probably originated. Synthesis of the style was the work of Mario Felice Boano. The flamboyant style tended to make cars large and gaudy by replacing the radiator grill with a chrome frame with wide vertical elements in the design of the mouth and teeth like some exotic animal. There was also an excess of chrome around the front lights. The lines as a whole were heavy and did nothing to lighten the plasticity and uniformity of the body panels. The flamboyant style was short-lived and it is unlikely anyone mourned its passing.

narwhal constructed by Figoni & Falaschi. These last two were usually neo-classical designers but on this project they were clearly either struck by incipient madness or an excessive degree of irony. The wheelhouses were drawn over the wheels so far that they were almost convex as in record breaking cars a few decades later. They hid roughly 70% of the wheels and it is pointless to ask how the front ones were capable of being steered. In comparison, American convertibles with fins and chrome seem positively retiring. Certainly they were stylistic exercises but often open-topped production cars are close to custom-built vehicles, a little like the relationship in the clothing industry between catwalk clothes and haute couture.

Pourtout's 1949 design was more compact but no less surprising. It was completely free of any edges or element that stood out on the smooth

pragmatic production model, the 1951 Peugeot Cabriolet 203. The small, unpretentious, no frills car with a small but sufficient engine allowed many Frenchmen to indulge in their own "American Dream". In Britain the fortunes of the cabriolet rested safely in the hands of Bentley, Daimler and Jaguar. In 1949 Bentley produced the Mark VI with body design by Pininfarina. Daimler produced the classic Conquest Drophead in 1953, compact, very powerful and destined to widen the market of the exclusive English marque. There was also a roadster version but this was no beauty. Jaguar's 1957 XK 150 Drophead Coupé was a beautiful wild beast with a six cylinder engine producing 253 HP which would take the car to 140 mph (assuming anyone would want to in an open-topped car). It could be argued that the XK 150 was close on being a sports car but the presence of a Roadster

160 top This car is one of the countless versions of the 135M chassis produced by the French company Delahaye from 1938 on. One wonders how the front wheels were able to be steered. Actually, the majority of the versions built were produced to impress spectators at car beauty contests. Arguably, in terms of excess, such contests were one of the worst developments in the history of the automobile.

160 bottom This is the DB2 MK 1 Convertible built by one of Britain's most elite marques, Aston Martin.

161 top The drawing shows an open-topped Mercedes used in 1950 to publicize the Type 170, an important cabriolet during the period of reconstruction after World War II.

161 bottom President J.F. Kennedy passing in a Mercedes 300, called Landaulette, during an official visit to Mexico in 1960.

SPORTS CARS, THE RENAISSANCE OF THE OPEN-TOPPED CAR

Postwar European cabriolets may not have been very exciting, though more graceful than their American counterparts, but this was not the case with sports cars. The wide variety of sports models included many beautiful examples, true cult objects which matched functionality with their ability to give pleasure. Sports cars and roadsters from the 1950's were balanced and competitive thanks to strides forward in technology which allowed metal to be treated like a malleable elastic mass according to the whim of the stylist.

More importantly, greater attention was paid to the torsional resistance of the car's structure. If we think of an open-topped car as a cardboard box with the top cut off, it is clear how necessary it is to create strengthening to give back the rigidity that is lost when the top is removed. If not, the chassis is likely to twist the first time torsional stress is imposed. Reinforced chassis give greater drive comfort, better roadholding and considerable passive safety.

Body shapes were studied in wind tunnels, which resulted in designs that tended to an athletic type of beauty rather than beauty simply for appearance's sake. Motors were more refined and the power they developed could be exploited to the full because of reliable transmissions and sophisticated suspension. Thanks to this wave of technological progress and a strong desire for freedom and the open air, during the 1950's sports cars experienced perhaps the best period in their history on both sides of the Atlantic.

With reference to the design and not the product, the sports car is here defined as a two-seater car (or a 2+2) without a roof panel though with a soft or hard top (allowing targas to be included), designed as an original car and not simply a version of a sedan or coupé, and above all where performance is more important than comfort or luxury. This is, in other words, a return to the concept of the GT and roadster but with a new design. Which?

162-163 top The picture shows the rear end of a Ferrari 166 Mille Miglia Barchetta from 1949-50. Note the right hand drive. The small engine, 2 liters, was already in the classic V12 configuration. The coachwork was designed by Touring. The car was raced by Clemente Biondetti, Felice Bonetto and Piero Taruffi.

162-163 center The 1958 Testa Rossa, often used for racing, was one of the most famous Ferraris of the 1950's. There were two V12 versions, which could only be told apart by the shape of the fender. The name came from the color of the cylinder head, and was used again in the 1980's on a roadgoing, mid-engined GT.

163 bottom The 1953 Ferrari 375 MM Spider Le Mans was designed by Pinin Farina. Note the two vertical elements on the ends of the grill that function as bumpers. The 375 MM Spider Le Mans differs from the 375 MM Spider Competizione by doing without the hollow behind the fender.

164 top This "flamboyant" Alfa Romeo, as European cars with particularly gaudy touches were called during the 1950's, is an unusual version of the 6C 2500. Generally, the 6C's were designed by Touring, Pinin Farina or Ghia and were successful both in racing and car beauty contests; the example in the picture seems to be heading for such a contest. Among the various oddities, note the bumper - a chrome tube.

164 bottom A three quarter picture of the front of the Alfa Romeo Giulietta Spider which came out in 1955. The nose dominated by the chrome triangular shield was characteristic of all Alfas. The car, designed and assembled by Pinin Farina, was created at the insistence of the American importer who understood how the North American market would receive a car which contrasted so strongly with the enormous national convertibles. The following year the Spider Veloce was marketed.

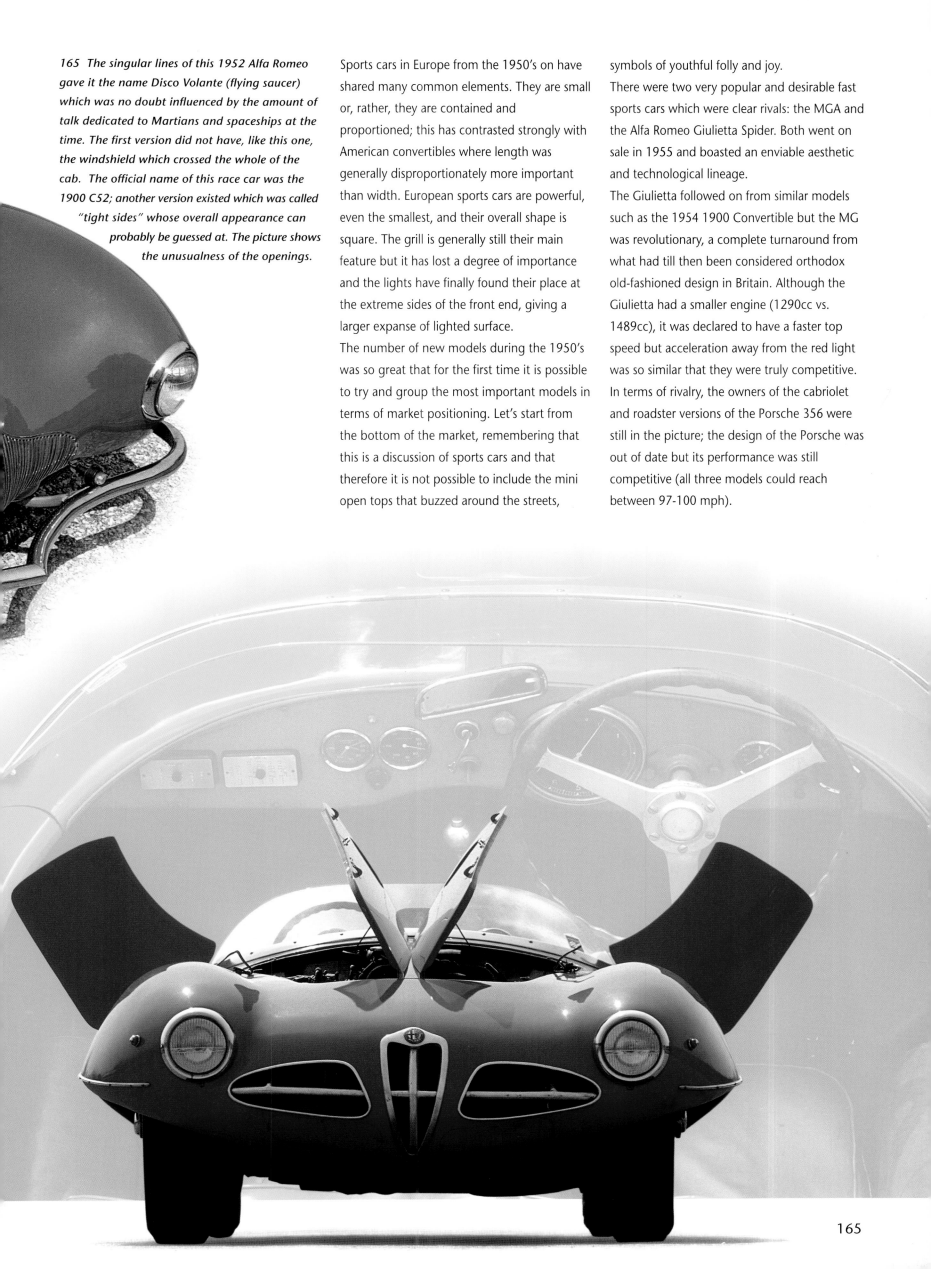

165 *The singular lines of this 1952 Alfa Romeo gave it the name Disco Volante (flying saucer) which was no doubt influenced by the amount of talk dedicated to Martians and spaceships at the time. The first version did not have, like this one, the windshield which crossed the whole of the cab. The official name of this race car was the 1900 C52; another version existed which was called "tight sides" whose overall appearance can probably be guessed at. The picture shows the unusualness of the openings.*

Sports cars in Europe from the 1950's on have shared many common elements. They are small or, rather, they are contained and proportioned; this has contrasted strongly with American convertibles where length was generally disproportionately more important than width. European sports cars are powerful, even the smallest, and their overall shape is square. The grill is generally still their main feature but it has lost a degree of importance and the lights have finally found their place at the extreme sides of the front end, giving a larger expanse of lighted surface.

The number of new models during the 1950's was so great that for the first time it is possible to try and group the most important models in terms of market positioning. Let's start from the bottom of the market, remembering that this is a discussion of sports cars and that therefore it is not possible to include the mini open tops that buzzed around the streets,

symbols of youthful folly and joy.

There were two very popular and desirable fast sports cars which were clear rivals: the MGA and the Alfa Romeo Giulietta Spider. Both went on sale in 1955 and boasted an enviable aesthetic and technological lineage.

The Giulietta followed on from similar models such as the 1954 1900 Convertible but the MG was revolutionary, a complete turnaround from what had till then been considered orthodox old-fashioned design in Britain. Although the Giulietta had a smaller engine (1290cc vs. 1489cc), it was declared to have a faster top speed but acceleration away from the red light was so similar that they were truly competitive. In terms of rivalry, the owners of the cabriolet and roadster versions of the Porsche 356 were still in the picture; the design of the Porsche was out of date but its performance was still competitive (all three models could reach between 97-100 mph).

In the same category but certainly less attractive were the 1953 Renault Ondine and the two Peugeots, the 403 and 404, respectively produced in 1957 and 1962. Mention should also be made of the 1959 Renault Floride and 1962 Caravelle and of course the MG Midget, which were all smaller with an engine of around 1000cc allowing the young and less well-off to have their own sports model.

The Lancia Appia Convertible and Cabriolet of 1959 had a small engine (1089cc) which could only produce 60 HP but they offered reasonably good performance and were extremely well equipped. They abandoned the fencer's mask type of grill and replaced it with a wide grill covered with a flat rectangular grate with large, right-angled weave. This feature had become frequent; it was seen in several Cadillacs and especially in the 1950's Ferraris from Pininfarina.

Both the Appia and the Alfa Romeo Giulietta had modest fins in recognition of what was happening in the US.

At the next level up where the cars were more powerful and aggressive; the body shapes remained the same but engines of two liters or more required more space. Hoods were thus longer, details and fittings more refined.

Lancia, BMW and Mercedes must all be cited but Triumph is the name that stands out. Unlike MG, Triumph remained faithful to the design of the traditional British roadster until the early 1960's, particularly with the TR2 and TR3. Then after a failed experiment with the small Herald came the TR4 in 1961 and the immensely popular Spitfire 4 in 1962.

The traditional and sporty TR3 was the last model that could truly be considered as "old-fashioned". The top of the door sloped sharply down at a diagonal so seeming to divide the car into two parts. The profile rose sharply towards the front where it created the frame of the dashboard, and towards the rear where it became the edge where the tonneau cover was fixed. The windshield seemed very high for the low driving position. The front end was characterized by the curve of the wheelhouse and the slight swelling of the motor compartment. Underneath there was a four cylinder, in-line 1991cc engine capable of 88 HP that gave a top speed of 111 mph and meant the Giulietta and company could be left behind. It would have been harder for the Triumph to do so if it had come up against the Lancia Aurelia B24 sports which could reach 112 mph thanks to its V6 motor. Unlike the Appia Convertible, the Aurelia still had the old style radiator grill. The B24 Aurelia is dealt with in detail in the section on the most beautiful open-topped cars of all time which leaves space here to mention the Mercedes 190 SL as another representative of the medium-high bracket of the market. This was a lovely, no frills model with little but striking chromework and balanced lines. This 1955 SL did not seem to have any competition among the luxury sports cars of the time. The performance was not exceptional as it had only

a small 4 cylinder, 105 HP motor but what impressed was the freshness, lightness and loveliness that the car exhibited. The 190 was not the only example to sport the glorious SL badge; the year before the most sought after car ever produced by Mercedes appeared, the Gullwing 300 SL, which took its name from the unique way the doors opened, upwards like the trunk, making it look like the wings of a seagull in flight. Unfortunately the original 300 SL was a coupé, so this work of art in movement has therefore been excluded from examination.

166 top A moment for pride: The 100,000th MG built, an MGA model from 1956.

166-167 This example is from the second series of the MGA produced between 1959 and 1962. Performance was slightly better than for the first series.

167 top This MG Midget MK III is from 1969. The little English sports car had a 1275cc engine and was nearly as popular as the MGA, selling 103,700 units in all.

167 bottom The Renault 4 HP prepared by Louis Rosier was a successful racing car.

167

The 190 SL could be considered one of the typical open tops from Stuttgart. However two years later brought the arrival of a gem that would leave even those most accustomed to expensive and elegant cars with their mouths open: the 300 SL Roadster, the open-topped version of the Gullwing. The motor compartment and side panels of the 190 were flat and straight. The hood sported a central ridge which made the surface less monotonous while the same function was performed on the sides of the car by two slight grooves at the top of the wheelhouses. This idea was to be repeated in different forms many times on successive models. The rear end was elegant and the luggage compartment occupied the

volume in the tail. 1,853 examples of the Roadster were produced in the years 1957-63 (as opposed to 1,400 Gullwings) despite the car's high price - 32,500 German marks. The heart of the Roadster was a 6 cylinder, 3 liter engine. It produced 215 HP and gave a top speed of 162 mph; it was truly a performer. Its appearance was dazzling and the details beautifully finished. The Roadster was the synthesis of the relatively modest 190 and the luxurious 300 SL sedan of 1954, from which it retained all the characteristics both inside and out except, of course, for the roof. The windshield did not seem to slope as much as the performance of the car merited.

The 190 and 300 were golden links in the SL chain which has had no equal in the history of the automobile. In stylistic terms, the SL's have almost represented perfection. They are recognizable by the absence of the Mercedes star traditionally placed on the top of the radiator; instead the star is centered in the face of the grill and accompanied by a horizontal chrome line. This positioning is aimed at rendering the radiator's air intake less imposing. Another German open top of the period was the BMW 507 Roadster. It cost 5000 marks less than the Mercedes 300 SL but had a powerful engine, a 3168cc V8 giving 150 HP for a top speed of 137 mph. The 507 was the first postwar BMW not to show the double bean radiator grill. It was designed by Albrecht Graf Goertz and is often considered the most beautiful of BMW's.

168 top A hymn to all sports cars sung by the Aston Martin DB2/4 MK II. Actually the conventional design of this car was very different, more rounded and more like the typical English sports car styles. The car was built between 1950-59 but Touring designer Michelotti proposed this version in 1956.

168 bottom The BMW 507 - together with the modern roadsters Z1, Z3 and Z07 and the previous 328 - was certainly one of the queens of BMW's open-topped production. The 1956 model did not have the vertical double kidney grill, which was sacrificed in favor of a shark's mouth that had been squashed down and broken up by a token flange. The 3168cc V8 produced 150 HP and could take the car to 137 mph. The 507 had no immediate successor.

169 top The Volkswagen Karmann-Ghia Convertible (here from 1973) achieved moderate fame and popularity. The name combined the names of two designers and therefore two designs, both famous in the world of open-topped cars: Karmann for the Beetle and Golf, and Ghia for a succession of Fords. VW, Ghia and Karmann cooperated in the production of convertibles as early as 1960.

169 center The 1955 BMW 503 came several years before the 507. The sporting theme was right on target with a basic, nervous and overall square design which was also very popular among small but lively Italian 2-seaters.

169 bottom The 1956 Austin Healey, like other Austins, was copied and reproduced many times. Here one can see combined the rounded fairings of English inspiration together with squarish panels more of continental origin.

This exciting roundup cannot end without discussing, for the first time, the open-topped Ferraris of the time: the 1952 212 Inter Pinin Farina and 1960 250 GT California.
The 212 Inter was the first Ferrari to be designed by Pinin Farina. Noticeable was the use, or abuse, of thick chromework on the sills, the rims around the windshield, the air intakes on the hood and the lights, and most of all in the huge radiator grill and its frame. The rear lights were small, pointed and ugly. It was called a cabriolet but really it was just a straight out sports car. The motor was a 60° V12 displacing only 2.5 liters but producing 150 HP and giving a maximum speed of 122 mph. In 1961 it was the turn of the

short wheelbase 250 GT California, also designed by Pininfarina (now one word) but assembled by Scaglietti. It is considered to be one of Ferrari's most representative sports cars. Its appearance was more menacing than the 212 as the car was set lower down and the position of the headlights, higher than the shark's mouth grill, fostered the aggressive image. The impression was one of nose-heavy dynamism. Another point to notice was the transparent and streamlined covering over the headlights. Besides the rearing horse emblem, the grill accommodated the two fog lights. There was no holder for a license plate, which would have to be screwed directly onto the body.

170 left This picture is of the Porsche production line in 1951. The coachwork is of the first series, the "pre-A", of the Porsche 356 produced from 1948-55. There were three engines available for this car: all were four cylinder boxer designs of 1.1, 1.3 and 1.5 liters that produced between 40-70 HP. Performance, naturally, was not overwhelming.

170-171 This aerial view shows a Porsche 356 ready for the American market. Note the rear-mounted boxer motor.

171 top This red Porsche is the Super 90 version of the 356 B with a 1.6 liter engine, on sale from 1959-63.

171 bottom This might be considered a holy place by sports car lovers - it is the Porsche production line putting the final touches to the 356 A Cabriolet (also seen are closed body versions). In the foreground is Ferry Porsche, Ferdinand's son.

The sides of the car were characterized by a ridge which ran from one wheelhouse to the other and by a chromed air outlet with three vertical slits, a common ornamental motif in sports cars of the period. The tail was surprisingly short and the two exhausts, chromed on the outside and painted red inside, stuck out like an affectation. The V12 engine displaced almost 3 liters and this time more power was there: 280 HP, which gave a declared top speed of 156 mph.

This chapter should have made it clear that the period from 1955 to 1961 was truly exciting for lovers of sports cars. It is not accidental that, considering only Europe, three of the sports cars from this period have been selected for entry in the section on the most representative models of all time (Lancia Aurelia B 24, Mercedes 300 SL and the Ferrari 250 GT California). And this does not include the E-type Jaguar, to be described later, or the American evergreens like the Cadillac Eldorado and Ford Thunderbird. In particular, the authors consider 1955 to be the most bountiful year for production of top quality models.

172 top and 173 bottom One of the most beautiful and desired open tops of all time, the Mercedes 300 SL, created as a spin-off from the Gullwing coupé. Evolution of the SL roadster has been continuously influenced by two factors. The first is stylistic - all SLs are slim in profile and have a strong personality (emphasized by the unusual placement of the three-pointed star not on the hood, but right in the grill). The second factor is technological - the SL range always tries to boast of the most sophisticated and advanced mechanical equipment. The original 300 SL Gullwing pioneered automotive fuel injection, for example. VIP's and movie stars soon adopted Mercedes' sports-car series as their own; in the photograph, actor Glenn Ford can be seen with his 300 SL roadster.

173 top The SL series boasted another roadster, the 190 SL, with body characteristics more linked to forms from previous models and with performance decidedly inferior to the 300 SL.

174 top A historic picture that shows the prototype Beetle cabriolet as it leaves the house of its "father", Ferdinand Porsche.

174 bottom Defining the Beetle created difficulties for its designers who could find nothing better than "closed body soft top". On the other hand, "cabrio limousine" seemed a little over the top. The semi-elliptic split window was rather strange. This configuration was the origin of other small-engined open tops like the Citroën 2CV, Renault 4, Fiat Topolino and Fiat 500.

175 left The very first Beetle convertible from coachbuilder Hebmüller can be recognized by the fact it was a 2-seater. When a fire destroyed the Hebmüller plant, the job passed to Karmann.

175 right Hitler's dream of a popular and cheap German car came true with the Volkswagen Beetle designed by Ferdinand Porsche. It cost just 990 marks, approximately half the price of the next cheapest car on sale in Germany.

THE ERA OF THE BEETLE

Unusual, clumsy, slow and with archaic lines, the definitive design of the open Volkswagen Beetle in 1948 seemed to have little chance of success with the lovers of top down motoring. Its expected public was those who had always wanted to drive with the wind in their hair but who did not have the means to buy themselves an elegant cabriolet or sporty two-seater. Overturning every prediction, the open-topped version of the Beetle was just as popular as the closed version and 331,847 units were sold. This amazing success of the Beetle Convertible was a pleasant surprise for Volkswagen and subcontractor Karmann. The car was designed by one of the greats of the automobile industry, Ferdinand Porsche. Porsche had worked for Mercedes and Auto Union but left to form his own company. Before doing so, he was asked by Adolf Hitler

The Beetle ("Kafer" in German) was designed during the late 1930's when there were already open-topped models in similar shapes on sale, for example, the 1936 Mercedes 170 H and the 1939 Adler 2.5. When production was restarted in 1948, responsibility for the curious cabriolet was given to coachbuilder Hebmüller who produced a two-seater. When a fire at the factory interrupted production, Karmann took over in 1949 and produced the definitive four-seater version. The body of both two and four-seater versions was identical to that of the sedan; it was as though a saw had simply taken off the part above the waist. It was a triumph for roundness! The funny little car was like an overturned oval cup with a snail shell at each corner (the fenders). The handle of the cup

to design a cheap, reliable and functional car ("Volkswagen" means "people's car"). The war interrupted production but the chassis continued to be used for military purposes. At the end of the war, the Beetle was involved in an amazing blunder. A British commission was specially set up to assess the car's potential and judged it to have no future, but Volkswagen's new manager, Heinz Nordhoff, was not prepared to give in and reduce production. Sales continued to grow and the Beetle became one of the most loved symbols of the young during the 1960's.

was the enormous roof which stuck out not just a little above the waist when folded.
There is little point in describing a model which is still fresh in the minds of all drivers and which is still not infrequently seen on the road. With regard to technical details however, when the Beetle first came out, it had a modest four cylinder boxer engine mounted in the rear. The size was 1131cc which produced a simple 25 HP. Both size and power increased as the years passed while most of the rest remained unchanged except, of course, for equipment relating to safety and comfort.

There were restylings but nothing which took away from the car's overall appeal.
The second series (if we discount the original two-seater) appeared in 1954 and remained in production until 1960. The quantity of chrome was increased, quality of finishing was improved, the body grew in length by 3 inches and the motor slightly increased in power.
Successive versions appeared every five years or so until 1979 when the Golf Cabrio made its triumphal entry on the back of a rich genetic inheritance from the Beetle, which regretfully went into retirement.

LARGE AMERICAN CONVERTIBLES

Is there a parallel between the European sports cars of the 1950's and the large American convertibles? What did the fast, sporty, elegant but basic open tops of Europe have in common with the flashy, self-propelled juke-boxes, the core business of American style of the 1950's and 1960's? On one side of the Atlantic "La Dolce Vita", and on the other "American Graffiti". It seems there was a huge divide. But there is a parallel and a strong one: an easy-going hymn to joy, pleasure, and, perhaps, irresponsibility, sung with the wind in one's hair and the sun or stars over one's head in a determined attempt to return to childhood.

To brand these large convertibles together as gaudy, useless, childish barges is not just wrong but shows a symptom of ignorance greater only than the superficiality which generated it. Were these cars so very vulgar? In our opinion, as will already be clear, decidedly not.

Certainly, if beauty is considered as an interpretation of the classical, sculptural and anthropomorphic inheritance handed down from the history of the car we have so far seen, the

Cadillac Eldorado et al had little to say. If, however, we consider beauty in the light of transgression, as a desire for novelty, surprise, excitement and freedom of thought etc., the finned wonders take on a regal dignity. Then, too, there is the taste of excess, the desire to show off, the knowledge of being over-the-top. This is surely just plain tongue-in-cheek, a need not to be taken seriously rather than youthful swaggering. It should not be forgotten that during the 1950's the United States was struggling with the Korean War, McCarthyism, civil rights, the Cold War, and the recession of 1958. There would be little to crow about in a society that continuously criticized and attacked itself. To imagine young American boys as interested simply in creating the perfect quiff, dancing to rock'n'roll and slipping out with Pop's car keys for wild nights, or riding around on Harley Davidsons in Easy Rider style, would be to accept blindly

empty stereotypes created for us by TV and the cinema. Decades on, these enormous witnesses of an era, the last in which fun was an option for youngsters, still travel the roads of the world. Consider for a moment; what is your first reaction when you see a large American convertible on the street? Most probably a smile in recognition of a past which is only available to most of us through the small and large screens. Then perhaps common sense spurs our critical reasoning, if not a veil of sanctimonious respectability, to ask, "What is that ostentatious sky-blue Buick Limited/Ford Skyliner/Cadillac Series 62 doing in a world that takes everything so seriously?" But we are talking about open-topped cars, about dreams and abstraction, the wish to smile, to explore and to imagine the road as an infinite ocean all to ourselves. These cars, half fish, half ship, allowed their drivers to surf on the crest of fantasy. They were a world apart.

176-177 This page shows three pictures of a car made in 1959, when the shiny, glittery era was almost at an end. This was a special-bodied Sedanca built on perhaps the 1950's most representative convertible, Cadillac's Eldorado. In the picture to the left note the shape of the roof, which resembles the limousine designs at the start of the century. ("Sedanca" refers to a car in which the folding roof only partly covers the passengers, though in fact this Eldorado is really a hard top with a central insert - in other words, a classic targa.) The closeup of the back end gives an excellent view of the most important design feature of 1950's convertibles, the fins. The idea of fins came from the most powerful designer in American auto history, Harley J. Earl, and was inspired by Lockheed's P-38 fighter. The rear lights were nearly always placed right at the tip of the tail, and sometimes they were used to conceal the fuel cap.

178 top This Nash Metropolitan was an American model built with English mechanicals that was sold between 1954-62. It definitely ran counter to the times, being absolutely tiny and having only a 4 cylinder engine.

178 center and bottom This elegant convertible, the Chrysler Town & Country, was sold from 1946-48. After the Crown Imperials it was the most expensive model in the Group.

179 top The front end of the 1951 Frazer Manhattan. The amount of chrome applied had started to increase inexorably.

There is an enormous jump between the rather awkward convertibles that existed throughout the 1940's and the sparkling models from about 1952 on. Let's consider their development chronologically. At the start of this period the car manufacturers started to lengthen the outline of their open-topped cars, the angle between the upper half and the side panels became cleaner and the edges more accentuated, in contrast to the curved and swollen surfaces of a few years before. Assimilation of the hood and fenders, elimination of the footboard, resizing of the grill and integration of the lights into the car body were difficulties which had been overcome. The body was now unified and heavy, and the grill was used to give identity to the car as had happened so often before. Two examples are the 1949 Packards, the Convertible and the Custom Eight. The first had a strange, large weave grill, round and rectangular lights and a "rail" type of bumper. The second seemed a composition formed from a curved rail-type bumper, three large pieces of chrome of equal length and a kind of long, chromed metallic protective chestpiece worn by knights in the Middle Ages, all topped by further decoration. It was horrendous. The 1950 Dodge Convertible limited itself to three very large chrome strips bent to resemble the front of a boat while the Mercury convertible of the same year had a long, narrow mouth without lips but with innumerable teeth (or even better, baleen, the cartilaginous bones in the mouth of a whale which trap the plankton). It resembled the grills of the flamboyant style designs in Italy and France. The list could go on and on, some more and some less bizarre. As for the rear, the only outstanding difference was the choice by the designer whether to cover part of the rear wheelhouse with a side panel or not.

But then came the first signs of the style that was to explode on the scene like a battery of fireworks.

Of particular importance was the evolution of details which were to characterize all models in the decades to come: the sides at the back of the car that were to be transformed into fins. Responsibility was once again due to aeronautical design and to one airplane in particular: a prototype of the Lockheed P-38 twin-boom fighter. The incorrigible Harley Earl, famous GM design head, was impressed by the oval shape of the plane's vertical stabilizers during a trip to California. The form buzzed in his head for five years until it was time to create the postwar generation of designs. A sensational model was the 1950 Buick LeSabre, the details of which were to resound like a refrain throughout all the following decade. They can be summarized as visual indications of opulence, transgression and neo-futurism.

Chrome was everywhere replacing the totemic forms of the stereotyped temple radiator shapes.

There were a number of air-intakes which cooled nothing; sparkling, shiny paintwork; aeronautical reminders to celebrate the new frontier of jet propulsion including the debatable and abnormal central air-intake which unhappily tempted Pininfarina in his first American experience. The rear fins finally swallowed up the lights and became hypertrophic appendages which competed with the front as the most zoomorphic element given that both ends unquestionably resembled the body of a dangerous, aggressive shark.

Apart from the appearance of the fins, there was another sign of what was unavoidably changing, the position of the driver and the front row of seats.

In the past and especially in sporting designs, the driver sat well back while in the convertibles he tended to sit in the center of the car. At the beginning of the 1950's this trend was emphasized and the driver found himself further and further forward towards his ever-larger V8 engine.

The tail grew further away to the limits of the known horizon until the rear volume was so large you could play a game of ping-pong on it. One model which suggested this trend was the 1952 Lincoln Capri. It had a large back end, fins, as much chrome as you could shake a stick at and a rather square shape.

180 The 1953 Buick Skylark was a classic model characterized by the chrome strip which ran down the side towards the rear fender. The dimensions of this model are definitely worth noting: the length was 17'10", width 6'7" and wheelbase 10'6". The V8 engine displaced 5276cc to give 157 HP and a maximum speed of 97 mph (which was increased to 103 mph in 1954). The most important detail was the shape of the grill; it was decidedly zoomorphic with the vertical bars resembling the baleen plates in the mouth of a whale. A parallel was the "flamboyant" style in Europe where the extravagant finishing touches seemed rather over the top.

180-181 This is the Buick engine control department at General Motors workshops.

181 top The front of a very popular car in the mid-50's, the Packard Caribbean. Note the two-tone coloring at the back that matches the interior. The front seems unexciting, probably because of the ugly design of the lights set against the rest of the body. It seems clear to the authors that Packard was unable to make up its mind whether to stick with the older styles or to adopt the new, extreme design themes.

181 bottom This customized Oldsmobile 98 seems to have a nautical inspiration. The similarity between the rear of the car and the stern of an average-sized yacht appears striking. The excuse is evidently the need to house the spare wheel, but what is more apparent is a simple taste for excessive display.

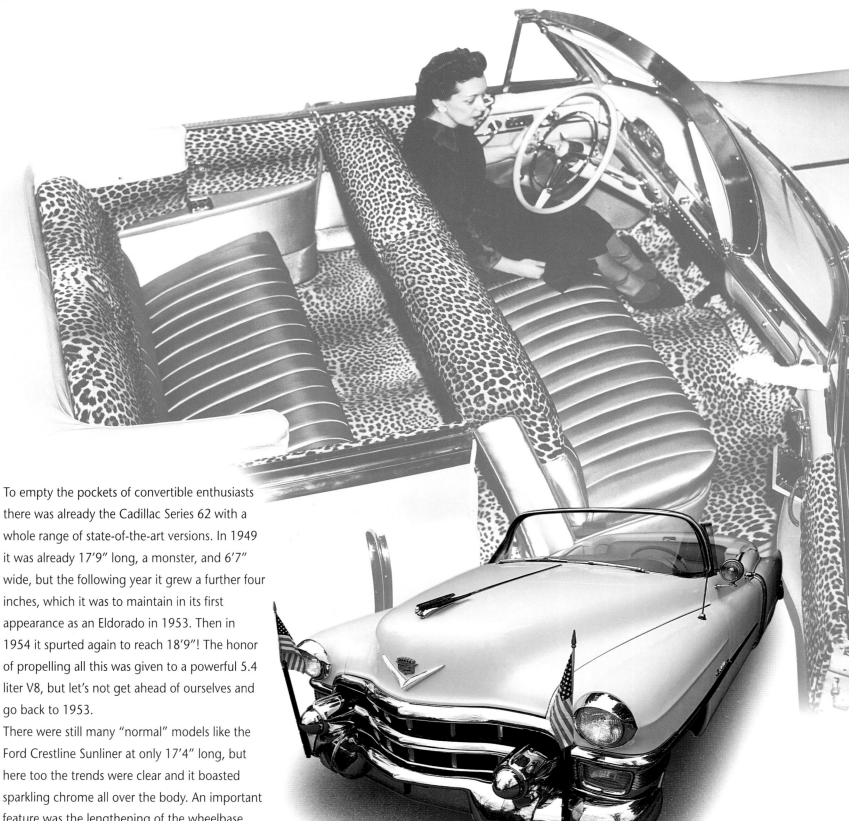

To empty the pockets of convertible enthusiasts there was already the Cadillac Series 62 with a whole range of state-of-the-art versions. In 1949 it was already 17'9" long, a monster, and 6'7" wide, but the following year it grew a further four inches, which it was to maintain in its first appearance as an Eldorado in 1953. Then in 1954 it spurted again to reach 18'9"! The honor of propelling all this was given to a powerful 5.4 liter V8, but let's not get ahead of ourselves and go back to 1953.

There were still many "normal" models like the Ford Crestline Sunliner at only 17'4" long, but here too the trends were clear and it boasted sparkling chrome all over the body. An important feature was the lengthening of the wheelbase which had two effects: first, the rear overhang was proportionally shortened and second, less emphasis was given to the rear volume. Less conventional were the Buick Super and Skylark of 1954 with some original chromework that widened towards the base; it resembled a wave to some extent and the marine theme was strengthened by the inclusion of three portholes taken from the previously mentioned Buick LeSabre.

And other makes? Hanging on to the older styles were Oldsmobile with the Fiesta, Packard with the Caribbean, and Plymouth with the Cranbrook, all dating from 1953. Dodge's 1954 Royal 500 and Hudson's Hornet of the same year moderated the new design ideas although the chrome was already running in rivers along the bodywork; however, it only took one more year

for those rivers to turn to torrents. At the other end of the spectrum, following the sports car Pininfarina was commissioned to design, Nash brought the Metropolitan to a market sated with excess. It was a tiny (12'5") three-seater open top which when placed next to the Cadillac Eldorado seemed like a Piper Cub next to a 747. The Metropolitan had an engine made by Austin in Great Britain.

Nash owed its name to Charles Nash, who had briefly been president of GM. His successor, George W. Mason, greatly admired the Cisitalia 202 SC designed by Battista "Pinin" Farina, and commissioned a design from him. This was a historic event, being the first time an Italian

coachbuilder had received such a major US production commission. The agreement was that the body would be mounted in Italy on an American frame, while the American designed engine would be tuned and installed in England by Healey. The resulting model was restrained and rather anonymous, distinguished only by the unusual, completely chromed grill which enclosed the circular headlights.

There were other important debuts in this period. In addition to the Eldorado in 1953 which grew out of the Series 62, the first appearance was made of America's most important sports car of all time, the Chevrolet Corvette.

182 top A moment from the General Motors Automobile Show in the Waldorf Astoria Hotel in New York. The car seems right at home in this famous hotel: note the leopard skin interior. The car is a Cadillac.

182 bottom One of the very many Cadillac Eldorados produced during the 1950's. The car belonged to President Eisenhower as can be surmised by the flags on the front bumper.

183 top The front of a 1954 Cadillac Eldorado. Note the thick weave grill. The front part of the hood can just be made out. This version was 18'5" long but this was not a record; the Cadillac Series 62 of the same year, closely related to the Eldorado, was 18'10" long.

183 bottom This 1959 Cadillac convertible is an Eldorado. Almost certainly, these were the most striking fins of the period.

184-185 top A classic shot from the cinema: a smiling Grace Kelly at the wheel looks at Cary Grant. The film, "To Catch a Thief", was directed by Alfred Hitchcock in 1955.

184 top The Ford Thunderbird was a car of great power and ambition sacrificed on the altar of sales figures. Successive cuts in its power and a softening of its appearance destroyed the sporting image of the car - but sales rose. The picture shows the second version of the Thunderbird from 1958.

184 bottom In 1958 the Thunderbird was still quite aggressive. The honeycomb grill sometimes held foglights.

185 top The T-bird in 1959 with its four headlights remaining. Note the silhouette of a rocket on the side which cited the start of the space age.

185 bottom A careful look at this car enables one to understand the mechanisms required to fold this roof into the T-bird's trunk (the short name of this Ford model).

and curved, the interior was compact, the back end was long and smooth; the chromework and the air intake in the center of the motor compartment only added to the similarity. Indeed, designs of the two means of transport often appeared to have borrowed freely from one another.

The market decreed that the T-bird initially won out over the Corvette - 17,500 1955 units sold compared to 700 - but while the Chevrolet was being steered towards a true sports personality, the Ford was aimed at performance and luxury accessories (electric seats and windows, power steering and braking), so much so that at the end of the 1950's the new four-seater outsold the two-seater 7 times. With the help of this success, Ford was Number One in sales overall between 1950-57. With regard to top range models, Cadillac offered both the Series 62 and the Series 62 Eldorado in 1954. In both cases the designers took their cue from the aeronautical industry in their hunt for reaction. The two models were very similar, though the Eldorado was 4 inches shorter and lower. The nose was dominated by two

enormous bumper guards but then everything was large including the Cadillac coat of arms over a golden "V". In the top-of-the-range model, the rear end was embellished with a metallic lining with fine horizontal lines. There was a transparent reflector which revolved on a pin in the rear lights. There were also decorations and friezes at the back, in this case small strips arranged vertically along the whole of the bumper. What were they made of? Chrome of course. And future versions of the Eldorado continued to offer sumptuous innovative extras to its well-to-do fans. Nineteen fifty-five was an exceptional year for the market as a whole with 8 million cars registered, a new American record. The car manufacturers launched into a wave of new models with convertibles in particular giving designers the opportunity to arouse the enthusiasm of younger generations. It was a heady period which lasted until the recession of 1958. Remember too that in Europe 1955 was a year of outstanding creativity with regard to open-topped cars.

And only two years later came the Ford Thunderbird, another model of major significance. The Thunderbird was Ford's answer to GM's Corvette. It was originally just a two-seater with an aluminum body (the Corvette was in glass-fiber) and a hard top available. The motor was a large V8, which compared favorably with the earlier 6 cylinder Chevy. The original design was of a fairly athletic sports car whose power was rather toned down by its pastel colors though these were fashionable at the time. The fins and front bumper guards were still modest. Features of the T-bird gave the car a strong resemblance to an elegant motorboat: the windshield was wide

186 top This set of rear lights belonged to a 1957 Chrysler New Yorker. Here the lights are set in the hollow of the upper part of the fin. Observe the decorations on the side, seven chrome shells.

186 bottom A convertible which had a much larger public than the elite Buicks, Packards and Cadillacs; this is the 1954 Chevrolet Bel Air. It cost little more than 2,000 dollars while the cheaper hard top version was called the Sport Coupé.

One of the successful convertibles was the 1955 Bel Air, Chevy's top model, which revolutionized the whole fleet presenting the celebrated and still current Smallblock V8. Something was stirring at Chrysler too. It is strange that one of the most courageous and purposeful companies should have been idle at the start of this turbulent period. Maybe its marketing managers were so caught on the hop by Harley J. Earl's creative innovations that it was only 1955 (when Chrysler too created completely new production lines with the exception of the New Yorker) before they had models to offer in line with contemporary trends. The Chrysler Windsor showed many similarities to the DeSoto Fireflite though their use of chrome and two-tone paintwork smacked of lack of practice when compared to the artistic details and the consistent design offered by Cadillac. The decisive reawakening was that of the DeSoto range which produced the Fireflite, Firesweep,

Firedome and Adventure models between 1954-59. The Dodge Custom Royal Lancer had a more defined personality. The hood had two-tone coloring, the grill was separated into two symmetrical horizontal elements and, being a five-seater, the rear volume was contained. Big fins were to arrive the following year.

Innovative coloring was the Oldsmobile Starfire and Super 88's first claim to fame: Their fronts were painted white that ended in a sort of arrow just above the wheelhouse. A piece of chrome separated the white half from the red or sky-blue of the other half which covered most of the sides and the rear end. 1956 continued the overwhelming success of the car industry, which continued to churn out new models and multiple versions. The market bubbled and Ford and GM battled it out at the top with continual price wars. Those who suffered were the smaller companies one of which seemed to fail every time you

opened a newspaper. Consequently, the Big Three just got bigger. One of the illustrious names to fall by the wayside was the traditionalist Packard, which was always the last to adapt to new design ideas. Its collapse was aided by its rash joining to another longstanding (and troubled) American marque, Studebaker. Packard's last new convertible was the 1955 Caribbean. In the meantime, an important development concerned the Eldorado which had acquired the additional name Biarritz to contrast with that of the coupé, the Seville. From a mechanical point of view, gas suspension was introduced for the first time. The Ford Thunderbird decided to store its spare wheel on the outside, a throwback to the roadsters of 20 years before (how things had changed! It seems a century had passed to judge by the differences between the T-bird and the Duesenberg J). The Ford's engine was made slightly more powerful which enabled it to reach 125 mph.

187 bottom The 1958 Buick Roadmaster. The name was old but the creativity in terms of chromework was very modern. Note the low grill made up of dozens of cubes looking like an echo chamber. The design of the lights was classic with headlights of equal size enclosed below a rectangular brow.

187 top The front profile of the Chrysler New Yorker from 1957. Although it may be considered a classic today and it included all the extreme concepts of the convertible of the day, it sold poorly - only a few more than a thousand examples were produced.

The Thunderbird's stablemate, the Skyliner, now offered a retractable hard top which entered the trunk electrically. Imagine the enormity of the task with the dampers, hydraulic jacks and motors necessary to ensure the functionality of the whole.

There seemed to be no end to the exaggeration of the rear end in 1957, to the point where it took over from the grill as the most distinctive element of the car.

The motors continued to grow more powerful which suited the youngsters just fine for their dangerous drag races.

Towards the end of the decade there were so many convertibles on the market that certainly we are bound to err in trying to make a list of the most representative models by leaving some out. However, we shall deal with the major events of the important models that soared through the 1950's and 60's like comets through space.

At the tip of the pyramid there was of course the most luxurious model, the Cadillac Eldorado Biarritz which was supplied to 1,800 rich customers. The rear lights became smaller and were moved to the end of the curve of the rear volume. This alteration underlined the presence of the fins which seemed actually to be detached from the car body.

Meanwhile, the Thunderbird changed its nose design, got flatter and wider, and grew fins - but these were not fins in the traditional sense at the back of the car; the Thunderbird fins started out from the back of the cab. At the time of purchase the buyer also had the choice of a version with a positive displacement blower.

A model of interest was the Chrysler 300 C with its robust 341 HP motor, which pushed this strangely light vehicle (under 2 tons, compared to the Eldorado's 2.3 tons) to 144 mph. The grill was unusual for its shape (having only two sides parallel) and massive size filled with a large weave mesh. The lights were modern in design, small and with double headlights. The 300 C

was certainly a very emphatic model and representative of its era.

Fortunately there were convertibles available at the cheaper end of the market like the Chevrolet Bel Air. This striking 17'3" long model cost only 2,611 dollars against the 7,286 of the Biarritz with the result that it sold 47,562 units. The Ford Sunliner 500, contemporary of the Skyliner and Fairlane, did even better: it cost 2,505 dollars and sold 77,726 units.

The 1958 Buick Limited, perhaps the most excessive design of all, was known as the "Glitter King". Its most distinctive feature was the side decoration that ran along beneath the fin. The fin was not especially large, but its importance was emphasized by thick chromework. Decoration was provided by a long curve which came to a point with three series of five vertical chrome lines and, as if that was not enough, the characteristic wave on previous models was still present. Behind there were two large bumper guards and a host of chrome bezels.

188 top This rare and exclusive convertible is the Chrysler Imperial Crown Southampton, completely redesigned in 1957.

188 bottom The front profile of the Pontiac Star Chief from 1957. At 17'1" long it was an average size convertible and sold at an average price. Note the curves of the windshield in the corners, the two-tone coloring and the trim panel on the sides, which further lengthened the profile. The use of wide whitewall tires was common during this period.

189 top The top of the Ford Skyliner in action; imagine the power needed to raise and lower it. Attempts had been made since the 1930's to create an electric motor for this job, but the batteries available were never powerful enough. Ford used electric motors which in turn operated hydraulic rams. Note the rear fender, which almost entirely covers the wheel.

189 bottom A three quarter shot of a car which, together with the Pacer of the same series, did not enjoy much success. This is the Edsel Citation Convertible Coupé from 1958 which was much appreciated but not bought. The characteristic front of the Edsels had an oval grill, vertically set . Performance was impressive thanks to its 320 HP engine - top speed was 119 mph.

1958 was a period of profound economic crisis but convertibles represented 5% of the market. One car which cost more than the Cadillac Series 62 (but naturally less than the Eldorado) was the Imperial Crown. This was another monumental machine distinguished by its grill made up of 4 very fine, narrow and serpentine coils like a refrigerator tray. The bumper was huge and thick and the double headlights were surmounted by chrome trappings. The spare wheel sat between the rear fins. Similar in terms of expanse of metal

was the gaudy Lincoln Continental Mark III. The 1958 Pontiac Bonneville boasted the same design of the rear sides as the Buick Limited, but more accentuated to become a deep hollow lined with chromed and grained metal. Another novelty was to be found on the 1959 Dynamic 88, the cheapest and best selling Oldsmobile of the year. Instead of fins, this car had two tubes with a "stopper" formed by the rear lights. These descriptions could go on and on, but they soon become boring.

Something new was needed once more, perhaps something less ostentatious after the excesses of the body and the competition to provide the most powerful engine.
One theme that was to prevail during the early 1960's was that the rear end tended to resemble an open tank or, more prosaically, a shovel. The fins curved outside the silhouette of the main body and the use of chrome diminished somewhat. Examples were Plymouth's Sport Fury and Buick's LeSabre and Electra 222. Going

against the tide of course was the Cadillac Eldorado Biarritz which kept its huge fins vertical and with the rear lights set right in the center. In the same category, the Dodge Custom Royal seemed bandaged up by a multitude of chrome strips while the fins, rather than curving out of the body shape, seemed stuck on afterwards. The result was one of rare ugliness.

The Chevrolet Corvette, however, continued on its way deserving of every honor it received. After its timid debut, the great American sports car took on its golden existence with the introduction of the Smallblock V8 engine. Between 1953 and 1955, the small roadster defied the design trends of the period by remaining "only" 13'10" long. Even after receiving the V8 in 1955, in '56 its length increased by no more than 10". For the whole of the 1950's the grill remained European in style, low and wide, with chrome toothing and two small bumper guards in place of bumpers. The first stylistic tweak to the flanks came in 1956 with a scallop behind the front wheel (usually in a contrasting color) that resembled the side of a mouth, so returning to zoomorphism. There were minor annual changes until 1963, when the Corvette received an all-new body, frame, and its first independent rear suspension.

190 top The picture shows one of the queens of the open-topped sports car world, the 1960 Chevrolet Corvette. The Corvette had been launched some years before but still no one imagined the successful future this powerful car with its Smallblock engine would enjoy. Note the toothy, mean-looking grill like the Packards of a decade before, the ovals beneath the lights and the simple, sporting windshield.

190 bottom A 1953 parade of Corvettes. Great emphasis was placed by Chevrolet on its new sports model destined to represent the classic American muscle car.

191 The front end of the 1953 Corvette. Note the single rather than double headlight (as was to appear in the 1958 model). The design in 1956 created a hollow in the side.

"LA DOLCE VITA" - STYLE IN THE 60's AND 70's
ITALIAN DESIGN - THE TRIUMPHS OF PININFARINA

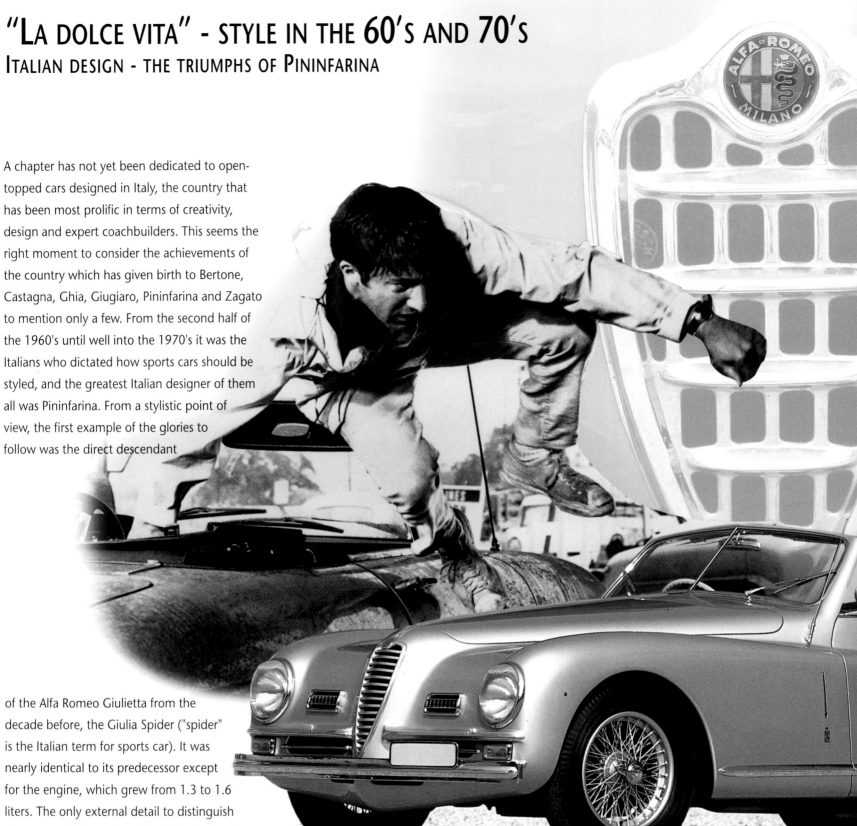

A chapter has not yet been dedicated to open-topped cars designed in Italy, the country that has been most prolific in terms of creativity, design and expert coachbuilders. This seems the right moment to consider the achievements of the country which has given birth to Bertone, Castagna, Ghia, Giugiaro, Pininfarina and Zagato to mention only a few. From the second half of the 1960's until well into the 1970's it was the Italians who dictated how sports cars should be styled, and the greatest Italian designer of them all was Pininfarina. From a stylistic point of view, the first example of the glories to follow was the direct descendant

of the Alfa Romeo Giulietta from the decade before, the Giulia Spider ("spider" is the Italian term for sports car). It was nearly identical to its predecessor except for the engine, which grew from 1.3 to 1.6 liters. The only external detail to distinguish the two models was that the Giulia had an air intake on the hood. The Giulia and Giulietta were therefore the forerunners of the magnificent Alfa Spider of the 1960's which was to make history and be the first in a long line of beautiful models. All these Alfas bore the mark of Pininfarina. A contemporary model of the Giulia was the Alfa Romeo 2600 Spider which was produced between 1962-65. This was designed by Touring and was derived from the 2000 which in turn had evolved from the 1900. Being a step up from the Giulia, it cost about 50% more. Stylistically, the Giulia Spider and 2600 Spider had a lot in common: the nose was made up of 3 parts, two chromed halves of a "moustache" and Alfa's characteristic triangle, in

this case very narrow. The 2600 had double headlights, one positioned more centrally than the other. Both had high doors and a large sill. The wheelhouses were well shaped, circular and hid no part of the wheel which generally had a chromed and decorated hubcap. The rear volume sloped gently down towards the bumper which was chopped short at the ends. The slope of the back meant that small fins were created from the taller sides and these fins encompassed the rear lights, perhaps the weakest feature in the design of these two exciting sports cars. The dimensions were quite different. The Giulia was 12'7" long while the 2600 was 14'7"; the

wheelbases were similarly proportioned, 7'4" against 8'1"; and the first was 5' wide while the second 5'6". The weight difference was proportional to everything else with the Giulia at 2470 lbs and the 2600 at 3640 lbs. There were notable differences in the motors: the Giulia had four cylinders in-line producing 91 HP which was later raised to 113 in the faster version of the car. Top speed was therefore increased from 107 to 113 mph. The 2600 had six cylinders in-line which produced 145 HP to give a top speed of 123 mph. The two models sold pretty well in the first three years of production - roughly 10,300 Giulias and 2,250 examples of the 2600.

192 top Dustin Hoffman jumps out of his Alfa Romeo Spider in the film "The Graduate". The low height of the car allowed for easy entry and exit; doors were often optional in roadsters.

192-193 Pinin Farina's interest in streamlining was always apparent. Note the homogeneity of the bodywork that resembles a hood fitted onto the chassis. The silver paint enhances the smooth surfaces and helps to soften the apparent overall solidity. This Alfa Romeo, immediately recognizable from the shield-shaped grill on the front, is the 6C 2500 SS from 1947.

193 top In the family of Italian open tops of the 1960's and 70's, the Giulia Spider came after the Giulietta and before the Duetto.

193 center At the start of the 1960's, Fiat brought out a small but finely detailed sports car, the 1500. In 1961 it was made slightly more powerful and the name was changed to the 1600 S. The power was raised from 80 to 100 HP and top speed increased from 106 to 109 mph.

193 bottom One thousand Alfa Romeo GTC cabriolets were built between 1966-67 but it was overshadowed by the launch of the Spider.

Nineteen sixty-three brought the Fiat 1500 Cabriolet, an upgrade of the 1959 Fiat 1200 sports car. Its lines were spare and square even in the later 1600S version. As was typical of the time, the grill consisted of rectangular elements which covered the whole of the nose only leaving the lights at the side.
This too was designed by Pininfarina and analogies with the Giulia Spider were to be seen; for instance, the rear lights were also housed in small fins though in the Fiat they were less obvious as the car's back end was flatter and squarer than the Alfa's. The Fiat also went out of production in 1965.

193

1966 was a year full of brilliant models and commercial successes. The first group comprised the Iso Grifo by Bertone, the Fiat Dino Spider and the Ferrari 365 California; the second group included the Fiat 124 Sport Spider and the Alfa Romeo Spider better known in Italy as the Duetto (and later in the US as the Graduate, from the film of the same name in which Dustin Hoffman drove one up the coast of California). With the exception of Bertone's Iso Grifo, the rest were designed by Pininfarina and his collaborators.

The Ferrari 365 California seems a bridge between the past and the future, and between Europe and the US. The rear, for example, had a flat and slightly sloping rear panel while the sides sloped outward to create a very wide "V"

like the flat of a shovel. This is the same design seen in American convertibles once the vertical fins from the 1950's were altered to form smooth, wide and flat surfaces. The Ferrari's door handles were unusual too in that they were made of thin metal strips laid over a deep futuristic hollow scooped partly out of the door and partly out of the rear volume. The nose was characterized by a flattened elliptical grill and the motor

compartment was very short so leaving room to the pop-up secondary lights.

The main beam lights were protected by a transparent streamlined cover. Under the hood lurked a 60° V12 capable of producing 320 HP. Maximum speed was 153 mph but only 14 were ever made.

Pininfarina's Fiat 124 Sport Spider was one the most elegant, balanced and mechanically valid sports cars of the decade

194-195 top Design of this Ferrari 275 GTS started out without the emphasis that was usually placed on non-mass produced models. It was built to compete in the growing market of small sports cars but it should be remembered that under the hood there was the usual 12 cylinder motor. Despite the efforts of the designer, the body seems a little uninspired in some details but overall it can be considered a pleasing and balanced car. The 275 GTS was introduced in 1964 and 200 were produced.

194 bottom and 195 bottom This is one of the most exciting and stylistically rich Ferraris, the Daytona. Cabriolet and closed body versions were produced by the coachbuilder Scaglietti based on designs by Pininfarina. This page shows the first, 1969, series with the lights visible though protected by a Plexiglas cover (left) and the later version with pop-up lights. This excellent and elegant car managed to combine sobriety and aggressiveness in its design. The shape of the front is strongly innovative, dominated by a narrow strip of lights just above the slender bumper. Only 121 examples of the 365 GTS/4 Daytona Spyder were produced which gives them a very high value today.

It made its debut at the 1966 Turin Motor Show beside the Fiat Dino Spider (close relation of the Ferrari Dino). It enjoyed great commercial and racing success, coming on as strongly as any other sports car in modern times. Although the World Rally Championship was held out of the Fiat's reach by the unbeatable Lancia Stratos, the 124 SS Abarth was runner up three times (1973, '74 and '75), it won two European titles (1972 and '75) and two Italian titles (1970 and '75). The Abarth version of the 124 was also available

car were just like the valves of a clam both at the front and behind. The zoological metaphor which stuck, however, was that of "cuttlebone" because of the particular shape of the rear. It must be said, though with all the respect due to such an important car as the Duetto, that the design of the rear volume had already been seen on the 1961 E-type Jaguar, another truly wonderful open-topped car; nor must it be forgotten that the 1900 Disco Volante from 1952

196-197 The Alfa Romeo 2600 Spider was extremely fast, reaching 125 mph with the top down. It was developed from the 2000 Spider and appeared for the first time in 1962. The elegant coachwork of this 2-seater was designed by Touring though the coupé was by Bertone. The picture shows actors Rossano Brazzi e Maureen O'Hara.

with an uprated 1.8 liter engine which offered 128 HP. Racing success apart, its simple and rational lines were a synopsis of Italian styling, perhaps even more so than the Alfa Romeo Duetto. Its back end was similar in shape to the Ferrari 275 GTS, though naturally with fewer details and poorer trim. Its tail, too, was chopped off. It is a pity that Fiat did not exploit the technological returns or commercial success of this wonderful model more, the only exception being the 850 mini sports car. The third great car to appear in 1966 was the Alfa Romeo Spider. As this model is discussed at length in the monographic section, only the basic points will be dealt with here and the reader is invited to consult the detailed section later on the most famous Italian open-topped car of all time. The first version of the Spider was distinguished by its general clam-like shape. The join between the upper and lower parts of the

196 top The 1.6 liter version of the Fiat 124 which appeared in 1969 was characterized, as it can be clearly seen in the image, by a honeycomb grill and two swellings on the hood to make space for the new engine.

196 bottom The open top version of the 1.4 liter Fiat 124 convertible by Pininfarina was called the Sport Spider. Its first appearance was at the Turin Motor Show in 1966. It had a 4 cylinder, double overhead cam engine and 5 speed gearbox.

the door and rear bumper, right around to the tail. The 1750's famous "cuttlebone" tail was even more tapered than that of the first series, and these were bought by 8,701 customers. 1968 brought the Duetto a younger brother, a 1.3 liter version called the 1300 Junior. Alfa's marketing department had suggested producing two versions of the 1.6 model, one with an upbeat motor, the other with a less powerful, less "race-like" engine which would also cost less: the 1750 Veloce cost 2,312,000 liras at the time, the 1300 Junior 1,796,000 liras. The 1300 had no transparent plastic covering over the front lights. Between 1968 and 1977 it sold 7,237 units. In 1969 both versions were given new looks which were to remain untouched until 1972. The most important innovation once again

concerned the tail which was now chopped short by 5 inches though the rear volume increased its baggage carrying capacity. The windshield became more inclined on both versions and the 1300 still had no light covers. The 2 liter version arrived in 1971, which was really designed for the American market; the US absorbed 60% of total production (38,379 units). Environmental pollution regulations meant that the car had to have mechanical fuel injection to meet the targets. The new engine took the new 2000 Veloce (name of the European version) to 124 mph. This basic version stayed in production until 1982 and the body design fortunately underwent no serious changes. Other versions were produced, but they were only different configurations of the existing motors and fittings.

designed by Touring more or less presented the same flattened oval shape. The first version of the Duetto was produced from 1966-68. Stylistically descended from the 1957 Superflow Disco Volante, it is considered the last production car conceived by Battista Pininfarina before his son Sergio took over. The chassis and mechanics were much the same as the Giulia it replaced. The 1750 Veloce came out in 1967, offering more refined lines and an even livelier motor. As the Alfa Romeo Spider had rear wheel drive, rigid suspension and a small cockpit, the driving experience was similar to that of a small racing car and the more vigorous engine was therefore in keeping with the spirit of the car. The Duetto-based models are all distinguished by a horizontal groove that stretches from the front wheelhouse, through

197 The 1969 Fiat Dino 2400 Spider was developed from the 2000 Spider presented three years before. The engine was originally developed by Ferrari for racing, but was later built by Fiat and used in the Dino 206 and 246

GT's. The Fiat 2400 mainly differed from the previous model by its mask-like grill with double chrome thread, by the absence of the wing nuts on the wheel hubs and by several alterations which were made to instrumentation.

197

198 top This model comes from a marque which, unfortunately, is mentioned rarely in this book, Maserati. The reason is that the company reduced marketing of open-topped cars to a minimum to be able to direct money towards racing. This is the A6GCS 2000 Sport Spider from 1955 designed by Pinin Farina. Note the curved and pronounced fairings and the slim windshield that was reduced to a small bell shape in the single seater version. It had no top of course.

198 center Here is one of the most controversial models in Ferrari's history, the Dino GTS. The car was designed at Pininfarina's urging, who insisted Ferrari build a mid-engined car. The Dino was a modest success and this 246 GTS could be considered the standard for small contemporary and future sporting GTs. Enzo Ferrari gave strict orders that the car should not bear the Ferrari badge.

The list of brilliant Italian sports cars certainly does not end here but there is no space to list the achievements of other great coachbuilders such as Vignale; just enough, though, to mention one of the great geniuses of automobile history, Giorgetto Giugiaro, whose functional interpretation of the car means he has been little involved with the design of convertibles.

Discussion of the 1960's will end with two superb Maseratis, the Ghibli by Ghia and the Mistral by Frua, and with another successful Ferrari convertible, the Daytona GTS/4 Pininfarina. These three all gave great performance. The Ghibli could touch 175 mph, an unforgettable experience in an open-topped car!

Following the Daytona, Ferrari offered the Dino 246 GTS with a heavy roll bar which categorizes it as a targa, i.e. a car with no soft top but with a removable hard top.

This was an epic time for GT's and Pininfarina's style infected many of his colleagues. Their splendid interpretations using the simple, square, sculptural lines that truly belong to open sports cars were certainly no less worthy than those of Pininfarina himself. The cars produced were very costly, gave great performance, had aggressive lines and were sporting to their marrow. They willingly sacrificed comfort and accessories to emphasize their racing aspirations.

After the end of the Second World War, the schools of car truly deserving of celebration are the old-fashioned English sports cars of the 1950's whose designs were evolutions of the prewar models based on the English interpretation of Art Deco and Baroque themes; the American styles of the 1950's for which appearance was everything, with enormous aerodynamic shapes and excessive chromework; and the Italian philosophy of sports car design in the 1960's and 70's which lasted until the second oil crisis.

The outstanding interpreter in this last school of design, as has been made clear simply by the arithmetic involved, was Pininfarina. It was during this period that Battista "Pinin" Farina died, on 3 April 1966, the importance of whom can be compared with that of Enzo Ferrari. Their repeated collaborations, with Battista's son Sergio, attest the great respect and esteem they held for each other. The death of the great coachbuilder and handover to Sergio created no crises for the company as Sergio had practically lived in the factory for years learning his trade as an apprentice. In 1961, the President of Italy decreed that the name "Pinin" Farina could be altered permanently to Pininfarina.

198-199 bottom Another representative Italian sports car, the 1978 Lamborghini Silhouette. Its particular feature is the convex shape of the upper part of the car interrupted only by the absence of a hard top. Starting with this prototype (the most recent model on this page), compare the development of details in the bodywork of GT's during the 1960's and 70's.

199 right This was one of the models that brought public attention closer to Maserati during the 1970's thanks to attractive design, top level performance and limited prices - all qualities that particularly interested the North American market. The model is the Ghibli Spyder, which followed Maserati tradition by being named after a famous wind.

SMALL SPORTS CARS THAT GENERATED GREAT EXCITEMENT

The English and Italian schools have just been championed as the European leaders in open-topped car design but it must also be stated plainly that in Germany, and particularly in the Mercedes design studio, models of historical importance and absolute prestige have continued to be produced with at least one "jewel" in every era. Moreover, Mercedes has always been a reference point for other manufacturers regarding stylistic and technological development.

Mercedes Benz's great talent has been to emphasize the factor that more than any other characterizes the car: functionality. They have shown how functionality can serve to highlight the beauty of a car's form or how it can be an object of admiration in itself. More simply, a car can be as functional as it is beautiful (the aesthetic aspect as a source of pleasure) or as beautiful as it is functional (practicality as a source of well-being). With regard to this last aspect, and outside the context of Mercedes, the world of automobiles in modern times has had its greatest seer in Giorgetto Giugiaro. It would be very interesting to see the results of a collaboration between the Mercedes design studio of Bruno Sacco and Giugiaro's Italdesign but that is just wishful thinking as this book goes to press. Returning to the 1960's, the Pininfarina star was at its apex just as Battista Farina, known as "Pinin", died. In the United States, as shall be described in the next chapter, the fairytale creations with their glittering chrome disappeared. But in Europe as a whole and particularly in Great Britain there was a wave of original sports cars, roadsters and cabriolets, big and small, economical and luxurious, powerful and less so.

The cabriolets were represented by the unique 1961 Citroën DS and the plethora of elegant, luxurious Mercedes but this chapter is more concerned with the production of roadsters and sports cars between 1960 and 1977 in Germany, Great Britain and France.

The principal German manufacturers were of course BMW and Mercedes, to which can be added Porsche with the 356 and the unfortunate 914; Volkswagen with the Beetle (at its peak throughout this period in its various guises); Opel with the ephemeral GT Cabrio; and DKW with the F12 roadster.

BMW had not considered the demand for open-topped cars as something incidental or sporadic, but their models were not an unbroken line. In the 1970's, however, their philosophy changed and their line of completely open cars ceased. The cause was an amazing stubbornness on the part of BMW and their trusty

200 top This model was a development of the Mercedes SL line that started with the 190 and 300 SL Roadster in the mid-50's. It is the 280 which went on sale in 1968. The engine was another 6 cylinder, in-line model that was able to produce 170 HP. Top speed was 125 mph.

200 bottom This picture proves how sight of a small part is often enough for a great car to be recognized. This is the Jaguar E-type's first series, here a 4.2 liter from 1964.

201 top This 4 cylinder Porsche 914 found little success with the public, maybe because it was so atypical of the Stuttgart (Germany) company. It was rather square with a targa top, i.e. a removable hard top.

201 bottom This Jensen Healey was sold from 1972-76. It had a smaller engine than Jensen usually used, a four cylinder, 1973cc model. Maximum speed was 122 mph. The best known model from Jensen was probably the V8 powered Interceptor.

coachbuilder Baur who together created a series of open tops with rigid uprights that made the cockpit look like an aquarium. It is better to pass straight on.

The open-topped Mercedes were divided into two ranges: the SL's, pure sports cars with above average performance, two sofa-like front seats and modern lines with a long, low grill decorated with the 3 pointed star; and the SE series, luxurious convertibles with soft lines and a traditional, large, square, temple-like grill. In both cases the forms are elegant without extravagance but with emphasis on driver and passenger comfort. There is no doubting the impression the SL's and Pagodas (the nickname given to the versions whose concave hard tops resembled the oriental building) made on drivers of all other types of car.

In Great Britain the strong presence of small marques specializing in the production of roadsters created a wide choice of models. The classic English style based on the designs of the 1930's continued to have its admirers but during the 1970's and 80's demand dropped as the oil crisis took its toll and consumers looked to more modern, equally exciting and certainly more comfortable models. Leaving aside the classic Morgan, here is a short list of the more important English models of this period. Winning a prize for being one of the ugliest cars of the decade, or longer, is the Daimler SP 250 of 1960 of which 2,648 examples were produced. Right from the shape of its nose, this open top declared its lack of appeal. The flattened oval grill stuck out and was decorated with an ugly metal frame; the headlights extended from two large pipes projecting from the fenders (like in the Porsche 911 but with the opposite effect); at the bottom of the front wheelhouse, the rim was continued towards the door thus creating an unnecessary curve which was copied at the back end (itself crowned with small fins). Only the spoked wheels saved the car with the traditional Jaguar wheel guards. While on the subject of Jaguar, an exciting

racing model well worthy of inclusion - and probably more a precursor of the immortal E-type than even the C and D-types - was the XK SS from 1957. Only 16 were ever made which has sent its value to the stars. Its shape can best be described by separating the front from the back. The front returned fenders to importance with large, well-shaped and very tapered models; the hood was unusually short (overall length was only 12'20", 18 inches shorter than the E-type) and ended at the base of the windshield that was so curved as to resemble a crash helmet visor. The doors were very square but curved in section. The rear of the XK SS was shaped in the form that was to be known in the 1966 Alfa Romeo Duetto as "cuttlebone". The transverse section has often been described as

convex but seems more of an ellipse. The bumper was a subtle chrome half-moon. The performance was remarkable thanks to the 3.5 liter, 6 cylinders in-line which produced 253 HP and gave a top speed of 147 mph. Shortly after, Roadster and Drophead Coupé (convertible) versions were produced. Aston Martin brought out the DB4 and DB5 models in 1961 and 1963 respectively. The latter was made famous by James Bond in the film "Goldfinger" with a model that had revolving license plates, cutting wheel guards, an oil spray, a bullet-proof shield, machine guns in the headlights and ejector seats. In reality, the DB5 was a very costly GT with ferocious power hidden under a sober exterior. Another top-of-the-range model was the Jensen

202 and 202-203 *This 1957 Jaguar XK SS was produced four years before the original and fascinating E-type. The rear is practically the same as the flying saucer shape of the E-type except for the shape and position of the lights and the curved fenders. Note the chrome double exhaust with baffle on the left side near the door.*

203 top *James Bond's most famous car, the Aston Martin DB5, produced from 1963-65. The front was slightly different from that of its predecessor, the DB4 - the headlights were protected by a sloping transparent cover - but the chrome weave of the trapezoid grill remained unchanged. The DB5 had a six cylinder, 3995cc engine that powered the car to 150 mph.*

Interceptor Mk III which was unusual for the size of its 8 cylinder Chrysler engine, 7.2 liters. Among the more reasonably priced models there was the 1961 Triumph TR4, the 1962 Lotus Elan and Austin Healey Mk II, the 1963 MGB and later the 1975 Triumph TR7. Besides the Citroën DS 19 (see the section of monographs) the French also produced two Peugeots, the 404 Pininfarina from 1966 and the 1968 504; Renault brought out the Caravelle in 1962 which sold alongside the Floride already on the market.

Both Renaults were tiny sports cars with small engines; the first series of the Floride was a great commercial success selling 177,122 units in 3 years. Both the Caravelle and the Floride had unpretentious simple lines; they were square like

the BMW 700 but more pleasing. The two models were very similar and it was not easy to distinguish them. Their dimensions were almost identical as were the fins, the wheelhouses and the ridges down the sides. The motors grew progressively in size: the 1959 Floride's 845cc increased to 956cc in the 1962 version and 1108cc in the 1962 Caravelle.

The two Peugeots were more powerful, more refined and in step with the trends of the time.

203 bottom *The Austin Healey 3000 was produced in three series called the MK I, MK II and MK III between 1959-68. All had a 2.9 liter engine but they were gradually increased in power until the last developed 149 HP. There were minimal differences aesthetically: the MK II differed from the MK I (shown) by having a hood that remained in sight when folded down while the MKIII was larger overall.*

204 left Brigitte Bardot relaxes on her Renault Caravelle S Spider. The picture was taken in 1962 at her villa in St. Tropez.

204 right An elegant blue example of the 1965 Citroën DS 21, known as the "shark" or the "iron" for its unusual body shape. Its real name, Désirée Speciale, was shortened to DS as the abbreviation sounds like the French word for goddess. This French cabriolet offered many technological novelties, such as an automatic clutch, steering-controlled headlight direction and hydropneumatic suspension.

Pininfarina and Peugeot often collaborated and in the case of the 404 this could be seen in the long, wide grill with its five horizontal chrome bars and in the clean lines of the side profile emphasized by a chrome strip the length of the body. The motor was a 1618cc, 4 cylinder, 70 HP unit. The 1969 504 was more aggressive and modern and in its three years of production, 7,803 examples were sold. Although common in the US, the 504's double headlights were still unusual for Europe. The car was as small as the 404 but the wheelhouses were wider and the nose narrower but heavy. This last feature was indicative of the styling of Peugeot convertibles to come in the 1970's, for example, the elegant,

restyled 504 that appeared in 1971; in that model the double headlights were replaced by a single, large and rectangular light and a lovely V6 engine was introduced in 1974.

The attentive reader may now be harboring the thought that something has been left out: very little, actually: the Porsche 911, Jaguar E-type, Lotus Seven and Triumph Spitfire. These open-topped beauties have been left till last to be the proverbial cherries on the cake. Unfortunately, there is only space for a superficial examination. The Porsche 911 was not Ferdinand Porsche's creation, but he was its spiritual father. The brilliant engineer's honored place in the history of the car is principally due to the Volkswagen

204-205 *The Renault Caravelle S. The 'S' stands for the second series made between 1962-63 and fitted with a slightly more powerful engine, 956cc instead of the original 845cc.*

205 top right *Advertising for the Targa version of the Porsche 911 from 1967. This is actually a hybrid: there is no glass rear window and the roll bar is clearly seen. The upper section of the illustration shows the various configurations possible, from the completely open to the completely closed version. The 911 Targa soon acquired a fixed glass rear window, however, for improved sealing and visibility.*

Beetle and the Porsche 356 which descended from it. But the 911 was clearly the next evolutionary step from the 356, so in truth every rear-engined Porsche is a logical descendant of Dr. Porsche's work.

The two open-topped versions of the 911 were the Targa and the Cabriolet. The latter will be discussed in the section on open-topped cars from the 1980's. The 911 Targa, on the other hand, has a fixed rear window and C-pillar as in a coupé. The space between the pillar and the windshield can be filled with a removable hard top. The widespread distribution of this version has made it natural to extend the name "targa" to models with similar characteristics, a practice

that is not at all welcomed by Porsche.
The Jaguar E-type was a thoroughbred open top and merits a place of honor on anybody's list. Its story began in 1961.
The E-type had many distinctive features, all noteworthy, which were combined with a generous motor and an overall line which married the development of several styling philosophies: the evolution of the old-fashioned 1930 styles, the search for balance between the front and rear volumes, the experience matured in Jaguar's many racing successes and the return to rounded forms in the design of the fender. Which of the three versions is more correct one cannot know.

The first series of E-type appeared in 1961 and without doubt had the most attractive rear end of all the production models. It appeared the sober maturation of the XK SS spoken of at the start of the chapter. The car had a remarkable overhang and the distance between the axles seemed a bridge over eternity. Such a long wheelbase emphasized the car's amazingly slender, lovely and fragile profile even more.
The second series appeared in 1968; it was largely identical to the first and supplanted not the 3.8 liter version (1961-64) but the 4.2 (1964-68). It kept the same engine but added a little zest (increased from 259 HP to 268); very little else was altered. The two series could only be

206 top This man, Colin Chapman, made automobile history as the creator of Lotus cars. Half expert technician and half successful salesman, his stubbornness helped him produce a small, powerful and easily handled racing car which enjoyed great success in its class. It was the Lotus Seven, seen here with its creator.

206 center and 206-207 top The Lotus Seven was practically a go kart that drove like a Formula 1 single seater. English convertible lovers saw in this car a continuation of the roadster style of the 1930's, 40's and 50's which was enough to bring the model success in a road version as well as on the track. The car's continued success was ensured by the company Caterham and others which still create more or less faithful replicas. The picture on the left shows the nose of the first, 1959, series. On the right, a Series 3 from 1965 which was fitted with an 85 HP Ford Cosworth engine. Note the rear trunk, a timid concession to functionality. The Lotus Seven was made in four series plus a Super Seven.

206-207 bottom This Jaguar E-type has its top up but nothing detracts from its aggressiveness. This 1964 example was fitted with a 4.2 liter engine which gave 259 HP.

differentiated externally by the different layout of the secondary lights. The dimensions of the third series (1971-75) were completely altered. The car was longer (15'4"), taller (4'0") and wider (5'5") but, more importantly, powered by the infinitely capable V12.

The engine size was 5343cc which developed 272 HP to give a maximum speed of 151 mph.

The wheelbase grew proportional to the increase in length to reach 8'8".

In the authors' opinion, the E-type is one of the five most beautiful open-topped cars of all time.

Still in Great Britain, the eclectic and inexhaustible genius of Colin Chapman was responsible for the Lotus Seven. Chapman was a passionate racer and managed to bolt together the Lotus Seven nearly, but not quite, infringing the racing regulations with his engineering contrivances. The Lotus Seven was an open top as ugly as it was exciting to drive. It had no doors, no top and no concession to comfort of any kind. In front it was almost a single seater racing car. The view from the front was mainly of the open suspension and an enormous radiator

boast the largest number of imitations and replicas. First of all there is the licensee, Caterham Motors, then the Dutch Donkervoort D8, the English Panther Kallista and the American Dakota F1 Roadster.

The MGB appeared in 1962 and was produced in three series until 1980. It was a commercial smash selling over 500,000 units which places it in the Olympus of best-selling open-topped cars of all time. Its English rival, the Triumph Spitfire (1962-81) sold 245,000 and was produced in four series. Triumph was also responsible for the

mouth that didn't cease growing over the years. The front fenders were taken from a motorcycle; those at the back were partly integrated into the bodywork. In 1961 the front fenders grew in length to resemble the old-fashioned classics which preceded it; in 1963 the relationship grew even closer when the car became almost comfortable with the addition of an inch or two in length. Over the years the engine size increased: from 1172cc in 1957 to 1498 in 1961 (the Super Seven) and to 1599 in 1963.

The Lotus Seven is one of the models that can

TR series, which was begun in the 1950's and ended in 1981 with the TR7 and TR8.

A comparison of the characteristics of the two models shows that the MGB had a 1.8 liter block that remained through all the years. The Spitfire's started much smaller at 1.1 liters. The power developed was naturally proportional to the engine size with the MGB giving 95 HP and the Spitfire 62 HP. The difference in top speed was 13 mph, 107 vs. 94. The differences in size were less marked with the Spitfire (11'11") giving away 12" to the larger MGB which was

208 top This famous English sports car from the 1960's is the TR4 from the even more famous Triumph company. The lines are very similar to the French and Italian style; the motor was more than acceptable with its 2138cc producing 100 HP for a top speed of 113 mph. All the TR series were very popular, particularly this model of which 40,000 were sold. The round headlights were its most characteristic feature with the two bumps they created in the hood.

208 center The English model MGB had the difficult job of replacing the successful MGA and it outdid its predecessor by far: 512,733 were sold to make it a standard among sports cars. It was quite able to match the lower-echelon Alfa Romeos and Porsches in performance. This small, lively and relatively cheap car with very sharp handling was very popular and even today there are many who value it highly. It had a 4 cylinder engine and was 12'8" long and 4'11" wide.

208 bottom Comparison of the 1960's models on this page against this Triumph TR6 from the 1970's gives an indication of how sports car styles changed. The friendly curves and rounded designs were replaced, especially at the rear, by squarer and more angular shapes.

209 The nose of one of the last MGAs - from 1962 - with its rectangular grill, in the center of which the trademark MG Octagon appears. The first MGA appeared in 1955.

also taller and wider and with a greater track. The wheelbase, on the other hand, was more differentiated, with the MGB's being considerably longer, 7'6" vs. 6'6". This gave it a much sleeker appearance.

As regards shape, the MGB had greater authority with its subdued, fundamental lines; the Spitfire however was admired for its brash and cheeky image which, despite having no claims to superiority, let the owner believe himself the equal of any MG.

ANYTHING GOES IN THE USA

After the splendid, unbridled 1950's when the attempt to maintain the ideals of fun and playfulness was becoming harder and harder in the face of reality, the 1960's saw the reshaping of American cars and a decrease in their decorative features. It is difficult to point to a trend in this decade that was to last and at the same time be common to all manufacturers.

The watchword for the 1950's had been "sparkle"; now it was "anything goes". A few examples are enough to demonstrate the most important stylisms that car design underwent, but it should not be forgotten that while engine sizes increased, the occasional technological innovation - the Corvair's rear engine, GM's early use of turbocharging, and Pontiac's fiberglass OHC drive belt - went largely unrewarded. The 1957 agreement between manufacturers that performance not be mentioned in car advertising had broken down by the mid 1960's, and a war to find brute power and acceleration was now on.

The development and events the country was living through were also of great relevance. America experienced constant economic acceleration after the recession of 1958 but the Cold War threatened and the nation placed its hopes on the youngest (and the first Catholic) president in its history, John F. Kennedy, whose personal impact on style, thought and interethnic and social relations was notable. Kennedy was attributed with being the true catalyst behind the space program which put a man on the moon in 1969 (like aeronautics, the space industry was also to influence car design).

During the 1960's, the overall dimensions of cars were reduced only slowly but the extravagant features at the rear end shrank much faster. Sometimes they changed shape, sometimes they folded over towards the outside of the body and then, faster and faster, they disappeared completely having been consigned to a style that was part of the past. Here are some examples of

those three categories. The first group comprises models whose fins persisted though in a smaller format: most prominent was the Cadillac Eldorado Biarritz, the model most compromised by its own style of ostentation, then there was the Buick LeSabre and Chrysler 300F, all three from 1960. In 1961, the Chrysler New Yorker and Imperial Crown still maintained noticeable fins. The second group preferred to lay their fins flat like a paper aeroplane; examples were the 1959 Chevrolet Impala and the Edsel Ranger and Oldsmobile Super 88 from 1960. The Dodge Polara was a curious case as its fins were transformed into light convex sections that resembled stabilizers on a boat keel. Functionally, all these styling tricks would have little if any effect on vehicle stability.

210 top and 210-211 center The Lincoln Continental Limousine, an amazing 21'6" long, in which Pope Paul VI visited the United States and took part in the Eucharist Congress in Bogotà, Colombia.

210 bottom This 1965 Chevrolet Impala has a tapered tail, light years away from the exaggerated rear fins of the 1950's and early 1960's.

211 top The 1964 Continental from Lincoln, a company that is part of the Ford group. It seems the car did not want to forget the fins of the previous decade and discreetly offered them once more on both front and rear fenders.

210-211 bottom The Pontiac GTO was produced from 1964-74. It started as no more than a sports version of the Pontiac Tempest with a 6.4 liter V8 engine producing 300 HP. Characteristic features of the early years were the double headlights arranged vertically and the supplementary lights integrated into the grill with telescopic sights.

The third group comprised nearly all other models. These designs dispensed with the fins altogether and had back ends that were square and flat with rounded edges. In the following 15 years there was a generally clean sophistication of line. The features were common to all the open-topped models and it is odd that in a period of great stylistic freedom (and particularly during a period that was very favorable to the sales of open-topped cars), the only models that refused to follow the herd were the Corvette and Mustang. Maybe it was the extreme popularity of convertibles which discouraged stylistic oddity or experiment. Among the first models of the new style was the popular 1961 convertible, the Chevrolet Impala, and the luxurious 1962 Ford 500XL Sunliner with its powerful V8 engine. The year that DeSoto went under, 1963, saw the arrival of a new Lincoln Continental, Oldsmobile Starfire, Pontiac Tempest and Ford Falcon Futura. A year

was clear the Mustang was to be a success, but that it would be one of the largest selling convertibles of all time was a real surprise. At the time, the work of destroying the lovely Thunderbird was still in progress. Over the years it was transformed into a sedan, and though this did nothing to harm sales, the car lost its aggressive, fiery character. It was a little like castrating a stud bull.

Meanwhile the Mustang brought a smile to Ford management, having been sold to a record 418,000+ owners in its first (extra-long) model year. The slender Ford was very much like the European sports cars of the period. In all versions it looked like a proportionally short sports car at only 15 feet long (10 inches more than the Corvette but two feet shorter than the 1955 Thunderbird, the convertible of the older generation) and with a wheelbase of 107 inches. The design was spare with little chrome. A galloping mustang was placed in the center of

later it was the turn of the Pontiac GTO and the Studebaker Daytona. At a time when many front end designs were similar (long and narrow with a large weave chrome grill and double headlights), the Studebaker's enormous, square and ugly nose resembled a luxurious English sedan. The Daytona was available as a station wagon, coupé or convertible but was not by any means the company's most beautiful model. Studebaker closed down in 1966.

Nineteen sixty-four was an important year because it celebrated the arrival of the Mustang. When it appeared in the Ford dealers' windows it

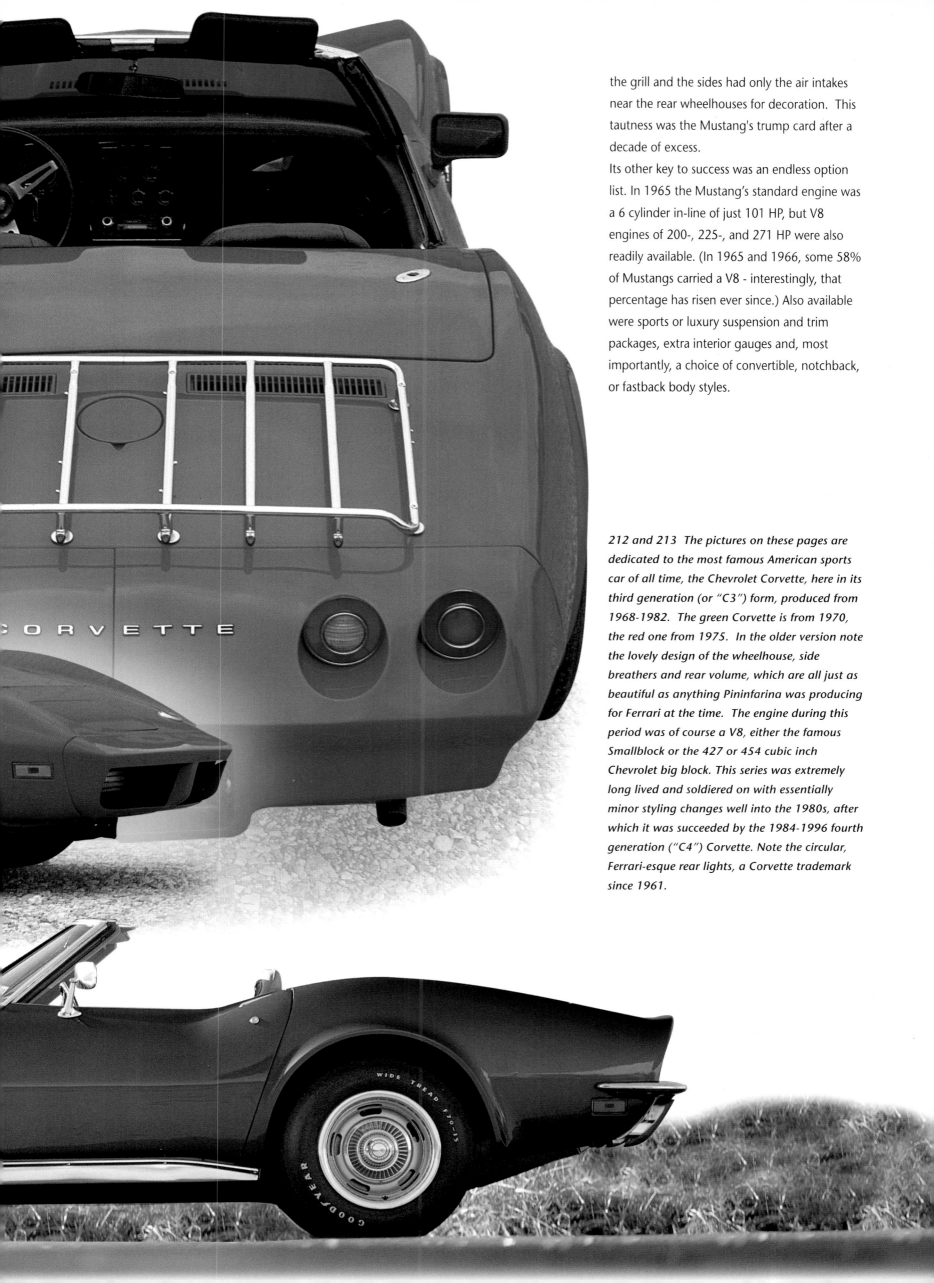

the grill and the sides had only the air intakes near the rear wheelhouses for decoration. This tautness was the Mustang's trump card after a decade of excess.

Its other key to success was an endless option list. In 1965 the Mustang's standard engine was a 6 cylinder in-line of just 101 HP, but V8 engines of 200-, 225-, and 271 HP were also readily available. (In 1965 and 1966, some 58% of Mustangs carried a V8 - interestingly, that percentage has risen ever since.) Also available were sports or luxury suspension and trim packages, extra interior gauges and, most importantly, a choice of convertible, notchback, or fastback body styles.

212 and 213 The pictures on these pages are dedicated to the most famous American sports car of all time, the Chevrolet Corvette, here in its third generation (or "C3") form, produced from 1968-1982. The green Corvette is from 1970, the red one from 1975. In the older version note the lovely design of the wheelhouse, side breathers and rear volume, which are all just as beautiful as anything Pininfarina was producing for Ferrari at the time. The engine during this period was of course a V8, either the famous Smallblock or the 427 or 454 cubic inch Chevrolet big block. This series was extremely long lived and soldiered on with essentially minor styling changes well into the 1980s, after which it was succeeded by the 1984-1996 fourth generation ("C4") Corvette. Note the circular, Ferrari-esque rear lights, a Corvette trademark since 1961.

In 1967 Chevrolet decided to bring out another model that, like the Mustang, Corvette and Mercury Cougar, was to stay in production for many years to come - the Camaro. When fit with one of a number of optional V8s, the lightweight Camaro was among the world's fastest cars. These small cars dominated the scene in the 1970's; their Mustang-like size earned them the nickname 'ponycars', and made them the American equivalent of the cheaper, smaller cabriolets in vogue in Europe. The European models would not have been popular in the US and would have been considered 'untrendy'. The extraordinary 1968 Mercury Park Lane stood out from the standardized packaging of other models - it was completely lined with wood-grained panels. By the middle 1960's, a move away from flat, bare sides started to appear; a gentle swelling grew just behind the doors, as seen on the Chevrolet Impala and Mercury Cougar of 1969, the Buick LeSabre of 1970 and

even more evident in the Oldsmobile Cutlass Supreme of the same year. Taken all in all, the 1960s saw American design reach perhaps its highest postwar form; shapes became taut, clean, and elegant, whether oversized or not. These harmonious, tension-filled shapes went far toward hiding excessive length. 1976 brought the end of an era when the Eldorado Convertible went out of production. It had been the most extreme representative of luxury, though luxury of a sparkling, outmoded and gaudy kind. The day the Eldo died, 21 April 1976, has been considered by some as the day American convertibles died. That is certainly wrong, as the Cadillac Eldorado had not represented the era of huge, splendid models for some time - not since it had bowed to the adoption of clean, essential and minimalist lines (as much as a Cadillac convertible is capable of doing). Therefore, either the era of the convertible had already ended or it was just undergoing a change. Not liking

epilogues we prefer the second version, although open-topped cars did see an enormous drop in availability, falling from 5.5% of total sales in 1965 to just 0.5% in 1974. After the early 1970's, Chrysler did not make another convertible until the K-cars of the 1980s, and an open Mustang was not available until 1982. 1975 was the end of the road for another prestigious open top, the Buick LeSabre, which had represented a fixed point for convertible lovers since the end of the 1940's. This twenty year period was marked by two distinct spells: The first saw record sales but little true innovation, while the second brought a crisis in sales but a certain development towards more modern and compact forms.

How did the Chevrolet Corvette cope during these two decades? For 1963, the muscular Corvette was an all-new car. Previously available only as an open top, the clean new model was now available as a coupe or convertible. The back was designed in the shape of an ellipse to give a

214-215 The sweeping side of the 1969 Cadillac Convertible De Ville. US open cars were not limited to just the Corvette and Thunderbird but also included luxurious and desirable models as in the 1950's. The rear seems an

unending table top (note the streamlining spats on the rear wheels). The engine was an 8 cylinder, 7.7 liter monster. Total length was almost identical to the Cadillac Eldorado Biarritz from the 1950's at 18'5".

strongly streamlined look to the tail and to balance the modern, pointed nose. The large, rounded wheelhouses were very fluid in their design. As previously mentioned, the standard Smallblock V8 engine gave impressive power and speed, which was combined with excellent balance. Then, in 1965, a big block was made optional, first at 396 cubic inches and later with 427 and finally 454 inches. The Corvette can be considered the model which most influenced the style and design of two-door sports cars throughout the decade, and its echo even reached Europe. In 1968 the car was redesigned again, its wheelhouses becoming even more accentuated to emphasize the longer, steeply sloping nose. Where the previous version of the Corvette had a tapered tail, the 1968 model's was cut short and swept into a vertical spoiler. In front, the headlights hid beneath pop-up lids. Still, the 1968 model was longer, heavier, and less pure than before.

215 top This Oldsmobile 4-4-2 is from 1968 and offered two basic motors, 260 and 300 HP. Special editions abounded.

215 center This elegant model, the 1970 Buick LeSabre, occupied the mid-high range of the convertible market. Although it was not as long as the Cadillac Convertible De Ville, it was still longer than average at 18'2".

215 bottom This 1973 Ford Mustang seems slightly tame in a white top and with whitewall tires. The completely redone, Pinto-based 1974 Mustang II was markedly smaller.

THE RECESSION: SMALL, NO-FRILLS CONVERTIBLES
CONVERTIBLES AND SPORTS CARS IN EUROPE

A couple of petrol crises were more than enough to rock the automobile industry. And if they were not enough alone, there were also economic crises and recessions throughout the western world plus wars, coups d'état, secessions and new geopolitical alignments which revolutionized the modes of thought, living and movement of Europeans and North Americans. If we add to this backdrop a greater, more pressing attention to devices aimed at increasing active and passive safety (seat belts, airbags, impact bars, progressive and programmed crumple zones, roll-bars, ABS and electronic

traction control), ably exploited by marketing experts to convince us to buy new and costly cars, in addition to the pressing need to build less polluting and more recyclable vehicles which share an increasing number of components, we find ourselves in an extensive and sad panorama of sameness, a widespread poverty of ideas and a lack of interest in convertibles and sports cars in general. On average, the open-topped cars of the 1980's were uglier, more anonymous and more devoid of ideas than during any other period in the history of the car.

Is it coincidence that an analogous situation was occurring in other industries where the creativity of designers and stylists was required? Certainly not, and it is not surprising that exciting convertibles were not produced in a period in which art, fashion and design were tired and unexciting. Those who thumb their noses at a gaudy 1950's convertible should humble themselves: Audacity, humor, a desire to amaze and the need to communicate through symbols and fetishes are preferable to boredom, uniformity and standardization - better bright colors than gray. Careful scrutiny of the ranges reveals, however, something interesting underneath. Starting with convertibles, there was nothing new at the top of the heap - the same old Rolls Royces, Bentleys and Mercedes. But it was the arrival of the mini-convertibles which comprised the huge majority of open-topped cars sold. They were small and cheeky, cheap to buy and cheap to run; these little cars took away the magic of the concept of the convertible with their lack of grace.
Among these were the Volkswagen Golf Cabrio (among the best-selling convertibles of all time), the Fiat Ritmo Bertone, the Ford Escort and the Peugeot 205. Sports cars offered a little more, but it was simply that being a step up the ladder they could offer a little more in terms of design and singleness of form.
Bear in mind that the terms sports car and roadster here also include models actually called cabriolets or convertibles in that they were open-topped versions of sedans or coupés, but which were closer in nature to sports cars with their dashing performance and line.

216 top This low, athletic sports car is a customized Turbo Esprit. The Esprit renewed the public's love affair with Lotus.

216 bottom The Maserati Spyder was very popular throughout Europe and the United States thanks to its name and low price. The Spyder in the picture was one of the first series sold from 1985-89 and had a 2.5 liter engine with double turbo. This model was followed by the 2.8 which was available until 1994.

217 top This model, the TR8, closed the glorious Triumph TR series and should go down in the history books for that reason alone. It had a 135 HP, V8 engine (the TR7 had only a four cylinder motor) that powered the car to 122 mph.

217 bottom This is a concrete example of how the style of square sports car bodies had become general. This is the Jaguar XJS Convertible which replaced the rounded E-type and was destined for a long, successful career.

217

218 top and 218-219 The rear and side view of a
Ferrari 348 Spider, designed by Pininfarina. It
differed from the GTS in that the latter was a
targa with a removable hard top. Both versions
had a 320 HP (310 for the US) engine able to
take the cars to 171 mph. The first series was
presented in 1989 but this model is from 1994.

218 bottom This Alfa Romeo Duetto belongs to
the fourth and final series but by the mid-1990's
this small and famous sports car had lost its
magic after its thirty year career. It was replaced
by the beautiful, front wheel drive car of the same
name.

219 bottom The Ferrari Mondial Cabriolet can
be recognized even by non-specialists by the central
grill just behind the cab close to the engine.

In general, roadsters began to demonstrate softer shapes than the angled models from the 1970's even if the sides and hood and trunk stayed flat. The search for the perfectly streamlined form went ahead in small steps so as not to upset profiles which, anyway, rarely excited the imagination.

As far as price goes, the Aston Martin DBS V8 and Lagonda were unbeatable. They were sold around the end of the decade and their discreet, fluid beauty was enhanced by their rarity. There were several Ferraris: the 308 GTS, the Mondial 8 and the Testarossa all in different versions and with different engine configurations. Ferrari fans will no doubt understand if the authors consider these, and those to come in the early 1990's, as among the worst Pininfarina products designed for mass production (relative to the capabilities of the manufacturer, that is). Until then, the intuitions of the designer had always struck gold but from this point on, he seemed stuck in a series of dry,

angled forms without the elegance and simplicity that could turn the most extreme design into a jewel that would shine in any setting. These three GT's - the 308 GTS, more targa than sports car; the dissatisfying Mondial 8 with its unrefined pop-up headlights and decoration along the hood; and the 1985 Testarossa coupe - were all clumsy, show-off designs adding nothing key to the history of open-topped cars. They were exhibitionist but without the self-parody needed that had been seen in models from the past with equally extravagant forms. The Testarossa should have been produced in a limited series to justify the furious infighting between collectors who offered ever larger sums of money, not for the car but just for the sales contract. Used cars were worth more than new ones so that anyone wanting to own one quickly had to pay thousands of dollars over the price. But in the cases of the Testarossa and 512 TR, this turned out to be unnecessary as more than enough of each were produced.

Even the fourth and last generation of the Alfa Romeo Spider, also by Pininfarina and which had won so many laurels on its first appearance, was certainly not exciting. It looked bulky and had nothing to say for itself.

At a lower price than the Ferraris but still in the luxury class was the Jaguar XJS-C. This had the unenviable task of replacing the E-type. Other English sports cars of the period were the TVR, Reliant Scimitar, Triumph TR7 and TR8 and the MG Midget; all were small, low, square and bursting with verve, if not perhaps speed.

The BMW 3-Series in its various engine sizes was more common. With elegant design and good performance, it marked the German carmaker's return to the production of a high quality open top. Then there was the popular Saab 900, the fast and cheap (but mechanically untrustworthy) Maserati Biturbo Spyder, and the Maserati-assembled Chrysler TC. The TC offered American styling with Italian construction - in other words, combining the worst of both

worlds.

The most important model of the 1980's on both sides of the Atlantic was the Porsche 911 Cabrio. However, this model was simply no more than the 911 Coupé devoid of any element above the waistline, windshield apart. The decision not to include it in the list of élite models, despite its fame, was not due to lack of space. Although nothing prohibits the inclusion of the Targa version (already referred to in the chapter of 1970's European open tops) from being defined as an open-topped car due to its removable hard top, it seems to us it is a bit of an impostor compared to sports cars, roadsters, cabriolets and convertibles. Targas try to be coupés but aren't, and due to their excellent qualities and versatility, they deserve a full but separate treatise.

The 911 Cabriolet had an unfortunate top which, when unfolded, deprived the car of the fluidity and rotundity which gave the closed version its wonderful character. At high speed it suffered from ballooning when low pressure created just above the car sucked the top up: the result was very noticeable and ugly. Although requested all over the world, the Cabrio was only a version of the 911 and seemed to have less personality than other open-topped cars included in the section of monographs. We hope the reader understands, if not agrees with, this choice.

In 1989 the Speedster version was produced. The name referred to the 1950's model with which it shared a high and aggressive rear end, more so than its reference model, the 911. The Speedster was also 1 inch lower.

The 1980's were overall a depressing decade though in 1986 a wonderful model was produced almost by chance, the BMW Z1 Roadster. It was small with many technological innovations which were then used in successive models, sedans and sports. The Z1 had a curious system for getting in: the doors did not open but slid down vertically to hide in the car body below. The welcome for this fun car was enthusiastic and the number of requests far outweighed expectations. It was the only true open top from BMW in this period that did not stint on functionality or investment. It was a real two-seater built for pure fun.

220 bottom The streamlined rear end of this 1989 Porsche 911 Speedster makes it look particularly aggressive. The name evoked the memory of the 356 Speedster of 1955 but the modern version did not have a long life. The most popular versions were the Targa and the Carreras 2 and 4.

220-221 The BMW Z1 originated as a styling exercise but was so enthusiastically received that it was put into production. It was a real roadster, predecessor of the magnificent Z3 and its successor, the evocative Z07 showcar. The most important feature of the Z1 was the electrically operated door which opened by sliding down into a bay under the body. The car's mechanical systems and geometry of the wheels contained innovations that were later adopted on more popular mass production models, sedans in particular. Only 8,000 examples of the Z1 were produced between 1988-91, making it very popular with collectors. Top speed was 143 mph.

221 top Before launching the MGF, which put the BMW-Rover group at the top of the roadster market around the world in the late 1990's, Rover brought MG out of hibernation with this model based on the MGB called the MG RV8. It was produced from 1992-95.

221 bottom The picture seems out of place but the car is actually contemporary to those on the same pages. It is the 1990 version of the Morgan Plus 8, which remains faithful to its original early postwar design except for certain modifications required to meet safety standards.

Too many Targas in the USA

The grayness of the 1980's spread its pallor over the whole of the automobile industry. It was barren of ideas but, more importantly, it had only limited desire to produce open-topped cars. If it is any comfort, the decade was also devoid of closed sports cars, known in Europe as coupés and in the US as two-door sports.

The American sports cars that were produced were largely the same, with only the Corvette standing out as a car with great personality. But by now the Corvette was a niche product for a small specialist market, and no longer able to affect the creativity of designers in a positive manner. It was not, however, entirely the fault of the designers that this trough existed: It was the pragmatic and rational public which no longer

expected great cars - or particularly fun cars. Even the glorious Mustang had lived through humiliating moments. One of the most famous models in the history of the American convertible, it had spent much of the 1970s as a spinoff of the economical, much-reviled Pinto model. Then, in 1979, it was totally revised with a new, squarish body based on the "sheer look" of the 1970's and placed on Ford's ubiquitous Fox platform (which also supported the Fairmont, LTD, and other cars). During the 1960's the Mustang had been a nervous, exciting open top which brought excitement to the lives of two generations; during the 1980s, this heritage would slowly be re-captured by a long succession of Mustang GT and Mustang LX

222-223 top The 1991 Mercury Capri XR2 shows how similar 1980-90 American and European open tops were in their flat, square and fairly impersonal designs before the "renaissance" of the mid-90's. The Capri's dimensions were typical of European cars as was the lively 4 cylinder engine.

models carrying Ford's powerful 4.9 liter V8. Called the "5 Liter" for marketing reasons, this powerplant grew ever stronger through the decade, and on the lightweight Fox platform, the Mustang V8's easily kept pace with the Chevy Smallblock powered Camaro and Firebird. Some saw the square shape of the 1979-1994 Mustang as vulgar; others considered it taut and aggressive. Either way, in T-top and convertible (debuted 1981) form, the Mustang spent the decade as America's most popular performance car - even though its base engines were always 4 or 6 cylinder cooking motors.

Meanwhile the Corvette, totally redesigned and released as the first 1984 model of the year (there were no 1983 Corvettes) put American sports cars once again on par with Europe's finest. With its Cross-Fire Injected Smallblock V8 and world-leading .90g cornering grip, the new Corvette leapfrogged its aging predecessor and once again competed head-on with Porsche and Ferrari, in performance if not price and status. In mid 1986 the Corvette Convertible made its reappearance after an 11-year hiatus, with an optional plastic hardtop and strategic chassis reinforcements to combat cowl shake. The decade ended for the Corvette with the announcement of the ultra-mean, ultra-powerful ZR1 option. Featuring a 4-cam, 32-valve, 385 HP all-aluminum V8 engine designed by Lotus and manufactured by Mercury Marine, the ZR1 was the fastest Corvette ever (180+ mph). Like all hardtop Corvettes of this generation, the ZR1's roof panel was fully removable, making it a true targa. No ZR1 convertibles were made for public consumption.

Cadillac had been a pilot fish during the 1950's and 1960's, charting the waters of open-air opulence. During the 1980's it produced more modest versions of the Eldorado and Biarritz, but the most interesting product from the firm in years was the Allante (designed and assembled by Pininfarina), a 2 seat luxury convertible based on a shortened front-wheel-drive Seville platform with a transversely mounted V8.

But perhaps the most representative American model of all during the 1980's was the trim, stylish LeBaron Convertible from Chrysler. Very cheaply priced with a host of standard accessories, the LeBaron Convertible grew from modest beginnings (88 HP from a transverse 4 cylinder engine driving the front wheels) to an impressive 152 turbocharged HP. The wasp-waist styling recalled American designs of the 1960's.

222-223 bottom This 1992 Pontiac Trans Am demonstrates the recent North American style of bare, functional lines; it might almost be a study in minimalism, despite its sporting character. Not to be missed are the small tail fillips.

223 top right This Cadillac Allanté was designed and assembled in the US before being shipped to the Pininfarina workshops in Italy where the electric top was installed and fittings were finished off.

The Japanese had made a name for themselves with technological ability, mechanical reliability and low prices during the 1970s, and during the early and middle 1980s they turned their attention to sports cars in a big way. Only one example - the Mazda RX7 Convertible - was a true open top, but the Nissan Z-car, Toyota Supra, Toyota MR2 and Mitsubishi Starion all offered T-top roofs as a widely ordered option. Japan's sports car history was not nearly as bereft as many Westerners imagined. From the early 1960s, Honda (Sports 360 through 800), Nissan (Fairlady 1200 through 2000) and Toyota (Publica Sport, 800 Sports) had all gained valuable experience with 2 seat open tops. Japan's history with closed GT models was even richer, including the radical rotary engined Mazda Cosmo L10A (1967), the Yamaha designed Toyota 2000 GT from the same year, and of course the now-legendary 6 cylinder Nissan 240Z, first revealed in 1969.

In the end, the most important open top of the 1980s would also be Japanese: the Mazda MX-5 Miata. Intentionally modeled on the best British and Italian offerings of the 1960s, it was small, fun to handle and the first true interpretation of a roadster since the bleak days of the 1970's. Blessed with a huge pent-up market for inexpensive, high quality, traditionally designed sports cars, the Miata was successful even against the the reborn Lotus Elan, the aging but classic Alfa Romeo Spider, and the admittedly uninspired Mercury Capri XR2. Introduced in mid 1989 as a 1990 model, more than 450,000 Miatas were sold before the redesigned 1999 model was debuted in January of 1998.

224 top The Mazda MX-5 debuted as a 1990 model, though Mazda began toying with the idea of a small, rear-drive, traditional open sports car in 1983. It went on sale in mid-1989.

224 center The Honda SSM was a prototype roadster made to commemorate the 1963 S500 Sport, Honda's first volume-built car.

224 bottom and 225 bottom The Honda del Sol is only 13' long, 5'6" wide and 4'1" high. It has an optional system for stowing the rigid hard top in the luggage compartment which operates either electrically or manually. This Japanese targa was introduced in 1992 to replace the coupe-only Honda CRX.

225 top The Toyota Celica cabrio is the open-topped version of the company's most famous coupé. The picture shows the profile of the latest version, which can be recognized by the four fixed round headlights in place of the pop-ups of its predecessor.

CONVERTIBLES HEADING FOR THE 21ST CENTURY

CONVERTIBLES AND SPORTS CARS ONCE MORE ON COURSE

226 top This model marked Rover's return to the small sports car and roadster market. The mid-mounted engine of this MGF gives excellent handling that makes it a joy to drive on twisting roads.

226 bottom and 227 bottom The Mercedes SLK is distinguished among late-1990 convertibles for its top. As seen in the image on the left, the rigid metal roof is automatically retracted by an electrohydraulic mechanism.

The 20th century, like this history, is coming to a close. Convertibles are now heading for the 21st century in a confident mood, having overturned the trend of falling sales during 1996-97. Now it is sports cars and roadsters which are leading the field. During the second half of the 1990's there have been many new models to awake the interest of motorists fed up with the same old anonymous boxes on wheels, and trend-setters are once again seen in powerful open tops. Some events were clear signs of the renaissance of open-topped cars: for example, the opening of the first BMW factory in the United States in South Carolina for the production of their

successful Z3 roadster, and the debut of a low-priced Mercedes convertible, the SLK, which reinterprets the concept of the electric retractable hard top.

At the same time, a quick look at social behavior around the western world shows that after decades of containment there has been a sudden reawakening of the desire to overstep the limits, to feel liberated in a car and less guilty of atmospheric pollution. The car producers are willing, as always, to welcome new trends and here all of a sudden is a flow of new convertibles to suit all tastes and pockets. The marketing departments understood that the average price

of an open top had to be relatively lower without the result, as in the 1960's, that all one got in return was a silly little bath-tub verging on the ridiculous. Now design even of the smallest is smart and innovative and engine performance is exciting even in the tiniest motors.

227 top The exciting BMW Z3 roadster, which is based on the firm's 3-Series Sedan. Note the letter M in the inset picture, which signifies that the car was prepared by BMW M GmbH, the motorsport division of BMW. This makes it a top-of-the-range version in terms of power.

228 top This Porsche Boxster was long awaited after being promoted as a prototype in one Motor Show after another. It finally saw the light in 1996. The Boxster has a longitudinal, 6 cylinder, 2.5 liter boxer engine. It produces 204 HP for a top speed of 150 mph.

228 center and bottom This is Renault's unusual interpretation of the sports car. It seems that this model was inspired by cars created by Colin Chapman like the Lotus Seven though it is less extreme. This Spider was actually designed for single marque racing but was then developed into a road version. It has a 150 HP engine which gives a top speed of 134 mph with 0-60 acceleration in 6.9 seconds. Note the side air intakes.

229 This semi-handmade Lotus Elise is an interpretation of the roadster theme. It is compact, aggressive and lively. Its 1.8 liter engine produces 118 HP. Note the design feature on the sides, the hollows which look like tracks made by landing meteorites.

These factors are enough to have given open-topped cars a boost although they are still confined to a niche market in Europe, the US and Japan. Fortunately the 1980's are long past and open top lovers sincerely hope they do not return. So what is available in the 1990's? For greater clarity, we have divided the most important models into arbitrary categories of market classification and given the year of presentation, entry into the market or restyling. The major creative impetus came in the middle of the decade so that we have excluded some cars that were not available after 1995.

Middle - high range roadsters and sports cars: these are statements of success by the drivers, vehicles for showing off and being seen in. The BMW Z3 (1995) and Mercedes SLK (1996) are leaders in the category, both with features that remind one of the 1930's grand prix racers but with covered wheels; their hoods are proportionally long, the driving position low and the sensitiveness

of the driver to vehicle response high. The 1995 MGF was mid-engined, like the 1996 Porsche Boxster and the Honda NSX, thanks to which the cars' trim and driveability are like small 1960's racing sedans. Renault's sports car offering is certainly curious, half way between a dune buggy and a modern interpretation of the Lotus Seven. It is called the Sport Spider and appeared in 1995.

230 The front and dashboard of the Jaguar XK8, the car which continues the glorious story of the E-type and XJS. It combines internal luxury with true sports car performance, the latter produced by an excellent engine and responsive driver controls.

231 top The Pontiac Firebird Trans Am from 1994. This is an interesting example of a modern, comfortable and sporting American convertible. The fuel injected 5.7 liter Smallblock V8 engine gives excellent acceleration, despite the chassis' considerable weight.

231 bottom Aston Martin is perhaps the world's best example of sporting luxury. This DB7 continues the tradition of prestigious, exclusive GT's. The 340 HP, 3.2 liter motor gives a top speed of 161 mph. There are several resemblances to the Jaguar XK8.

Middle market sports cars: these are more or less pure sports cars but at a more affordable cost which are aimed at those who wish to have a second car purely for fun. Certainly they are less attractive than those above but they are important in terms of the market; often they are simply convertible versions of Japanese or American liftback coupés. This category includes the extremely popular 1994 Alfa Romeo Spider, completely different to the previous series of the same name. The following models have no particular aesthetic characteristics and even their standard motors often coincide with those of their own previous series: the Chevrolet Camaro (1993), the Japanese Toyota Celica (1993) and Mitsubishi Eclipse (1994), the Fiat Barchetta (1995) and the Audi TT (1998).

Power houses: some sports cars distinguish themselves for their engine and the performance it generates, often being revised versions of less than amazing convertibles. Their appearance does not appear much influenced by their new sporting nature and thankfully there are no extreme or grotesque designs. Falling into this classification are the BMW M3, the classic American Pontiac Firebird and Porsche 911 Carrera all from 1994, and the very elegant Jaguar XK8 (1996).

Gran turismo: real GT's, open-topped by chance, with powerful performance and reserved for the most able drivers. Some of these models are rare, like the TVR Griffith 500 (1990) and the Aston Martin DB7 Volante (1993); some are more well-known, like the Chevrolet Corvette (edition dates 1986 and 1998), the Ferrari F355 Spider and the Honda NSX Targa, both from 1995.

232 top This largely handbuilt Dodge Viper RT/10 has gone against the grain of traditional open top design during the 1990's. It is uncomfortable and flashy but may be the only car apart from the Ferrari F40 or F50 able to give the lucky driver the sensation of driving a Formula 1 car. The massive 8 liter engine is capable of producing 400 HP which enables the car to accelerate from 0-60 in 4.3 seconds and reach 169 mph.

232 bottom This is a real and rare road monster, the Lamborghini Diablo Roadster, in which it is possible to touch 201 mph, given the right conditions of course. It even beats the Viper on acceleration reaching 60 mph in just 4 seconds. Despite the name Roadster, it is more in line with a targa.

233 This is the front of a car that is difficult to consider as a road model given its seating arrangement and handling characteristics. It is the Ferrari F50, a 2-seater Formula 1 machine, which for top speed (203 mph) and 0-60 acceleration (3.7 seconds) cannot be beaten.

Road monsters: expensive, uncomfortable, totally non-functional and with truly monstrous fuel consumption, these are the cars longed for by those who believe pure speed is the maximum of human aspiration. Traveling at 180 mph is one thing but if you can do it with the top down, like being in a dark tunnel with a violent and mean roar coming from the engine, so much the better. But really these cars are nothing but toys and they do not last long. The best known among them are the Chrysler/Dodge Viper RT/10 (1992), the Ferrari F50 (1995), the Lamborghini Diablo (1995) and the Maserati Barchetta (1991). The ever-present: these are cars that were conceived years ago but which have modern lines, fittings and performance. Generally they are subject to regular restylings, as in the case of the Porsche 911 which dates from 1980, or were

brought to the market during the 1980's and left unchanged, as with the Mazda Miata (1989). The Morgan Plus 8 is still identical to past versions but it had a slight touch-up in 1988, the same year the Maserati Spyder was presented. Other similar models are the reborn Lotus Elan (1989), the Honda del Sol (1992) and the Volkswagen Golf Cabrio (1993). Convertibles: open-topped vehicles but very functional, seating 4-5 people and furnishing driver comfort and plenty of luggage space. These characteristics mean they can be used as first cars without having to make do with a hard top as, once the soft top is up, they are as functional as a sedan. They are to us particularly refined, elegant, comfortable, well-finished and with all the power one could wish for. Their design is generally sober and, windshield apart,

nothing rises above the waist of the body. Typical examples in terms of commercial success and design balance are the Saab 900 (1993) and the BMW series 3 (1992); the former is curiously oyster-shaped when looked at from the side, i.e. its ends are very tapered compared to the rounded central volume. The American representatives are also very fine: there is our old friend, the Ford Mustang (1993) which ends the century halfway between the exciting creature it was devised as and the square, coarse and ugly machine of the 1980's. There are many others which are part of this list - the elegant Audi Cabriolet (1991), the Mercedes E Class (1993), the Chevrolet Cavalier and Pontiac Sunfire (1994), the Chrysler Stratus/Sebring (1995), the Renault Mégane (1996) and the Volvo C70 (1997).

The babies: these are generally preferred by women and by the young in preference to off-road vehicles. They allow drivers to show a certain statement of non-conformity and to show off without any excessive economic investment and without creating any difficulty in terms of driving or parking. It is easily the largest group in terms of sales but the least interesting visually. In comparison to other open tops they are nothing but bath tubs with four wheels, a motor, a roll-bar, and a top which balloons at 60 mph. But they are popular and deserve a mention: there is the Ford Escort (1990), the Opel Astra (1991) in Europe, the Suzuki Cappuccino and Toyota Paseo (1991) in Japan, the Rover 200 Cabriolet (1992) and the Peugeot 306 and Fiat Punto (1994).

Luxury models: at the other end of the world from the above are these luxurious convertibles at the very pinnacle of quality and beauty. Their prices, naturally, are stratospheric and

234 top right This Alfa Romeo replaced the Spider or Duetto. It has the same name and several of its features are similar but it has not received the same enthusiastic response from lovers of its noble predecessor.

234 top left The Audi TTS Roadster is the German company's follow-up to the modest success of the Audi 80 Cabriolet. This model is also available in a closed body version and will be remembered for its extensive use of aluminum.

234 center The rear end of the Fiat Barchetta. The Barchetta marks a return to the sports car market for Fiat which, with the exception of cabriolets, has been absent for some time.

234 bottom Chrysler has cut out a niche in the European market with the Stratus. In dimensions, price and engine size (also available is a 2 liter version), the Stratus matches European needs.

inaccessible to common mortals, their engines guarantee power to spare at any speed, and their drive comfort is such that you might think you were parked. The major jewels in this range are the Mercedes SL (updated 1989), the Aston Martin Virage Volante (1990) and the glorious Bentley Azure (1994). Overall the choice of open-topped cars is very rich but, we repeat, the return to interest in convertibles is due, we believe, most of all to those in the first category, in which appear suggestions of the design themes to come. It is as if these roadsters were repositories for innovations which will later be applied to all other cars.

The world of open-topped vehicles is also a world for people who like to demonstrate they are different; some of them are old-fashioned gentlemen, some jesters, and a few are nostalgic motorcyclists. All of them, however, dislike being considered as one of the masses. For them there exist many, almost unknown, makes of open tops, many of which are built to order. In Great Britain especially there is a strong following for such cars. Here is a short list, some of which may be familiar: Ginetta G27 (1992), AC Ace (1993), Caterham 21 and Reliant Scimitar (1994), Rinspeed Roadster (1995) and the Panoz AIV (1996), but the list could go on and on.

At last there is an open-topped car available for every taste like there used to be in the 1950's. On both sides of the Atlantic, with Japan a little behind, sports cars and convertibles (together with their semantic and stylistic variants which we have attempted to illustrate without going into learned and unnecessary lessons of style) seem to have survived economic crises and recessions, but more importantly they appear to be on equal terms with their natural and most dangerous enemy: raggedness.

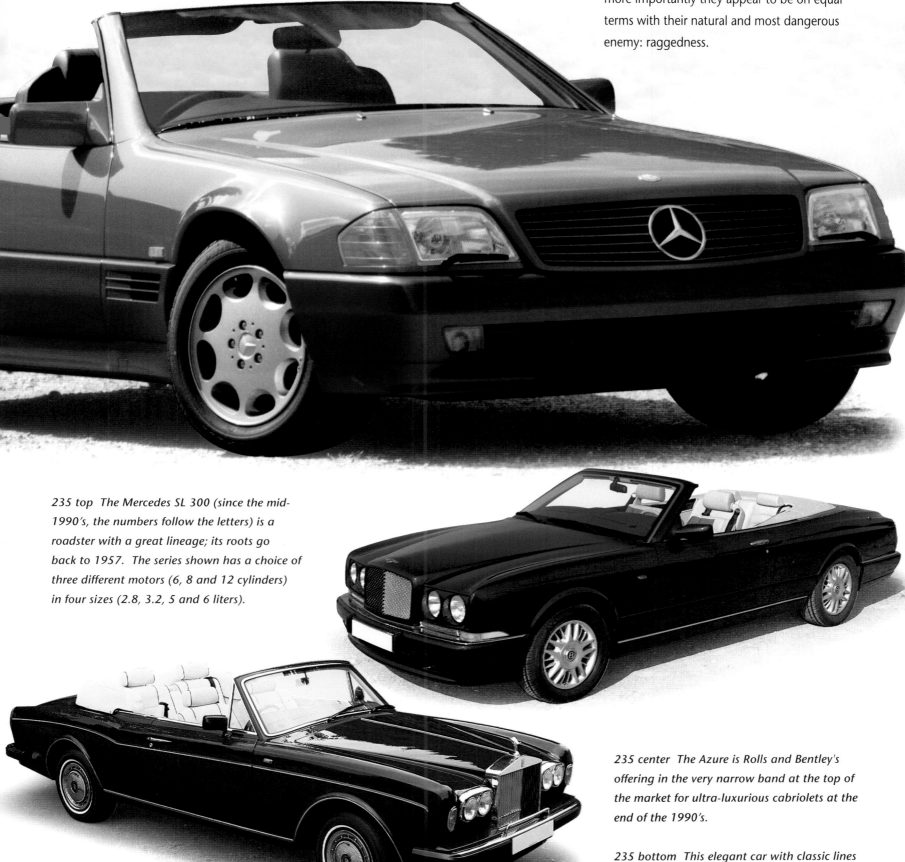

235 top The Mercedes SL 300 (since the mid-1990's, the numbers follow the letters) is a roadster with a great lineage; its roots go back to 1957. The series shown has a choice of three different motors (6, 8 and 12 cylinders) in four sizes (2.8, 3.2, 5 and 6 liters).

235 center The Azure is Rolls and Bentley's offering in the very narrow band at the top of the market for ultra-luxurious cabriolets at the end of the 1990's.

235 bottom This elegant car with classic lines is the 1992 Rolls Royce Corniche Anniversary.

WHO WILL BE THE NEXT DESIGN GENIUS?

This book has been written during a period when waves of fluid curves and streamlined forms have been applied to sporting cars, particularly if open-topped. Beautiful, stunning designs are to be seen that have given new life and vigor to the range of open tops across the world, cars that reflect the correct evolution of forms, details and proportions matured in 100 years of the history of the automobile.

But, too, there are some cases where their features seem weighed down, repetitive, afraid to take chances.

We have already dwelled on the role of open-topped cars: besides bringing pride to the owner, they stimulate the imagination of the designer and herald unusual and innovative designs for the cars of the future.

They are like top models in fashion shows, "dressed" by designers to surprise and signal the emerging trends.

Just now, apart from a few cases in the second half of the 1990's, the convertibles of the decade are undergoing a crisis of identity despite being available in great numbers and looking good. Often they are clones of coupés or, if they are designed as independent models, they do not take chances. Overall, they are too pedantic. Our feeling, backed up by the work of outstanding designers like Philippe Starck who created the Aprilia Motò and the Ford Ka and Escort, is that new and exciting paths are about

to be trod. It seems that we are moving towards a car that is prepared to take risks, have a strong individuality and sense of irony, that is able to anticipate trends and which is free of similarities and conformity.

The designs of Starck, described as a "politician of forms", seem generated by intersections of curves. The forms seem to result, not from the union of concepts with three dimensional forms, but from sections of lines that start and finish outside the car itself. These line sections are generated by each feature Starck has made visible (lights, bumpers, grill, roof panel, door etc.) but it could equally be argued that the shape of each feature is only the result of the crossing of two, sometimes three, curves.

This creative chaos is wonderfully dynamic and the eye of the beholder does not tire from running along the lines of the whole car body, searching for the primary thread from which all the forms evolve and without ever understanding whether the cuts in the bodywork are responsible for "creating" the objects or vice versa.

Starck's ideas have been taken and adapted on many prototypes, more or less functional, and exhibited at international shows, in particular Detroit, Frankfurt, Geneva and Tokyo from 1995 on. But Starck's ideas are not the only ones: even more in evidence is a strong return to more elaborate styles such as Art Déco, and the

creation of vertical and rectangular sets of lights like prisms which were seen hanging from lamps during the 1920's.

A tangible example was the extraordinary Plymouth Prowler, of which only 5,000 examples were planned and which earned immediate attention. It was a real 1950's hot rod design, with wheels separate from the car body, motorcycle type fenders, visible suspension, a large and biomorphic motor compartment (with a nod in the direction of the "coffin hood" of Gordon Buehrig's Cord), bumpers like mini rails, false footboards and a boattail rear end rounded like the top of a trunk. The design was a great success even without the curious revival of functionality in the form of a trailer in the same color and style. At the end of the century, here is an opportunity that convertibles cannot allow to go begging: what type of car can best embody the idea of "Differentiation"?

We may be mistaken but we are convinced that from the start of the 21st century, strange, postmodern forms will be seen, perhaps childish, exaggerated and also disquieting.

We really need a wind of change in all schools of industrial design with a brilliant designer of strong personality and charm at center stage. Maybe it will be Starck when he is allowed to design a sports car; maybe Alfa Romeo's De Silva if he is able to develop the beautiful new Nivola coupé; maybe BMW's Chris Bangle, currently the

236-237 Chrysler conceived the Plymouth Prowler as a showcar, but it entered production in 1997. The lines are a clear reference to the hot rods of America's past, especially at the front, where we see the modern version of a fencing-mask grill. Note also the motorcycle type fenders separate

from the body and the curious, government-mandated hammer-shaped bumpers with turn indicators incorporated. A two-wheeled mini trailer was also presented in the exact same color and overall formula of the rear of the car; it functioned as a supplementary luggage compartment.

most successful and courageous modernizer of convertibles; or maybe the successors to Pininfarina and Giugiaro who are already pawing the ground with a wave of new ideas backed up by an enormous technological patrimony; or then again maybe a young, unknown designer who, still ignored by the car manufacturers and media, works the midnight hours in some Californian or Japanese design studio trying to bring his ideas to reality. We like to think of him still working with a pencil and paper rather than computer aided design programs.

The design genius of the 21st century will be part architect, part child, part poet, part standard-bearer of hyper-technology; he will have a passion for cars but not be a slave to them; he will welcome new discoveries and try to exploit them to the maximum and in an original manner; he will abhor sameness but will not attempt to achieve effects at any cost; he will love speed but not aggression or excess; he will be flexible with materials, generous with colors, miserly with gadgets. A prodigy, no less. We like to think of him, for reasons of historical balance, as.a descendant of the gentleman at the beginning of the story who was left powerless and indignant as one of the first mechanical contraptions spattered him with mud. It is unnecessary to continue with further descriptions of abstruse models filled to the brim with electronic gadgets and original ideas, sometimes ingenious and sometimes just plain vulgar.

The reader who has come with us this far will be tired of reading, he will want a breath of fresh air, perhaps in an open-topped car. He can at least dream if he doesn't have one, and enjoy it if he already does. Very probably he will see direct descendants of the cars described in this volume, perhaps the spirited Argento Vivo by Pininfarina, the Formula by Giugiaro, the legendary Audi TT Roadster, the ambiguous De Tomaso Bigua, the small Ghia Focus, the technological Honda SSM or the modern replica of the Volkswagen Beetle.

As for us, we love this romantic world filled with incorrigible dreamers, regretful motorcyclists and adults who refuse to grow up. A world where vanity, if moderated, is not a failing and a sense of irony, if unconditioned, is a quality. A world where everyone is convinced that convertibles have a soul.

PURE BEAUTY

This is an organized trip into the world of open-topped cars, a trip in time among models that are timeless, a guided visit to twenty-two convertible "temples" from the 1919 Isotta Fraschini Type 8 to the 1997 Chevrolet Corvette. For each of these temples we shall try to illustrate their outer architecture (the bodywork), their supporting frame (the chassis and mechanics) and, above all, their genesis. In the authors' modest opinion, it is fascinating and intriguing to discover how many models, some of which are sculptures in motion, came into being quite by chance; the original lines of some were often an expedient answer to

technical requirements while the prototypes, simple styling exercises, were sometimes so thrilling that the public, far-sighted dealers, marketing geniuses and stubborn coachbuilders demanded they be put into production. Some examples? The Chevrolet Corvette, Citroën DS, Ferrari Dino, Mercedes 300 SL and Porsche 356 Speedster.
Even military conflicts have had a hand in the creation of some. Twelve of the following collection were produced during the 1950's and 60's when the desire to forget the misery, destruction and suffering of war resulted in imaginative and joyful design.

238 The 1996 XK8 is the last sports Jaguar of the 20th century, the worthy heir and representative of the company that has given us the class, elegance and performance of unforgettable models like the E-type and the XK series.

239 The 1936 Mercedes 540K has an extraordinary and eternal glamour that it partly inherited from the 500K Spezial Roadster, one of the most widely sought after collector cars. World War II unfortunately interrupted a certain and sparkling future for this superb model.

A final geographic note: the succession of models has meant continual crossings of the Atlantic Ocean that is mirrored in the production of some European models aimed at the American market: the Alfa Romeo Spider America, Ferrari 250 GT Spyder California, Ferrari Daytona and Lancia Aurelia B24 Spider America.

Like the historical text, this section is no less subject to possible imperfections or omissions. Some readers will quite rightly lament the absence of some models but lack of space has constrained us, reluctantly, to limit the number of "guests".

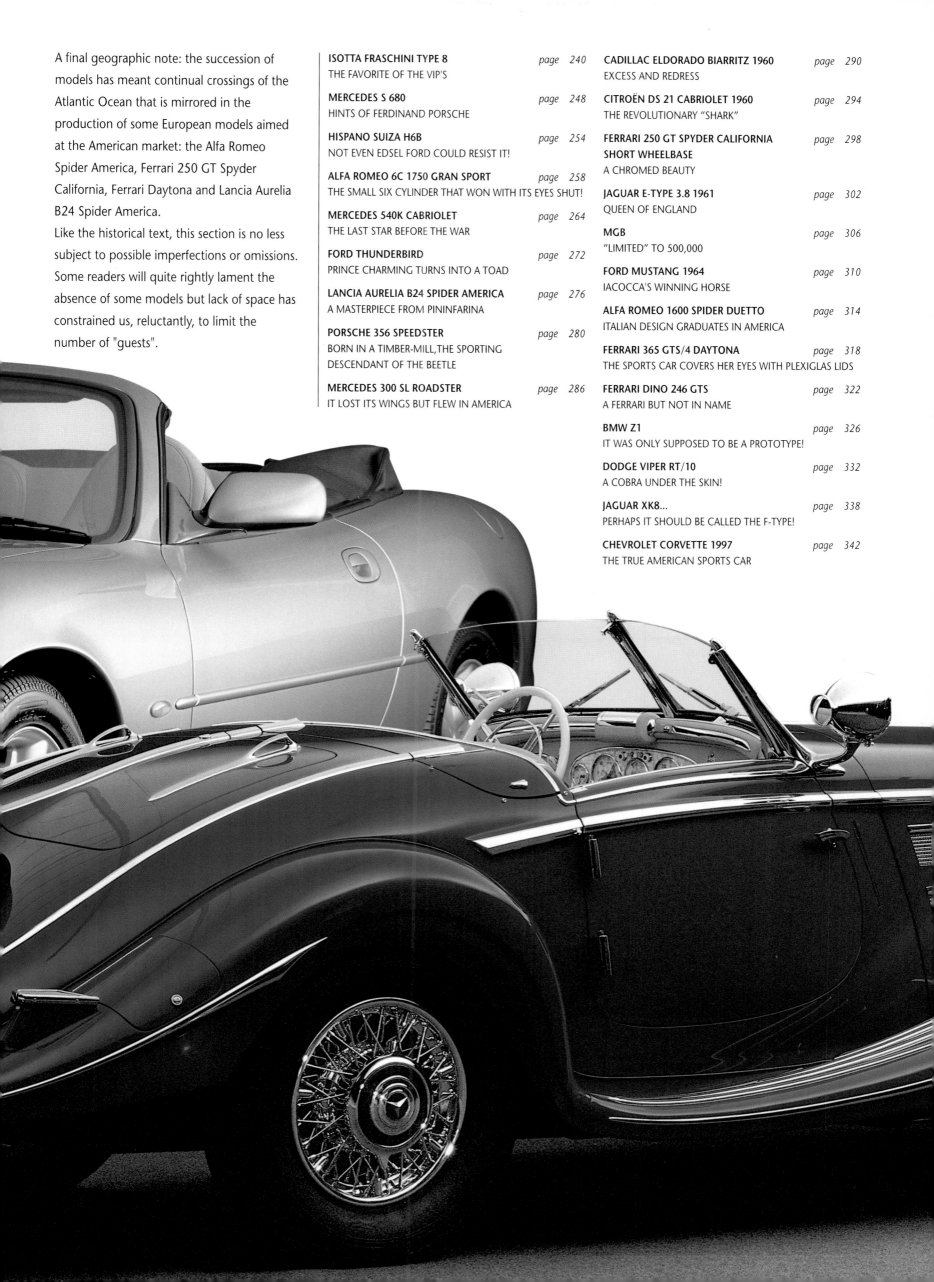

ISOTTA FRASCHINI TYPE 8
THE FAVORITE OF THE VIP'S

The Isotta Fraschini Type 8 inspired coachbuilders all over the world who, like expert tailors, "dressed" the chassis in exclusive outfits using the most luxurious materials to create the greatest elegance. It was a great success with film stars: the world's most handsome man, Rudolf Valentino, and the divas of the silent screen, Clara Bow and Gloria Swanson, each had at least one. It was included in several films and was unforgettable in the final sequence of "Sunset Boulevard" when its bulky outline is

official car of the Italian Ministry of Internal Affairs and the Soviet Ambassador to Rome. One was even given to Pope Pius XI by the Italian Automobile Club.

This was the client list that the Isotta Fraschini Type 8 could boast, made by the Italian company which made up the trio of European luxury car manufacturers during the 1920's and 1930's with Hispano Suiza and Rolls Royce. Perhaps having a double barreled name gave these marques an aristocratic stamp.

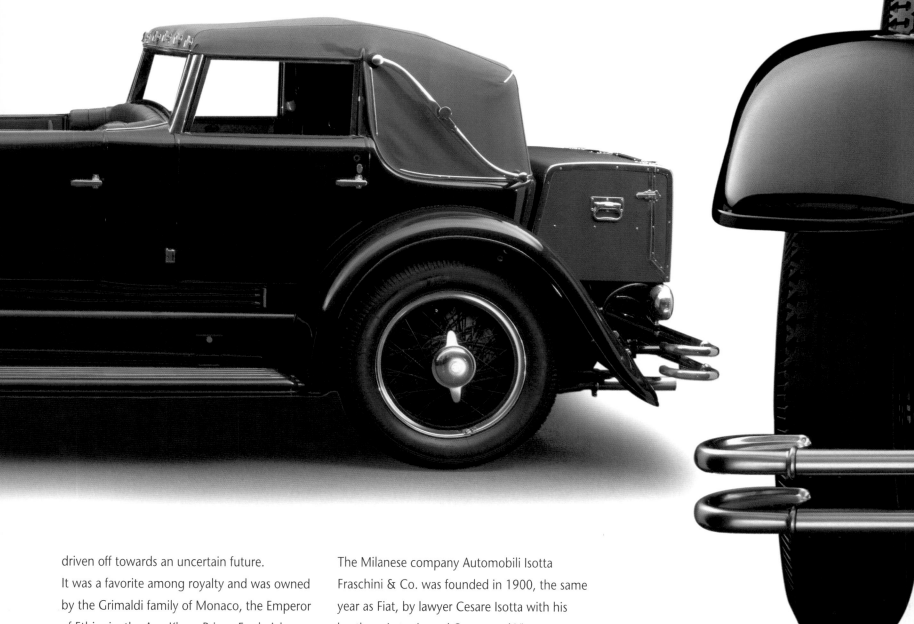

driven off towards an uncertain future.

It was a favorite among royalty and was owned by the Grimaldi family of Monaco, the Emperor of Ethiopia, the Aga Khan, Prince Frederick Leopold of Prussia and King Umberto of Italy; and of course there were the industrial magnates like the margarine king, Van Den Berg from Holland, men of letters like Gabriele d'Annunzio and politicians like Mussolini. It was also the

The Milanese company Automobili Isotta Fraschini & Co. was founded in 1900, the same year as Fiat, by lawyer Cesare Isotta with his brothers Antonio and Oreste and Vincenzo Fraschini. The company immediately dedicated itself to the construction of top quality cars. When the First World War started, the company was converted to produce military vehicles and engines for airplanes and motor boats but, once

ended, the need to forget the period was accompanied by the determination to construct a better world and the owners of Isotta Fraschini intended to build the very best. They opted for production of a single model, a courageous decision given the difficulties associated with reconversion, but they had technological knowledge learned before the war to exploit. They started again from scratch. The chassis (the company did not make the bodies) was designed for the American market as it was the richest and the most receptive to high quality

machines. A powerful, multi-cylinder engine was needed; four cylinders were clearly not sufficient, and even six cylinders were not exclusive enough. The next logical option was to use eight, marking the first eight cylinder series-built automobile motor made in Italy. The talented Giustino Cattaneo was charged with designing and developing it.

The experience Cattaneo had gained during the war with airplane engines came to bear in the production of his masterpiece. It took 17 months and 20 experimentation models to perfect and

in December 1919 the eight cylinder engine with cast iron block and cylinder head was ready. It displaced 5898cc, produced 80-90 HP and could take the car to 75 mph.

Only a short time later the Type 8 chassis, mechanics, radiator and hood were in the company's showrooms. Until 1935 the car remained largely unchanged. It became the Type 8A in 1924 with an increase in engine size to 7.3 liters, the "S" (extra powerful) versions giving 160 HP. In 1931 it became the Type B which was Isotta Fraschini's attempt to relaunch

the marque in the US following the economic crash of 1929. The differences between the two versions were minor: the chassis was strengthened and the option of a Wilson preselector-type gearbox was added.

It was on the Type 8B that the most beautiful examples of the Isotta Fraschini were produced. The radiator and hood were the only elements that were standard; the rest of the body was left to the imagination and skill of the coachbuilders. The radiator with black grill was in a classic and imposing square shape. The radiator's chrome frame sported the company badge, round till 1924 then rectangular. Often a chrome supporting strut that united the two large headlights was designed to recreate the badge in the center of the radiator. Although a third headlight was provided as a sporting touch, it subtracted somewhat from the car's regal bearing and few coachbuilders included it in their designs. The long hood with its vertical strip air intake excited the imagination of the coachbuilders who embellished it with large fenders and spare wheels often protected by a wheelcover painted the same color as the body. From the windshield back, the coachbuilders were free to interpret the car as they wished. Their job was to take the wishes of their customers as a base (the customers were always looking for new personal touches) and to let their fancy fly. There was no limit to the use of costly materials in the attempt to create details which would make each example unique. The coachbuilders who worked most on the Type 8 were the Italians Sala, Castagna and the Farina workshops but then there were also Touring,

Figoni & Falaschi, Fleetwood, Hooper, Lancefield, LeBaron and Ramseier. Each one produced customized models and each version was unique. It is impossible to say that one was more beautiful than any other; they were all magnificent. Here are some just to give an idea of the glamorous world of the Type 8.

Castagna produced the unforgettable "Closed Body" which transformed the Type 8 into a landaulet or torpedo using the Baehr system of folding hood, windows and hinges. "Landaulet" meant the car was partly open, usually the front where the driver sat. The doors were very large and not particularly beautiful but they were the only kind able to support the enormous weight of the transformation kit.

Then there was Castagna's version which was featured in the film "Sunset Boulevard". The black car was very dignified, almost austere: the only touches of color were the shiny gray of the footboard, the fenders, the folding mechanism of the hood, the side of the hood itself, the frame of the windshield and the grill and the

spokes and hubs of the wheels while the wooden drawers of the tool box were brown. The initials "N.D.", for Norma Desmond, the character in the film played by Gloria Swanson, were painted at the height of the waist. The driver's seat had no top. Behind the chauffeur there was another windshield which marked the limit of the covered area; inside there were two rows of seats. A distinguishing feature was the keyboard for giving instructions to the driver - slow, fast, stop, back, right, left, home - which activated an indicator beside the steering wheel. The "Ogni Tempo" (All Weather) Type 8A came from the Farina workshops. It had flat lines, large doors, a vertical windshield and the spare wheel attached to the hood. The 8A S (the S meant it

was a more powerful version) was a torpedo with more sinuous lines than the 8A with a windshield for each row of seats, a lowered waistline near the doors, and fenders which integrated the housing for the spare wheel. The roadster prepared by Fleetwood for Rudolf Valentino was also unforgettable. The glamour of the car was no less than that of the man himself. The shape resembled that of Touring's Flying Star; the lines were sinuous, the hood tapered and the fenders described a long S. Nor was there any lack of elegant chromework on the handles at the height of the waist. The splendor of the Isotta Fraschini Type 8 started to fail at the end of the 1920's the day after the Wall Street Crash. Despite the wonderful creations that continued the Type 8's agony until the middle of the next decade, the economic crisis did not leave much room for luxury. Chauffeurs became an unnecessary cost and the new rich preferred to drive their own cars. It was the start of the decline for the Italian manufacturer, which slowly started its own drive down Sunset Boulevard.

TECHNICAL DESCRIPTION OF THE ISOTTA FRASCHINI TYPE 8

YEARS OF PRODUCTION	1919-1935	**BORE AND STROKE (MM)**	85 X 130, 95 X 130
CHASSIS	STEEL SHEET SIDE STRUTS AND CROSS MEMBERS	**PISTON DISPLACEMENT**	5898, 7370 CC
SUSPENSION	FRONT AND REAR: RIGID AXLE AND SEMIELLIPTICAL LEAF SPRINGS; HYDRAULIC SHOCK ABSORBERS	**HORSEPOWER**	80-160 AT 2200-2800 RPM
		TIMING SYSTEM	TWO OVERHEAD VALVES PER CYLINDER, 1 CAMSHAFT IN THE BLOCK
WHEELS & TIRES	SPOKED WHEELS, 700 X 21 TIRES		
STEERING	WORM WHEEL AND HELICAL GEAR	**FUEL SUPPLY**	2 CARBURETORS
FRONT TRACK (INCHES)	55	**GEARBOX**	MANUAL 3 SPEED + REVERSE; CENTRAL GEARSHIFT
REAR TRACK (INCHES)	55		
WHEELBASE (INCHES)	144	**DRIVE**	REAR
ENGINE	FRONT LONGITUDINAL, EIGHT CYLINDERS, IN-LINE	**MAX. SPEED (MPH)**	87 - 100

MERCEDES S 680
HINTS OF FERDINAND PORSCHE

Eight years after the end of the First World War, the memory of the bombing was still fresh in German minds and the wounds inflicted on the economic and social fabric had not healed. Two events that took place in 1926 were direct consequences of that war: The founding of the Daimler-Benz company and the production of the S 680 with supercharged engine.
Back in 1915, orders from the Luftwaffe (the German air force) to Daimler Motoren (as it then was) had obliged the company to manufacture airplanes. The need to construct airplanes able to fly higher than their opponents to achieve supremacy in dogfights was responsible for Paul Daimler's development of the supercharged engine, though this concept had first been experimented with by Gottlieb Daimler as early as 1885 on his first motor. The concept was

TECHNICAL DESCRIPTION OF THE MERCEDES S 680

YEARS OF PRODUCTION	1926-1930	REAR TRACK (INCHES)	55	TIMING SYSTEM	TWO VALVES PER CYLINDER, SINGLE OVERHEAD CAMSHAFT
CHASSIS	TUBULAR STRUCTURE IN STEEL PLATE (FROM 1928 IT WAS LOWERED AND MADE FROM STAMPED STEEL PLATE)	WHEELBASE (INCHES)	133		
		ENGINE	FRONT LONGITUDINAL, SIX CYLINDERS, IN-LINE	FUEL SUPPLY	SPECIAL CARBURETOR (FROM 1928 TWO MERCEDES THREE JET CARBURETORS AND RING FLOAT)
WHEELS & TIRES	SPOKED WHEELS, 5 X 30 HIGH-PRESSURE TIRES (FROM 1928, 6.50 X 20 O & 7.00 X 20 BALLOON STEEL CORD)	BORE AND STROKE (MM)	98x150		
		PISTON DISPLACEMENT	6789 CC	GEARBOX	MANUAL 4 SPEED + REVERSE; CENTRAL GEARSHIFT
		HORSEPOWER	FROM 120 TO 250 AT 3000-3300 RPM	DRIVE	REAR
FRONT TRACK (INCHES)	55			MAX. SPEED (MPH)	FROM 103 TO 122

transferred to the car engine and in 1921 the first Mercedes cars with driver-controlled superchargers were presented at the Berlin Motor Show. Supercharging meant extra power and therefore sports models. Together with the attractive design and racing successes of their cars, supercharged engines contributed to the image of quality that the company is still famous for. When the war ended, Daimler was hit just as hard as all other manufacturers of top-of-the-market cars by the economic crisis, nor could it continue to produce airplanes as this had been prohibited by the Allies. The difficult situation that resulted was responsible for the merger of

the Daimler and Benz companies which had in fact been working in collaboration since 1924. The first model that came out of this union was the S 680. It was derived from the model K which in turn descended from the 15/70/100 PS prototype, the founder of the family of S models (the SS, SSK and SSKL) which filled Daimler Benz's production until the Second World War. The designer behind the 15/70/100 PS was none other than the engineer Ferdinand Porsche who became technical director of Daimler in 1923. The S 680 inherited the dimensions of the body from the K though the chassis was lowered. The motor was set back by 12 inches

for a lower seat on the chassis and better weight distribution. The 6.8 liter, 6 cylinder engine with driver-controlled supercharger was prepared by Porsche to be used also for racing; it developed 120 HP with the supercharger off and 170 HP with it on. The versions that followed the S 680 had power increased up to 250 HP and several modifications to the chassis, the fuel supply and tires as listed in the technical description. The open-topped versions of the S 680 were a roadster and a four-seater cabriolet. The roadster was fitted out in a very sporty manner: to the large "V" shaped grill with chrome frame, the long hood with external exhaust and leather

closure straps (aesthetic elements that could not be altered as they formed part of the chassis) were added fenders separate from the body. To the roadster a drop-shaped footboard separate from the fenders was added. The fenders seemed to have been designed in a wind tunnel; the back ends were wider and ended in a point. The cab was made for two people and even the windshield was designed to save an inch or two. The frame of the windshield was slim and often flanked by two additional headlights that were even larger than those on the grill. The two-door, four-seater cabriolet was decidedly more attractive. The waist was low, there was more

chrome and the finishing was of better quality than the roadster. The fenders were traditionally shaped: the slender front ones were joined to a large footboard that in turn developed into the rear fenders. The S 680 had no rear volume; just behind the slightly raised rear seats there was only space for the top to be folded before the body slid down towards the rear bumper. The two spare wheels were carried on the back of the car. The S 680 generated the S 700 and S 710 which differed mainly by the size of the engine (increased to 7 liters). The S series came to an end in 1930, two years into the production of the SS series.

HISPANO SUIZA H6B
NOT EVEN EDSEL FORD COULD RESIST IT!

The Hispano Suiza was the most expensive car during the 1920's, more than a Rolls Royce or an Isotta Fraschini. Its symbol was a stork.
The stork in flight seemed caught on the radiator cap like a still-shot with only its long, powerful wings in contact with the car and its body stretched out behind. It seemed to inspire liberty and gracefulness - and it was a symbol of birth, too!
The symbol of the stork appeared on Hispano Suiza cars from 1919. It was a present from Mark Birkigt, the technical director of the Barcelona based company, to his friend Georges Guynemer, a pilot in the First World War who disappeared on a mission, so that Guynemer's plane, fitted with a Hispano Suiza engine, would have a bird as a symbol. The choice of a symbol more suitable for a plane than a car

manufacturer was not limited to Hispano Suiza: The rearing horse that first appeared on the racing Alfa Romeos driven by Enzo Ferrari and which was later transferred onto Ferrari's own racing and road cars was a reproduction of the symbol the Italian pilot Francesco Baracca kept on his fighter plane. Enzo received this symbol from Baracca's parents the day after his victory at the Savio track at Ravenna in 1923.
Hispano Suiza Fàbrica de Automòviles was founded in 1904 by Damian Mateu. The technical contribution by the young and brilliant Birkigt brought the newly formed company to international attention immediately. It acquired celebrity in 1905 when King Alfonso XIII of Spain bought a 20 HP chassis: from that moment on, the first example of each new model was sent to the Spanish royal family. In 1911 the first factory was opened in France and Jean Lacoste, father of the famous tennis player who later started the

sports clothes business, became a director.
During the Great War, the company was employed in making military equipment: lorries, industrial motors and airplane engines. Birkigt designed an aeronautical V8 motor which was fitted to a number of Allied warplanes, but it was from the prototype of another airplane engine, this time a V12, that the six cylinder motor which powered the H6 chassis was derived. The H6 represented the very best of Hispano Suiza; it was the machine that propelled the company to the top of the heap amongst luxury cars, easily on a par with Rolls Royce and Isotta Fraschini. The H6 chassis was designed by Birkigt with the clear intention of competing with Rolls Royce. The car's mechanical innovations, for example, drum brakes on all four wheels with mechanical servo steering, combined with its strong performance (94 mph) and exceptional elasticity, roused the passion of sports car lovers. But it was not only enthusiasts of fast cars that

255

were thrilled; the rich were attracted by its luxury and exclusivity and by the elegance and magnificence of the car bodies the coachbuilders designed for it.

Parisian coachbuilders dedicated themselves to the H6 most, taking advantage of the proximity of the French factory where the car was produced. Million Guiet (responsible for a sports Torpedo version which won a car beauty contest in 1929), Labourdette, Hibbard and Darrin produced torpedoes, cabriolets, dual cowls and landaulets from the H6, all of them unique creative responses to the requests of the customers and the possibilities offered by the chassis. A common feature between all these versions tended to be the shape of the fenders which for the most part were slender and very streamlined and that also served as a support for the spare wheels. The wheels were usually spoked but occasionally had hubcaps in the same color as the body. The chassis components obviously did not change: the long, imposing hood, the large grill with vertical chrome bars and the large round headlights.

The wish to "dress" a Hispano Suiza was not limited to France. In Great Britain the H6 was well treated by Park Ward (despite their absolute loyalty to Rolls Royce) and the serene Mulliner; in Belgium, by Van den Plas; and in the United States, where most of the company's production went, by Brewster and Brunn.

Many famous people became owners of the H6, including Pablo Picasso, and then of the successive H6B of 1922 and H6C of 1924. The B series did not really offer any alterations which merited a change in name - possibly it was done simply to ensure alphabetical continuity with the series officially identified as "C" with an engine increased to 8 liters.

Besides the usual maharajahs, magnates, aristocrats and film stars, one of the most illustrious owners of a Hispano Suiza H6 was Edsel Ford, son of Henry, who preferred a powerful but manageable Hispano to a stately Rolls Royce, a glamorous Isotta, an opulent Duesenberg or a technical Mercedes.

TECHNICAL DESCRIPTION OF THE **HISPANO SUIZA H6B**			
YEARS OF PRODUCTION	1922-1933	BORE AND STROKE (MM)	100 X 140
CHASSIS	STAMPED STEEL PLATE	PISTON DISPLACEMENT	6597 cc
SUSPENSION	FRONT: RIGID "H" SECTION AXLE AND LONGITUDINAL LEAF SPRINGS; REAR: RIGID AXLE, LONGITUDINAL LEAF SPRINGS, FRICTION SHOCK ABSORBERS	HORSEPOWER	135 AT 3000 RPM
		TIMING SYSTEM	TWO OVERHEAD VALVES PER CYLINDER
		FUEL SUPPLY	GRAVITY OPERATED PRESSURE FUEL FEED
WHEELS & TIRES	SPOKED WHEELS, 7.00 X 18 TIRES		
FRONT TRACK (INCHES)	59	GEARBOX	3 SPEED + REVERSE, CENTRAL GEARSHIFT
REAR TRACK (INCHES)	59		
WHEELBASE (INCHES)	144	DRIVE	REAR
ENGINE	FRONT LONGITUDINAL, SIX CYLINDERS, IN-LINE	MAX. SPEED (MPH)	62-80

ALFA ROMEO 6C 1750 GRAN SPORT
THE SMALL SIX CYLINDER THAT WON WITH ITS EYES SHUT!

In 1929 the Italian Motor Show celebrated its second year as an international exhibition and was held in Rome instead of Milan. The reasons for the transfer were both political and strategic: political because King Vittorio Emmanuele II and the head of the government, Benito Mussolini, wanted the Italian capital to assume once again its imperial greatness and become the nation's center of cultural activities; strategic because they wanted the car to become popular in the center and south of Italy which were economically depressed compared to the industrial north.

The stars of that single Roman motor show were American: Buick, Cadillac, Chevrolet, Oldsmobile, Packard, Pontiac and Studebaker grabbed the attention of the visitors as though they had been beautiful Mediterranean girls. The rooms were adorned with carpets, tapestries, paintings, statues and flowers with the aim of making the visitors forget they were in an industrial exhibition, but this atmosphere also

had a negative side: there was the risk that important novelties would pass unobserved by a public still reeling from the economic earthquake recently unleashed in New York. Unfortunately for Alfa Romeo, their stand was relegated to one of the many corridors where the cars were parked along the length of the wall as though they were in a city street. It was in this line of cars that the 6C 1750 was presented to the public for the first time. Actually it was only the chassis of the car as there had not been the time to produce a suitable body.

The 6C 1750 had been developed from the 6C 1500, a model created in 1925 by Vittorio Jano who had been asked by Alfa Romeo to design a light, medium engined car with excellent performance - just what the market was asking for. The 1920's had seen a rise in popularity of small economical cars with four cylinder engines of about 1 liter as opposed to the six cylinder, 2 liter or more, luxury models.

Jano took the best of each of the two current trends and produced a winning compromise, the 6C 1500. When the chassis received its debut at the 1925 Milan Motor Show, the car was presented under the name "N.R." with a 6 cylinder, 1.5 liter motor. Experience was accumulated with the racing version, the P2, which brought many victories to the company as well as its first World Championship in 1925. This experience was put to good use by Jano and he was able to make the new car light and manageable. The two most important technical features of the 6C 1500 were, first, the fixed head for sports use rather than the normal cast iron head that could be removed from the cylinder block, and second, the compressor that could not be cut out of operation. For the first time a new device was used to govern the play in the valves and this system would be used by Alfa Romeo up until the Giulietta during the 1950's: by inserting and turning a special key in the tappet head,

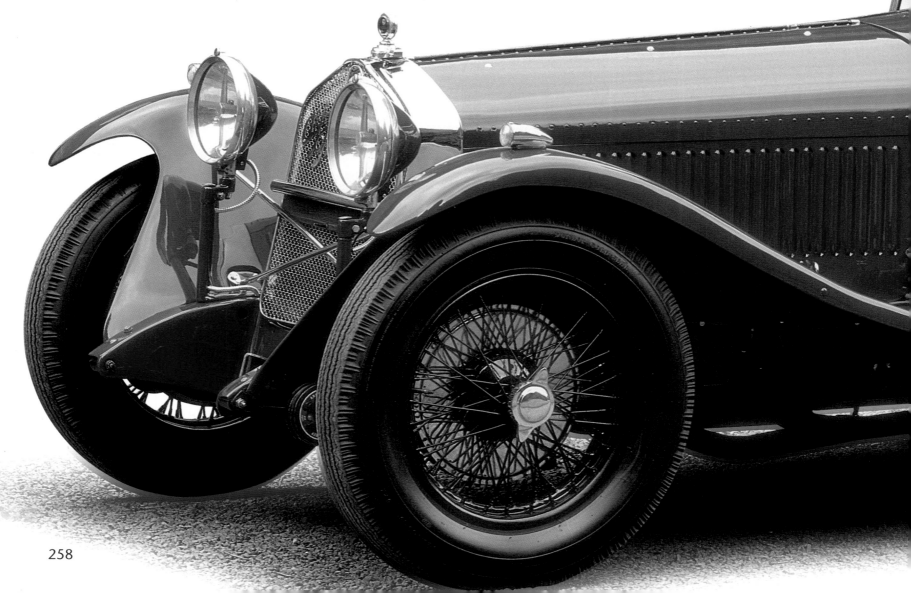

the play between cam and tappets could be adjusted. These features were also to be found in the 6C 1750 which was available in the following versions: Touring, Sports or Gran Turismo (GT), Super Sport or Gran Sport. Their engines could operate both with or without the compressor. As always, supercharged cars were suitable for racing and the 6C 1750 was successful like the P2 had been. The Gran Sport in particular stood out: among its many victories was the unforgettable Mille Miglia of 1930 won by the famous Nuvolari (partnered by Guidotti) who showed the genius and astuteness of a champion by overtaking his teammate Achille Varzi with the car lights off! Not seeing the lights of his rival behind him, Varzi had relaxed and slowed down believing Nuvolari to be out of the race.

The Gran Sport was also a favorite of the coachbuilders. The first 6C 1750's to leave the Alfa Romeo factory were supplied with just the working chassis, dashboard, hood and one or two spare wheels. Coachbuilders such as Castagna, Touring, Zagato, Young and Van den Plas would then create a made-to-measure body. The Gran Sport model also lent itself to sports bodies due to its shorter wheelbase: it was 8'11" long compared to the 9'6" of the Sport and Gran Turismo models, and the 10'0"

of the Turismo.

The bodywork designs by Zagato and Touring were the most requested for the Gran Sport. The Ugo Zagato workshop in Milan provided a two seater that housed the motor's auxiliary oil tank on the lower left hand side of the cab, i.e. by the passenger's feet, because at that time the car had right hand drive. The dashboard of the Gran Sport had instruments on a black background rather than the white background of the Sport, Super Sport and Turismo versions. The dials were circular with a plated rim and lit internally rather than with the traditional external light. The accelerator pedal was round and positioned between the brake and the clutch.

The passengers were protected from the rush of air by a sloping windshield on a fixed base which ran the width of the long curved hood. The side windows were not small and ineffective but wide and functional. The large chromed radiator grill had an oval cooling liquid thermometer with ornate chromed rim mounted on the top; with the two headlights (three for the racing version) it was certainly one of the two main features of the front of the car. The sides of the vehicle had traditional fenders joined to each other via the footboard, a grill for ventilating the cab near the door, another to cool the motor and, at the bottom, the Zagato name. A decorative chrome

TECHNICAL DESCRIPTION OF THE ALFA ROMEO 6C 1750 GRAN SPORT		

YEARS OF PRODUCTION	1930-1932	**ENGINE**	FRONT LONGITUDINAL, SIX CYLINDERS IN-LINE, ONE-PIECE CAST-IRON BLOCK
CHASSIS	"C" STAMPED PLATE WITH SIDE STRUTS AND CROSSMEMBERS		
SUSPENSION	FRONT AND REAR WITH SEMI-ELLIPTICAL LEAF SPRINGS AND FRICTION SHOCK ABSORBERS	**BORE AND STROKE (MM)**	65 X 88
		DISPLACEMENT	1752 CC
		HORSEPOWER	85 AT 4500 RPM
WHEELS & TIRES	WHEELS WITH TOUCHING SPOKES, 28 X 5.25 TIRES	**TIMING SYSTEM**	2 X 90° OVERHEAD VALVES PER CYLINDER
STEERING	WORM WHEEL AND HELICAL GEAR, LONGITUDINAL AND TRANSVERSAL BAR, RIGHT HAND DRIVE	**FUEL SUPPLY**	1 VERTICAL TWIN CARBURETOR
		CLUTCH	MULTIPLE DRY PLATES
		GEARBOX	4 SPEED + REVERSE; CENTRAL GEARSHIFT
FRONT TRACK (INCHES)	54	**DRIVE**	REAR
REAR TRACK (INCHES)	54	**MAX. SPEED (MPH)**	81
WHEELBASE (INCHES)	107		

band ran from the hood to the rear of the car where the one, or two, spare wheels were kept. The Touring workshop, also of Milan, produced the attractive Flying Star which was so elegant that a white model bought by Mrs. Josette Pozzo of Genoa won several prizes at car beauty contests. Much of the admiration the Touring version engendered was caused by the sides of the body: the vertical cooling grill was substituted by three horizontal strips which finished on the doors. It was these that gave the design the name "Flying Star". The upper section of the doors was covered with chrome which continued to the rear of the side panels to create an elegant "V". The fenders were not joined as in the Zagato design but ended at the height of the doors to give the car great character.

MERCEDES 540K CABRIOLET
THE LAST STAR BEFORE THE WAR

As the war came to a close and the defeat of the Reich approached, there were many who believed that the German car manufacturers had no future. Their ideas and projects lay under the ruins, what factories were still operating produced war machines and the men who were still alive were barely surviving. Among the marques that might have disappeared forever was Mercedes. Were their splendid prewar models to be their last production jewels? Fortunately, or perhaps because of the tenacity and determination of the German people, it was not the case. Once peace was restored, the prewar works of art that had been hidden in huts and haystacks to preserve their splendor returned to the roads. Among the most magnificent was the luxurious and exclusive Mercedes 540K, where the letter K signified for the first time "Kompressor" (supercharger) rather than "Kurz" (short wheelbase).

The 540K was the final expression of the stylistic and technical developments of a series of cars Mercedes had started in 1933 with the 380. The debut of the 540K was in 1936 (the same year

another German star was born, the Volkswagen Beetle by Ferdinand Porsche) and it would probably have had a future if the war had not interrupted production.

The new model inherited many innovative mechanical features from the 380 and its successor, the 500K; for example, four wheel independent suspension and supercharging at will by the driver. This last feature gave the car a Dr Jekyll and Mr Hyde nature, transforming it from a comfortable and tranquil convertible into a fast "gran turismo" model.

Aesthetically, the 540K inherited a little of the looks of the 500K Spezial Roadster, the dream of many collectors. The 540K differs little from the 500K and actually is almost the same car with a larger, supercharged engine. The 8 cylinders displaced 5.4 liters rather than 5 and that increased the power to 180 HP. Production continued until 1942 and the replacement, the 580, was ready for production having been presented in its experimental state at the Berlin Motor Show as early as 1939 but the war dictated otherwise.

The chassis of the 540K was used for several types of bodywork of which the cabriolet was the most interesting. The front of the 540K was without doubt the most imposing view; of the car's overall 16'3" length, half was devoted to the hood and front end. The nose was a collection of attractions; it is difficult to choose which was the most distinguishing feature between the fenders, grill and headlights. The bumper consisted of two curved pieces joined by the license plate and behind it, rather than the grill as one would assume, there was the part of the bodywork which joined the two large but light fenders looking like waves thrown up by a passing boat. The flat surface created behind the bumper was excellent for attaching rally plates or the results of car beauty competitions in which the 540K was as at home as a racing car on a track.

Like the curtain raised over a stage during a performance, the fenders were gathered at the sides of the nose over the grill. The "V" shaped central section of the grill was a model of elegance made entirely from chrome while the tight internal mesh was partially covered by the shiny metal member used to anchor the two large headlights and third, smaller, central one. A three pointed star on a blue background on the central grill complemented the grill's angles while just above it, on top of the radiator itself, was a second Mercedes star that looked like the sights of a gun aiming at any other vehicle that dared to get in the driver's way. Mercedes was the only maker to display two badges so close. The long hood stretched away from the radiator towards the windshield. There was certainly much more space inside than the 8 cylinder engine required. The top of the hood was free of all embellishments such as air intakes, ribbing or chromework which were relegated to the sides. The air intakes were as long as the hood itself and decorated with thin vertical chrome bars. Continuing the Mercedes tradition which started in the 1920's, the external chrome exhaust pipes, like the tubes from a diver's helmet to the oxygen tank, stood out from the sides of the hood but they were partly hidden by the spare wheels positioned just behind the fender. The fenders curled around the wheels in an obvious representation of a wave. The two lights mounted on top looked just like boat lights and the footboard created from the join of the two wheelhouses was a clear invitation to climb aboard.

The rest of the side view was taken up by the outline of the door.

A chrome molding ran along the top all the way to the rear wheelhouse. The waist of the car was very high and the windows above were short, just a quarter of their own width. The top's folding mechanism was visible, two articulated chrome arms that also acted as aesthetic adornments. The rear end was anonymous but the 540K already had enough distinguishing features for one car.

To have an idea of how much comfort was available to the passengers, the huge, stuffed and extra soft seats are sufficient indication. There was also a small sofa at the back provided in case of need but it was light years from the comfort provided by the front seats. The steering wheel was enormous, seeming to compete with the size of the headlights. It had four spokes in the shape of a cross splayed out from a small center. The whole of the instrument panel was white including the background of the dials and the buttons.

TECHNICAL DESCRIPTION OF THE MERCEDES 540K CABRIOLET

YEARS OF PRODUCTION	1936-1942	BORE AND STROKE (MM)	88 X 111
CHASSIS	LOWERED, BOXED STAMPED STEEL PLATES	PISTON DISPLACEMENT	5401 CC
SUSPENSION	FRONT: INDEPENDENT WHEELS, SPIRAL SPRINGS; REAR: INDEPENDENT WHEELS, FLOATING AXLE SHAFTS, SPIRAL SPRINGS; TUBULAR HYDRAULIC SHOCK ABSORBERS	HORSEPOWER	180 AT 5800 RPM
		MAX. TORQUE (KGM)	28 AT 3600 RPM
		TIMING SYSTEM	TWO OVERHEAD VALVES PER CYLINDER, CAM IN BLOCK
		FUEL SUPPLY	SINGLE VERTICAL TWIN CARBURETOR, SUPERCHARGING WITH POSITIVE DISPLACEMENT COMPRESSOR AND DIAPHRAGM PUMP
WHEELS & TIRES	17" SPOKED WHEELS, 7.00 X 17 TIRES		
FRONT TRACK (INCHES)	59		
REAR TRACK (INCHES)	58	GEARBOX	MANUAL 4 SPEED + REVERSE; CENTRAL GEARSHIFT
WHEELBASE (INCHES)	128	DRIVE	REAR
ENGINE	FRONT LONGITUDINAL, EIGHT CYLINDERS, IN-LINE	MAX. SPEED (MPH)	106

FORD THUNDERBIRD

PRINCE CHARMING TURNS INTO A TOAD

First the Thunderbird was a sports car, then it became a convertible and finally ended up as a sedan. This is an unusual evolution for any car and was entirely unpredictable for the Thunderbird, which was created for precise marketing reasons to meet new market demands rather than serve old ones. The Thunderbird was Ford's answer to the Corvette, and the Thunderbird and Corvette together were the American majors' reply to the European sports cars which were growing in popularity in the US. The models that arrived from Europe - Jaguar in particular - were the answer to the demand for small, high performance cars that the national manufacturers did not satisfy. The Thunderbird met the Corvette's challenge between its debut in 1955 and 1958, when it was transformed into a four-seater convertible. By placing emphasis on comfort, a wide range of accessories and a powerful motor, it was truly competitive to GM's new model. Unlike the Corvette, the new Ford disdained plastic and offered electric windows, electric seats, power steering, power brakes, three types of transmission - manual with and without overdrive, and automatic - and a V8 engine. The public soon showed which model it

preferred: in 1955 the Thunderbird sold 16,500 units against the Corvette's 700. But in 1958 the Thunderbird was changed from a prince into a toad, from a zippy sports car into a sedate convertible. The T-bird's enthusiasts cried out as the car changed its personality, grew larger, and saw its lines become heavier and squat.

But from a commercial point of view it was a great success - sales increased from 21,380 in 1957 to 37,892 in 1958 - because the new Thunderbird was ahead of its time despite its change in nature. It had a unitized body (a relative novelty), powerful engines, a high degree of comfort (including a steering wheel that moved sideways to facilitate getting in and out), and a competitive price.

But successful sales could not restore the attraction of the sports model. The two-seater had had a balanced body, contained dimensions, well-proportioned volumes and was as sporty as could be wished. The nose emphasized the round headlights under their protective cover which seemed like eyes without brows. Under the eyes, naturally, there was the mouth; in this case it was a shark's mouth created by a chrome grill and

frame with two bullets on the one-piece bumper. The hood displayed a wide, narrow air intake with an oval hole which was always a sign of sporting pedigree and synonymous with power. The windshield wrapped around to the sides where a faux air outlet was positioned, elegant with diagonal chrome strips. A slight pleat lightened the side view and emphasized the small fin at the rear by separating it from the rest of the body.

The Thunderbird had a full wheelhouse that hid some of the rear wheel, which was a pity as the white-walled tires were very elegant. The tail was a near copy of the front. Without the presence of the fins and aeronautical bumper bullets the tapering trunk would have seemed convex, a style which appeared in the 1960's. The cab design followed the sobriety and elegance of the outside. A piece of chrome ran the width of the dashboard creating a frame for the controls, ventilation buttons and radio. The instrument panel comprised three separate components. The first was semicircular and placed in the center consisting of the speedometer and principal dials. The second and third were smaller and round and placed on either side of the speedo; they contained the rev counter and clock. If the three components are seen upside down, they resemble the nose of the car without the bumper and bullets.

In 1956 the Thunderbird was improved with the addition of two air intakes on the front bumper for better internal ventilation, the spare wheel was placed outside to create more loading space and the V8 engine was made available as a 5.2 as well as 4.8. 1957 brought more important alterations: the bumpers were made larger and of a different design to accommodate the bigger grill; the bumper bullets disappeared and the fins became more extreme; inside there was a new, more readable instrument panel; the wheels were altered from 15" to 14" to give the car a lower stance and make it look more slender; and a positive displacement supercharger became available on request, enabling the fastest Thunderbirds to reach 131 mph. Even so equipped, competition use was minimal.

TECHNICAL DESCRIPTION OF THE FORD THUNDERBIRD

YEARS OF PRODUCTION	1955-1957	BORE AND STROKE (MM)	95.3 X 83.8; FROM 1956, 96.5 X 87.4
CHASSIS	UNITIZED STEEL BODY	DISPLACEMENT	4785 CC; FROM 1956, 5112 ALSO AVAILABLE
SUSPENSION	FRONT: INDEPENDENT A-ARMS WITH COILS; REAR: SEMI-ELLIPTICAL LEAF SPRINGS	HORSEPOWER	169-177; FROM 1957, 214
		TIMING SYSTEM	TWO VALVES/CYL., CAM IN BLOCK
WHEELS	15" WHEELS; FROM 1957, 14"	GEARBOX	MANUAL 3 SPEED; ON REQUEST, MANUAL 3 SPEED + OVERDRIVE; OPTIONAL 2 SPEED AUTOMATIC
STEERING	SERVO-ASSISTED		
FRONT TRACK (INCHES)	55		
REAR TRACK (INCHES)	55		
WHEELBASE (INCHES)	101	DRIVE	REAR
ENGINE	FRONT LONGITUDINAL, V8	MAX. SPEED (MPH)	119 - 137

LANCIA AURELIA B24 SPIDER AMERICA

A MASTERPIECE FROM PININFARINA

Once postwar Italy had forgotten the misery and brutality of the Second World War, America represented the model that everyone wanted to follow, American fashions and trends were the ones to copy. Everything "stars and stripes" was avidly welcomed and every Italian product was inspired by and aimed for success in America. Cars were no exception: Ferrari even called some of its versions "America", Fiat produced the 1400 that looked like a small American car covered in chrome, and Alfa Romeo attempted to export its Giulietta to the US. There was certainly no shortage of new ideas - they had been put aside during the war

following year's Turin Motor Show. Its success led to the B20 coupé (1951), to further developments of the B10 and B20 and to increases in size and power of the engine which eventually reached 2.5 liters and produced 115 HP. The cherry on the cake arrived with the B24 Spider in 1955 designed by Pininfarina and named "America" in an attempt to break into the lucrative US market. The car had all the attributes for overseas success; it had lovely lines, looked like a racing sedan and had marvelous performance (112 mph). Gianni Lancia took every opportunity to drive it and even Pininfarina gave it a spin.

to make room for military production. Lancia geared up too. Management returned to Turin after a year of internment in Padua to work on the design of a new V6 engine, an idea that Lancia had cultivated for some time and which designer De Virgilio had had in mind since 1943. Later on they thought of a new model which was more than a revised version of the Aprilia. This culminated in the Aurelia B10 and the new 60° V6 motor produced in 1949. Presentation of the car to the public was delayed till the

The B24 was a Spartan sports car following the English style but it was also elegant as only Italian designs can be. The cab was moved forward (like the "cab forward" concept taken up again by Chrysler in the 1990's), the windshield wrapped round with the uprights set back and the doors had no handles like racing cars. To open the car it was necessary to pull on the cord on the inside of the door. The windows were fixed and could not be opened; the external rear view mirror was set on the fender too far away to be adjusted by the

driver. The side of the vehicle sported only the Pinin Farina name, behind the door and low down. The two small door panels interrupted the sweeps of the fenders which finished at the lights at either end of the body. There were two large round headlights in a chrome rim and two small lights below. At the rear, there was one light in the shape of a drop and a small round light below which together formed an exclamation mark. The bumpers were divided into two parts like a moustache, in the front

turned up towards the chrome radiator grill and behind towards the license plate holder with side light; the two exhaust pipes sat below. The grill and headlights were the concluding elements of the central rib of the hood which sported a narrow, rectangular and sporty air intake above. Given the need to open the door by pulling on a cord, one would expect a Spartan interior but the two seats were soft and in fake leather. The steering wheel was a wooden, 3 spoke Nardi and the dashboard had

an anti-reflection cover as protection against the sunlight. The instrument panel had three circular dials, one large central speedometer and two smaller dials for the rev counter and fuel and oil indicators. On the road the B24 was impressive. Even the British press - which liked to remind everyone that the sports car was a British invention and was therefore critical of foreign competition - was enthusiastic about the brilliant performance and temperament of the 2.5 liter, 118 HP motor and the enjoyable ride compared

to the other Aurelias provided by the independent rear wheel suspension. Production of the B24 began and ended in 1955: 240 were made including the 1954 prototype, 59 with right hand drive and 180 with left hand drive (the latter distinguished by the letter "S" which many thought meant "sports"). Between 1956-58 it was the turn of the convertible (of which 521 were produced) that was aimed even more at the American market. It differed from the sports version by its single piece bumpers, the appearance of door handles, vent windows and main windows that opened, a less rounded windshield, a larger air intake on the hood and a two dial instrument panel. Sales of the B24 could have been higher but Lancias were mainly handmade, the body panels were hand-beaten for instance, and the company could not keep pace with the number of orders which arrived mainly from the US.

The looks of the convertible were mostly the

Trintignant is imprisoned in the car. In the film, the car that crashed was not actually a B24 but a disguised Fiat. During shooting 2 B24's were used; one crashed so another had to be found to finish the film, not an easy task when they had been out of production for 4 years. When a replacement was eventually found, it was a different color from the first - light blue rather than light green - but because the film was in black and white, nobody noticed.

same as those of the sports car but it was a little more respectable and had lost some of the America's personality.

The B24 was also made famous by the cinema as was to happen to the Alfa Romeo Duetto years later; the B24 was used in the film called "Overtaking" (Il Sorpasso) by Dino Risi starring Vittorio Gassman and Jean Louis Trintignant. In the final scene Gassman travels with Trintignant at top speed along the Italian coast road suitably called the "Aurelia"; during the last overtaking maneuver the car goes off the road and over a drop. Gassman manages to escape but

TECHNICAL DESCRIPTION OF THE LANCIA AURELIA B24 SPIDER AMERICA

YEARS OF PRODUCTION	1955	WHEELBASE (INCHES)	98
CHASSIS	STAMPED STEEL SHEETS WELDED TO THE BODY	ENGINE	FRONT LONGITUDINAL, 60° V6
SUSPENSION	FRONT: INDEPENDENT WHEELS WITH CYLINDRICAL SPIRAL SPRING AND ADJUSTABLE INTERNAL HYDRAULIC SHOCK ABSORBERS; REAR: SEMI-INDEPENDENT WHEELS, RIGID AXLE WITH SEMI-ELLIPTICAL LEAF SPRINGS; TELESCOPIC HYDRAULIC SHOCK ABSORBERS	BORE AND STROKE (MM)	78 X 85.5
		DISPLACEMENT	2451 CC
		HORSEPOWER	118 AT 5300 RPM
		MAX. TORQUE (KGM)	18.5 AT 3000-4000 RPM
		TIMING SYSTEM	CAMSHAFTS IN THE BLOCK, HEMISPHERICAL FIRING CHAMBERS
		FUEL SUPPLY	TWIN CARBURETOR
		CLUTCH	DRY SINGLE-PLATE
WHEELS & TIRES	DISK WHEELS, 165 X 400 TIRES	GEARBOX	4 SPEED + REVERSE; CENTRAL GEARSHIFT
STEERING	WORM AND ROLLER		
FRONT TRACK (INCHES)	50	DRIVE	REAR
REAR TRACK (INCHES)	51	MAX. SPEED (MPH)	112

Porsche 356 speedster

Born in a timber-mill,
the sporting descendant of the Beetle

Large round dreaming eyes that look up to the sky in a dreamy, innocent gaze; this is the impression given by the headlights of the 356, the first car to bear the Porsche badge. This look was directly inherited from the Volkswagen Beetle which also supplied the 356 with many mechanical parts as well as innovative features like the air-cooled, rear-mounted boxer engine with four cylinders. The same look returned on the 356's descendant, the 911, which remained unaltered until 1998, when the two large eyes gave way to four small headlights grouped with the indicators under a shell-shaped cover.

The 356 was dreamt up in prison and realized in a timber-mill. In 1946 the Austrian designer, Ferdinand Porsche - creator of the Volkswagen Type 60, better known as the Beetle, and the beautiful Mercedes SSK among other things - was working off a prison sentence for his war-time collaboration with the German Reich. He was sentenced to 22 months in a French prison which aggravated his poor health.

In the meantime in Austria, his son Ferry re-established the family business with a few partners in an old timber-mill converted into a design studio and managed to scrape together the one million French francs necessary to pay his father's bail. Once back in Austria, Porsche Sr. went straight back to work with his son and together they began to build the 356 using parts from a Beetle. Two prototypes were built in 1948: the first was a mid-engined sports model with roadster-type body, tubular chassis

and rear wheel drive; the second was more functional and less costly as it cannibalized mechanical parts from Volkswagen production (steering, brakes, wheels, suspension). Its body could be either coupé or cabriolet, the reinforced chassis was made with stamped steel sheets welded to the body and both drive and engine were located at the rear. Final choice fell on the second prototype. That was the start of the 356; the first model had an aluminum body and a 1.1 liter boxer engine.

Between 1948 and 1965 Porsche produced 79,366 examples of the 356. There were several series, the "pre-A", "A", "B", "C" and "GS" or "Carrera", closed bodies (coupés) and open bodies (cabriolets, roadsters). All the engines were the 4 cylinder boxer type varying between 1.1 and 2 liters to give from 40 to 130 HP. It is difficult to categorize the 356 series into the best or the most beautiful. Each variant has its own strong points and elegance. The first series represents the origins of the model when production still took place in the timber-mill. The A series brought a series of aesthetic and

mechanical alterations which became the basis for successive development of the model. These alterations were so decisive that the previous series became known as "pre-A". The B and C series were the maximum expression of the 356 encapsulating its maturity and perfection with increased power, new steel bodies, disk brakes and the appearance of the roadster.

The GS Carrera series distinguished themselves for their power and victories on the race track and in long distance road events like the 1954 Carrera Panamericana.

The wins were due to the new double overhead camshaft engines designed for racing but then adapted to the 356 road models.

The most famous version of the 356 was without doubt the Speedster which was produced between 1954-58 in both the pre-A and A series. James Dean bought one of the first series and though he died in a car crash with a Porsche, it was not the 356 as many think, but rather a 550 sports racing model that he was testing.

The Speedster was designed for the American market. Porsche's American importer, Max Hoffman, asked the company for a cheaper, lighter and more Spartan model to compete with the English sports cars: The result was a car lightened by 198 lbs. The Speedster differs from the cabriolet by its lower and more wrap-around windshield, its simpler range of accessories, the reclinable and removable windows and the smaller, unpadded top. The Americans went wild for this version of the 356.

The overall lines of the car remained more or less unchanged, exceptionally aerodynamic. The rounded body, which today seems the prerogative of Japanese designs, was the leit motif of the 356. The sides were convex and free of molding, interrupted only by the door handles. The 16" wheels matched the color of the car body in the pre-A series but were 15" and colored metallic silver in the A.

The front of the car did not have to accommodate the engine or its air intakes. Instead there were two small intakes for the horn inside the small lights which, together with the bumper guards requested by American dealers, bring life to the front view of the car. The Porsche name sat between the front lights and the U shape of the hood resembled a nose between two eyes. The split windshield was joined by a chrome rim in the first series and the wipers were placed symmetrically at either end. The A series changed this layout to a one-piece curved windshield with wipers in the traditional position close together. The motor's modest cooling intake was positioned high on the rear of the car; there were four round lights and two small rectangular reflectors.

The cab was very basic: the dashboard in the first series had two large dials and a third smaller one and the steering wheel had three spokes.

The A series had a newly designed dashboard with three round indicators and padding for safety. The two spoke steering wheel had a white grip and the ignition key and starting lever had become a single control.

In 1957 the 356A Speedster benefited from other changes. The circular rear lights became drop-shaped and the front lights gained a chrome rim. The two exhausts were integrated into the bumper guards; the license plate light was moved from above to below; the rear window was made larger and a hard top (removable) was made available. The door handles took on a new shape and the door lock hooks were also modified; vent windows appeared and the name Porsche was added to the hubcaps. In the cab the speedometer was moved from the left to the right and was replaced by the indicators showing panel lights, fuel level and oil temperature. The ashtray was moved under the dashboard, the gearshift was moved slightly back and gearshift travel was shortened. The Speedster was available with a choice of engines: the 44 HP 1300 was the smallest (60 HP in the S version); then there was the 55 HP 1500 (75 HP in the S); from 1956 the new 60 HP 1600 (75 HP in the S) replaced the 1500; at the top of the range came the new twin camshaft 1600 in 1958 which was a motor derived from racing and which became the origin of the GS Carrera versions.

The next series of the 356, the B, was built from 1959-63 while the C was produced between 1963-65. Both continued the trend of improvement begun with the A: there were new chassis and in 1961 the 130 HP 2 liter Carrera engine arrived. Production of the Speedster ended with the A Series 356 in 1958. In 1965

the entire cycle of the 356 came to an end to make way for the 911 which had appeared two years earlier. Ferdinand Porsche died in 1951 and could not enjoy the success of the 356 as had already happened to the Beetle. At the end of the war a commission of experts was formed by the Allies to evaluate the possibility of producing the Beetle in their own factories. Their judgement? The Beetle was a lemon! But that is another story....

TECHNICAL DESCRIPTION OF THE PORSCHE SPEEDSTER

YEARS OF PRODUCTION	1954-58
VERSIONS	1300/1300S/1500/1500S/1600/1600S/1600GS
CHASSIS	STEEL STAMPED PLATE WELDED TO THE BODYWORK
SUSPENSION	FRONT: INDEPENDENT WHEELS, DOUBLE TRAILING ARMS, SQUARE SECTION TORSION BARS, STABILIZER BAR; REAR: INDEPENDENT WHEELS, OSCILLATING AXLE SHAFTS, ROUND SECTION TORSION BARS; TELESCOPIC HYDRAULIC SHOCK ABSORBERS
WHEELS & TIRES	WHEELS IN STAMPED PLATE, 5.60-15 TIRES
STEERING	WORM AND ROLLER
FRONT TRACK (INCHES)	51
REAR TRACK (INCHES)	49
WHEELBASE (INCHES)	82
ENGINE	REAR-MOUNTED, FOUR OPPOSED CYLINDERS, AIR COOLED
BORE AND STROKE (MM)	74.5 X 74 (1300/1300S); 80 X 74 (1500/1500S); 82.5 X 74 (1600/1600S); 87.5 X 66 (1600GS)

PISTON DISPLACEMENT (CC)	1289 (1300/1300S); 1488 (1500/1500S); 1582 (1600/1600S); 1588 (1600 GS)
HORSEPOWER	44 AT 4400 RPM (1300); 60 AT 5500 RPM (1300S); 55 AT 4400 RPM (1500); 70 AT 5000 RPM (1500S); 60 AT 4400 RPM (1600); 75 AT 5000 RPM (1600S); 115 AT 6500 RPM (1600GS)
MAX. TORQUE (KGM)	8.3 AT 2500 RPM (1300); 9 AT 3600 RPM (1300S); 10.8 AT 2800 RPM (1500); 11 AT 3600 RPM (1500S); 11.2 AT 2800 RPM (1600); 11.9 AT 3700 RPM (1600S); 12.8 AT 5500 RPM (1600GS)
TIMING SYSTEM	2 OVERHEAD VALVES, PUSHROD OPERATED FROM A CENTRAL CAMSHAFT (1300/1300S/1500/1500S/1600/1600S); TWIN OVERHEAD CAMSHAFTS PER CYLINDER BANK (1600 GS)
FUEL SUPPLY	2 TWIN CARBURETORS
CLUTCH	DRY SINGLE-PLATE
GEARBOX	4 SPEED + REVERSE; CENTRAL GEARSHIFT
DRIVE	REAR
MAX. SPEED (MPH)	FROM 91 TO 106

MERCEDES 300 SL ROADSTER

IT LOST ITS WINGS BUT FLEW IN AMERICA

The Mercedes 300 SL's lineage was illustrious but its existence was owed to one man, Max Hoffman, the American importer of many European marques, one of which was Mercedes. The 300 SL roadster was the open-topped version of the celebrated Gullwing coupé where the doors opened vertically like the wings of the bird. Mass production of the 300 SL only got off the ground when Max Hoffman flew to Stuttgart to sign a purchase contract for 1,000 examples of the car. Mercedes management would otherwise never have produced a road version of the 300 SL.

Hoffman's was a very courageous move that has ensured him a place of honor in automobile history. However, Hoffman was not new to introducing sports cars to the US; he was responsible for the debut in the American market of, among others, the Porsche 356 Speedster, the Alfa Romeo Giulietta Spider and the BMW 507, often fitted out especially to suit American requirements.

The Mercedes management had not considered a road version of the 300 SL because the purpose of its creation had already been served: to show the world that Mercedes had returned to the pinnacle of racing after the disaster of the Second World War. When the war ended, Mercedes' star had ceased to shine. Most of their factories had been destroyed except the Mannheim plant, and this was being used by the Allies to repair their own vehicles. But once Mercedes had obtained the necessary permits, they restarted production with a prewar model, the Type 170.

In 1951, two events changed the course of the company's history: production of the new 220, 300 and 300 S models, and the granting of permission to return to racing. Mercedes first used the 300 S with its reliable but not brilliant 3 liter, 6 cylinder motor but the body had to be redesigned as it was too heavy to compete against the likes of Jaguar and Ferrari.

The Mercedes technicians worked to produce a new chassis and the result was a trestle structure in thin steel tubes having an overall weight of just 154 lbs. Adequate resistance to flexional and torsional stress meant that the sides of the trestle

had to be high, which in turn affected the space available for the doors. It was this fact that determined the characteristic feature of the car: instead of standard doors with hinges at the side, the car was fitted with doors with hinges at the top so that they opened vertically. The bodywork was made from aluminum and the engine was inclined at 50°.

The racing version of the 300 Sport Leicht ("light" in German) was ready. It was 1952 and victory after victory fell to the new model, including the Carrera Panamericana which served as the 300 SL's presentation to America. A year later, Mercedes management decided to retire the 300 SL as they were thinking of moving into Formula 1, but they had not estimated the enthusiasm the American public had had for the car at the Carrera Panamericana.

It was so great that many had requested a road version and Hoffman understood the market so well that he felt sure of underwriting his large purchase order.

This was the story behind construction of the road version of the 300 SL. The 3 liter, 6 cylinder engine remained unchanged, a tubular chassis was used instead of the trestle model despite its extra weight as it gave more comfort and, above all, the original body design had to stay. But of course, it all had to be elegant and exclusive in keeping with Mercedes' style. The roadgoing Gullwing made its debut in 1954. Its price was decidedly high at 29,000 German marks - more than a 12 cylinder Ferrari - but less than the 1957 SL roadster that replaced it. The 300 SL remained in production until 1963.

The roadster was designed for comfort with particular attention to the accessories the American market was accustomed to. The lines were sleeker than the coupé's aided by the absence of a fixed top and 2 inches added to the length of the tail.

There were few other differences from the Gullwing. The front had rectangular sets of lights with integrated indicators and fog lights instead of the original round lights with separate indicators. The grill was still rectangular but had rounded corners and a chrome three pointed star as large as could fit in the center; bumpers were available on request. The nose had a sporting air: The moderately long curved hood started from the top of the pronounced bumpers. It had two ribs which ended at the chrome rimmed windshield. A hard top was also available with a wide rear window.

The design of the sides was lovely: two protruding panel strips each functioned as a wheelhouse; a pronounced diamond-shaped air intake which cooled both the engine and the cab was positioned between the front fender and door; and two chrome strips followed the flare of the wheelhouse making the side view of the car even slimmer.

Not having a fixed roof, the doors had to open in the traditional manner but this was certainly more comfortable for the user.

The lengthening of the tapered rear end gave the rear and front volumes similar dimensions. The luggage compartment housed the spare wheel and fuel tank. A set of suitcases especially made for the 300 SL was also available. If mounted, the bumpers and their huge guards

caught the eye. The rear lights were like tight smiles which stretched round to the sides. The cab was a declaration of conservative elegance and luxury. The system to fold the steering wheel was innovative - the crown of the wheel could be twisted horizontal to facilitate getting in and out.

The roadster's instrument panel was slightly different to that of the coupé: between the rev counter and speedometer (which read up to 170 mph), there was a rectangular display for the water and oil temperatures, oil pressure and fuel level as well as a series of panel lights. The leather seats were well shaped. To increase comfort further, the roadster had a horizontal spring which compensated the rear suspension. The result was a smooth and comfortable ride. The 300 SL's performance was outstanding: 135 mph top speed which could be increased to 156 mph if the rear axle ratios were changed - almost a matter of pride to a car which started life as a racer and ended its cycle as an elegant open top for wealthy American customers.

TECHNICAL DESCRIPTION OF THE MERCEDES 300 SL ROADSTER

YEARS OF PRODUCTION	1957-1963	REAR TRACK (INCHES)	56
CHASSIS	PARALLEL TUBES WITH SUPPORTING TRESTLE DESIGN	WHEELBASE (INCHES)	94
SUSPENSION	FRONT: INDEPENDENT WHEELS, TRIANGULAR TRANSVERSAL	ENGINE	FRONT LONGITUDINAL MOUNTED AT 50°, SIX CYLINDERS, IN-LINE
	WISHBONES, SPIRAL SPRINGS WITH RUBBER COMPONENTS, TRANSVERSAL	BORE AND STROKE (MM)	85 X 88
	ANTI-ROLL BAR; REAR: INDEPENDENT	DISPLACEMENT	2996 CC
	WHEELS, FLOATING AXLE SHAFT WITH	HORSEPOWER	215 AT 5800 RPM
	CENTRAL SINGLE JOINT	MAX. TORQUE (KGM)	28 AT 4600 RPM
	ON A LOWERED PIN, SPIRAL SIDE SPRINGS PLUS TRANSVERSAL CENTRAL	TIMING SYSTEM	TWIN OVERHEAD VALVES PER CYLINDER, 1 OVERHEAD CAM
	COMPENSATION SPRING; HYDRAULIC	FUEL SUPPLY	DIRECT INJECTION
	TELESCOPIC SHOCK ABSORBERS	GEARBOX	MANUAL, 4 SPEED + REVERSE; CENTRAL GEARSHIFT
WHEELS & TIRES	15" STEEL WHEELS, 6.70 X 15 TIRES		
STEERING	CONTINUOUS BALL-TYPE	DRIVE	REAR
FRONT TRACK (INCHES)	54	MAX. SPEED (MPH)	134-156

CADILLAC ELDORADO BIARRITZ 1960

EXCESS AND REDRESS

The name Eldorado comes from the Spanish "el Dorado", the golden land, which was what the Spanish conquistadors called the legendary area supposedly situated somewhere between the Amazon and the Orinoco rivers where gold simply lay underfoot for the taking. But this opulent Cadillac is golden, too. It was made in a limited series in 1953 at the end of the Korean War purportedly as a technology showpiece for General Motors, although its actual function was to bring attention to Cadillac's less expensive models. Like a shapely, attractive dancer who stands at the door of the nightclub inviting the public to enter, the Eldorado stood in the window of the Cadillac showrooms exercising the same function. The hope was of course that they would be tempted into the showroom to admire the Eldorado and end up buying one of the cheaper Cadillacs.

Many in the public had already seen the Eldorado when president-elect Dwight Eisenhower traveled in it to his swearing-in ceremony. The Eldorado went to a few, wealthy customers. The price was very high, double that of a Series 62 sedan and five times that of a Chevrolet coupé. The finishings were of course magnificent: luxury, elegance and extravagance defined the style of the American car during the 1950's. The shapes were excessive, the lines tense, angles acute, edges aggressive and the

rear fins were extreme for their day. There were also bumper bullets, high bumper guards and chrome trimmings.

The 1953 Eldorado was the American luxury manufacturer's top model, and the Eldo was to remain a "special" Cadillac of one sort or another over the following years. The Eldorado's role was to change with the fashions of the time; the target and mechanical underpinnings of the car would be altered but the name always remained, like the Thunderbird and Mustang. The first Eldorado was based on the Series 62 convertible. The intention was to give the new car a sporty look, so GM lowered the windshield and wrapped it around, a modification later extended to all Cadillacs and soon common on American cars of all kinds for years to come. The doors were reduced in height so as to lower the waistline and make the car appear more slender.

When the top was down it disappeared, laying inside the body covered by a metal panel on the same level as the trunk. The cab was completely lined with leather, including the dashboard, and the quantity of accessories provided would make cars fifty years on envious: electrically controlled seats, windows and antenna, radio, hydraulically operated roof, power braking and steering and automatic transmission. All Eldorados shared these luxuries, and naturally a V8 engine.

The model was subject to continuous variation during the years 1953-60, but always on the basis of existing Cadillac platforms. It wasn't until 1967 that a truly radical Eldorado appeared, a fabulous front-wheel-drive GT based on the chassis of the 1966 Olds Toronado. Every year the admiral of the Cadillac fleet benefited from improvements to the bodywork, the mechanicals and the interior fittings. The

lines became slimmer, the fins were lengthened and shortened again at an extraordinary rate, the grill, air intakes and bumpers were all altered, and the engine was made more powerful. In the 1950's, it was almost as though Eldorado designers wanted to confuse the public and hide the fact that the car differed less and less from the Series 62 it was based on. The result was that sales peaked in 1955, and then started to decline with the introduction of the Biarritz variation of the convertible and the Seville variation of the coupé in 1956. Attempts at buoying sales in 1958-59 were unsuccessful. From 1958 a system of air springs was introduced as an optional extra that maintained the car's height from the ground regardless of the load. This was a sophisticated system but did not find many buyers.

The 1959 version of the Biarritz differed from

TECHNICAL DESCRIPTION OF THE CADILLAC ELDORADO BIARRITZ 1960

YEARS OF PRODUCTION	1960	BORE AND STROKE (MM)	101.6 X 98.4
CHASSIS	UNITIZED BODY	DISPLACEMENT	6382 CC
SUSPENSION	FRONT: INDEPENDENT WHEELS, WITH DEFORMABLE TRANSVERSAL A-ARM, SPIRAL SPRINGS; REAR: RIGID AXLE AND LONGITUDINAL LEAF SPRINGS; TELESCOPIC HYDRAULIC SHOCK ABSORBERS, AIR SPRINGS ON REQUEST	HORSEPOWER	325 HP AT 4800 RPM
		MAX. TORQUE (KGM)	59.5 AT 3100 RPM
		TIMING SYSTEM	2 VALVES PER CYLINDER, 1 CENTRAL CAMSHAFT
		FUEL SUPPLY	FOUR-BARREL, DOWN-DRAFT CARBURETOR
WHEELS & TIRES	STEEL WHEELS; 8 X 15 TIRES	GEARBOX	AUTOMATIC HYDRAMATIC, 3 SPEED + REVERSE, GEARSHIFT ON THE STEERING COLUMN
STEERING	CONTINUOUS BALL-TYPE WITH SERVO-ASSIST		
WHEELBASE (INCHES)	128	DRIVE	REAR
ENGINE	FRONT LONGITUDINAL, 90° V8	MAX. SPEED (MPH)	110

previous Eldorados even more. Radical changes were made to the engineering and the bodywork: the engine was increased in size to 6.4 liters producing 325 HP, and the automatic transmission and chassis were altered. The car became lower, wider and longer (18'3"), the windshield got larger, wrapped around more and was fitted with vent windows. The taller and sharper fins now started from the cab and reached all the way to the rear end where they supported rocket-shaped tail lights. The lines of the 1959 Eldorado were sensational and excessive, the front end covered in a chromium concert of headlights, glittering eggcrate grill, and enormous bumpers integrating the supplementary lights and the license plate. The sides of the car ran smoothly (and seemingly unendingly) to the rear, incorporating an extraordinary piece of chromework that started at the front fender and reached uninterrupted to the back. The length of this spear - close on 16 feet - should be eligible for a Guinness record. At the tail, an exaggerated, imposing set of huge vertical fins capped off the opulence.

The interior was equally extravagant. An expanse of color-matched leather covered the plush, comfortable seats. The dash contained a rectangular frame for the main indicators which was flanked by two round, protruding dials and heating controls under the steering wheel.

In the topline Biarritz comfort was extreme, and the performance - notwithstanding the massive weight - was impressive, reaching a maximum speed of 110 mph.

But the 1959 Eldorado would truly be the zenith of the old Cadillac; the kind designed strictly as an unselfconscious, high-visibility paean to glitter and opulence.

The 1959 model represented the very pinnacle of 1950's excess, a concept largely driven by GM design boss Harley Earl. But a new head of design came to GM in late 1958, William L. Mitchell, and Mitchell had other ideas. He was too late to affect the 1959 Cadillac, and too late to have a major impact on the 1960 model. However, Mitchell did intend to create a new, cleaner, more sophisticated aesthetic, and one of the first results was a 1960 Cadillac line shorn of much of its gaudiness. The giant chrome swaths of '59 gave way to dignified spears, while the towering fins became tapered and more airy. It took the all-new 1961 Cadillac to truly establish this look, but the 1960 model may be even more interesting as a fascinating transition point between the old and new. Above the bulbous, overblown body of the Earl years, in the 1960 Cadillacs Mitchell laid the foundations of a brilliant new American style.

CITROËN DS 21 CABRIOLET
THE REVOLUTIONARY "SHARK"

André Citroën, founder of the company of that name, never saw it but would certainly have been proud and a little surprised to discover how much the substitute for the revolutionary Traction Avant, which appeared twenty years before, was to be just as innovative. It was 1955, twenty years since Citroën's death and the best tribute to his memory was perhaps the unveiling of the DS (Désirée Spéciale, which in French is pronounced "déesse", meaning goddess) at the Paris Motor Show. On that day, 6 October, many car experts and enthusiasts recognized that they were present at an important moment in the history of the car. The sculptor Flaminio Bertoni had designed a body in a completely original, futuristic shape. The body was self-bearing in separate elements. The integral streamlining and absence of a radiator grill fixed new standards in design and aerodynamics.

From a mechanical point of view, the revolution was in the constant height hydro-pneumatic suspension with trim adjustment on four independent wheels which gave it a quality of roadholding and drive comfort till then unknown. A control on the dashboard governed the height off the ground of the car - low in

normal drive conditions, high for uneven surfaces and very high for changing a tire. The old car jack was therefore redundant and was substituted by a safety stand on which the car was placed.

Other innovations were the automatic clutch and gearbox, the hydraulically assisted braking system and, for the first time on a mass produced car, front disk brakes.

Five years later in 1960, on the threshold of an economic boom, the scene was repeated. The Paris Motor Show was the setting for the debut of the convertible version of the Citroën DS 19. The absence of a hard top made the lines of the car even sleeker so that it resembled a motorboat; it was truly a car capable of offering competition to the large American convertibles.

Despite the sedan version's revolutionary design, the DS 19 cabriolet displayed a personality that was even stronger than that of the hard top, maybe too strong. It aroused contrasting feelings: either it was loved completely or it was scorned. Its unusual shape earned it the nicknames "shark" and "iron": an extremely long curved hood which ended at

the bumper, a high waistline, slightly curved sides and free of any chrome or molding. The tucked in rear was almost half the length of the front and tapered right down to nothing. The DS cabriolet was the work of French coachbuilder Henry Chapron, who had already presented a prototype of the DS called "La Croisette" as early as the 1958 Paris Motor Show. The public acclaimed the prototype immediately and Chapron asked Citroën to provide him with some chassis but the company did not wish to collaborate. Chapron however did not give in: he bought 25 new sedans from dealers and turned them into 25 convertibles intending to convince Citroën to design a chassis with reinforced side struts which would get around the lack of a roof panel. Production of the car was then entrusted to Chapron and the DS 19 appeared to the public in 1960.

The first version differed from the following series by the position of the chrome-rimmed air intakes inside the front fenders, by the lack of fairing on the front sets of lights (this appeared in 1965 together with the directional headlights controlled by the steering) and by the wheels attached to the axle by a single central bolt. All DS models had in common the single spoke steering wheel, the internal rear view mirror, the gearshift sited on the steering column and the extremely comfortable padded seats. The 1960

engine was derived from the Traction Avant: it was a 4 cylinder, 2 liter motor capable of 75 HP and 88 mph. The 1960 DS had a lesser powered (66 HP) and less well-finished model, the "ID", as a stablemate. The DS was updated in 1962 with an 82 HP engine, integral fairing around the lower part of the front of the car, rubber bumper guards and modifications to the dash. In 1965 the engine received another dose of power taking it to 90 HP and 106 mph, but then the 19 series was replaced by the 21 in which another engine was made available, the 2.1 liter, 109 HP motor capable of 116 mph. Some modifications were made to the car's appearance and cab in 1967; for example, headrests were introduced, and in 1969 the instrument panel was altered to contain three circular indicators. The last retouches were made in 1970 when fuel injection was made available.

Production of the DS cabriolet ended in 1971 but Chapron continued to assemble them until 1974 with Citroën's permission, producing very rare examples of the DS 23 (141 HP, fuel injection, 122 mph), the most powerful series of the DS cabriolet.

Overall production of the convertible was only 1,325 units, a limited volume determined by its higher price than that of the sedan. This of course now makes it a very sought after and exclusive model.

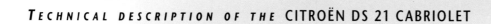

TECHNICAL DESCRIPTION OF THE CITROËN DS 21 CABRIOLET

YEARS OF PRODUCTION	1965-71		DISPLACEMENT	2175 CC
CHASSIS	UNITIZED BODY		HORSEPOWER	109 AT 5500 RPM
SUSPENSION	ALL INDEPENDENT, HYDRO-PNEUMATIC WITH SHOCK ABSORBERS, STABILIZING BAR AND TRIM CORRECTOR		MAX. TORQUE (KGM)	17.7 AT 2500 RPM
			TIMING SYSTEM	TWO OVERHEAD VALVES PER CYLINDER, CAMSHAFT IN BLOCK
WHEELS & TIRES	185-15		FUEL SUPPLY	TWIN CARBURETOR
STEERING	SERVO ASSISTED RACK AND PINION		CLUTCH	DRY SINGLE-PLATE WITH AUTOMATIC HYDRAULIC CONTROL
FRONT TRACK (INCHES)	59			
REAR TRACK (INCHES)	51		GEARBOX	4 SPEED + REVERSE; STEERING COLUMN GEARSHIFT
WHEELBASE (INCHES)	122			
ENGINE	FRONT, FOUR CYLINDERS, IN-LINE		DRIVE	FRONT
BORE AND STROKE (MM)	78 X 100		MAX. SPEED (MPH)	116

FERRARI 250 GT SPYDER CALIFORNIA SHORT WHEELBASE

A CHROMED BEAUTY

Only 106 examples were made of this splendid convertible, or "Spyder" as it was officially called at its presentation in December 1957. Like in a film, the cast of the blockbuster "Ferrari 250 GT California Spyder", produced by Ferrari Automobili of Modena, turned again to a design by Pininfarina, a body by master coachbuilders Carrozzeria Scaglietti of Modena, wheels by Borrani and steering wheel by Nardi. The final result, the "film" itself, made of metal plate, chrome, cylinders and horsepower, immediately became a cult object. Highly sought after and highly valued, it commanded huge prices among collectors - preferably the Spyder rather than the Cabriolet and preferably the short wheelbase version than the long. The success of the California was not only posthumous, as happens to many cars. Famous people queued up for one, for example, the last long wheelbase version went to Pininfarina himself; a short wheelbase version with a racing engine was sold to the French film director Roger Vadim who gave it to Brigitte Bardot; another belonged to Vittorio Emanuele, member of the Italian royal family, but it was destroyed in a crash; the American actor James Coburn had another. The last California, produced in February 1963, was delivered to Luigi Chinetti, Ferrari's American importer. Many buyers wanted it customized. The sixth short wheelbase California made had its bodywork made completely from aluminum to take part in the Le Mans 24 hour race. Another Spyder had a special console on the transmission while a Swiss customer asked for the side air intakes to be removed and for the instrumentation to be placed directly in front of the driver.

As suggested by the name, the Spyder California was designed for the American market which was always the most receptive and appreciative for the company from Modena. At the beginning of the 1960's, Ferrari had barely been in business for ten years - enough, though, to create a legend. The story started with Enzo Ferrari, ex-Alfa Romeo driver, and Ferrari's history of successes on the Formula 1 race track. As early as the 1951 British Grand Prix, a Ferrari came home ahead of the previously unbeatable Alfa Romeos which had won the World Championship the previous year and were to win again that year. Ferrari then won the Championship in 1952 and '53 and came second in 1954 behind the Mercedes driven by Manuel Fangio. Production of road models followed, a beautiful mix of elegance and sportiness, which borrowed from the experience gained on the race track and that were "dressed" in the outfits of the finest designer, "Pinin" Farina. The Spyder first appeared in December 1957

together with the 250 Cabriolet Pinin Farina. The similarities between the two are numerous but the success of the Spyder brought production of the cabriolet to a halt just a year later.

The first Spyders had a wheelbase of 8'5" which was shortened to 7'10" in 1960. There were few differences between the two but most importantly the short wheelbase version weighed less, had a wider track, a lower trim and an air intake on the hood.

It was not the distance between the axles though that was responsible for the attraction of the California. The car's beauty was tangible in a series of exterior and interior details, for example, slightly convex sides, the wide tires, the lowered trim and the top which disappeared behind the seats so making the body even sleeker. The car also had almost an obsessive presence of chrome right from the tip of the decidedly aggressive nose, which makes no attempt to hide the intentions of the 200 HP

developed by its 12 cylinder engine. All the following were chromed or polished metal: the square shark's mouth grill and the rearing horse in the center, the rim of the grill and the supplementary headlights (the pre-series examples did not have them), the one-piece bumper and bumper guards, the rim of the round headlights burrowed into the hood (protected by a plexiglas cover which dictated the curvature of the sides) and the rim of the fairly upright windshield. Chromed also were the door handles and the air intake housed between the front fender and the door, these being the only details to "disturb" the car's muscular flanks. Then there were the chromed aluminum crossed spoke wheels with fluting and wing nut on the hub cap, four works of art by Borrani; the rims around the small square reflectors and the tall, narrow rear lights; and the last part of the fins that started at the cab which, together with the curved trunk, make the back end higher than

the front. Finally, the ends of the two pairs of round exhaust pipes and the trunk handle were also chromed. The cab was the opposite of the Spartan and uncomfortable interiors of English sports cars. It was filled with leather, wood and chrome (!) and had a level of finishing that touched on perfection. The comfortable leather seats were padded and were deeply sculpted to hold the body in place; inclination of the seatback was adjusted by two bolts.

The dashboard was an absolute novelty: only the rev counter and the speedometer were in front of the driver, the other instruments being located in the center of the dash. This type of display was to characterize thoroughbred sports cars in the years to come. The two principal dials were fitted with a chrome rim and anti-reflection peak and both had a two-tone background: the central part was white while the differently sized white numbers were set on a black background. The dial hands were red and the speedometer

read up to 190 mph! The steering wheel was designed and manufactured by Nardi. It had a wooden grip, three chromed spokes and the yellow Ferrari shield with black horse in the center. That is all the driver of a California needed to control the 220-240 HP V12 capable of giving him a maximum speed of 155 mph. The other instruments were on the central console below the rearview mirror, all with chrome rims of course: oil temperature and pressure, water, fuel and a clock. Below those was a set of black buttons which were difficult to identify as they were similar to the black leather background of the console. They controlled the windshield wipers, the internal and external lights, the horn switch (one for the city and the other, more powerful, for high speeds), adjustment of the clock and the auxiliary electric fuel pump. This mechanical pump was a back-up for the two pumps on the motor and was designed to help the carburetors on cold starts.

TECHNICAL DESCRIPTION OF THE FERRARI 250 GT SPYDER CALIFORNIA SHORT WHEELBASE

YEARS OF PRODUCTION	1960-1962	WHEELS & TIRES	16" SPOKED WHEELS; 6.00-16 TIRES	HORSEPOWER	220-240 HP AT 7000 RPM
CHASSIS	ONE PIECE MADE FROM ELLIPTICAL STEEL TUBES	STEERING	WORM WHEEL AND HELICAL GEAR	TIMING SYSTEM	2 VALVES PER CYLINDER, SINGLE OVERHEAD CAMSHAFT
SUSPENSION	FRONT: INDEPENDENT WHEELS, DEFORMABLE WISHBONES, SPIRAL SPRINGS; REAR: RIGID AXLE AND SEMI-ELLIPTICAL LEAF SPRINGS; HYDRAULIC SHOCK ABSORBERS	FRONT TRACK (INCHES)	54	FUEL SUPPLY	THREE CARBURETORS
		REAR TRACK (INCHES)	53	GEARBOX	MANUAL, 4 SPEED + REVERSE, CENTRAL GEARSHIFT
		WHEELBASE (INCHES)	94	DRIVE	REAR
		ENGINE	FRONT LONGITUDINAL, 60° V12	MAX. SPEED (MPH)	155
		BORE AND STROKE (MM)	73 X 58.8		
		DISPLACEMENT	2953 CC		

Jaguar E-type 3.8 1961
Queen of England

Spring 1961 had almost arrived but the nights were still cold and damp. It was March and, as happens every year, the Geneva Motor Show was to be held, an important international shop window for the automobile industry.

Opening day was to be Wednesday, 15th March but a new car had only started its journey the night before. It came from the Jaguar factory in Browns Lane, Coventry in Great Britain. It took the Dover-Calais ferry at midnight and crossed France quickly through the dark and foggy night. The driver of the sports car with the long nose and flying saucer tail was Jaguar's Assistant Advertising Manager, Bob Berry. It was a race against time. A delay in the supply of some parts meant the car had not been able to leave until the last moment. This missile on wheels had an appointment with history in the Parc des Eaux Vives at midday. It arrived bang on with just enough time for a rub down: the body, wet from the damp night air, like a sweating horse after a brisk gallop, had to be shined to meet the public.

The efforts of the six cylinder engine and its driver were not in vain; public gratitude for the car lasted fourteen years, their love for it always. The E-type, or "XKE" as it was first called as a continuation of the dynasty of Jaguar sports cars that started with the 1948 XK 120, entered straight into the Olympus of automobile sensations as the maximum stylistic expression of the English marque. It had an absolutely innovative and original line and incorporated the valuable experience garnered from racing the C-type and D-type models.

The road going E-type benefited from many racing technical developments: the double camshaft, six cylinders in-line 3.8 engine which produced 265 HP, the three carburetor fuel supply, the tubular chassis with unitized body, disk brakes, the self-locking differential and the geometry of the rear suspension. And naturally performance was exalting, equivalent to the Jaguars that had won the Le Mans 24 hour race in 1951, '53 and '55-'57. The E-type ran like the wind and indeed seemed sculpted by the wind. The design of the new Jaguar was the work of Malcolm Sayer, the aeronautic engineer who had already designed the C-type, D-type and XJ13. Sir William Lloyd had asked for a model to replace the glorious XK series which had been on the market for nine years. The originality of the E-type's body design was more the result of research into aerodynamic efficiency than a new stylistic theme. The coupé version made its appearance at the same time as the roadster; with the top up or with the hard top version, the cab set back on the body looked like the turret on a submarine. It was obviously impossible for the driver to have a clear view of the long length of the hood which seemed to hide at least 8 cylinders; the power underneath was obvious. The nose was an example of rare power without the adoption of any particular aesthetic characteristics. The most important feature was the hood which everybody wanted to look beneath: when lifted, it also raised the fenders leaving the mechanical parts and even the tire tread in sight. The central swelling ensured the three carburetors plenty of air. Two side air intakes near the windshield (with its three wipers) helped keep the engine cool. Set further back than the grill, the lights were housed in the curved fenders and protected by Plexiglas. The grill looked just like a mouth despite having no rim or chromework; in fact the only chrome to be found was the part that cut the grill horizontally in two, joining the two parts of the bumper, and which held the Jaguar badge.

It is not clear which was more responsible for the extraordinary beauty of the sides - their subtle forms or their extremely clean extension. The door handles and chrome external mirror almost seemed to get in the way of the continuation of the car's side profile and functionality was the only justification for their presence. The balanced shape of the sides that ended in a point at each end enhanced the classic spoked wheels with their solid wheelnuts on the hub. The back end was a masterpiece of beauty; rarely has a sports car shown so much power and determination in the tail. The finely tapered form left little space for ornamentation which is why the rear lights above the narrow bumper were so slight. Getting into the cab was a real test: the underdoor side-members were 12 inches high so that it was necessary to drop into the seats. Another surprise was that the thinly padded, leather seats could not be reclined or even move forward or backward! This was a serious state of affairs for a driver of average height who was forced to drive with his knees forced upwards and with little lateral space left by the massive transmission tunnel. And if the size of the transmission interfering with posture wasn't enough, the heat it radiated made life even less comfortable. It was just as well that one of the first modifications was to replace the flat transmission panel with a curved one to give a little more space.

The steering wheel and dashboard emphasized the car's sporting temperament. The wheel had a wooden grip and three steel spokes. The dash had two main dials (speedometer, rev counter and clock) in front of the driver, and the other instruments set in the center of the console lined within a sheet of aluminum - these were the water temperature, oil gauge, fuel gauge and ammeter set in circular dials plus the ignition

key, start button and secondary instruments operated by small steel lever switches. The aluminum sheet also covered the transmission tunnel and hand-brake.

The E-type continued throughout the 1960's and halfway through the 1970's. The first modifications, apart from the panel in 1962, were made in 1964 with alterations to the mechanics: the 3.8 engine was replaced by a 4.2, first gear was synchromeshed, the seats received increased padding and the aluminum sheet was replaced by leather.

1967 saw the introduction of the so-called "one and a half" series. The Plexiglas cover over the front headlights disappeared and the elegant steel lever switches on the dash were replaced by anonymous rocker switches.

The second series appeared in 1968: the grill was larger and fitted with a mesh, the rear lights were given a new and unattractive shape and fitted under the bumper to suit American regulations. The third and last series was brought out in 1971. The grill was enlarged again and a new V12, 5.3 engine was installed on a longer chassis.

Sales of the E-type were brought to an end in 1975. The second oil crisis had created serious problems for Jaguar and production was aimed towards the new XJS. There was no longer space for a sports car like the E-type. But it was better that it ended this way - any alterations to this splendid machine to match it to the new and gloomy market conditions could only have reduced its appeal and robbed it of its personality. Better to quit while on top.

YEARS OF PRODUCTION	1961-63	WHEELS & TIRES	15" SPOKED WHEELS, 6.40-15 TIRES	HORSEPOWER	265 AT 5500 RPM	
CHASSIS	TUBULAR FRAME, SEMI-UNITIZED BODY	STEERING	RACK AND PINION	MAX. TORQUE (KGM)	36 AT 4000 RPM	
SUSPENSION	FRONT: INDEPENDENT WHEELS, A-ARMS, TORSION BARS, STABILIZING BAR; REAR: INDEPENDENT WHEELS, TRIANGULAR LOWER WISHBONES, DOUBLE JOINTED OSCILLATING AXLE SHAFTS, DOUBLE SPIRAL SPRINGS; HYDRAULIC TELESCOPIC SHOCK ABSORBERS	FRONT TRACK (INCHES)	49	TIMING SYSTEM	TWO OVERHEAD VALVES PER CYLINDER, DOUBLE OVERHEAD CAMSHAFT	
		REAR TRACK (INCHES)	49	FUEL SUPPLY	THREE HORIZONTAL CARBURETORS	
		WHEELBASE (INCHES)	95	GEARBOX	MANUAL 4-SPEED + REVERSE, CENTRAL GEARSHIFT	
		ENGINE	FRONT LONGITUDINAL, SIX CYLINDERS IN-LINE	DRIVE	REAR	
		BORE AND STROKE (MM)	87 X 106	MAX. SPEED (MPH)	150	
		PISTON DISPLACEMENT	3781 CC			

MGB
"LIMITED" TO 500,000

The atmosphere was full of excitement in England during the early 1960's. The wind of change was blowing strong and customs, clothes and attitudes were all undergoing radical revision. Miniskirts and flashily colored clothes arrived while four boys from Liverpool who called themselves "The Beatles" were doing well. The sounds of their early songs were to be heard everywhere music was played: radios, tape-recorders, record players at home, in the pubs, in the shops and even in the car. Who knows, maybe they would become famous!

The letter "B" was auspicious too in the motoring field in this period as the MGB, successor to the "A" series and English sports car par excellence, took its first steps. The MGB was basic with simple lines, an accessible price and good performance. Although the Abingdon manufacturer's latest open top gave no concessions to luxury, it was more comfortable than the previous series and, most important of all, its sporting temperament was everything one would ask of an MG.

Work on the design of the new sports car had been going on since 1957. MG had asked the Italian coachbuilder, Pietro Frua, to produce a more comfortable model "A" with lowerable windows and a larger trunk. The result was a copy of the Maserati 2000 - another of Frua's creations - that did not convince the management at the British Motor Corporation, owners of MG and fourth largest car manufacturer in the world after Chrysler, Ford and General Motors. The car was heavy with modest performance and had little sporting appeal so the company started again from scratch with the production of a new body. The new project was entrusted to Donald Hayter of the Pressed Steel Co. which specialized in metal dies. The fruits of Hayter's efforts were welcomed by BMC: the laconic and imperturbable comment, "the prototype has met with approval", from management was the start of the MGB's career.

The very first example of the new car came off the assembly line in April 1962. It had left hand drive as it was destined as part of a batch of 500 for the wealthy and important American market. The MGB was immediately welcomed by the public for its simple lines; the absence of frills was its winning card - what you saw was what you got.

Compared to the "A", the "B" was less sinuous and less affected. The "A" had an inclined grill which followed the curve of the hood; it was limited in width to the two bumper guards and did not even reach the headlights. The sides of the car were flat and straight without chromework or even door handles (you had to pull on a cord in the internal lining of the door); the only features to be seen were the concave rear fenders.

The new model was very different. The front had a hood cut short by the wide, narrow grill with vertical chrome bars. At either end of the grill were the indicators and set back in the fenders, but not protected by a Plexiglas cover, were the two circular headlights. The chrome one-piece bumper held the license plate and, for the American market, the bumper guards and supplementary protection bar in front of the grill. The hood was very long and seemed to house a multi-cylinder motor but there were no air intakes or other demonstrations of power. The sides were more "furnished" than the previous model with a ridge straight as a ruled line the length of the body at the height of the front wheelhouse (the rear wheelhouse was

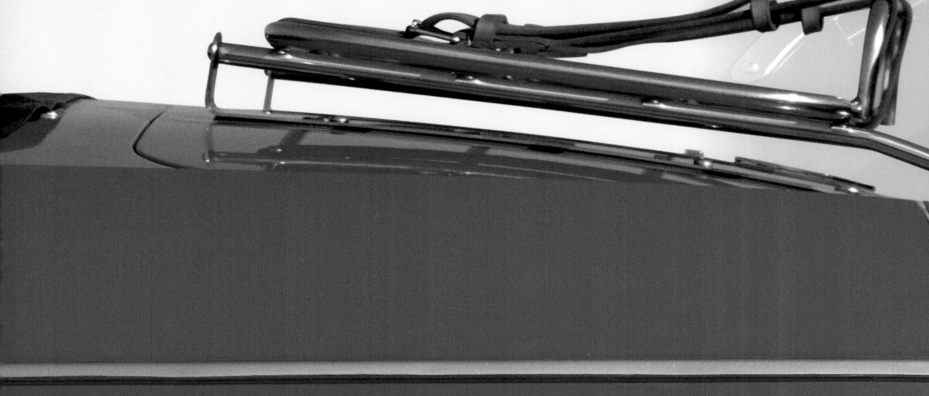

TECHNICAL DESCRIPTION OF THE MGB SERIES 1 1962

YEARS OF PRODUCTION	1962-67		ENGINE	FRONT LONGITUDINAL, FOUR CYLINDERS, IN-LINE
CHASSIS	UNITIZED BODY		BORE AND STROKE (MM)	80.2 X 88.9
SUSPENSION	FRONT: INDEPENDENT WHEELS, DEFORMABLE WISHBONES, SPIRAL SPRINGS; REAR: RIGID AXLE, SEMI-ELLIPTICAL LEAF SPRINGS; HYDRAULIC SHOCK ABSORBERS		PISTON DISPLACEMENT (CC)	1798
			HORSEPOWER	95 AT 5400 RPM
			MAX. TORQUE (KGM)	15 AT 3000 RPM
			TIMING SYSTEM	TWO VALVES PER CYLINDER
WHEELS & TIRES	14" SPOKED WHEELS, 5.60-14 TIRES		FUEL SUPPLY	TWO CARBURETORS
STEERING	RACK AND PINION		GEARBOX	MANUAL 4 SPEED + REVERSE, CENTRAL GEARSHIFT
FRONT TRACK (INCHES)	48			
REAR TRACK (INCHES)	49		DRIVE	REAR
WHEELBASE (INCHES)	90		MAX. SPEED (MPH)	106

slightly lower because it had a shorter radius); below the ridge was the side indicator light and above, the door handle (a novelty for an open MG). In the center of the slightly curved trunk, the MG badge was proudly displayed. The lights were set vertically with a chrome rim while the chrome fuel cap was off-center. The cab was much more comfortable than the "A" due mainly to the adoption of a unitized body, another first for MG. The sober exterior was mirrored inside: the dashboard was sparsely populated by buttons and dials without any attempt at ergonomic design. Square instruments were mixed haphazardly with round and rectangular ones. The steering wheel was original: the three spokes each comprised three thin metal tubes which met in the round central body topped by the MG badge on a red background; apart from the lining of the sides of the leather seats, this was the only splash of color found in the predominantly black interior.

From a modern viewpoint, the optional extras available were curious. The oddest was surely the heater, followed by a cigarette lighter, ashtray and external rear view mirrors. The others remained the same over the years: spoked wheels with a large central wheelnut, radio, tonneau cover, external luggage carrier and stabilizing bars.

The MGB had a four cylinder, 1.8 liter engine initially designed for the new Austin sedan (another marque belonging to BMC). Being powerful enough, it had no problem pushing a car that weighed only a little over 2,000 lbs to 106 mph. The MGB ended its first series in 1967 and the two that followed offered new details and slight aesthetic and mechanical modifications. Some features, due to the American safety requirements, rendered the car less attractive, for example, the polyurethane bumpers on the late 1974 version made the front of the car look like a toad. Production came to a halt in 1980, not because a new model was to substitute it but because 500,000 had been made and there was little incentive to keep flogging a former winner whose time had clearly passed. Besides, the Abingdon factory was being shut and the MG marque was being suspended - thankfully, only temporarily. The "B" returned after a long forced break in a 1990's edition called the RV8 powered by an all-alloy Rover V8 engine. After sporadically appearing on sporting versions of Austin-Morris sedans during the 1980's, the MG badge was resuscitated in the second half of the 1990's with the creation of the MGF.

FORD MUSTANG 1964

IACOCCA'S WINNING HORSE

The Mustang was launched in the United States in 1964 and on the first day of sales, 22 thousand orders were received. The enthusiastic response was so great that one dealer in Chicago was forced to lock the doors of his showroom for fear that harm might come to the huge number of people crammed inside.

At Garland, Texas, one of the lucky new owners was unable to take his new car away until his check was cashed the next day so he spent the night asleep in it afraid that somebody else would offer more money for it.

The 400,000 units expected to be sold in the first year were gone in fewer than four months. Two years after the launch there were 472 Mustang clubs with over 32,000 members. This was the extraordinary welcome given to the

Ford Mustang that, like the Chevrolet Corvette, has always been synonymous with the American sports car.

The Mustang's name was chosen to reflect the qualities of the small, strong, usually Arab horse with long mane and tail that lives half-wild on the North American plains and South American pampas. Naturally the horse is unbroken, fast, proud and has a free spirit, just the attributes Ford president Lee Iacocca wanted for his new, inexpensive sports car. These were characteristics that no other Ford model was able to provide during the 1960's as the 1955-57 two-seater Thunderbird had gone out of production. The gap was only partially filled by the more expensive Chevrolet Corvette, the Chevy Corvair Corsa and by European models.

Iacocca had started at Ford in 1945 and thanks to his winning marketing strategies had rapidly climbed the corporate ladder to become Vice President. He had an instinctive understanding of the market and once he replaced Robert McNamara as President he radically changed the direction of the company.

It all started from the idea of a small, inexpensive coupe and open top featuring 2+2 seating, relatively low entry price, average performance, but lots of style. This all came together under a project called T-5, which was later to be renamed Mustang.

The Mustang moniker first surfaced on a high performance early 1960's sports prototype equipped with a mid-placed V4 engine, a long nose and a short tail. That car never amounted to much, but when Iacocca gave the green light to the production of the new youthful four-seater, the name eventually resurfaced.

The basic concept of this new model was made up in clay in less than six weeks, and briefly it was called the Cougar. Iacocca liked the car but not the name, so "Mustang" was reinstated. (The "Cougar" name would return in 1967 for Mercury's Mustang-based ponycar.)

The lines of the production Mustang did not vary much from the prototype. The body rested on the chassis of the sedate Falcon economy car; the front volume was very long with a square hood, while the rectangular grill protruded further than the round headlights. The grill was a fine chrome mesh accentuated by a horizontal and a vertical bar which seemed to indicate the Mustang's coordinates. A deep pleat ran the length of the sides and ended near the rear fender at a false air intake. Where the sides met the tail there was a vestigial fin.

On the convertible version, polished edging on the body behind the interior marked the limit of the folded top, and a soft top protector could be attached to the body with fasteners. The base model featured conical stamped wheelcovers, and the interior was relatively sober, befitting a car designed for a low entry price.

Once that entry price was met, however, watch out. There was a huge variety of options available to allow the owner to customize the Mustang in sportier or more luxurious trappings. In place of the base 6 cylinder in-line engine one could have a cooking V8 or even a "Hi-Po" 289 cubic inch, 271 HP V8 with four-barrel carburetor and

truly high performance. Suitably modified by Shelby American into the homologation-special Shelby GT350, the Hi-Po 289 Mustang was capable of dominating US production racing, vanquishing many more outwardly sporty cars with ease. Responding to its low price, neat styling, and wide option book, an astounding 418,000 buyers took a Mustang home during the extra-long 1965 model year, the car's first.

The option-rich Mustang was designed to be a chameleon, and it has remained one ever

since - though not always in the way Ford intended. As time has passed, the Mustang has weathered recessions, oil crises, and changes in fashion by adapting and renewing itself in many different forms. The current model - lithe, trendy, and alternately cheap (with a V6 engine) or powerful (with an all aluminum, 32 valve, 4 cam V8) - may be more similar to the first than any other edition. No matter what form it takes, however, the name Mustang will always resonate not only with Americans, but with car enthusiasts all around the world.

YEARS OF PRODUCTION	1964-66
CHASSIS	STEEL UNITIZED BODY
SUSPENSION	FRONT: INDEPENDENT WHEELS, A-ARMS, TORSION BARS, SPIRAL SPRINGS, STABILIZING BAR; REAR: LIVE AXLE WITH HALF ELLIPTIC LONGITUDINAL LEAF SPRINGS AND HYDRAULIC TELESCOPIC SHOCK ABSORBERS
WHEELS & TIRES	14" STAMPED STEEL, 6.50-14 TIRES
STEERING	RACK AND PINION, POWER ASSIST OPTIONAL
FRONT TRACK (INCHES)	56
REAR TRACK (INCHES)	56
WHEELBASE (INCHES)	106

ENGINE	FRONT LONGITUDINAL, 90° V8
BORE AND STROKE (MM)	101.6 X 72.9
DISPLACEMENT (CC)	4728
HORSEPOWER	271 AT4500 RPM
MAX. TORQUE (KGM)	36 AT 4000 RPM
TIMING SYSTEM	TWO OVERHEAD VALVES PER CYLINDER, CAM IN BLOCK
FUEL SUPPLY	2- OR 4-BARREL CARBURETOR
GEARBOX	3- OR 4-SPEED MANUAL, 3-SPEED AUTOMATIC + REVERSE, CENTRAL GEARSHIFT
DRIVE	REAR
MAX. SPEED (MPH)	127

ALFA ROMEO 1600 SPIDER DUETTO
ITALIAN DESIGN GRADUATES IN AMERICA

The Duetto was one of Alfa Romeo's most famous cars and represented Italy's answer to the classic English sports cars with their rounded lines. For twenty years it was the company's only open-topped car, the perfect incarnation of Alfa's sporting philosophy. Design was by Pininfarina: He was responsible for the convex sides, a feature very similar to the Jaguar E-type but which traced its own heritage more to Alfa's Disco Volante specials of the 1950's.

The Duetto made its appearance at the 1966 Geneva Motor Show with the rather anonymous name of Spider 1600, but Alfa Romeo was looking for a more imaginative name and in an unusual move, left it to the public to choose in a competition. An entry form could be had from the local Alfa Romeo dealer, the prize being of course a Spider 1600. The competition was a

great success and over 140 thousand entries were received. The winning name in the competition was "Pinin/Pininfarina" in memory of the designer who had just died, but Alfa did not give its approval and choice fell instead on "Duetto". Unfortunately a confectionery company already produced a biscuit with this name obliging Alfa to give up on it - fortunately, only briefly. The Spider was then known by two nicknames: the more famous was "cuttlebone", given by the Alfa workers to describe the shape of the back of the car. The other nickname, which applied in the US, was the "Graduate", from the film of the same name in which Dustin Hoffman drove the Alfa up the California coast. The car he used was the more powerful version fitted out for the American market.

The Duetto was the first of four generations of

Alfa Spider, which were produced until 1994. They were distinguishable mainly by the shape of the rear. The Duetto's appearance was a complete break with the past having nothing to do with the Giulietta Sprint which it replaced. The body was slim, especially with the roof down. The overhangs, i.e. the parts of the body that stretch from the wheels to the respective ends of the car, were symmetrical; apart from being convex (more technically, having a curved transversal section), the sides were also characterized by a tapered indent starting from the front wheelhouse and running to the rear lights. This was an aesthetic motif which lightened the sides of the vehicle and gave rigidity to the body. The external mirror had a chromed protective hood and was positioned much further forward than the windshield,

making it difficult to adjust from the driving seat. The small radiator grill with its chromed rim acted as a bumper together with the two sections that contained the indicator lights and air intakes. The lights were set back in the hood forming a very pronounced hollow which was covered by a removable perspex fairing to allow cleaning and maintenance, or which could be replaced by a chromed rim.

The rear was the leit motif of the Duetto. Its curved section combined with the flat rear trunk was both attractive and innovative for the period; the chrome bumper had rubber bumper guards and housed small round reflectors; the lights were positioned at the extreme edges of the tail and wrapped around to the side of the car close to the indent. The canvas soft top was only available in black; the top's cover and the large rear window were both made of vinyl. The soft top was attached to the windshield using an effective over-center fastener, a novelty at that time. Also available was a black hard top made from plastic and lined with fake leather. Black was also the dominant color in the relatively comfortable interior; behind the two seats there was even room for a little baggage. Only the fundamental instruments and controls were provided, reflecting the Spartan interiors of English sports cars. The instrumentation panel included the speedometer, rev counter, partial and total mile counter in addition to the usual panel lights and was protected by a non-reflecting plastic cover. In the center of the dash and facing towards the driver were three other indicators (fuel level, oil pressure and water temperature), a radio bay and the air conditioning controls. The floor change gearshift had first a plastic, then a leather, boot. The steering wheel had three metal spokes, on each of which was a horn button. The seats were covered in elasticized leather.

The mechanics of the Duetto were derived from the Giulia TI. The motor was front longitudinal, it had rear wheel drive, a rigid rear axle and the front axle had independent wheels. The engine was a twin camshaft, four cylinder 1.6 which produced 109 HP. Performance was better than its rivals with a top speed of over 114 mph against the 100 mph of the Fiat 1500 cabriolet and MGB, though equal to the Porsche 912 Targa. Between 1966-68, 6,235 examples of the Duetto were produced, then two variants were added to the range: the 1750 Veloce and the

TECHNICAL DESCRIPTION OF THE ALFA ROMEO SPIDER DUETTO

YEARS OF PRODUCTION	1966-1968
CHASSIS	UNITIZED BODY IN STEEL PLATE
SUSPENSION	FRONT: INDEPENDENT WHEELS, TRANSVERSAL WISHBONES, OBLIQUE CONNECTING ROD, SPIRAL SPRING, STABILIZING BAR; REAR: RIGID REAR AXLE, LONGITUDINAL WISHBONE, "T" STABILIZER, SPIRAL SPRING; HYDRAULIC TELESCOPIC SHOCK ABSORBERS
WHEELS & TIRES	STAMPED PLATE WHEELS, 155 X 15" TIRES
STEERING	CONTINUOUS BALL-TYPE OR WORM AND ROLLER STEERING
FRONT TRACK (INCHES)	51
REAR TRACK (INCHES)	49

WHEELBASE (INCHES)	88
ENGINE	FRONT LONGITUDINAL, FOUR CYLINDERS, IN-LINE
BORE AND STROKE (MM)	78 X 82
DISPLACEMENT (CC)	1570
HORSEPOWER	110 AT 6000 RPM
MAX. TORQUE (KGM)	14.2 AT 2800 RPM
TIMING SYSTEM	TWIN OVERHEAD VALVES, TWIN OVERHEAD CAMS, DOUBLE CHAIN
FUEL SUPPLY	2 HORIZONTAL TWIN CARBURETORS
CLUTCH	DRY SINGLE-PLATE
GEARBOX	5 SPEED + REVERSE; CENTRAL GEARSHIFT
DRIVE	REAR
MAX. SPEED (MPH)	114

1300 Junior. Externally the 1750 could be distinguished from the 1600 by the different design of the hubcaps, the position of the door mirror and the logo on the back. The 1300 lacked headlight fairings, had differently designed hubcaps and the side indicator lights were set further forward. Inside, the 1750 Veloce was more elegantly finished than the 1600; the seats were more deeply padded and the steering wheel was wooden. The 1300 on the other hand was finished rather meagerly. The 1750's engine was the same design as the 1600 but enlarged to 1779cc and with 10 extra horsepower - 119 compared to 109. The improvement in performance was modest: 119 mph rather than 114 mph. The four cylinder engine of the 1300 Junior was reduced to 1290cc and 89 HP giving 106 mph.

In 1970 the second generation of the Duetto (now "Spider") appeared, the "Kamm-tail" series: The bumpers were made from a single piece and the engine range was altered to 1.6-2 liters. The third series was the "aerodynamic" variant with the very obvious spoiler and other attachments (unconvincing from an aesthetic point of view) which was in production from 1982-89. The engine sizes remained unaltered although the range of power outputs was changed. The last series was available from 1989 to 1994. The Spider was always very popular in the United States, where more than half of the examples produced were sold. The first US-specific version was the 1750 Veloce, a "cuttlebone" model from 1968. Modifications to the bumpers, the removal of the fairings from the headlights and later the introduction of Spica mechanical fuel injection were all required to make the car conform to American safety and emissions laws. These alterations evolved in the successive versions. The 2000 Veloce USA was the best selling variant; 22,059 were sold, some 20% of total production.

FERRARI 365 GTS/4 "DAYTONA"
THE SPORTS CAR COVERS HER EYES WITH PLEXIGLAS LIDS

In the United States the Daytona was so appreciated that many converted the coupé into the sports version by removing the roof panel and replacing it with a soft top. This did not meet with the approval of the Ferrari technicians who believed that removing the top ruined the performance of this beautiful machine. This was just one aspect of the Daytona phenomenon which was always dogged by controversy. It started with the name which was chosen to celebrate the amazing victory of the Ferrari P4 and 412P at the 1967 Daytona 24 Hours, the grueling sports-prototype event second only to Le Mans in prestige. The name of the new GT leaked out of Maranello and was made public before the car's official presentation. Enzo Ferrari responded by repudiating this name and calling the car the "365 GTB/4" which, according to Ferrari coding of the time, indicated the cubic capacity of each cylinder (365 x 12 = 4380cc, the displacement of the prototype which was increased to 4390.3cc in the production models); GTB for Gran Turismo Berlinetta (i.e. GT coupe) and GTS for Gran Turismo Spider (GT spider); and 4 for 4 cams. However, the car has always been known as the Daytona by Ferrari enthusiasts just as the Alfa Romeo Spider Duetto is known as the Cuttlebone. The creation of the mechanical standards for high performance GT's. But once the Daytona was on the road its performance supported Enzo Ferrari who said, "The oxen should always be in front of the cart". The car was extremely quick and stable and it showed that although a rear mounted engine helped produce high performance, it was not indispensable if you knew how to build a car right. And that didn't take into consideration that an engine in the back gave problems of heat and noise. Ferrari remained faithful to its philosophy so that the company's devoted (and rich) customers should not be frightened by a new model with radical innovations.

Daytona was driven by market needs. The competition at the end of the 1960's from Maserati, Iso Rivolta, Aston Martin and Lamborghini urgently required replacement of the 275 GTB/4. Two years of feverish work were needed to make the prototype ready for presentation in 1968 but the immediate response was criticism: although it displayed an exciting and innovative body shape from the genius of Pininfarina, mechanically the car was based on a traditional layout with front mounted engine. It seemed like a lack of courage on Ferrari's part. Just a stone's throw from Maranello at Sant'Agata Bolognese, the Lamborghini Miura went into production with a rear mounted engine right at the time the Daytona was shown. Combined with its sporty body, the Miura seemed to lay down the stylistic and Enzo Ferrari was shown to be right in the end and the Daytona was recognized as a prestige model - but it was to be the last front engined 2-seat Ferrari for the next 25 years.

The Daytona sports version was produced in 1969 and was first shown at the Frankfurt Car Show. The open-topped version was more indicative than the coupé in expressing sports car style at the end of the 1960's, which was populated by cars with elegant, angled, slim volumes and no-frill bodies. The Daytona Sports was produced from 1969 to 1973; 121 were made of which 96 went to the United States, although conversions carried out on the coupé version to turn it into a sports model upped the numbers. The conversion did not take place simply because the sports car was so attractive, but also because prices for the sports version

YEARS OF PRODUCTION	1969-1973		BORE AND STROKE (MM)	81 X 71
CHASSIS	ONE PIECE MADE FROM STEEL TUBES		PISTON DISPLACEMENT (CC)	4390
SUSPENSION	FRONT AND REAR INDEPENDENT WHEELS, DEFORMABLE WISHBONES, SPIRAL SPRINGS; HYDRAULIC SHOCK ABSORBERS		HORSEPOWER	352 HP AT 7500 RPM
			TIMING SYSTEM	2 VALVES PER CYLINDER, 2 OVERHEAD CAMSHAFTS PER BANK
WHEELS & TIRES	SPOKED 15" WHEELS; 215/70-15 TIRES		FUEL SUPPLY	SIX CARBURETORS
STEERING	RACK AND PINION		GEARBOX	MANUAL, 5 SPEED + REVERSE, CENTRAL GEARSHIFT
FRONT TRACK (INCHES)	55			
REAR TRACK (INCHES)	55		DRIVE	REAR
WHEELBASE (INCHES)	94		MAX. SPEED (MPH)	175
ENGINE	FRONT LONGITUDINAL, 60° V12			

were sky-high and it behooved unscrupulous individuals to take a saw to the roof panel of the hard top. Apart from the top, differences between the Daytona sports and coupé were the Borrani spoked wheels with wing nut on the hubcap rather than the star version (the former allowed the brake caliper to be seen), and the less inclined windshield. In 1975 when the Daytona was already out of production, the coachbuilder Michelotti presented a sports version with an electrically retractable top at the Turin Motor Show.

A characteristic detail of some Daytonas was the Plexiglas cover over the front lights. This was one of Pininfarina's favorite features which he proposed on many of his production designs; this touch predated similar protection on sports models of the 1990's by at least 25 years.

But the Plexiglas had to be removed early in 1969 as American regulations stipulated that the headlights had to be housed behind retractable metal hoods. This meant an undoubted loss of originality and, worse, over the years many owners who were obliged to replace the lights after an accident opted for the metal hood rather than the Plexiglas cover as it was cheaper. Despite this loss, even with metal hoods the front of the Daytona had a true sports appearance. The square grill was placed just below the two-piece bumper and the smooth line of the hood was broken only by two air vents. The direction indicators folded round onto the sides of the car and there was a marked pleat at mid height where the sides and the rear of the car met. Another nice touch was that the door handles were set within the door panels.

Pininfarina introduced this feature mainly for reasons of safety, just as he had included rounded corners and inlaid handles in his own home to prevent injury.

The rear of the car was notable for the two sets of round lights that were to reappear even larger on the 308. They were set on a sloping surface beneath the overhanging lip of the trunk which acted as a mini spoiler as well as housing the license plate light. The rear bumper also comprised two elements; the reversing light was positioned in the center and the four large exhaust pipes below. The pipes were the most obvious external signs of the power of the 352 HP, V12 engine with its unmistakable growl. The engine was capable of pushing the sports car to 175 mph, a speed at which it would be absolutely crazy to drive with the top down without wearing at least a helmet and goggles like the great drivers of the 1950's.

The cab was traditionally fitted out with a profusion of leather, eight round instrument dials framed with chrome in front of the driver and the air conditioning controls to one side. The central console was a sweep of leather flanked by the two seats, a huge span only minimally filled by the traditional gearshift layout, the hand brake, the chrome ashtray, the radio and a few less important controls. The bucket seats had an adjustable headrest, a perforated cushion for air circulation and high sides to prevent sliding during fast cornering.

FERRARI DINO 246 GTS
A FERRARI BUT NOT IN NAME

What a lot of difficult choices had to be made in the production of the Dino! Enzo Ferrari was afraid it would not be successful and would compromise Ferrari's image. He did not feel confident building a mid-engined car because he did not have enough experience of the issues involved.

He had given way on the competition front; the company's racing department had converted to rear engined cars following the 1961 successes in England, but Enzo said road cars were not to be touched; the GT's had to have "the oxen in front of the cart".

This had been demonstrated by the Daytona, a GT that gave tremendous performance and was extremely driveable even with the engine in the front. A front mounted engine ensures a degree of comfort that a mid-engined sports car can never do because the proximity of the motor to the cab brings an increase in heat and noise which is only tolerable up to a certain limit even among the most passionate of enthusiasts. And this does not take into consideration the additional poor motor ventilation which creates problems of cooling.

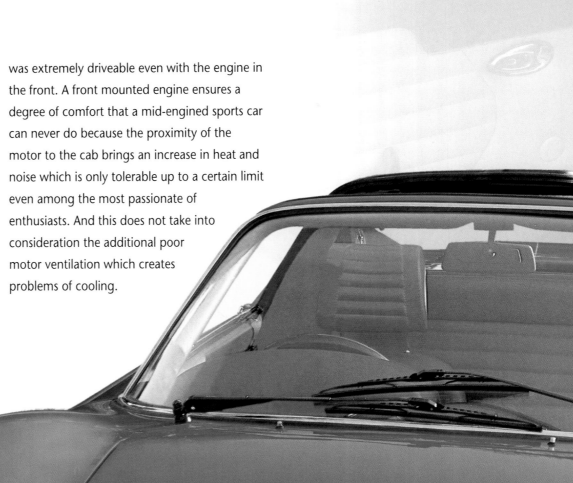

But time and Pininfarina, who had been longing to design a small coupe with a central rear mounted engine to bring Ferrari abreast of the revolutionary Lamborghini Miura, were able to make the obstinate Enzo Ferrari change his mind. He at last agreed to produce a small GT with central-mounted motor but on one condition, that it would not bear the Ferrari badge. The new car would have to be produced around the Dino motor which had been the result of an agreement between Fiat and Ferrari. The Dino was the result of a commission to Vittorio Jano, the famous Alfa Romeo designer, to produce a V6 with the help of Enzo's son, Alfredo, known as Dino. Dino's early death (at age 24 of a viral infection, June 1956) left a lasting pain with Enzo, and the father later named this engine for his son. The ultimate road version would be a 65° V6 of 2.4 liters and 195 HP. Models for the American market were fitted with anti-pollution devices as required.

In the meantime Pininfarina worked on the Dino 85 racing chassis provided by Ferrari, but three years and four prototypes had passed before the production model was finally arrived at. In 1967 the roadgoing 2 liter Dino 206 GT appeared, followed by the 2.4 liter 246 GT in 1969. Both were made jointly by Fiat and Ferrari, and Dino therefore became a marque - a rectangular logo

with blue writing on a yellow background. This was a marketing ploy that would reappear in the 1990's used by Japanese companies to sell exclusive sports cars and luxury sedans (for example, Toyota with Lexus and Honda with Acura).

In Ferrari's case the purpose was the opposite; to disassociate the manufacturer from the car which was considered not exclusive enough! The Dino ran counter to the Ferrari tradition even if the 6 cylinders beneath the hood had the unmistakable verve of the engines from Maranello. After the 246 GT of 1969 came the L, M and 1971 E series which was the origin of the GTS sports. This version had a reinforced back end to make up for the lack of roof and could only be told apart from the closed version by the different C-pillar, the black targa roof panel and by the roller blinds in place of sun flaps.

The E series was the best finished and best equipped even if the cab was still as basic as could be: some of the optional accessories offered were electric windows, leather upholstery, air-conditioning, "Daytona" seats and widened wheelhouse flares to permit wider diameter wheels. The car body was the result of the development and improvement of the three preceding series: the convex nose had a low, wide grill placed in the center of the two-piece bumper which meant it was right in the path of any collision, however slight. The side lights and indicators were sited above the bumper. The round headlights were set in the fender without a fairing to cover them. Two air intakes were placed on the hood each with three rectangular elements containing a grill. The windshield was very inclined and was fitted with a rim in the same color as the car body. The doors had a deep indent which ended at the air intake on the rear fender. The door locks were set below the indent though in the coupé they were positioned in the lower rim of the window. Unlike the small sedan, the sports version did not have rear windows at the sides. The removable plastic hard top was only supplied in black. There were chrome rims for the vent windows and for the three slits used to ventilate the interior. The slits were mounted where the back of the roof attached to the body. They also formed two small fins which joined to the rounded rear panel where there were two small air intakes to cool the engine. The rear end had two round lights similar to those on the Daytona. The bumper was also in two chromed parts and the alloy wheels were star-shaped. Production of the 246 GTS continued until 1974 for a total of 1,274 units out of the 3,661 making up the entire Dino series. The uncertainties Enzo Ferrari had at the start of the project were proved unjustified by the sales, which were excellent. But while this was the first road Ferrari with a mid-mounted engine - a feature that went on to characterize Maranello models until the 1990's - it would never have as much glamour as the 250 GT Spyder California or 365 GTS/4 Daytona.

TECHNICAL DESCRIPTION OF THE FERRARI DINO 246 GTS

YEARS OF PRODUCTION	1972-1974	STEERING	RACK AND PINION	TIMING SYSTEM	2 VALVES PER CYLINDER, 2 OVERHEAD CAMSHAFTS
CHASSIS	TUBULAR	FRONT TRACK (INCHES)	55		
SUSPENSION	FRONT: INDEPENDENT WHEELS, DEFORMABLE WISHBONES, SPIRAL SPRINGS; REAR: INDEPENDENT WITH WISHBONES, SPIRAL SPRINGS, AND HYDRAULIC SHOCK ABSORBERS	REAR TRACK (INCHES)	56	FUEL SUPPLY	THREE CARBURETORS
		WHEELBASE (INCHES)	91	GEARBOX	MANUAL, 5 SPEED + REVERSE, CENTRAL GEARSHIFT
		ENGINE	REAR TRANSVERSAL, 65° V6		
		BORE AND STROKE (MM)	92.5 X 60	DRIVE	REAR
WHEELS & TIRES	14" ALLOY WHEELS; 205-70 VR 14 TIRES	DISPLACEMENT (CC)	2419	MAX. SPEED (MPH)	150
		HORSEPOWER	195 HP AT 7500 RPM		

BMW Z1
IT WAS ONLY SUPPOSED TO BE A PROTOTYPE!

At the beginning of the 1980's the range of open-topped cars available was depressing; after the wonderful models produced in the 1950's and 60's the market was suddenly bereft. Manufacturers, particularly the Europeans, turned the economic worries and climate of uncertainty produced by two oil crises onto their new cars. There was no excitement, no style, no daring. The result was anonymous designs where the cars all appeared the same: two volume, enclosed bodies surrounded by plastic bumpers. It was as if open-topped cars had never existed. It became a matter

of waiting for the tide to turn and when it did the cars were powerful, top-of-the-market models such as the Jaguar XJS Convertible.

It was not until the end of the 1980's that cars appeared that were an economic possibility for most people. Among the first companies to react was BMW. At the 1987 Frankfurt Motor Show the Bavarian manufacturer presented the Z1, a compact sports prototype. It was a two seater without a central roll-bar and it had a futuristic system of electrically sliding the doors up and down requiring the passenger to climb in.

The public reaction was enthusiastic, so much so that BMW management decided to produce a mini series of 1000 units. A year after its Frankfurt debut the Z1 concept car went into production. The "Z" stood for "Zukunft" which is German for future, the "1" left one to imagine that this was just the start of a series of Z2's, Z3's etc. that would continue ad infinitum. BMW continued production until 8,000 Z1's had been built, 8 times the planned number. It was a real success.

The attraction of the Z1 can be attributed to

the team of young designers who created it. They had wanted to recreate the myth of the open-topped sports cars of the 60's like the Porsche 356, MGB series, Alfa Romeo Giulietta Spider and so on, cars they would probably have ridden in beside their father or elder brother. They wanted to approach this sporting concept using new technologies; besides the sophisticated electro-mechanical door opening system, they used a body made from panels of thermoplastic material which could be individually replaced if damaged.

The Z1 was just under 13 feet but long enough to accommodate a host of original aesthetic features: the front was tapered and looked like a cuttlebone thickened by the bumper which integrated the grill, two air intakes, the lights and indicators. The lights sat on top of the hood and were protected by a cover. The dipped lights were ellipsoidal and cylindrical sticking further out than the rectangular full beam lights. Two ribs ran up the hood to the windshield where the two streamlined door mirrors were attached. The front of the cab was strengthened by a thick round bar which performed the double function of a central roll-bar (missing) and support to the passenger as he lowered himself into the seats. The wraparound seats themselves were like something out of a science fiction film; in the same color as the car and with a built in headrest and strengthened back, they almost "contained" the passenger.

The materials and components used for the console were those of a normal BMW production model as were the mechanical elements and the quiet, refined 6 cylinder, 2.5 liter engine capable of producing 170 HP. The steering wheel however was original. It was made up of 3 thick spokes with a small central body and thumbrest on the grip. The instrument panel was minimal with four circular indicators protected by an anti-reflection lid which appeared stuck onto the dashboard. The single outstanding detail was a red rev counter hand; the rest of the instrumentation was white. The sides of the car emphasized the wedge shape of the Z1. The waist was very high so it could flow smoothly into the solid rear end dominated by the bumper into which the two oval exhaust pipes were integrated. The rear lights were rectangular and wrapped around on to the car flanks. Placed between the trunk and the bumper was an outlet for the streams of air from the smooth sandwich-structured chassis.

TECHNICAL DESCRIPTION OF THE BMW Z1

EARS OF PRODUCTION 1988-1991

CHASSIS MONOCOQUE WITH SANDWICH CHASSIS IN SYNTHETIC MATERIAL AND BODYWORK MADE FROM THERMOPLASTIC PANELS

SUSPENSION FRONT: VARIABLE INCIDENCE SINGLE JOINT UPRIGHT, POSITIVE KINGPIN OFFSET, COMPENSATION OF TRANSVERSAL FORCES, ANTIDIVE BRAKING; REAR: CENTRALLY GUIDED, DOUBLE WISHBONE AXLE, 3 ARM AXLE (ONE LONGITUDINAL, TWO TRANSVERSAL), ANTIDIVE START AND BRAKING, SEPARATE SHOCK ABSORBER AND

SPRINGS; TELESCOPIC HYDRAULIC SHOCK ABSORBERS

WHEELS & TIRES LIGHT 16" ALLOY WHEELS, 225/45 VR16 TIRES

STEERING RACK AND PINION WITH HYDRAULIC SERVO ASSIST CONTROLLED BY THE MOTOR SPEED

FRONT TRACK (INCHES) 57

REAR TRACK (INCHES) 57

WHEELBASE (INCHES) 96

ENGINE FRONT LONGITUDINAL, SIX CYLINDERS, IN-LINE

BORE AND STROKE (MM) 84 X 75

DISPLACEMENT 2494 CC

HORSEPOWER 170 AT 5800 RPM

MAX. TORQUE (N/M) 222 AT 4300 RPM

TIMING SYSTEM TWO VALVES PER CYLINDER, SOHC

FUEL SUPPLY ELECTRONIC INJECTION

CLUTCH DRY SINGLE-PLATE

GEARBOX 5 SPEED + REVERSE; CENTRAL GEARSHIFT

DRIVE REAR

MAX. SPEED (MPH) 140

DODGE VIPER RT/10
A COBRA UNDER THE SKIN!

When the Viper prototype made its debut at the Detroit Motor Show in 1989, many car enthusiasts, particularly those who had come of age twenty years before, had a shock when they came to the Chrysler stand. The concept car they were looking at with the unequivocally menacing name "Viper" had something familiar about it. The aggressive roadster - with its harmonious, rounded lines without the smallest edge or corner and its extra long hood, which promised huge power beneath - certainly had a skeleton in the closet.

The skeleton was 27 years old and belonged to the Shelby Cobra from 1962. The Cobra was another "reptile", a superb, magnificently curved sports car created by the famous American ex-driver Carroll Shelby. It was in the early 1960's that Shelby had the idea of producing a racing and street car with an American V8 engine set on an English AC chassis.

The idea was rejected by General Motors which already produced the Corvette. Shelby then went to Ford during the period that Lee Iacocca was launching his "Total Performance" program. Few believe it was a simple coincidence; Shelby's

idea was received with the greatest enthusiasm, with the result that the Shelby Cobra was born in 1962 based around a 4.3 liter Ford V8. This engine was later increased to 4.7 and then 7 liters, and the car remained until 1968.

Twenty years later, the Cobra returned in shape and philosophy: The marque this time was either Chrysler or Dodge (depending on the destination market) and the name was Viper, perhaps as a sign of continuity or maybe just from a love for reptiles!

The moving spirits behind the car were Chrysler design boss Tom gale and Chrysler president Bob Lutz, two hardcore car nuts who wanted a machine that represented the American tradition of street monsters. (According to Lutz, "...nothing can replace large engines!") Serious production of the Viper got under way in 1992. Similarity with the Cobra is mainly based on the car's body, its parallel-tube chassis structure and its engine philosophy. The Viper's powerplant was an 8 liter, 90° V10 with 400 horsepower and limitless torque. The antiquated pushrod-operated valve layout contrasted with its modern all-alloy construction.

In 1996 the Viper underwent several changes introduced by the new GTS coupé: mechanical modifications saw the V10 increased in power from the 364-400 HP of the previous generation to 450 HP, and aluminum suspension arms lightened the corners of the car by 66 lbs. Aesthetically, the "shark mouth" air intake was reduced in size, optional side windows and electromagnetic locks were introduced, new polished alloy wheels appeared and a rigid, double-bubble targa top was made available in the same color as the body.

The menace of the Viper was tangible: The intentions and possibilities of its powerful V10 were not hidden beneath the hood but screamed at the viewer in every detail of the body and cab design. The front view truly resembled a viper with the waves over the long hood looking like the snake's head and the narrow, wide, wary eyes indicating readiness to attack. Other notable details were the bumper shield that gave an idea of the car's power, the gigantic, shark's mouth air intake and the huge round supplementary headlights carved out of the shield and protected by a cover so large that

it was wider than the main sets of lights and ended on the body flanks.

But the car's brutal power was not just obvious from the front: the sides continued the convex shape of the hood and displayed curved air vents as tall as the car's flank between the door and fender. The body included miniskirts housing the visible side exhausts and the mighty 17" wheels which had an open, 3 spoke design to better cool the brake plant. There was less exhibitionism at the back end which was only half the length of the front; the only features were the oval sets of lights which curved round to the sides of the body. The cab was less striking than the exterior but just as interesting. There were two heavily padded bucket seats, the instruments scooped out of the dash had a white background while the main instruments in front of the driver each were covered by an anti-reflection peak. The only concession to a normal production car was the air conditioning controls ... to make it just that little bit more human!

YEARS OF PRODUCTION	1992 - CURRENT	STEERING	RACK AND PINION	TIMING SYSTEM	2 VALVES PER CYLINDER	
CHASSIS	TUBULAR STRUCTURE; BODY MADE FROM COMPOSITE MATERIALS	FRONT TRACK (INCHES)	59	FUEL SUPPLY	MULTIPOINT ELECTRONIC INJECTION	
SUSPENSION	FRONT AND REAR INDEPENDENT WHEELS, SPIRAL SPRINGS, ASYMMETRICAL UPPER AND LOWER ARMS, TRANSVERSAL STABILIZERS; GAS SHOCK ABSORBERS	REAR TRACK (INCHES)	60	CLUTCH	DRY SINGLE-PLATE	
		WHEELBASE (INCHES)	95	GEARBOX	6 SPEED + REVERSE; CENTRAL GEARSHIFT	
		ENGINE	FRONT LONGITUDINAL, 90° V10	DRIVE	REAR	
		BORE AND STROKE (MM)	101.6 X 91.6	MAX. SPEED (MPH)	166 - 168*	
WHEELS & TIRES	FRONT ALLOY WHEELS 17 X 10JJ, REAR 17 X 13JJ: FRONT TIRES 275/40 ZR 17, REAR TIRES 335/35 ZR 17	DISPLACEMENT	7986 CC			
		HORSEPOWER	364-450 HP AT 5000-5150 RPM*	*DEPENDING ON THE DESTINATION MARKET		
		MAX. TORQUE (KGM)	61.5 - 63.5 AT 3600 RPM*			

Jaguar XK8...
Perhaps it should be called the F-type!

In 1996 Jaguar produced their first completely new car for 21 years and their first new sports car for 25 years. The engine too was completely new, the fourth in the history of this glorious English marque which was bought by Ford in 1989. This was Jaguar's first 8 cylinder engine, the worthy successor to the 1948 XK series' 6 cylinder motor which was only replaced 45 years later by the AJ6 series' engine with multivalve distribution: The third Jaguar engine was the 1971 V12 designed for the American market. Even the XK8's 5-speed automatic gearbox was a first. To say that the XK8 was only a new Jaguar

is not to understand the importance of the event. If everything was new, who knew what revolution of form and style the car would offer. None thank heavens! The resemblance to that masterpiece, the E-type, was clear and the influence of the XK120 was felt. The XK8 was more Jaguar than ever, the prodigal son of the glorious past and the English manufacturer's worthy representative for the third millennium. The proportions of the body closely follow those of the E-type: the long hood and cab that sits way back are the same as the former queen of Coventry, but the rear volume is larger than the

earlier model. The XK8's ogival form is more similar to the front than the flying saucer tail of the 1961 Jaguar.

The XK8 is the natural heir of the E-type. The XJS that came out between the two seems just a transition model, a car that has temporarily (for over twenty years) had to hold the affection of Jaguar lovers. The takeover by Ford made a large contribution to the splendor of the XK8. Ford's mighty financial backing provided the necessary investment to develop the X100 project, started in 1992, to the maximum. The result was a new sports car that completely respects Jaguar's

design philosophy. There was no violence and no cultural invasion by the American owners. What luck for car lovers!

The XK8 was ready in just 30 months. The tests were extensive to perfect the car in every way: 100 prototypes were used to determine the final model. Severe reliability tests were carried out all over the world: 500,000 miles were driven in Arctic temperatures in Canada and in the heat of the Arizona desert; 25,000 miles were driven without stopping in WOT conditions (Wide Open Throttle, i.e. with the accelerator permanently on the floor) on a circular track in

Italy 8 miles long; the convertible also underwent supplementary tests in the wind tunnel with water spray to guarantee the watertightness and soundproofing of the top. Aesthetically the lines of the XK8 mark it out from the rich panorama of luxury open-topped cars it is in competition with. The only rival with a resemblance is the closely related Aston Martin DB7, as though the high-range English sports cars wanted to redefine "English style".

The XK8 represents pure harmony of forms and it is difficult to find an edge anywhere. The examples of chromework can be counted on the

TECHNICAL DESCRIPTION OF THE JAGUAR XK8

YEARS OF PRODUCTION	1996 - STILL CURRENT
CHASSIS	STEEL MONOCOQUE WITH FRONT AND REAR CRUMPLE ZONES
SUSPENSION	FRONT: INDEPENDENT WHEELS, UNEQUAL TRAPEZOIDAL WISHBONES, BRAKING ANTIDIVE SYSTEM, SPIRAL SPRINGS, STABILIZING BAR; REAR: INDEPENDENT WHEELS WITH DIE-CAST LOWER TRAILING ARMS AND AXLESHAFTS SERVING AS UPPER WISHBONES, ACCELERATION/ DECELERATION ANTIDIVE SYSTEM, STABILIZING BAR, SPIRAL SPRINGS; TELESCOPIC HYDRAULIC SHOCK ABSORBERS

WHEELS AND TIRES	8" X 17" ALLOY WHEELS, 245/50 ZR 17 TIRES
STEERING	RACK AND PINION, SERVO ASSIST PROPORTIONAL TO SPEED
FRONT TRACK (INCHES)	59
REAR TRACK (INCHES)	59
WHEELBASE (INCHES)	101
ENGINE	FRONT LONGITUDINAL, 90° V8
BORE AND STROKE (MM)	86 X 86
DISPLACEMENT	3996 (CC)
HORSEPOWER	281 HP AT 6100 RPM
MAX. TORQUE (KGM)	38 AT 4250 RPM

TIMING SYSTEM	FOUR VALVES PER CYLINDER, DOUBLE OVERHEAD CAMSHAFTS, VARIABLE TIMING SYSTEM
FUEL SUPPLY	ELECTRONIC MULTIPOINT FUEL INJECTION
GEARBOX	AUTOMATIC, ELECTRONICALLY CONTROLLED 5 SPEED + REVERSE, CENTRAL GEARSHIFT
DRIVE	REAR
TOP SPEED (MPH)	155

fingers of one hand, appearing only on the vertical element that divides the shark's mouth grill in two, on the ends of the exhaust and on the antenna of the audio system.

The nose is similar to a reptile - it is difficult not to think of the Chrysler Viper and its half-sister, the AC Cobra. The XK8's resembles the expression of a viper before it unleashes its attack on its unfortunate prey.

The fenders and hood are curved almost to swollen proportions and each hides something important: the fenders announce the presence of the small, round headlights set back from the grill and protected by an elliptical cover; the hood hides the badge, the classic leaping jaguar with "Jaguar 4 litre" that describes the treasure

hidden below, the new all-aluminum V8, as powerful and fast as anyone could wish, angry when needed, sweet at all other times and always silent. The bumper is an extension of the smooth, uninterrupted hood. It accommodates the grill and supplementary headlights in seatings carved out of the shield. The heavily inclined windshield has a reinforced frame to protect the passengers in case of overturning and anchors the solid side mirrors. The flanks of the XK8 are slightly curved. A section in the same color as the bodywork joins the bumpers to the body and is interrupted only by the wheelhouses containing the enormous 17" wheels. At the rear, the bumper shield protrudes and wraps

around to the sides, getting thinner as it does so, until it disappears on the wheelhouses. The sets of rear lights mirror the elliptical shape of those at the front. The electric top covers or uncovers the XK8 in under twenty seconds. When folded down it is protected by a soft cover the same color as the interior. There is no hard top as the comfort provided by the steel framed soft top is such that a hard top is not necessary. The cab is an opulent drawing room for two and, when necessary, for four, though not for long journeys. Leather and wood cover every inch of the dashboard and surround the controls and instrument dials. The steering wheel automatically moves back towards the dash to facilitate getting in and out.

CHEVROLET CORVETTE 1997
THE TRUE AMERICAN SPORTS CAR

The history of the car is marked by an infinite series of ideas, men, projects and models. It is also the repository of two legends: the Corvette and the Ferrari. Certainly they are very different: The first refers just to a car while the second, more complex, revolves around a man, the world of racing and his red thoroughbreds. The legend of the Corvette is characterized by one element: unpredictability. This excellent American sports car was first produced as a one-off stylistic exercise to be displayed in the ballroom of the Waldorf Astoria Hotel in New York in 1953. The aim was to show that General Motors was able to produce a car in the style of the English sports cars which were so loved in the United States. Such a design ran counter to

GM's typically oversized production cars with their enormous grills and nascent fins.
The name Corvette came about by chance. GM wanted their new sports model to have a name which emphasized the car's bubbly personality and which was synonymous with power, speed and dynamism. A GM photographer proposed "Corvette", after the small, fast naval warship used in WWII as an escort or for antisubmarine defense. GM management must have been delighted. The Corvette made its first appearance as a brilliant white convertible showcar in 1953.
The lines were sober, the overall size small, the hood very long and tail short. The clear differences between it and the general

American production models in the 1950's was accentuated by one factor in particular: the bodywork was made of glass-fiber. The advantages of this material are that it can be molded into any shape the designer wishes, its lightness improves performance, and it is rustproof.
Unexpectedly, the car met with overwhelming appreciation from the public, so much so that it was decided to turn it into a production model. Already the signs of a dazzling future were apparent: The brilliant white brought to mind a wedding, the wedding of the car to drivers all over the world, while the rustproof fiberglass body meant it was an evergreen, destined to remain young forever. In 1953 the Corvette was

on the crest of a wave; it was one of the most desirable sports cars around, and stylistically quite advanced. It was a trendsetter. Certainly some mistakes were made, however. The motor chosen for its debut - Chevy's OHV in-line 6 cylinder - is often regarded as a loser. In truth, at 150 HP this engine beat the contemporary Maserati and approached the 160 HP Jaguar XK. It was the sluggish, mandatory 2 speed automatic that truly hampered the car, a choice definitely not in line with its sporting ambitions. This false step slowed initial sales and cooled the original enthusiasm, but GM put this brilliantly right in 1955. A team led by Chevrolet chief engineer Ed Cole had created another legend - the celebrated, light and compact Chevy Smallblock V8 - and this matched the sports car perfectly. (The Smallblock would in fact have as long a life as the Corvette; over 60 million copies have been made to date.) The V8 kept the car alive, and the rest is history. The successive generations are unforgettable. The 1963 version brought breathtaking lines and was also available as a coupé. The third generation came in 1968, a mod design with a tight waist, wide fenders and long hood. At the same time the "T-top" appeared, a coupé with removable roof panels that was the only open top version available from 1976-85. The fourth generation was dedicated to sheer performance and had a new steel chassis, while the Smallblock engine remained unchanged from the previous model.

In 1996 the challenge to technicians and designers was once more taken up. Something original had to be created, but still respecting the characteristics which had endured for forty years. Radical changes might not be appreciated by Corvette enthusiasts.

The result was the fifth generation, initially just as a targa coupé, with the convertible arriving in 1997. The Smallblock engine was so thoroughly updated that it is effectively an all-new motor - for the first time since 1955. Still retaining the pushrod-operated 2 valve layout, bore spacing and 5.7 liter displacement of the previous engine, this new V8 produces 344 HP and is made entirely of light alloy.

John Cafaro, the Corvette design manager, succeeded in the delicate task of perpetuating the legend. Starting from inviolable aesthetic parameters such as the proportion of the volumes (long hood and short tail), pop-up headlights and four round rear lights, he developed a more sinuous, slim and aggressive body than the previous model.

The front resembles a reptile (the 1990's were full of them), with two ribs and curvatures on the hood which house the main headlights. There is no grill, but two wide, narrow air intakes hold small auxiliary headlights. It is difficult to know where the hood ends and the bumpers and fenders begin, but the result is unarguably attractive. On each side a vertical air intake is positioned near the widely curved front fender. The handles are set in the doors and, being the same color as the body, they are effectively camouflaged. The waist rises as

it approaches the rear making a back end that is heavy and impressive, a demonstration of strength as powerful as the front. There is no bumper, but the round reflectors carved out of the body are essential: When taken with the rectangular lights below, they seem like two laughing faces. The rear air vents and four huge round exhausts almost touch the ground. Inside, the seats are locked into the small spaces remaining on either side of a central console as wide as a landing strip. The driving position is practically horizontal, and the rest of the interior is just as sporting.

This design was originally conceived in the early 1990's, at which time it would have been considered quite radical. However, since the existing Corvette was still selling well, its replacement had to wait. In the meantime, an all-new Mazda RX7 for 1994 stole some of the Corvette's thunder by espousing similar ideas of proportion and line, albeit less aggressively. Still, this doesn't affect the new Corvette's beauty: We look forward to the sixth generation.

YEARS OF PRODUCTION	1997 - STILL CURRENT
CHASSIS	STEEL CHASSIS WITH GLASS-FIBER BODY
SUSPENSION	FRONT: INDEPENDENT, SHORT LONG ARM, FORGED ALUMINUM UPPER AND PRESSURE CAST LOWER WISHBONES, TRANSVERSE MONOLEAF SPRING AND STEEL STABILIZER BAR; REAR: INDEPENDENT 5 LINK DESIGN WITH TOE AND CAMBER ADJUSTMENT, CAST ALUMINUM UPPER AND LOWER WISHBONES AND KNUCKLE, TRANSVERSE MONOLEAF SPRING, STEEL STABILIZER BAR AND TIE RODS,

	TUBULAR U-JOINTED METAL MATRIX COMPOSITE DRIVESHAFTS
WHEELS & TIRES	CAST MAGNESIUM WHEELS, FRONT 8.5 X 17, REAR 9.5 X 18; FRONT TIRES 245/45 ZR17, REAR 275/40 ZR18
STEERING	RACK AND PINION WITH SERVO ASSIST DEPENDING ON SPEED
FRONT TRACK (INCHES)	62
REAR TRACK (INCHES)	62
WHEELBASE (INCHES)	104
ENGINE	FRONT LONGITUDINAL, V8
BORE AND STROKE (MM)	102 X 88

PISTON DISPLACEMENT	5666 (CC)
HORSEPOWER	344 HP AT 5400 RPM
MAXIMUM TORQUE (KGM)	42.2 AT 3200 RPM
TIMING SYSTEM	2 VALVES PER CYLINDER, CAMSHAFT IN THE BLOCK
FUEL SUPPLY	SEQUENTIAL ELECTRONIC INJECTION
GEARBOX	AUTOMATIC, 4 SPEED + REVERSE AND OVERDRIVE OR MANUAL 6 SPEED + REVERSE, CENTRAL GEARSHIFT
DRIVE	REAR
MAX. SPEED (MPH)	172

GLOSSARY

- **Ballooning** - The aerodynamic effect which forces the rear part of the top to swell when the car is traveling at high speed. The effect is caused by the drop in air pressure resulting from the direction of the airflow over the convex shape of the windshield/roof. It is as if the top were being sucked up by the air above.

- **Baquet** - Literally "bath tub". It refers to cars at the beginning of the century in Europe with two rows of raised seats (single seats or divans) similar to those used in turn of the century horse-drawn carriages. Baquets were generally without front doors, a top or a windshield. The motor usually had four cylinders and displaced 3-4 liters. In the United States the term "touring" was often used. See Phaéton.

- **Barchetta** - An open top dedicated to racing without doors or a top and with uniform and streamlined bodywork. It had either one or two separate seats.

- **Bateau** - The shape of the rear end of open-topped racers at the beginning of the century which looked like the hull of a boat.

- **Bellows** - A part of the soft top, made from leather, plastic or canvas.

- **Boattail** - The tapered form of the rear end. The term literally describes the shape of the vehicle's tail which resembled the bow of a boat. It was much used in racing.

- **Break** - A motorized carriage without side protection but with a fixed, non-rigid cover held up by rods like a canopy. Breaks were very basic vehicles in use at the turn of the century.

- **Bullnose** - A term in use in Great Britain during the 1920's to indicate a type of radiator which resembled the nose of a bull.

- **Cabriolet** - This term has changed meaning significantly over the years and in different countries. During the 1920's and 30's in continental Europe it meant an open top with a top, two doors and four seats which was often derived from a sedan. The equivalent in Great Britain was called a Drophead Coupé while the English used the term cabriolet to mean a four-door open top. Concurrently in the United States, the term used was Convertible Coupé. Today a cabriolet describes open-topped cars derived from a sedan or coupé (i.e. from a hard top). It could also be understood to mean an open top with two rows of seats (4-5 seats) with just two doors.

- **Chummy** - In Great Britain from the 1920's and later, a chummy was an open-topped car. The vehicle was usually a 2+2, i.e. two full-size seats in front and two very small seats behind.

- **Convertible** - In the US from 1927 on, the term was used to mean a car with a soft, retractable top provided the top was hooked permanently to the bodywork, and therefore not removeable like for some roadsters. Other requisites were side windows (that opened) and the absence of lateral uprights and any framework above the waist of the car apart from the windshield. The most common and exact type had two doors and was therefore called a Convertible Coupé: those with four doors were called Convertible Sedans. In both cases, four or five people could be seated.

- **Convertible Coupé** - A two seater convertible. In the US in the 1930's the term was often synonymous with cabriolet though not with the modern usage of the word.

- **Convertible Sedan** - A four door convertible.

- **Drophead Coupé** - A drophead coupé was the British term for the equivalent of the American term 'Convertible Coupé' and continental European 'Cabriolet' from the 1930's on.

- **Dual Cowl** - A design of car which saw the cab divided into two compartments - front and back - and separated by metal panels and a supplementary windshield. It was a typical configuration of luxury cabriolets during the 1930's, 40's and 50's.

- **Fencer's Mask** - The term describes a type of radiator grill designed from the 1930's which resembled a fencer's mask for its shape and the tight weave of the grill.

- **Hard Top** - A removable top to replace the soft top. It is made from plastic and usually of the same color as the car body. It has a Plexiglas or glass rear window. In Targa models, the hard top fits between the windshield and a central upright.

- **Landau** - A partially open limousine. The open part was usually the front where the driver sat.

- **Landaulet** - A Landau with the rear part of the roof (hard or soft) which could be opened or folded down.

- **Phaéton** - A French term taken from the name of the son of Helios, Greek god of the sun. It means an open-topped car with four seats. At the beginning of the century the term was used instead of baquet. During the 1930's, it was synonymous in the US with Convertible Sedan and Convertible Phaéton. The term Double Phaéton was also used.

- **Ragtop** - the same as soft top.

- **Rib** - A rigid arc of metal or wood which makes up part of the rigid or semi-rigid frame of the top.

- **Roadster** - The term 'roadster' has had several meanings depending on the origin and the period. In the US and sometimes in Europe at the start of the century, it meant models that were successors to, and sometimes contemporary with, Runabouts but which were more powerful and fitted with a jump seat. They did not have a top. More recently, the term has meant 'sports car' in Anglo Saxon countries. Generally it is a two seater sports car, small and powerful.

- **Roll bar** - A metal bar to protect the car in case it rolls over. If located in the center of the cab in place of the central upright, it may be a single piece in the form of an arc or it may be a 'pop-up' bar which appears when the car overturns. If placed behind the headrests, it may be composed of two pieces, either fixed or 'pop-up'.

- **Runabout** - A small, light two-seater. Runabout was a term used mainly in the United States to indicate a small open car, generally without a top. It was basic, cheap and generally had a single cylinder motor.

- **Sedanca** - A type of early body design in which the top extended for a quarter of a circle and covered only the passengers in the rear seats.

- **Spider** - The continental European equivalent of the English term Roadster. It was first used to describe small, fast horse-drawn carriages but came to describe open-topped two seaters or 2+2's. From a commercial point of view, in Europe the term Spider is used when talking about an open top that is an independent design, i.e. not derived from a sedan (unlike a cabriolet).

- **Streamlined** - A term which simply means aerodynamic. It was predominantly used to describe convertibles during the 1950's and 60's but its origin is drawn from futuristic American models from the 1930's based on airplane design. The coachwork is uniform with all features designed to offer least wind resistance.

- **Tank** - Denotes open tops with completely closed and uniform bodywork except for the opening of the cab. See Barchetta.

- **Targa** - An open-topped car with a hard top provided. It is a halfway house between a spider and a coupé. It sometimes has a longitudinal crosspiece. In this case the hard top is made up of two pieces.

- **Tonneau** - The rear part of the cab (see Phaéton).

- **Tonneau Cover** - Soft cover used on parked roadsters to protect the cab from the rain when the top is down.

- **Top** - Soft covering laid over a framework, generally made of metal, with joints and a rib to hold it taut both crossways and lengthways. Tops were for a long time made from waxed canvas, and occasionally still are, although today plastic materials are usually used. They often have two layers and sometimes are made from two separate pieces. The tops on modern convertibles are partially or totally opened and closed electrically taking approximately 25 seconds depending on the complexity of the mechanism.

- **Torpedo** - Long wheelbase open tops from the top to the bottom end of the market. They succeeded Tourers and Phaétons. The coachwork was made of flat panels, the doors were low and the sides offered no protection from the weather. The soft top turned around a pin placed in the center of the body. It was held taut by ribs and fixed in place by uprights or tie-rods. With the top down, the metallic upper part of the torpedo seemed very flat; with the top up, there was a huge expanse between the pin and the front fastener.

- **Touring/tourer** - Used in the USA at the start of the century to mean the equivalent of a European baquet. During the 1920's in the US, it came to mean a four-seater open top with four doors, generally in the medium-low segment of the market.

- **Vis a vis** - A very early type of car, almost always open-topped, in which the two rows of passengers sat face to face.

B I B L I O G R A P H Y

AA. VV., *Daimler 1896-1996*, Jaguar Italia SpA, 1996

AA. VV., *Der Unschützbare Cabrio*, Hamr Verlag Gmbh, 1995

AA. VV., *Detroit style automotive form 1925-1950*, Detroit Institute of Arts, 1985

AA. VV., *Ferrari 1946-1990 Opera Omnia*, Automobilia, 1990

AA. VV., *Museo Vincenzo Lancia*, Lancia, 1972

AA. VV., *Peugeot 60 ans de cabriolets*, Automobiles Peugeot, 1987

AA. VV., *Pininfarina catalogue raisonné 1930-1990*, Automobilia, 1990

AA. VV., *Tempi di mobilità*, Audi Ag, 1992

AA. VV., *The Great American Convertibles*, Beekman House, 1991

AA. VV., *Tutte le Alfa Romeo 1910-1995*, Editoriale Domus, 1995

AA. VV., *Tutte le Fiat*, Editoriale Domus, 1970

AA. VV., *Volvo 1927-1996*, Volvo Car Corporation, 1996

Adcock, I., *The birth of the MG F*, Bloomsbury Publishing, 1996

Alfieri, B., *Form Mercedes Benz*, Automobilia, 1995

Alfieri, B., Casucci, P., *Ferrari Spider 1949-1990*, Automobilia, 1989

Altieri, P., Lurani, G., *Alfa Romeo catalogue raisonné 1910-1989*, Automobilia, 1988

Amatori, F., *Storia della Lancia 1906-1969*, Fabbri Editori, 1992

Burgess Wise, D., *Tutta la storia della Ford*, Automobilia, 1982

Cancellieri, G., De Agostini, C., *La storia della Maserati*, Automobilia, 1995

Cherret, A., *Alfa Romeo Tipo 6C 1500, 1750, 1900*, Giorgio Nada Editore, 1990

De Serres, O., *Cabriolets Francais 1945-1995*, Epa Editions, 1995

Dumont, P., *Tutta la storia della Renault*, Automobilia, 1982

Flammang, J., *Chronicle of the American Automobile*, Publications International, 1994

Flammang, J., *Chrysler Chronicle*, Publications International, 1995

Fusi, L., *Alfa Romeo, tutte le vetture dal 1910*, Emmeti Grafica Editrice, 1978

Lewandowski, J., *Mercedes Benz catalogue raisonné 1886-1990*, Automobilia, 1990

Lewandowski, J., *Opel*, Sudwest, 1995

Lorieux, G., Wolgensinger, J., *Genealogie*, Citroën, 1988

Madaro, G., *Alfa Romeo Duetto*, Giorgio Nada Editore, 1990

Moretti, V., *Ghia*, Automobilia, 1991

Newbery, J., *Classic Convertibles*, Grange Books, 1994

Norris, I., *Jaguar catalogue raisonné 1922-1992*, Automobilia, 1991

Pasini S., Solieri, S., *Porsche 356*, Edizioni Rebecchi, 1987

Schrader, H., *BMW Automobili*, Editoriale Semelfin, 1992

Schrader, H., *Klassische Cabriolets*, Blv, 1986

Turinetto, M., *Automobile: le forme del design*, Progetto Leonardo, 1991

Wolgensinger, J., *André Citroën*, Flammarion, 1991

• **Specialized magazines and periodicals**

Auto, Conti Editore SpA

AutoCapital, Editoriale Motori srl

La Manovella e ruote a raggi, Giorgio Nada Editore

Le Grandi Automobili, Automobilia

Ruoteclassiche, Editoriale Internazionale Milano SpA

Guida all'acquisto di tutto, Edizioni Errezeta

Radar Coupé & Spider, Studio Zeta Editore

A C K N O W L E D G M E N T S

Press Offices:
- *Augerma*
- *BMW Italia*
- *Chrysler Italia*
- *Citroën Italia*
- *De Tomaso*
- *Ford Italia*
- *Jaguar Italia*
- *Mercedes Italia*
- *Nissan Italia*
- *Peugeot Italia*
- *Porsche Italia*
- *Renault Italia*
- *Rover Italia*
- *Sidauto*
- *Suzuki Italia*
- *Toyota Italia*

Petra Nemeth and Karin Ammach BMW Mobile Tradition,

Massimo Castagnola Archivio Storico Fiat,

Robert Denham Studebaker National Museum,

John Emery Auburn Cord Duesenberg Museum,

Mrs. Figini Quattroruote,

Cathy Latendresse and Alene Soloway Henry Ford Museum & Greenfield Village,

Isotta Fraschini Fabbrica Automobili S.p.A.,

Philip Hall The Sir Henry Royce Memorial Foundation,

Thomas A. Kayser Gilmore CCCA Museum,

Leo W. Lincourt Corvette Americana Hall of Fame,

Lotus

Laura Mancini GM Media Archives,

Aston Martin Lagonda Limited,

Stefano Mazza,

Charles Morgan,

Francesco Pagni Pininfarina Collection,

Klaus Stekkönig and Jens Torner Porsche,

Elvira Ruocco Archivio Storico Alfa Romeo,

The Triumph Sports Six Club,

Loris Tryon Blackhawk Automotive Museum,

Weimper Mercedes-Benz Classic Archives Team

PHOTO CREDITS

Dennis Adler/Autostockhaus: pages 172 top, 172-173, 287, 299 bottom.

Alfa Romeo Historical Archive: pages 48 centre, 48 bottom, 113 top, 124 bottom, 124-125, 135 bottom left, 196-197, 218 bottom, 262-263.

Archive Photos: pages 16-17, 18 top right, 22 top, 23 top, 27 top, 51 bottom, 92 bottom.

Arkiv für Kunst und Geschichte: pages 14 centre, 15 bottom, 28 bottom, 30 bottom, 31 bottom right, 46 bottom, 56-57, 56 bottom, 61 top, 70 centre, 73 centre, 76 centre, 78 bottom, 98 centre, 129 top, 161 top, 174 bottom.

Aston Martin Lagonda Archive: page 231 bottom.

Auburn Cord Duesenberg Museum: pages 93, 94, 95 top, 107 top, 107 bottom.

Autogerma Archive: pages 78 top, 122 centre, 128 top, 128 centre, 130 bottom.

Sandro Bacchi: pages 112 top, 114, 115 bottom, 116-117, 117, 164 centre, 164 bottom, 165, 192 top right, 192 bottom, 193 centre, 260, 261 bottom.

Bagview Books: pages 204 right, 294, 295, 296, 297.

BMW Artwork Service: pages 60 top, 60-61, 136 bottom.

British Motor Industry Heritage Trust: pages 152 centre, 152-153, 154-155, 203 bottom.

Neill Bruce: pages 1 bottom, 6-7, 8-9 top, 9, 14 top, 14 bottom, 15 top, 16 top, 16 left, 17, 18 top left, 18-19, 19, 22 bottom, 24 top left, 24 bottom, 25, 26, 27 centre right, 27 bottom, 28 centre, 28-29, 29 top, 29 bottom, 30 top, 30 centre, 31 top, 31 centre, 32-33, 32, 33 bottom, 37, 38, 39 bottom, 42, 43, 44-45, 56 top, 57 top, 57 bottom, 58 centre, 61 bottom, 62 top, 65 bottom, 68 top, 69, 71 bottom, 72, 74 bottom, 75 bottom, 80-81, 82 bottom, 88 top, 96 bottom, 113 bottom, 115 top, 118 top, 119 top, 120, 120-121 bottom, 129 bottom, 131 top, 132 top, 133 bottom, 134, 140 centre, 140-141 bottom, 146-147, 148 bottom, 149, 152 top, 152 bottom, 153, 154 top, 156 centre, 160 bottom, 163 top, 166 bottom, 167 top, 168 top, 172 bottom, 173 top, 184 top, 185 bottom, 194-195 top, 195 bottom, 198 top, 198 centre, 199, 200 bottom, 201 bottom, 202, 202-203, 203 top, 206 centre, 206 bottom, 207, 208 centre, 208 bottom, 212 top, 213 top, 214, 216 bottom, 218 top, 218-219, 219 bottom, 220 bottom, 223 bottom, 226 top, 227 bottom, 228, 229, 232, 234 top left, 234 top right, 234 centre, 235 bottom left, 258, 259, 261 top, 274, 275, 299 top, 304 top, 312-313, 318, 319, 322, 323, 324, 325, 333, 334, 337 top.

The Bugatti Trust: pages 28 top, 77 top, 108 top, 108 bottom, 109 top, 109 bottom, 125 bottom, 128 bottom.

Chrysler Archive: pages 234 bottom, 236, 237, 332-333, 336-337.

Citroën Archive: page 125 top.

Corbis Bettman: pages 22 centre, 23 bottom, 99 bottom, 110-111, 138 top left, 138 top right, 159 bottom, 169 top, 175 top, 182 top, 184-185, 192 top left, 204 left.

Jim Fets: pages 8-9 bottom, 342, 343, 344, 345.

Fiat Historical Archive: pages 20, 21, 27 centre left, 40, 41, 50 top, 51 centre, 62 bottom, 62-63, 63, 76 top, 76 bottom, 77 bottom, 78 centre, 79 top, 102 top, 116 top, 166-167, 196, 197.

Henry Ford Museum & Greenfield Village: pages 91 top, 128 top, 210 top, 211 centre.

Fotostudio Zumbrunn, Zürich: pages 4-5, 10-11, 12-13, 118 bottom, 119 bottom, 136-137, 137, 176, 177, 178 centre, 178 bottom, 233, 238-239 bottom, 240, 241, 242, 243, 244, 245, 246, 247, 248, 249, 250, 251, 252, 253, 254, 255, 256, 257, 264, 265, 266, 267, 268, 269, 270-271, 272, 273, 326, 327, 328, 329, 330, 331.

GM Media Archives: pages 49 top, 49 bottom, 53 bottom, 72-73, 73 top, 73 bottom, 86, 87, 143 centre, 180 top, 180-181, 190 bottom.

Martyn Goddard: pages 60 bottom, 128 bottom.

Honda Archive: page 224 centre.

Ian Kuah: pages 340, 341.

Image Bank: pages 29 centre, 53 top, 200 top.

Jaguar Archive: pages 156 bottom, 230.

Pierpaolo Krak: pages 282-283 top, 285.

Maggi e Maggi: page 290, 291, 292, 293, 352.

Mary Evans Picture Library: page 31 bottom left.

Mercedes Benz AG: pages 2-3, 16 bottom right, 46 top, 50-51, 122-123, 123, 148 top, 161 bottom, 173 bottom.

National Motor Museum/Nicky Wright: pages 7, 77 centre, 98 bottom, 104 centre, 105, 109 centre, 130 centre, 140-141 top, 150 top, 151 top, 151 bottom, 154 bottom, 158 bottom, 159 top, 160 top, 164 top, 169 bottom, 170 bottom, 171 top, 186-187 bottom, 189 centre, 193 top, 205 bottom, 208 top, 216 top, 216-217, 217 bottom, 221, 224 top, 302, 304 bottom, 305.

National Motor Museum Beaulieu: pages 238-239 top.

Nissan Archive: page 52 top.

Peugeot Archive: pages 66 centre, 66 bottom, 66-67, 67, 110.

Pininfarina Archive: page 86 bottom.

Porsche Archive: pages 170 centre, 171 bottom, 201 top, 205 top, 280, 281, 282-283 bottom, 284.

Quadrant Picture Library: pages 224-225.

Henry Rasmussen: pages 1 top, 54, 55 top, 83 bottom, 84, 85, 88 bottom, 89, 92 top, 95 bottom, 96 top, 96 centre, 97 top, 103 top, 104 bottom, 106, 107 centre, 131 bottom, 138-139, 139, 146 bottom, 157, 158-159, 162, 163 centre, 163 bottom, 170-171, 181 bottom, 182 bottom, 190 top, 191, 194, 194-195 bottom, 212-213 bottom, 215 bottom, 286, 288, 289,300, 301, 302 left, 320, 321.

Sergio Reggiani: pages 224 bottom, 225 bottom, 276, 277, 278, 279, 306, 307, 308, 309, 314, 315, 316, 317.

Renault Archive: pages 68 bottom, 122 top, 167 bottom.

Peter Roberts Collection c/o Neill Bruce: 34 top, 35, 36, 39 top, 39 centre, 47, 48 top, 50 bottom, 51 top, 52-53, 55 centre, 57 centre, 58 top, 58 bottom, 59, 64, 65 top, 66 top, 68-69, 70 top, 70 bottom, 71 top, 74 top, 74 centre, 75 top, 79 bottom, 82 top, 90 top, 90 bottom, 99 top, 102 bottom, 113 centre, 116 centre, 124 top, 129 centre, 130 top, 132 bottom, 133 top, 143 top, 150 bottom right, 166 top, 169 centre, 174 top, 175 bottom, 206 top, 226 bottom, 231 top, 235 top.

The Sir Henry Royce Memorial Foundation: page 55 bottom.

Reiner W. Schlegelmilch: pages 168 bottom, 220-221 top, 220-221 centre, 227 top, 227 centre.

Hans Schwarz & Partners Archive: page 235 bottom right.

Studebaker National Museum: pages 98 top, 108-109.

Nicky Wright: pages 24 top right, 33 top, 34 centre, 34 bottom, 49 bottom, 82 top, 90 centre, 91 bottom, 97 bottom, 100, 101, 102-103, 103 bottom, 104 top, 111 top, 112 bottom, 120-121 top, 121, 129, 135 top, 135 bottom right, 136 top, 142, 143 bottom, 144-145, 146 top, 147, 148 centre, 150 bottom left, 151 right, 155, 156 top, 178 top, 179 top, 180 bottom, 181 top, 183, 184 bottom, 185 top, 186, 186-187 top, 187 bottom, 188, 189 centre, 189 bottom, 193 bottom, 198 bottom, 209, 210 bottom, 211 top, 211 bottom, 215 top, 215 centre, 217 top, 222-223 top, 222-223 bottom, 223 top, 310, 311, 335.

White Star Archive: pages 52 centre, 52 bottom, 130-131, 338, 339.